THE CULTURE OF "THE CULTURE"

Liverpool Science Fiction Texts and Studies, 65

Liverpool Science Fiction Texts and Studies

Editors
David Seed, *University of Liverpool*
Sherryl Vint, *University of California Riverside*

Editorial Board
Stacey Abbott, *University of Roehampton*
Mark Bould, *University of the West of England*
Veronica Hollinger, *Trent University*
Roger Luckhurst, *Birkbeck College, University of London*
Andrew Milner, *Monash University*
Andy Sawyer, *University of Liverpool*

Recent titles in the series

46. *Stanislaw Lem: Selected Letters to Michael Kandel* (edited, translated and with an introduction by Peter Swirski)
47. Sonja Fritzsche, *The Liverpool Companion to World Science Fiction Film*
48. Jack Fennel, *Irish Science Fiction*
49. Peter Swirski and Waclaw M. Osadnik: *Lemography: Stanislaw Lem in the Eyes of the World*
50. Gavin Parkinson (ed.), *Surrealism, Science Fiction and Comics*
51. Peter Swirski, *Stanislaw Lem: Philosopher of the Future*
52. J. P. Telotte and Gerald Duchovnay, *Science Fiction Double Feature: The Science Fiction Film as Cult Text*
53. Tom Shippey, *Hard Reading: Learning from Science Fiction*
54. Mike Ashley, *Science Fiction Rebels: The Story of the Science-Fiction Magazines from 1981 to 1990*
55. Chris Pak, *Terraforming: Ecopolitical Transformations and Environmentalism in Science Fiction*
56. Lars Schmeink, *Biopunk Dystopias: Genetic Engineering, Society, and Science Fiction*
57. Shawn Malley, *Excavating the Future: Archaeology and Geopolitics in Contemporary North American Science Fiction Film and Television*
58. Derek J. Thiess, *Sport and Monstrosity in Science Fiction*
59. Glyn Morgan and Charul Palmer-Patel, *Sideways in Time: Critical Essays on Alternate History Fiction*
60. Curtis D. Carbonell, *Dread Trident: Tabletop Role-Playing Games and the Modern Fantastic*
61. Upamanyu Pablo Mukherjee, *Final Frontiers: Science Fiction and Techno-Science in Non-Aligned India*
62. Gavin Miller, *Science Fiction and Psychology*
63. Andrew Milner and J.R. Burgmann, *Science Fiction and Climate Change: A Sociological Approach*
64. Regina Yung Lee and Una McCormack (eds), *Biology and Manners: Essays on the Worlds and Works of Lois McMaster Bujold*

THE CULTURE OF "THE CULTURE"

Utopian Processes in Iain M. Banks's
Space Opera Series

JOSEPH S. NORMAN

LIVERPOOL UNIVERSITY PRESS

First published 2021 by
Liverpool University Press
4 Cambridge Street
Liverpool
L69 7ZU

Copyright © 2021 Joseph S. Norman

The right of Joseph S. Norman to be identified as the author of
this book has been asserted by him in accordance with
the Copyright, Designs and Patents Act 1988.

All rights reserved. No part of this book may be reproduced, stored in a
retrieval system, or transmitted, in any form or by any means, electronic,
mechanical, photocopying, recording, or otherwise, without the prior
written permission of the publisher.

British Library Cataloguing-in-Publication data
A British Library CIP record is available

ISBN 978-1-78962-174-7 cased

Typeset by Carnegie Book Production, Lancaster
Printed and bound by CPI Group (UK) Ltd, Croydon CR0 4YY

Contents

The Culture Series (List of Abbreviations)		vii
Acknowledgements		ix
Introduction		1
1	World Systems: Imperialism, Interventions, the *Technologiade*	37
2	Thinking the Break: The Culture as Postscarcity Utopia	69
3	Posthuman Culture: Senescence, Rejuvenescence, (Im)mortality	111
4	The Handy Wo/Man: Feminism, Space Opera, Ambisexuality	141
5	Reason Shapes the Future: Atheism, Humanism, Quasi-Religion	179
6	Whole-Tone Scales Reaching Forever: Art in Utopia, Utopian Art	213
Concluding Postscript		259
Bibliography		263
Index		281

The Culture Series

The following is a list of the series in chronological order of publication with the abbreviations (where applicable) used in this book:

- *Consider Phlebas* (1987) – *Phlebas*
- *The Player of Games* (1988) – *Player*
- *Use of Weapons* (1990) – *Weapons*
- *The State of the Art* (1991) – *State*
    - 'The State of the Art' (1988) – 'State'
    - 'A Gift from the Culture' (1987) – 'Gift'
    - 'Descendent' (1987)
- *Excession* (1996)
- *Inversions* (1998)
- *Look to Windward* (2000) – *Windward*
- *Matter* (2008)
- *Surface Detail* (2010) – *Surface*
- *The Hydrogen Sonata* (2012) – *Hydrogen*
- 'Zakalwe's Song' (*Poems*, 2015)
- 'Slight Mechanical Destruction' (*Poems*, 2015) – 'Slight'

Acknowledgements

I began researching *The Culture of "The Culture"* in 2010, and I am especially grateful to Nick Hubble, who supported my research from the outset. When I first met Nick to discuss my ideas, he said that this project "had legs": thanks so much to him for helping it to walk, guiding it down the road, and steering it away from potholes. Thanks also to all from the Brunel Department of Arts and Humanities who supported my research, including the students whom I taught during this time and with whom I discussed Banks's work. I was proud to co-host The State of the Culture conference at Brunel in 2013, at which several writers cited in this book were in attendance, discussing some of the content that would eventually be contained within; I am grateful to all who took part in the conference, but especially to Ken MacLeod for speaking so eloquently and at such a difficult time. Thanks also to Gary Lloyd for his correspondence, for discussing the music he created with Iain, as well as for providing unique insight into his friend's musical tastes and background. I was also fortunate to be granted permission by Banks's estate to view items from his archive at the University of Stirling in 2019, prior to granting general access to researchers. Thank you to the archive staff, who enabled me to incorporate some material from the archive into this book; I certainly intend to return. Every writer that I mention in this book has helped to shape my thinking in some way, and I am proud to be a part of such an academic community. I am indebted to Liverpool University Press for accepting and publishing this book, especially for the help of my editor, Christabel Scaife, and for the careful and considered comments of the reviewer chosen to read my manuscript.

Mum and Dad – to say that I could not have done this without you is a massive understatement: you've always supported my decisions, however unorthodox. Thanks for years of love, slap-up dinners, lifts, London jaunts, and everything else. Finally, more thanks than I can effectively articulate in words to my partner Em, who has supported this project in many ways from the outset. I really appreciate you reading various forms of my work throughout the years, and thanks for putting up with my occasional meltdowns, usually late at night.

Then there's the man himself: Iain (M.) Banks. I did not have the opportunity to meet Iain properly, although I mentioned my research to him very briefly at a book signing. As a researcher it's a strange and challenging thing to hear the author you're working on has died quite suddenly, right in the middle of your research; and, as a fan, it's pretty devastating. It is with some personal regret that, after Iain left me with his email address, I procrastinated about writing to him until I had the most pertinent questions ready. Even though I can only claim to have known Iain in a vague, vicarious way from reading his writing and hearing him speak, he was clearly a wonderful guy, not to mention a talented and fearless writer. I toast both Iain Banks and Iain M. Banks, whiskey in hand. Thank you for leaving us with such an extensive, varied, and exciting oeuvre: the process of analysing it all has really only just begun.

Introduction

On 2 March 2019, Iain M. Banks's series of fictional texts concerned with the galactic meta-civilisation known as the "Culture" played a subtle part in the history of space travel when the first private mission to launch a spacecraft to the moon paid tribute to these works. Taking part in the Google Lunar X Prize, the *Beresheet* lander, owned by the Israeli non-profit organisation SpaceIL, was launched to the lunar surface using the Falcon 9 rocket owned by US company SpaceX. Following *Beresheet*'s successful launch in its first stage, the Falcon 9 was able to return to Earth in a second stage by landing on a drone ship in the Atlantic Ocean called the *Of Course I Still Love You*. The drone ship's idiosyncratic name was drawn directly from one of the Culture's spacecraft. Elon Musk, tech entrepreneur, futurist, and SpaceX CEO, is well known to be an SF fan, naming the Falcon 9 after the Millennium Falcon from the *Star Wars* franchise (1977–) and the mission's human-sized dummy "Ripley" after the protagonist of Ridley Scott's *Alien* (1979). This triad of references is significant as it locates Banks's series alongside two of the most iconic SF visions of all time. Yet Musk describes his relationship with the Culture as something deeper than a fan's appreciation, tweeting the following declaration on 16 June 2018: "If you must know, I am a utopian anarchist of the kind best described by Iain Banks".[1] In pursuit of this goal, Musk has tested other rocket pads with Culture names (*Just Read the Instructions*, *A Shortfall of Gravitas*) and his company Neuralink began the more speculative project of developing a "Neural Lace" in 2016, a kind of Brain–Machine Interface (BMI) intended to perform the same function as its namesake in Banks's fiction. Never lacking in ambition, Musk describes the ultimate goal of SpaceX and "the most important

---

[1] Elon Musk (@elonmusk), 'If you must know, I am a utopian anarchist of the kind best described by Iain Banks', Tweet, 16 June 2018. https://twitter.com/elonmusk/status/1008120904759402501?lang=en.

project in the world" as: interplanetary colonisation,[2] something like the point at which the Culture series begins.

Such projects clearly indicate the extent to which contemporary technoscience is both inspired by, and catching up with, the fictional speculations of SF. As Istvan Csicsery-Ronay Jr. comments with minimal hyperbole, "the world has grown into sf".[3] Ranking 21st in the 2018 edition of *Forbes'* list of the World's Most Powerful People, Musk is one of the key individuals with the necessary financial backing and influence to affect such growth. Yet the extent to which multi-billionaire entrepreneurs can truly achieve such goals in the public interest should be called into question, as it was by Banks on a number of occasions. Banks died on 9 June 2013, of gallbladder cancer, having announced the diagnosis on his website two months previously, so we can only speculate on the nature of his response to Musk's ambitions. While it seems broadly clear why a futurist such as Musk would look to SF for inspiration, it seems odd that Banks specifically should inspire wealthy venture capitalists from Silicon Valley (Facebook CEO Mark Zuckerberg is also a Culture fan[4]), given the vigour with which Banks would denounce the "American Libertarianism" that such figures represent. Despite this, Banks expressed optimism about privately funded space flights in 2010, even though his socialist politics clash with such entrepreneurship, suggesting that he, like Musk, advocates getting humans out into space in any manner possible.[5]

Other commentators were more critical, with Stuart Kelly – a friend and regular critic of Banks – publishing an article in the *Guardian* newspaper asking 'Does Elon Musk really understand Iain M Banks's "utopian anarchist" Culture?' Banks himself certainly conceived of the Culture as his "personal utopia" and "secular heaven", based upon

---

[2] Maureen Dowd, 'Elon Musk's Billion-Dollar Crusade To Stop The A.I. Apocalypse', *Vanity Fair*, April 2017. https://www.vanityfair.com/news/2017/03/elon-musk-billion-dollar-crusade-to-stop-ai-space-x.

[3] Istvan Csicsery-Ronay Jr., *The Seven Beauties of Science Fiction* (Middletown, CT: Wesleyan University Press, 2008), 1.

[4] In 2015, Zuckerberg chose *The Player of Games* for A Year of Books, his fortnightly book club dedicated to "big ideas that influence society and business". Exactly to what extent he has been directly influenced by the Culture is difficult to ascertain, although Facebook finds something of a mirror in the Culture's advanced techno-neurological communications network.

[5] Val Nolan, '"Utopia is a way of saying we can do better": Iain M. Banks and Kim Stanley Robinson in Conversation', *Foundation* 43, no. 119 (2014): 65–77.

egalitarian principles, and such an understanding of the Culture is widely shared by fans and critics alike. Yet Kelly's rebuke illustrates another major strand of thought in scholarship on the Culture, describing Banks's civilisation as a "totalitarian, interventionist monolith".[6] As such, this debate frames a major task of my book: exploring the Culture through a dialectic relationship between utopia and utopianism on the one hand, and empire and imperialism on the other. Despite the conviction of his utopian intentions, Banks foregrounds such ambiguities in the Culture from the first published text in the series, *Consider Phlebas* (1987), which begins with the utopian Culture reluctantly engaged in a hugely destructive, pan-galactic war with the imperial Idirans. Three-quarters of the way through the novel, a character of Culture origin named Fal 'Ngeestra experiences a crisis of identity regarding the nature of her own people when the line between utopia and empire becomes blurred: "Not even sure of our own identity: just who is Culture? Where exactly does it begin and end? Who is and who isn't? [...] no clear boundaries to the Culture, then; it just fades away at the edges, both fraying and spreading. So who are we?" (*Phlebas*, 334) 'Ngeestra's language here seems confused, initially describing the Culture with the pronoun "it", then, in the following sentence, using "we". Does the term refer to a particular group of people? or to a place (an "it" with no clear borders)? Maybe, as this book will argue, the Culture is exactly as its name describes: a collective philosophy, an identity, a shared way of living.

My book begins with a similar question to 'Ngeestra's – what is the Culture? – that demands a complicated answer. The Culture series, consisting of nine novels, three short stories, and two poems, is a huge and sprawling sequence that Banks shaped and reshaped in response to the historical period of almost 40 years (roughly 1974–2012) in which he wrote. This period encompasses the (so-called) end of the Cold War, the Fall of the Soviet Union, the implementation of the Neoliberal capitalist world order, the 9/11 attacks, and the subsequent War on Terror: a time of huge economic, political, and cultural changes in the contexts of Britain, Banks's native Scotland, Europe, and indeed the whole globe. As such, the answer to the question of what the Culture itself represents, as well as the broader meanings of the entire sequence, changes accordingly, and Banks forces his readers to consider and reconsider that which he describes from text to text, chapter to chapter, page by page, even line by line.

---

[6] Stuart Kelly, 'Does Elon Musk really understand Iain M Banks's "utopian anarchist" Culture?' *Guardian*, 18 June 2018. https://www.theguardian.com/books/booksblog/2018/jun/19/elon-musk-iain-banks-culture-novels.

I provide an in-depth analysis of Banks's creation itself, working to offer a clearer understanding of its ambiguities and complexities, showing how the Culture develops and changes, and how perceptions of it are (re)shaped across the series. I ask how these texts can inspire such varied interpretations, which cannot always be straightforwardly attributed to differences in political orientation. More broadly, I also explore how the ten texts function as a space-opera series, subverting and reimagining the tropes of the sub-genre as New Space Opera. Placing the series within the political and cultural period of the post-Cold War era, and the economic climate of Neoliberalism, I argue that Banks's fiction provides both a complex response to the dynamic historical context in which he wrote, as well as a radical, fictional alternative. But before we go further, it is necessary to understand something of Banks the writer, as well as the basic components of the Culture.

Iain M. Banks (1954–2013)

Iain Banks was born in Fife, Scotland, on 16 February 1954, to middle-class, Protestant parents: his mother was an ice skater whilst his father was an officer in the Admiralty.[7] An only child, Banks declared his ambition to be "a Writer with a capital W" from age 11,[8] and had written what he intended to be his first novel (actually a novella) by age 14.[9] Whilst attending Gourock and Greenock high schools, Banks met Ken MacLeod, who became a life-long friend, and who also forged a successful career writing SF. Banks studied English, Philosophy and Psychology at the University of Stirling,[10] where he wrote poetry and experimented further with novel writing, graduating in 1975. In his youth he travelled around Europe and North America, and lived in London for several years employed in various jobs, until achieving his ambition of becoming a full-time writer in 1985.[11]

Throughout his career, Banks adopted a split writing persona at the request of his publisher. He published thirteen works of SF as "Iain

---

[7] Colin Hughes, 'Doing the Business', *Guardian*, 7 August 1999, www.theguardian.com/books/1999/aug/07/fiction.iainbanks; Isobel Murray, 'Interview with Iain Banks, 29th November 1988', in *Scottish Writers Talking 2*, Isobel Murray, ed., 2–3.
[8] Murray, 'Interview', 13.
[9] Hughes, 'Doing the Business'. Web.
[10] Murray, 'Interview', 13.
[11] Hughes, 'Doing the Business'. Web.

M. Banks", adopting the middle name "Menzies", which his father had mistakenly omitted from Iain's birth certificate. As "Iain Banks", he published fifteen so-called mainstream fictions, a poetry collection, and a memoir. *Transition* (2009) was the only text to be published as both: as SF in the US and mainstream in the UK.[12] Banks won the British Science Fiction Award twice: for the non-Culture SF novel *Feersum Endjinn* in 1994, and *Excession* in 1996.[13] Banks's third non-Culture SF novel, *The Algebraist*, was nominated for a Hugo Award in 2005.[14] Banks identified himself as an atheist,[15] humanist,[16] and feminist[17] throughout his life, as well as a socialist[18] with complex left-wing political views. Banks regularly wrote letters to national newspapers, especially the *Guardian*, expressing firm views on topical political issues.[19]

Known for his passion for whisky, Banks's hobbies also included composing music, playing computer games (especially *Civilization*), and as he admitted, occasionally using recreational drugs. Banks amassed a large collection of sports cars, narrowly avoiding death in a crash, and later selling this collection for environmental reasons.[20] Banks's friends, including MacLeod and Banks's biographer Craig Cabell, frequently recall one of his wilder moments: climbing from one third-floor balcony to another at an SF convention, unaware of a robbery occurring in a nearby suite, and narrowly avoiding arrest.

[12] *Telegraph*, 'Obituary: Iain Banks', 9 June 2003. www.telegraph.co.uk/news/obituaries/culture-obituaries/books-obituaries/10108884/Iain-Banks.html.
[13] BSFA Website, 'About the British Science Fiction Awards'. www.bsfa.co.uk/bsfa-awards/.
[14] The Official Site of the Hugo Awards, '2005 Hugo Awards', n.d. www.thehugoawards.org/hugo-history/2005-hugo-awards/.
[15] Secularism.org, 'Profile of Iain Banks', n.d. www.secularism.org.uk/iainbanks.html.
[16] *Ontario Humanist Society*, 'In memoriam: Iain Banks, novelist, humanist, "evangelical atheist"', 10 June 2003. http://www.ontariohumanists.ca/events/in-memoriam-iain-banks-novelist-humanist-evangelical-atheist-national-humanist.
[17] Iain Banks, 'Out of this World', *Guardian*, 12 July 2008. www.theguardian.com/books/2008/jul/12/saturdayreviewsfeatres.guardianreview5.
[18] Scott Beauchamp, 'The Future Might Be a Hoot: How Iain M. Banks Imagines Utopia', *Atlantic*, 15 January 2013. www.theatlantic.com/entertainment/archive/2013/01/the-future-might-be-a-hoot-how-iain-m-banks-imagines-utopia/267211/.
[19] For example, on 5 April 2013, Banks wrote a letter to the *Guardian* entitled 'Why I'm supporting a cultural boycott of Israel' (www.theguardian.com/books/2013/apr/05/iain-banks-cultural-boycott-israel).
[20] Craig Cabell, *Iain Banks: The Biography* (John Blake Publishing Ltd, 2014). Ebook.

Banks announced that he had been diagnosed with terminal gallbladder cancer on his website in 2013, and was widely praised for the bravery with which he handled his final few months. Banks died on 9 June 2013, shortly before the publication of his final novel, *The Quarry*, in the same year. An asteroid, (5099) Iainbanks, was named in his honour the same year. During the handful of occasions that I heard Banks speak in public – at SF cons, book signings, and Q&As – he came across as deeply intelligent, friendly, and self-deprecating, but, perhaps most of all, extremely funny, in an exuberant and natural manner. MacLeod confirms that Banks greatly enjoyed these public appearances, and John Mullan's comment in Banks's obituary for the *Guardian* newspaper that Banks "was an author whose readers felt in close touch with him" certainly rings true to me.[21]

The Culture: An Overview

The essay 'A Few Notes on the Culture', originally published in 1994, was the closest Banks came to detailing the fictional history of his creation. Banks's series is set within our Milky Way: imagined to be populated by a diaspora of humans and Artificial Intelligences (AIs), as well as a multitude of extraterrestrial life forms, his stories are largely concerned with planets outside of our solar system. The Culture is a kind of civilisation, or group of civilisations, "formed from seven or eight humanoid species, [...] which established a loose federation approximately nine thousand years ago."[22] According to the fictional timeline of the series, the texts cover events that precede our own time, occur concurrently, and also in our relative future, for example: *Consider Phlebas* is set in 1331 CE during the Late Medieval Period in the European history of Earth; 'The State of the Art', the only text in the series to depict Earth, is set during the time of its composition in 1977 CE; while the final text, *The Hydrogen Sonata*, takes place in the far future of approximately 2375 CE. The Culture has achieved an almost complete mastery of technoscience; therefore, its citizens live on a variety of self-built artificial habitats, especially huge planet-sized spaceships called General Systems Vehicles (GSVs) and ring-shaped "bracelet worlds" known as Orbitals (or Os), whose environments offer almost unlimited freedom for all,

---

[21] John Mullan, 'Iain Banks Obituary', *Guardian*, 10 June 2013. https://www.theguardian.com/books/2013/jun/09/iain-banks-dies-59-cancer.

[22] Iain M. Banks, 'A Few Notes on the Culture', *Vavatch*, 10 August 1994. www.vavatch.co.uk/books/banks/cultnote.htm.

including almost total control over, and artificial augmentation of, an individual's own physiology and built environment.

The Minds are AIs whose intellectual capacity greatly exceeds that of human beings, and who seem to maintain the day-to-day bureaucracy of the Culture as a mere fraction of their potential capabilities. While the Minds technically have no need to exist in physical space, they often manifest as Avatars, humanoid figures designed to interact with human beings, or inhabit and power the substrate of spacecraft or Os (the latter form known as Hubs). Drones are another type of AI, with an intellectual capacity somewhere between people and the Minds, who regularly enact with Culture people as part of their daily lives, in an arrangement, said to be voluntary, which covers friendship, servanthood, and varieties of pastoral care. Both the Minds and drones are considered equal in status to Culture people; they are therefore also considered citizens.

Contact is a division of the Culture concerned with establishing and maintaining peaceful diplomatic relations with other civilisations in the galaxy. While the Culture has moved entirely beyond conflict within its own environments, Contact developed from earlier Culture military organisations, and therefore potentially fulfils external military functions if necessary, especially in relation to its subdivision known as Special Circumstances (SC). SC handles more difficult relationships, especially when the Culture feels it necessary to intentionally affect the course of another society's development. SC's work is frequently controversial, and for this reason it sometimes employs mercenaries from outside the Culture to carry out its missions, although Culture people, as well as the Minds and drones, are also drawn in to service.

Everyone in the Culture has free and mostly unlimited access to its hugely powerful data network, available to AIs directly, and for others through "terminals" and/or a neural lace. A terminal is a small, convenient device that enables instant communication with others in the Culture, which can take seemingly any form according to personal preference or, when used by SC, operational need. Most Culture people are fitted with neural laces: a kind of synthetic mesh that grows with an organic brain, allowing for a huge range of benefits, including instantaneous data access, mood control, storage of memories and personality, even resurrection.

Other civilisations that have achieved a level of technological development equivalent to the Culture, of which there are several, are known as the "Involved"; they cover a variety of species types, philosophies, and ideologies. The Culture is spread widely across the galaxy, although it is said to be wary of the extent of its influence, and seemingly imposes no restrictions or formal processes upon allowing others to join. The Culture is said to have moved completely beyond material scarcity as well as mandatory labour.

The Sublimed are mysterious enlightened entities that exist within the "pure energy" realm of the Sublime, which exists in another dimension. While they have very little contact with people, some from the Culture claim to have met them in some capacity. Many civilisations are able to become Sublimed themselves at a certain point of development, often making this conversion en masse, yet the Culture is known for discouraging Subliming amongst its citizens. Contact has the highly secretive division of Numina, exclusively responsible for managing relations between the Culture and the Sublimed.

Texts and Contexts: Developing the Culture in the Apocalyptic 1970s

Beginning with the composition of 'Zakalwe's Song' in December 1973 and ending with the publication of *The Hydrogen Sonata* in October 2012 (or even the republication of Banks's Culture poems in 2015), the Culture series was developed, written and published across a period of almost 40 years. Given the social, economic, and political complexity of this period in history, there are several overlapping periodisations in which Banks's series should be considered. Firstly, the importance of the 1970s – which has come to represent probably the most controversial and contested decade in British politics – as formative context for the series cannot be understated. Secondly, William Davies's periodisation of Neoliberalism, published in the *New Left Review* as "The New Neoliberalism" – which outlines three distinct developmental and political phases: "Combative", "Normative", and "Punitive" – neatly maps the shifting economics that radically rearranged Britain and the globe over the years in which Banks worked, and to which his works responded with vitriol. Thirdly, Philip Wegner's book *Life Between Two Deaths, 1989–2001* (2009) explores the period of the "long nineties" as falling between two symbolic deaths; while he focuses upon US culture at this time, Wegner's book provides detailed, contextual discussion applicable to a British and global context, which he expands upon and develops further in *Shockwaves of Possibility* (2014). Finally, Fredric Jameson's influential periodisation of the historical development of postmodernism – its "early" period from 1945 to the late '70s, "high" phase in the '80s, "late" phase in the '90s, and our current era known variously as post-postmodern, post-Cold War, or simply that of Globalisation.

Davies's first phase, "Combative Neoliberalism", spanning roughly 1974–1989, aligns with the early period of Banks's career, from initial development of the Culture, Banks's publication debut, and three other mainstream works; the eventual publication of the first Culture book on 23 April 1987; and two other novels, several stories, and a novella also set in the Culture.[23] Many accounts of the 1970s emphasise a sense of economic decline and political crisis: as Dominic Sandbrook explains, the decade was dominated by "a pervasive sense of crisis and discontent with few parallels in our modern history. [...] And within a few years, the image of the 1970s as a uniquely drab, depressing period in modern British history has become deeply embedded in the popular imagination."[24] While the years following World War Two saw an economic boom in Britain, as in many other parts of the world, the economy in much of the Western World stagnated in recession between 1973 and 1975 – the exact period of Banks's undergraduate study at the University of Stirling. Scotland, in particular, was affected by the widespread decline of heavy industries and its economy did not start to improve until the 1980s, when it benefited from the exploitation of North Sea petroleum and natural gas. Yet Stéphane Porion looks beyond the "clichés and the popular memory of events" in the '70s, calling for a "reappraisal of the key terms of 'crisis' and 'decline'", given the ease with which they were manipulated for political ends.[25] Rather than the 1970s marking something approximating an apocalypse for British society – a *complete* breakdown – then, it should be characterised as "the breakdown of a particular phase in post-war British politics; ostensibly the post-war consensus of welfare-capitalism with its Keynesian commitment to full employment, a strong state and meaningful partnerships with the trades unions."[26] And it was exactly this kind of communitarian, social democratic politics that was being eroded around him which Banks channelled into his vision of a utopian society, providing a truly radical alternative to the real-world status quo.

However the decade is characterised, Banks clearly began writing the Culture books during a time of great political and economic change, producing a first draft of what became *Use of Weapons* in 1974, using

---

[23] William Davies, 'The New Neoliberalism', *New Left Review* 101 (September–October 2016): 124–127.

[24] Dominic Sandbrook, *State of Emergency: The Way We Were: Britain 1970–1974* (London: Penguin, 2011), 9.

[25] Stéphane Porion, 'Reassessing a Turbulent Decade: the Historiography of 1970s Britain in Crisis', *Etudes Anglaises* 69, no. 3 (2016): 310.

[26] Nick Hubble, J. MacLeod, and P. Tew, eds., *The 1970s: A Decade of Contemporary British Fiction* (London: Bloomsbury Publishing PLC, 2014), 8.

"the Aliens" as a working title for the Culture. *Weapons* was not just the first Culture book that Banks wrote, however; as Ken MacLeod explains, it is "arguably, the first *novel* Iain Banks ever wrote",[27] for although Banks had written drafts of at least three others previously, amounting to around half-a-million unpublished "but hilarious" words,[28] *Weapons* was the first that was strong enough to be – eventually – published. While the Culture is often understandably seen as the focus of the series, Banks's writing did not begin with the idea of developing his personal utopia: before a setting came a character, Zakalwe, protagonist of *Weapons*. Banks explained that the series truly began with the notion that Zakalwe is "a mercenary, a bad guy, but without knowing it he was working for the good guys", and the Culture itself, "created more by accident than design, sort of grew from there."[29] Even at this early stage, Banks knew that he wished to write works of space opera that would appeal to established fans of the sub-genre whilst working to radically subvert its conventions, as he would help achieve with Zakalwe's moral ambiguity – an idea to which we'll return in more detail below. The idea of the Culture as intended utopia may have been influenced, to a certain extent, by Banks's context at the time as a student, writing within the picturesque surroundings of the Stirling campus, in the shadow of the William Wallace Monument (honouring the thirteenth-century Scottish hero), an educational enclave that Banks himself would later speak of in idealised terms as a form of utopia. Rather than identifying mere youthful wish fulfilment as the inspiration for development of the "good guys", however, Nick Hubble instead describes Banks's positive view of AI, the early development of which was occurring at the time, as the key to the Culture's genesis:

> a young Iain M. Banks earning money during his student vacations, witnessed the way manual workers were using newly-available pocket calculators to check that they weren't being cheated in their pay packets. From this small example of the social benefits arising from artificial intelligence was born the idea of the Culture, a pan-galactic Utopian collective of machines and people.[30]

[27] Ken MacLeod, 'Iain Banks: A science fiction star first and foremost', *Guardian*, 10 June 2013. Emphasis added. https://www.theguardian.com/books/2013/jun/10/iain-banks-ken-macleod-science-fiction.
[28] MacLeod, 'Iain Banks'. Web.
[29] Hughes, 'Doing the Business'. Web.
[30] Nick Hubble, 'Science Fiction in the U.K.', in 'The Mass Market Era (1945–1960)', *Sense of Wonder: A Century of Science Fiction*, Leigh Ronald Grossman, ed. (Wildside Press, 2011). Ebook.

Without the Minds and drones – AIs vastly more intelligent than humans – the Culture could not exist in the form depicted in the stories. Extrapolating from this idea that a society controlled by computers could provide "social benefits", such as freeing human beings from mandatory employment and material inequality, we can start to understand how Banks's thinking along these lines would start to shape the rest of the broader shape of the Culture as developed in the books that followed. By having a utopia closely involved with an ethically dubious anti-hero such as Zakalwe at the heart of the first book in the series, Banks set up the theme of moral grey areas that would continue throughout. This complicated the Culture's status as a positive utopia from the outset and would provoke much heated discussion amongst Banks's fans and critics. In formulating a fictional society underpinned by social, communitarian values, Banks responded directly to the radical, right-wing reshaping of the world's economic landscape by Neoliberalism.

The origins of Neoliberalism are often traced back to the Bretton Woods conference of July 1944, which "addressed a perceived need to prevent another Great Depression and to rebuild Europe in the post-war period."[31] Thatcherism mixed Neoconservatism with Neoliberalism, leading to policies such as "the privatization of public assets, the selling of council houses and deregulation of the City and banks", and represented powerfully ideological rhetoric that held great sway on the culture of Britain in the 1980s. Thatcher supported the regime of General Pinochet, the Chilean dictator who came to power on 11 September 1973, and oversaw Pinochet's establishment of Neoliberalism in that country for the first time in the world's history; I demonstrate the relevance of this context to *The Player of Games* (drafted in 1979) in Chapter Two. Around three months after Pinochet's rise, Banks wrote the poem 'Zakalwe's Song' – a proto-Culture work, likely to predate the first draft of *Weapons* – which would eventually be included in *Weapons* as epilogue, with 'Slight Mechanical Destruction', another poem from March 1978, as epigraph. Here 'Slight' is attributed to the Culture character, Rasd-Coduresa Diziet Embless Sma da' Marenhide, better known as Diziet Sma – a significant detail given that Sma is one of the few characters to reoccur in the series, and that she plays an important role in understanding the Culture itself. The novel describes Sma (and a drone Skaffen-Amtiskaw) attempting and finally succeeding to recruit Zakalwe into Special Circumstances, as well as the way in which their relationship develops. Sma regularly engages in debates

---

[31] Jerome Winter, *Science Fiction, New Space Opera, and Neoliberal Globalism* (Melksham: University of Wales Press, 2016), 3.

about the nature of the Culture with individuals such as Zakalwe who oppose it to some extent, and she ceaselessly argues in its favour, in a manner that its other official ambassadors (such as Shohobohaum Za in *Player*) do not always do. Therefore, she comes to operate as an advocate for the Culture, with her own personal views acting metonymically for those of her broader society. Following the ways in which Banks would frequently align his own thoughts and views with those of the Culture, there is often a sense that to read Sma's views is to read those of the author himself.

Whilst living in London in 1976, Banks drafted his next book, *Against a Dark Background*, which was not published with the label "A Culture novel" on its cover, and the vast majority of commentators – including myself – do not consider it part of the series. Yet, with a female protagonist fighting a threat from within her family, a pan-galactic scale, and a quest for a "Big Dumb Object", it has certain thematic parallels with the Culture texts, as Kincaid has explored.[32] *Against a Dark Background* was published a few months before *Star Wars* was released to cinemas on 25 May 1977, instigating one of the all-time most significant space-opera franchises, and Banks would pay a brief, humorous homage to George Lucas's films in his next Culture work. Banks completed his first draft of 'The State of the Art' in late-1978, a novella that would draw upon his experiences travelling around Europe three years previously, again featuring Diziet Sma in dialogue with a man who has become disillusioned with the Culture's way of life. This theme would continue in *The Player of Games*, which is concerned with the titular figure Gurgeh and the ways in which his reluctant completion of an SC mission transforms an empire, and helps him to personally embrace the Culture's values. Banks first drafted *Player* in 1979 during a brief return to Scotland, in the same year that Margaret Thatcher (1925–2003) was elected prime minister of the United Kingdom on 4 May.

Texts and Contexts: Normative Neoliberalism and "The Iron Lady"

Fed up with rejection of his SF by publishers, Banks wrote a first draft of *The Wasp Factory* between May and June 1981, before returning to the Culture to complete a draft of *Consider Phlebas* between July and December 1982. Banks made his publishing debut with *The Wasp Factory*

---

[32] See Paul Kincaid, *Modern Masters of Science Fiction: Iain M. Banks* (Oxfordshire: University of Illinois Press, 2017), 54–62.

in 1984. Having admitted that he "had deliberately turned away from science fiction" because there were more available outlets for mainstream publishing, and therefore more chances for him to secure some kind of publication and begin his career, *The Wasp Factory* was published as "mainstream" fiction under the name "Iain Banks".[33] Yet he had "quite deliberately chosen a book which still had a setting and a character that gave you some of the freedoms you have in science fiction, making up your own society and religion [...] There is some feeling of remoteness of the island almost being another planet."[34] *The Wasp Factory*, with its graphic depictions of animal cruelty, torture, and infanticide, sharply divided critics who generally either praised the originality and intelligence it brought to the Gothic horror genre or – especially amongst the right-wing press – offered scathing indictments arguing the exact opposite (extracts from which Banks would gleefully republish in the jacket of future editions). Even so, *The Wasp Factory* became a controversial "overnight success" and paved the way for Banks to achieve his ambition of being published by the age of 30. Berthold Schoene-Harwood identifies *The Wasp Factory* as a satirical allegory on the reassertion of masculine warrior culture and imperial values that Margaret Thatcher encouraged during the Falklands War in 1982,[35] foregrounding a major theme of Banks's life and work. If he held a "life-long, heart-felt hatred for the Conservative and Unionist Party",[36] Banks was especially vitriolic about the "Iron Lady", from the outset of his career. And it is in the increasingly atomised and individualised culture of Thatcherism that Banks continued to develop the self-motivated, morally grey, multi-fractured identity of the mercenary Zakalwe. We can therefore start to build a picture of the Culture texts as Banks's way of responding to the political climate of the time, both in terms of critique as well as a way of developing and maintaining radical political alternatives.

This success as a mainstream writer was followed by two other books under his mainstream moniker, *Walking on Glass* (1985) and *The Bridge* (1986), both of which merge SF, the fantastic, and realism through coexisting planes of reality, either psychological or interdimensional. While neither book was published as science fiction, let alone as a

---

[33] Murray, 'Interview', 29.
[34] Murray, 'Interview', 29.
[35] Berthold Schoene-Harwood, 'Dams Burst: Devolving Gender in Iain Banks's "The Wasp Factory"', *Ariel* 30, no. 1 (1999): 146.
[36] Ken MacLeod, 'Ken MacLeod on Iain Banks', *Internationalist Socialist Network*, 23 July 2013. http://internationalsocialistnetwork.org/index.php/ideas-and-arguments/analysis/193-ken-macleod-on-iain-banks-use-of-calculators.

Culture novel, some fans and critics have argued for a direct link to Banks's ongoing series in the former (a thinly veiled reference to a "Knife Missile", a type of Culture drone) and broad, thematic parallels in the latter (a paranoid character from London who believes himself to be living in an interstellar setting that mirrors the plots of pulp space opera; the playing of vastly complex games). Banks finally published a Culture book in 1987, making the unusual decision to publish the first three novels in the reverse order to that in which they were written. He therefore introduced his readers to his personal utopia through *Phlebas*, told from an anti-Culture perspective and set largely outside its realms, rather than *Player*, for example, not published until 1988, which begins with scenes set on a Culture Orbital featuring prominent pro-Culture perspectives.

Texts and Contexts: Post-Cold War Culture "Between Two Deaths"

Davis's second phase, "Normative Neoliberalism", spans the reopening of the Berlin Wall in 1989 to the global financial crisis of 2008, with the next six Culture texts published during this time. On 9 November 1989, the Berlin Wall was opened by the East German government, allowing access between West Germany and West Berlin for the first time in over 20 years. The events of 1989 mark the first of Wegner's "deaths" and the beginning of the period that he describes as "the strange space between an ending (of the Cold War) and a beginning (of our post-9/11 world), one of those transitional phases that, once again following the leads of Lacan and Žižek, I call the 'place between two deaths'".[37] If the fall of the Berlin Wall marks Wegner's first "death", then the "toppling of the World Trade Centre buildings should be understood as a form of what Jacques Lacan theorizes as the 'second death', an event that repeats an earlier 'fall'".[38] This in-between place, then,

> located as it is between the Real Event and its symbolic repetition, is strictly speaking "non-historical," and such an "empty place" is experienced in its lived reality, as Žižek suggests, in a Janus-faced fashion. On the one hand, it feels like a moment of "terrifying monsters," of hauntings by a living dead past. Yet it is also

---

[37] Phillip E. Wegner, *Life Between Two Deaths, 1989–2001: U.S. Culture in the Long Nineties* (United States of America: Duke University Press, 2009), 9.
[38] Wegner, *Life Between Two Deaths*, 9.

experienced as a moment of "sublime beauty," of openness and instability, of experimentation and opportunity, of conflict and insecurity – a place, in other words, wherein history might move in a number of very different directions.[39]

Banks would capture a similar impression of this period writing later in *Transition* (2009):

> those retrospectively blessed dozen years lasted from the chilly, fevered Central European night of November 9th, 1989 to that bright morning on the Eastern Seaboard of America of September 11th, 2001. One event symbolized the lifted threat of a worldwide nuclear holocaust, something which had been hanging over humanity for nearly forty years, and so ended an age of idiocy. The other ushered in a new one.[40]

Here the narrator looks back upon this time in history, sometimes known as the "long nineties", with longing for a period of relative peace between two cataclysmic events – a time in which Banks published five Culture novels (*Weapons*, *Excession*, *Inversions*, *Windward* and *Matter*), and six mainstream novels (*Canal Dreams* [1989], *The Crow Road* [1992], *Complicity* [1993], *Whit* [1995], *A Song of Stone* [1997], and *The Business* [1999]).[41] The first of Wegner's deaths, the opening of the Berlin Wall, signalled not just the end of the Soviet Union, but led many to declare the death of communism in the popular imagination, as well as in reality in Eastern Europe. As a result, the British "New Labour" government of prime ministers Tony Blair and Gordon Brown from the mid-1990s to 2010 led an ideologically altered Labour party, causing Banks – like so many on the Left – to become disillusioned with the party that he had supported for many years: as MacLeod confirms, Banks "switched his practical vote to the Scottish National Party" (SNP), and his "protest vote to the Scottish Socialists" or UK Green Party.[42] Banks was one of many in Scotland who turned to the SNP, whose support had built steadily since the 1970s, whose motivation "didn't come from nationalism but from reformism".[43] Voting for Scotland to leave the United Kingdom,

---

[39] Wegner, *Life Between Two Deaths*, 9.
[40] Iain Banks, *Transition* (Great Britain: Little, Brown, 2009), 1.
[41] Writing in *Shockwaves of Possibility*, Wegner discusses *Transition* at length, alongside MacLeod's *The Human Front* (2001), in terms of 'Alternate Histories, Periodization, and Geopolitical Aesthetics' (200–233).
[42] MacLeod, 'Ken MacLeod on Iain Banks'. Web.
[43] MacLeod, 'Ken MacLeod on Iain Banks'. Web.

then, was for Banks the only way that his country could separate itself from an unwanted Tory government for whom they had not voted, rather than a specific dislike of the union itself.[44] The post-9/11 era became defined by the endless War on Terror perpetuated by the U.S. and U.K. governments. On such matters of Western imperialism, with which his Culture series engages extensively, MacLeod states that Banks "opposed every war the British state waged in his lifetime, with the one exception of NATO's war over Kosovo," and, in particular, Banks was "vehemently opposed"[45] to the Iraq War in 2003. In response to Blair's invasion of Iraq, Banks performed one of several idiosyncratic acts of political protest for which he became known throughout his life: physically cutting up his passport and posting it to the prime minister at Downing Street.[46] Seeing the Iraq War as illegal and immoral, to Banks the blame lay squarely with Blair, despite Gordon Brown's involvement: "There is the technicality of cabinet responsibility," Banks argued, "but it was Blair who bowed to Bush in the first place, and Blair who convinced the Labour party and parliament of the need to go to war with a dossier that was so close to lying that it makes no difference."[47] Following this, in 2004, Banks became a signatory on a campaign to impeach Tony Blair on the grounds of "Misleading Parliament and the country over Iraq", "Negligence and incompetence over weapons of mass destruction", "Undermining the constitution", and "Entering into a secret agreement with the US president".[48] The campaign, however, which was reportedly also signed by up to 23 MPs and included other celebrities such as Brian Eno and Susan Wooldridge, was ultimately not selected for debate in the House of Commons.

Banks finally published *Weapons* in 1990 – over 20 years after it was first drafted – and *The State of the Art* collection in the following year. Containing the eponymous novella and two Culture short stories – 'A Gift from the Culture' originally published in *Interzone* and 'Descendent' in an anthology, *Tales from the Forbidden Planet*, both in 1987 – *State* marked the end of the publication of the first wave of Banks's writing on the Culture. It was not until the 1990s that Banks would again begin writing a Culture story from scratch, releasing *Excession* on 13 June 1996, followed by *Inversions* on 27 May 1998. *Look to Windward*, a text concerned

---

[44] MacLeod, 'Ken MacLeod on Iain Banks'. Web.
[45] MacLeod, 'Ken MacLeod on Iain Banks'. Web.
[46] Stuart Jeffries, 'A Man of Culture', *Guardian*, 25 May 2007. www.theguardian.com/books/2007/may/25/hayfestival2007.hayfestival.
[47] Jeffries, 'A Man of Culture'. Web.
[48] BBC, 'Blair Impeachment Campaign Starts', 27 August 2004. http://news.bbc.co.uk/1/hi/uk_politics/3600438.stm.

with a thwarted terrorist attack on the Culture by a fundamentalist religious empire, was published on 17 September 2000, almost a year prior to the attacks in New York City of 11 September 2001. Paul Kincaid is convinced that *Windward* was intended as the final Culture text because Banks's civilisation "is reaching the end of the line", and comments that, in that book, Banks "caught the spirit of the times far more effectively than in books in which he consciously tried to reflect that moment", such as *Dead Air* (2002).[49] Whether or not *Windward* was intended as the end, there was certainly an eight-year gap in Banks's publication of Culture texts between 2000 and 2008, during which time his output included two non-SF novels, the whisky memoir *Raw Spirit* (2003), and the non-Culture space opera *The Algebraist*.

Returning to the Culture with *Matter* in 2008, the year of the global economic crisis, Banks then published *Surface Detail* in 2010. While promoting *Surface* at the Roundhouse, London, in 2010, he explained that he did not have any ideas relating to the end of the Culture within its fictional universe, intending to keep writing stories set in the Culture, seemingly indefinitely. Davis marks the start of the third phase of his schema, "Punitive Neoliberalism", as beginning in 2008 and continuing into the present time of writing. *Transition*, published a year later, can be considered the culmination of a kind of loose stylistic trilogy (alongside *The Bridge* and *Walking*) for its generic blending and its return to the theme of a multiverse; and Banks's utopia is again referenced obliquely through the presence of a "drug bowl", a quintessential Culture vice, again suggesting that the dimension-hopping protagonist may have visited an O or a GSV. Yet Banks's life, and therefore the series, was cut tragically short and *The Hydrogen Sonata* (2012) proved to be the last Culture book. Porion identifies 2009 as the year in which the decade began to be reappraised and revised, moving away from the influential right-wing narrative of 1980s Thatcherism, which blamed post-World War Two social democracy for the nation's perceived decline.[50] Instead, twenty-first-century accounts have emphasised the relativism of notions of crisis and decline, particularly, for example, when applied to the retreat of the British Empire during this time. Others have emphasised that recent studies highlight Britain's similar economic performance to many other countries during that decade, its rising living standards, low unemployment by today's standards, and the vibrant cultural life of the era.[51]

---

[49] Kincaid, *Iain M. Banks*, 101–103.
[50] Porion, 'Reassessing a Turbulent Decade'.
[51] See Hubble, McLeod, and Tew, eds., *The 1970s*, 1–13.

Having received his cancer diagnosis on 4 March 2013, Banks and his publishers worked to release his final book, the mainstream novel *The Quarry*, before he passed away, but were unsuccessful. Discussing his last publications, Banks allowed himself a note of regret: "let's face it; in the end the real best way to sign off would have been with a great big rollicking Culture novel."[52] While MacLeod revealed that towards the very end of his life Banks had asked him to continue writing Culture novels in his own style, Banks had been unable to leave substantial notes on the ideas he had for what would have been the eleventh text in the series. This, coupled with MacLeod's already conflicted feelings on the request, therefore leaves this prospect unlikely.[53] According to Banks's wishes, a volume of poetry featuring both his own work and that of MacLeod was released in 2015. This volume, simply entitled *Poems*, reprinted the two poems which bookend *Weapons*, 'Zakalwe's Song' and 'Slight Mechanical Destruction', and therefore returns to the ideas that first inspired his series, providing something of a sense of artistic closure.

Texts and Contexts: Punitive Neoliberalism and Globalisation

While Banks would not live to comment explicitly on the new global crises that define the time of writing in 2019, it is feeding into this general context that the Culture books must be considered. Tensions between nationalism and internationalism in Britain and across the globe developed alongside the writing and publication of the Culture stories. Britain entered the European Economic Community (becoming the European Union [EU] in 1993) under Edward Heath's Conservative government while Banks was an undergraduate, with scepticism toward the EU building throughout his lifetime, eventually resulting in the "Brexit" referendum in 2016, which Banks would not live to witness. The political and social divisions associated with Brexit dominate discussion at the time of writing, as they will no doubt continue to do beyond the scheduled beginning of the EU withdrawal process on 29 March 2019. The current leader of the opposition for Great Britain, Jeremy Corbyn, argues for the potential for Brexit to enable an alternative to

---

[52] Stuart Kelly, 'Iain Banks: The Final Interview', *Guardian*, 15 June 2013. https://www.theguardian.com/books/2013/jun/15/iain-banks-the-final-interview.

[53] Xantha Leatham, 'Dying Wish of Scots Author Revealed', *Scotsman*, 15 February 2015. www.scotsman.com/lifestyle/dying-wish-of-scots-author-iain-banks-revealed-1-3690835.

Globalisation, and the accompanying wave of populism continues to spread throughout Europe, raising the potential for further countries to vote on leaving the EU. Populism, nationalism, terrorism (both jihadist and from the political Right), and corporate greed dominate the headlines, and I write at a time of great uncertainty, both within Britain, and across the globe. The overall tone of the contemporary moment is marked by a great feeling of uncertainty and apocalypticism, perhaps not dissimilar to that of the 1970s.

Created by a man engaged with and invested in the dynamic political, cultural, and economic period in which he wrote, the Culture series inevitably captures and comments upon elements of this real-world historical context even as Banks worked to depict a fictional concurrent, near- and far-future history. But the scope of Banks's commentary was not closed by his untimely death or the release of the final Culture text for, as Hubble argues, "Banks's fiction from the start anticipated concerns which would become central to the twenty-first century future we now inhabit, including a committed anti-fascism, a new gender politics and a reawakened sense of Scottish identity."[54] We will return to Banks's legacy in general, and these themes in particular, later in this book.

Traditional Space Opera

Unlike the often generically slippery fiction published under Banks's mainstream moniker, the Culture series is straightforwardly identifiable as SF because most texts take "the most quintessential form of sf narrative": space opera. Csicsery-Ronay describes this sub-genre as "spectacular romances set in vast, exotic outer spaces, where larger-than-life protagonists encounter a variety of alien species, planetary cultures, futuristic technologies (especially weapons, spaceships and space stations), and sublime physical phenomena."[55] Most of the Culture series are space operas, with the exception of *Inversions* (and perhaps *Player*), a planetary romance, as discussed in Chapter One.

E.E. "Doc" Smith's *The Skylark of Space* – written between 1915 and 1921, serialised in *Amazing Stories* in 1928, and published in book form in 1946 – is frequently identified as the first space opera in prose.

---

[54] Nick Hubble, 'Iain M. Banks by Paul Kincaid', *Strange Horizons*, 18 December 2017. http://strangehorizons.com/non-fiction/reviews/iain-m-banks-by-paul-kincaid/.

[55] Csicsery-Ronay, *Seven Beauties*, 218.

Smith's tale of scientists competing to create a working space drive and their subsequent rivalry for resources in deep space proved to be highly influential. Fredrick Pohl argued that, "With the exception of the works of H.G. Wells, possibly those of Jules Verne", *The Skylark in Space* "has inspired more imitators and done more to change the nature of all the science fiction written after it than almost any other single work."[56] With its scientist–adventurer protagonist, traditional gender roles, binary sense of morality, and fast-paced thriller narrative, Smith's story established many traditional tropes of the sub-genre. But it was not until the first Golden Age of SF (1938–1946) that space opera would become established as a popular narrative form. Writers such as Smith, A.E. "Van" Vogt, Leigh Brackett, and Edmond Hamilton produced narratives of heroic galactic exploration and conquest, fighting laser wars on alien habitats, and discovering strange artefacts and technologies, which grew to dominate the field. Csicsery-Ronay and Brian Aldiss trace space opera's roots back to the classical epic tradition – from *The Epic of Gilgamesh*, Homer, Virgil and others up to the Renaissance – and emphasise the sub-genre as a modern reimagining of this ancient form.[57] Aldiss describes space opera in epic terms:

> Ideally the Earth must be in peril, there must be a quest and a man to match the mighty hour. That man must confront aliens and exotic creatures. Space must flow past the ports like wine from a pitcher. Blood must run down the palace step, and ships launch out into the louring dark. There must be a woman fairer than the skies and a villain darker than a Black Hole. And all must come right in the end.[58]

Both critics emphasise the sense of huge interplanetary, even intergalactic, scale necessary for space opera and the prominence of encounters with radical Otherness, with Aldiss adding the importance of a central quest narrative, violent conflict, clear-cut morality, patriarchal gender norms (the hero is a man in search of a female love interest), and conservative narrative closure.

The foundations for an eventual reformulation of space opera were in fact laid from the very moment that the sub-genre's name was coined.

---

[56] Frederik Pohl, 'Introduction', in E.E. "Doc" Smith, *The Skylark of Space* (Connecticut: Easton Press, 1991).

[57] Brian Aldiss, ed., *Space Opera: An Anthology of Way-Back-When Futures* (London: Book Club Associates, 1974), 10.

[58] Aldiss, *Space Opera*, 10.

Originally known as "super-science epics" during the 1920s and '30s, in 1941 Wilson Tucker famously compared the "hacky, grinding, stinking, outworn spaceship yarn" with TV Westerns, known as "horse operas", and "morning housewife tearjerkers" known as "soap operas", and thus produced the term "space opera."[59] By this point, as Westfahl observes, space opera had already cemented its reputation as the "least respected form of science fiction".[60]

Space Opera During the New Wave

The reputation of space opera was to sink even further during the 1960s and '70s, related to the "New Wave" of Science Fiction at this time: a loose movement of radical SF writers and critics who sought to reimagine the genre's politics and aesthetics. In 1963, Michael Moorcock used a guest editorial in *New Worlds* magazine to bemoan the state of SF at the time; when he spoke of fiction that suffered from serious deficiencies in "passion, subtlety, irony, original characterization, original and good style, a sense of involvement in human affairs, colour, density, depth", he was undoubtedly referring to space opera.[61] During Moorcock's period as editor of *New Worlds*, then, "galactic wars went out; drugs came in; there were fewer encounters with aliens, more in the bedroom."[62] While Aldiss edited a prominent anthology of short stories in the sub-genre, published in 1974, his *Space Opera* collection demonstrates an oddly ambivalent attitude towards its content: while Aldiss warns that "this is not a serious anthology", which is "for fun" and features "screwy ideas",[63] the stories are also "one of the repositories of narrative art; furthermore, they say a great deal about fundamental hopes and fears when confronted by the unknowns of distant frontiers".[64]

Yet the New Wave did not completely abandon space opera. Some New Wave writers applied radical politics and aesthetics to the sub-genre,

---

[59] Gary Westfahl, 'Space Opera', in *The Cambridge Companion to Science Fiction*, E. James and F. Mendlesohn, eds. (Cambridge: Cambridge University Press, 2003), 197.
[60] Westfahl, 'Space Opera', 197.
[61] Michael Moorcock, 'Guest Editorial', *New Worlds* 129 (April 1963), 2 and 123; reprinted in *Science Fiction in the 20th Century*, Edward James, ed. (Oxford: Oxford University Press, 1994), 168.
[62] Brian W. Aldiss, *The Detached Retina* (Liverpool: Liverpool University Press, 1995).
[63] Aldiss, *Space Opera*, 9–10.
[64] Aldiss, *Space Opera*, 9–10.

such as Ursula Le Guin in her "Hainish Cycle". In her classic *Left Hand of Darkness* (1969), Le Guin reimagined the intergalactic empire as a federation between humans and aliens, and addressed gender politics through the relationship between Genly Ai, an Earth human, and Estraven, of the ambisexual Gethenians. In *The Dispossessed* (1974), she placed the dialectic of anarchism and capitalism at the heart of the planetary romance. Westfahl also notes a *general* lack of space opera published during this time, with the exception of parodic works (perhaps referring to Douglas Adams's *The Hitchhiker's Guide to the Galaxy* [1979]), suggesting that enthusiasm amongst the reading public also waned.[65] Yet there were several notable exceptions, including Jack Vance's *Space Opera* (1965), Robert Heinlein's classics *Stranger in a Strange Land* (1961) and *The Moon is a Harsh Mistress* (1966), the first three novels in Frank Herbert's Dune saga (*Dune* [1965], *Dune Messiah* [1969], *Children of Dune* [1976]), several books by Samuel Delany including *Nova* (1968) and *Triton* (1976), Larry Niven's *Ringworld* (1970), Fredrik Pohl's *Gateway* (1977, winning the Hugo Award for Best Novel the following year), and C.J. Cherryh's Faded Sun trilogy (1978–1979). In film and TV, this period actually marked the appearance of the two most famous and enduring examples of space opera ever created: *Star Trek: The Original Series* (initial run 1966–1969) and *Star Wars: Episode IV – A New Hope* (1977), which went on to become two of the highest-grossing franchises of all time, in any genre. The original series of the BBC show *Blakes7* was broadcast from 1979–1981, working to subvert many of the space-opera tropes established in the two, earlier and more popular franchises established around this time.

Making Space Opera New

Roger Luckhurst, Jerome Winter, Westfahl, Hartwell, and Cramer have all identified Banks's Culture novels and other SF works, such as *The Algebraist* and *Against a Dark Background*, as crucial to "New Space Opera". This was a loose movement, emerging during the late 1980s and early 1990s, which marked a conscious reformulation of the original sub-genre. It formed part of a specific boom in British SF during this time, as well as a revitalisation of British literary culture more broadly during the '80s, especially in Scotland.[66] British writers

---

[65] Westfahl, 'Space Opera', 197.
[66] See Andrew M. Butler, 'Thirteen Ways of Looking at the British Boom', *Science Fiction Studies* 30, no. 3 (November 2003): 20; and Monica Germana,

of New Space Opera include Neal Asher, Steven Baxter, C.J. Cherryh, Colin Greenland, M. John Harrison, Ken MacLeod, and Alastair Reynolds, while John Scalzi, Dan Simmons, and Lois McMaster Bujold are amongst the most prominent from the US. Luckhurst notes that the general resurgent popularity of New Space Opera seems "mildly odd" given the prior extent of its bad reputation, but remarks that it is *"strikingly* odd" that a "quintessentially American sub-genre should reappear in Britain."[67] Butler explains that "To some extent a genre is always a parody of itself [... P]erhaps where British science fiction has become most systematically parodic and revisionary is in its revival of the subgenre of space opera".[68] Again, Banks provides a strong example of this revisionism through his identification of American space opera as politically problematic.[69] The boom during this time marked a renewal in confidence for British writers to sell their work to an American audience, following a relative lack of interest in previous years, perhaps inspired by a renewed interest in British culture more generally during this time.

But how exactly does New Space Opera reformulate the sub-genre? From the outset, Banks had a clear idea of his political and aesthetic intentions for the Culture series. David Haddock notes that the "underlying idea" of the Culture was Banks's desire for a "moral, intellectual high-ground in space opera that had to be reclaimed for the Left"[70] as a "reaction against the 'right-wing, dystopian SF' that he read as a kid".[71] Haddock cites Robert Heinlein as an example, noting that *Phlebas* was written as "a radical version of *Starship Troopers*," which could also be read as "an old-fashioned space opera."[72] Ursula Le Guin described the politics of traditional space opera as follows:

'Special Topic 1: The Awakening of Caledonias? Scottish Literature in the 1980s', in *The 1980s: A Decade of Contemporary British Fiction*, Emily Horton, Philip Tew, and Leigh Wilson, eds. (Bloomsbury Publishing PLC, 2014), 52.

[67] Csicsery-Ronay, *Seven Beauties*, 222.
[68] A. Butler, 'British Boom', 20.
[69] "Literary merits aside, and generalising unfairly, the field as Iain found it presented a dilemma: American SF was optimistic about the human future, but deeply conservative in its politics; British SF was more thoughtful and experimental, but too often depressive." – MacLeod, 'Iain Banks: A science fiction star first and foremost'. Web.
[70] Oliver Morton, 'A Cultured Man', *Wired* 2.6, June 1996. yoz.com/wired/2.06/features/banks.html.
[71] *Interzone* 16, 'Interview with Kim Newman', cited in David Haddock, ed., *The Banksonian: An Iain (M.) Banks Fanzine* 4, November 2004, 6.
[72] *Interzone* 16, 'Interview with Kim Newman'.

Socialism is never considered as an alternative, and democracy is quite forgotten. Military virtues are taken as ethical ones. Wealth is assumed to be a righteous goal and a personal virtue. Competitive free-enterprise capitalism is the economic destiny of the entire Galaxy.[73]

We can see an example of this in Smith's Lensman universe (including *Galactic Patrol* [1937] and *First Lensman* [1950]), for example, in which Winter notes a "secret history of intergalactic, racially-inflected eugenics", inspiring Samuel Delany to declare him a "reactionary purveyor of fascist mysticism".[74] If, in the galactic empires and wide-spread unitary environments of 'old' and pre-dominantly American space opera, "military virtues are taken as ethical ones", then Banks's work would eradicate the need for an army altogether or reduce the presence of its military to a minimum, consider ethical values as paramount, and consider almost obsessively any decision to commit acts of violence or intervention, in the name of peace and harmony. If space opera were to enjoy a renaissance, then, it would necessarily have to be shorn of its reactionary politics and ideologies, and brought up to date with the era in which he was writing. Banks applied feminist principles to the Culture, for example, critiquing the patriarchal, sexist values of much SF from the Golden Age and Pulp era, and portrayed the Culture as fundamentally pacifist, with no need for martial structures.

Banks's polemical stance was shared by MacLeod, the pair inspired by reading Moorcock's *New Worlds Quarterly* in the 1970s.[75] Upon first reading Harrison's *The Centauri Device* (1974), Banks himself would ironically make the same mistake as some *Phlebas* reviewers years later: reading *Centauri* "naively" as "straight space opera".[76] So Banks was motivated to write *Phlebas* by a "pure love" of space opera, as Greenland's early review suggests, but combined with the cynicism and calculation that Greenland had "no reason to doubt" were present. As Aldiss notes, "space opera has certain conventions which are essential to

---

[73] Ursula Le Guin, 'American SF and the Other', *Science Fiction Studies* 7, vol. 2:3 (November 1975). http://www.depauw.edu/sfs/backissues/7/leguin7art.htm.

[74] Samuel R. Delany, 'The Necessity of Tomorrow(s)', in *Starboard Wine* (Middletown, CT: Wesleyan University Press, 2012), 1–14, quoted in Winter, *Science Fiction, New Space Opera, and Neoliberal Globalism*, 35.

[75] See Brian M. Stableford, Peter Nicholls, Mike Ashley, and David Langford, 'New Worlds', in *The Encyclopedia of Science Fiction*, Clute et al., eds. (London: Gollancz, 2018), updated 31 August 2018. http://www.sf-encyclopedia.com/entry/new_worlds.

[76] Ken MacLeod, 'Telephone interview', 2:05pm, Friday 17 May 2013.

it, which are, in a way, its raison *d'etre*; one may either like it or dislike those conventions, but they cannot be altered except at expense to the whole."[77] Banks and MacLeod were well aware of this, and – following Harrison's lead – both became expert at subverting these conventions, without losing the fundamental essence of the sub-genre.

An Ambiguous Reception

Many early reviews emphasised Banks's SF debut, *Consider Phlebas*, as "a stunning departure" in terms of style and genre from his mainstream debut, *The Wasp Factory*, despite the parallels between *The Wasp Factory* and SF that Banks identified. While *Phlebas* did not polarise reviewers as much as *The Wasp Factory*, being received largely in a very positive manner, it did provoke debate, disagreement, and critical ambiguity, often stemming from Banks's playful and contrarian attitude to the space-opera sub-genre. New Space Opera was generally explicitly identified as such after the fact, with many reviewers of *Phlebas* expressing uncertainty about the tone and ultimate intentions of Banks's novel in relation to sub-genre. Did the author intend for the book to be read as straightforward space opera or sub-genre satire? Did *Phlebas* simply mark a return to a previously maligned sub-genre, albeit better written; or was there something more politically radical occurring under the surface of Banks's fast-paced, violent work? Even MacMillan's own press material described *Phlebas* as "an epic space opera in the highest traditions of Science Fiction",[78] despite Banks's outspoken desire to reinvent the sub-genre. Colin Greenland, reviewing for *Foundation*, did not detect Banks's subversive intentions. He was disappointed that *Consider Phlebas* "does not transcend genre", as had Banks's three previously published mainstream novels at the time (*The Wasp Factory*, *Walking on Glass* and *The Bridge*), arguing that it "conforms throughout". To Greenland, *Phlebas* demonstrated "a determination to work in original and distinctive areas and shapes,"[79] but, in further contrast to Clute's opinion and Banks's intentions, he argues that "There is no reason to suspect that Banks has written *Consider Phlebas* as an exercise in cynicism, or calculation, or anything other than pure love".[80] Similarly, reviewing

---

[77] Aldiss, *Space Opera*, 10.
[78] The Iain Banks Archive, University of Stirling.
[79] Colin Greenland, 'Consider Phlebas by Iain M. Banks', *Foundation: The International Review of Science-Fiction* 40 (Summer 1987): 93.
[80] Greenland, 'Consider Phlebas', 93.

Phlebas for *Futura Reviews*, Gerry McCarthy argued that "Even for the late eighties, when science fiction had withdrawn from the excesses of the New Wave and scuttled back to its conventions for safety, this is a remarkably conventional piece of work."[81] While John Clute's review for *Interzone* was lukewarm overall, he was one of the few to acknowledge the complexity of Banks's space opera: "what began as seemingly orthodox space opera, turns into a subversion of all that's holy to the form."[82]

So what was the cause of such ambiguity? This question prefigures the debates central to scholarship on the Culture that have developed, especially as criticism gained in pace over the last decade. In part, the ambiguous effect is achieved by the perspective through which Banks chooses to tell his story: *Phlebas*'s most prominent view-point character is Bora Horza Gobuchul, a morally dubious and self-motivated mercenary similar to *Centauri*'s protagonist, John Truck. *Phlebas*, concerned with a war between the secular Culture and an almost equally powerful religious race, the Idirans, is one of clashing ideologies; yet unusually, as Andrew M. Butler describes, "the mercenary hero, Bora Horza Gobuchal [*sic*], is actually fighting for the wrong side, against the Culture."[83] Horza hates the Culture, but harbours few ideological sympathies with the Idirans either, being merely allied with them temporarily against a common enemy; his identification with either side is free to fluctuate, based on personal whim. Again, similarities can be drawn in this regard between *Phlebas* and *Centauri* as, in the latter, Martin Lewis notes: "Both the capitalism of the Israeli World Government and the socialism of the United Arab Socialist Republics comes equally under attack."[84] The initial confusion and ambiguity towards *Phlebas*, then, would seem to indicate a degree of success in Banks's aims: deliberately creating tension between a desire for his work to be recognizable as belonging to a certain mode of SF, while simultaneously deconstructing and critiquing it: appealing to space-opera fans and acknowledging his own influences, whilst foregrounding the sub-genre's faults. The ways in which Banks subverts the conventions of space opera – its heroes, antagonists, galactic world systems, plethora of speculative technologies, narrative formulations, tropes and clichés – continue to be examined throughout this book.

---

[81] Gerry McCarthy, *Futura Reviews*, June 1988, Dublin, in the Iain Banks Archive, University of Stirling.
[82] Haddock, ed., *The Banksonian*, 4, 7.
[83] A. Butler, 'British Boom'.
[84] Martin Lewis, 'The Centauri Device, M. John Harrison', *SFsite*, 2002. www.sfsite.com/04a/cd125.htm.

Methodology: The Dialectic of Utopia and Empire

Similar debates also run through academic consideration of the Culture, which has emerged sporadically from the outset, significantly increasing in volume shortly before and especially after Banks's death in 2013. Critics have paid more attention to his mainstream work than his SF, generally speaking, although his place in the literary canon seems less secure than in that of SF.[85] The prominent SF journal *Foundation* published two special editions dedicated to Banks's work, in 1999 and 2013. The majority of critical material available that considers Banks's SF focuses on the Culture series, with consideration of non-Culture SF novels such as *The Algebraist*, *Feersum Endjinn* and *Against a Dark Background* forming the least-discussed aspect of his works. Those who have discussed the Culture – fans, reviewers, Banks himself – seem to agree, in its most basic form, that the Culture is a kind of society or civilisation, but their understandings of the exact nature of this society differ greatly, and can be grouped into two general categories, which exist potentially in a dialectical relationship. As Sherryl Vint observes, "much of the criticism on Iain M. Banks's Culture novels" reads the series in accordance with its author's intentions to some extent, focusing on "the question of whether the Culture can be considered a utopia."[86] Yet there are just as many critics – Vint included – who read the Culture as in fact asserting some kind of imperialist project, and describe the Culture as a kind of empire. The Culture is often discussed as either utopia or dystopia, commonwealth or empire, freedom or totalitarianism, whilst occasionally as a grey area between the two.

Following Vint, there are as many different varieties of utopian form attributed to the Culture as there are different critics making such arguments. When examining these different varieties side by side, they form a reasonably comprehensive taxonomy of the various utopian forms that exist generally, despite their application to only one society. Elon Musk described it as "anarchist" and "utopian", as we have heard. The Culture has been called: a "limitless utopia";[87] a "critical utopia";[88] an "ambiguous

---

[85] See Martyn Colebrook, 'Reading Double, Writing Double', *Bottle Imp* 8 (November 2010): 5.
[86] Sherryl Vint, 'Cultural Imperialism and the Ends of Empire', *Journal of the Fantastic in the Arts* 18, no. 1 (Winter 2008): 83–98.
[87] British Library, 'Exhibitions and Events: April–August 2011', 10.
[88] Simon Guerrier, 'Culture Theory: Iain M. Banks's "Culture" as Utopia', *Foundation: The International Review of Science-Fiction* 28, no. 76 (1999): 36.

utopia";[89] a "techno utopia";[90] a "liberal utopia";[91] a "political utopia";[92] "anarcho-communist";[93] an "ostensibly utopian meta-civilisation";[94] a "spacefaring socialist minarchy";[95] and an "anarchist",[96] "socialist",[97] and/or "communist utopia" (*Phlebas*, 35). Suggesting a similar definition, Hubble uses the term "pan-galactic Utopian collective";[98] Garnett echoes this with the phrase "Galactic Cooperative";[99] and Thomas Christie has called the Culture an "astro-political community" and a "quasi-technocratic civilisation which is loosely structured upon utopian ideals."[100] By focusing upon the perceived utopian aspects of Banks's society, then, these descriptions portray the Culture in a largely positive light. Similarly, descriptions of the Culture that highlight its less positive aspects are equally varied, paying less attention to utopian readings or issues of utopian verification. Just as Stuart Kelly rebutted Musk's

[89] Allan Jacobs, 'The Ambiguous Utopia of Iain M. Banks', *New Atlantis: A Journal of Science Technology* (Summer 2009): 45–58.

[90] Ronnie Lippens, 'Imachinations of Peace: Scientifications of Peace in Iain M. Banks's *The Player of Games*', *Utopian Studies: Journal of the Society for Utopian Studies* 13, no. 1 (2002): 1.

[91] Chris Brown, '"Special Circumstances": Intervention by a Liberal Utopia,' *Millennium – Journal of International Studies* 30, no. 3 (December 2001): 625–633; Patrick Thaddeus Jackson and James Heilman, '"Outside Context Problems": Liberalism and the Other in the Works of Iain M. Banks', in *New Boundaries in Political Science Fiction*, Hassler and Wilcox, eds. (South Carolina: University of South Carolina, 2008): 257.

[92] Mike Christie, 'Review of "The State of the Art"', *Foundation: The International Review of Science Fiction* 49: 80.

[93] Stephen Poole, 'Culture Clashes: Review: *Matter* by Iain M. Banks', *Guardian*, 8 February 2008. www.theguardian.com/books/2008/feb/09/fiction.iainbanks.

[94] Felix Danczak, 'Look to Windward: T.S. Eliot's *The Waste Land* as a Template for the sf of Iain M. Banks', *Vector* 264 (Autumn 2010): 23.

[95] Farnell, 'Preemptive regime change in Iain M. Banks's *The Player of Games*', *Fukuoka University Review of Literature & Humanities* 41, no. 4 (16 January 2010): 1,506. ci.nii.ac.jp/naid/110007530075/en/

[96] Banks, 'A Few Notes on the Culture'; Patricia Kerslake, *Science Fiction and Empire* (Liverpool: Liverpool University Press, 2007), 177.

[97] Banks, 'A Few Notes on the Culture'. Web.

[98] Nick Hubble, 'Science Fiction in the U.K.', in *Sense of Wonder: A Century of Science Fiction*, Leigh Ronald Grossman, ed. (Wildside Press, 2011). Ebook.

[99] *Wired* 1, 'Interview with David Garnett', in David Haddock, ed., *The Banksoniain*, 9, 6.

[100] Thomas Christie, 'Chapter Two: Iain M. Banks's *The State of the Art* (1989) and Ken MacLeod's *The Stone Canal* (1996)', in *Notional Identities: Ideology, Genre and National Identity in Popular Genres* (Newcastle upon Tyne: Cambridge Scholars Publishing, 2013), 28.

"utopian anarchist" view of the Culture with his own reading of it as a "totalitarian, interventionist monolith", Banks's creation has been described as: a "hedonistic" and "essentially decadent" society;[101] "imperialist propaganda";[102] a "hegemony";[103] a "fallible dystopia";[104] a "liberal empire";[105] a "Galactic Empire";[106] and a "meta-empire".[107]

Patricia Kerslake's *Science Fiction and Empire* (1997) is the most comprehensive critical study of imperialism, colonialism, and postcolonialism in the SF field to date, as a part of which she provides a complex, largely anti-utopian reading of the Culture as "meta-empire". Kerslake argues that the Culture uses its utopian elitism as a lure to achieve a totalising web of imperial power around the galaxy, leading to a homogenous monoculture – a similar argument to that which Sherryl Vint develops in her two essays on the Culture: 'Iain M. Banks: The Culture-al Body' (2007) and 'Cultural Imperialism and the Ends of Empire: Iain M. Banks's *Look to Windward*' (2008). Similarly, an anti-utopian reading shapes Paul Kincaid's thinking on the Culture in his *Modern Masters of Science Fiction* monograph, *Iain M. Banks*, where he argues that the incomplete picture of the Culture's internal workings makes it "a personal utopia, but not a political or a social one".[108] Banks's utopia may lie in the "individual experience of those living in the Culture", Kincaid argues, but cannot be taken at face value because, "when it comes to interaction with others, particularly those with other societies, therein lies anti-utopia."[109] Simone Caroti's Culture monograph, *The Culture Series of Iain M. Banks: A Critical Introduction* (2015), is "meant as an introduction to the Culture series, not any sort of presumptive final

---

[101] Farah Mendlesohn, 'The Dialectic of Decadence and Utopia in Iain M. Banks's Culture Novels', *Foundation: The International Review of Science-Fiction* 93 (2005): 116–124.

[102] The Shrieking Man, 'Iain M Banks: Imperialist Propagandist?' 23 March 2008. hismastersvoice.wordpress.com/tag/iain-banks/.

[103] William Hardesty, 'Space Opera without the Space: The Culture Novels of Iain M. Banks', in *Space and Beyond: The Frontier Theme in Science Fiction*, Gary Westfahl, ed. (Praeger, 2000), 116.

[104] Darko Suvin, 'Theses on Dystopia 2001', in Michal Kulbicki, 'Iain M. Banks, Ernst Bloch and Utopian Interventions', *Colloquy: Text Theory Critique* 17 (August 2009): 1.

[105] Jackson and Heilman, 'Outside Context Problems', 257.

[106] Christopher Palmer, 'Galactic Empires and the Contemporary Extravaganza: Dan Simmons and Iain M. Banks', *Science-fiction Studies* 26, no. 77 (March 1999): 73.

[107] Brown, '"Special Circumstances": Intervention by a Liberal Utopia'.

[108] Kincaid, *Iain M. Banks*, 142.

[109] Kincaid, *Iain M. Banks*, 48.

word on it."[110] As such, it focuses on providing plot summaries and begins to examine the series critically, advancing a utopian reading of the Culture. Finally, *Gothic Dimensions: Iain Banks – Timelord* (2013) by Moira Martingale – while largely focussed on Banks's non-SF work – does locate the Culture within the important context of the Gothic tradition, and discusses Banks's depiction of gender identity in the series' "cyber females".

Two edited collections of essays dedicated to Banks's work have been published to date. *The Transgressive Iain Banks: Essays on a Writer Beyond Boundaries* (2013) focuses largely on Banks's mainstream works, while *The Science Fiction of Iain M. Banks* (2018) covers his SF,[111] and both explore common themes of genre and game-play. Jude Roberts's PhD thesis from the University of Nottingham focuses on Banks's conceptualisation of "the subject as fundamentally and foundationally vulnerable".[112]

Methodology: Thinking the Break and Post-Apocalypse

In this book I contend that, despite its ambiguities, the Culture is ultimately best regarded as a kind of utopia, according to the open and inclusive definition of the term provided by Ruth Levitas in *Utopia as Method*: "the expression of desire for a better way of living and of being." By choosing an "analytic rather than descriptive definition" in this manner, Levitas works to reveal "the utopian aspects of forms of cultural expression rather than creating binary separation between utopia/non-utopia."[113] Following Levitas, then, this current book applies a similarly "holistic, reflexive method"[114] to the Culture series, drawing upon a variety of disciplines and critical perspectives to explore how Banks expresses his utopian desire. Working from a similarly fluid understanding of utopian thought, Fredric Jameson conceives of utopia in terms of process rather than focusing upon an end result. Radical left-wing thinkers of the nineteenth century, such as Karl Marx, Friedrich Engels, and Leon Trotsky, viewed utopian thinking as dreaming that

---

[110] Simone Caroti, *The Culture Series of Iain M. Banks: A Critical Introduction* (North Carolina: MacFarland & Company, Inc., Publishers, 2015), 2.

[111] Nick Hubble, Joseph Norman, and Esther MacCallum-Stewart, eds., *The Science Fiction of Iain M. Banks* (Exeter: Glyphi Publications, 2018).

[112] Jude Roberts, 'Culture-al Subjectivities: the Constitution of the Self in Iain M. Banks's Culture Texts' (PhD thesis, University of Nottingham, 2013).

[113] Ruth Levitas, *Utopia as Method: The Imaginary Reconstituion of Society* (Hampshire: Palgrave MacMillan, 2013), 11.

[114] Levitas, *Utopia as Method*, back cover.

distracts from the process of political engagement of actually achieving socialism. Jameson, however, argues for utopia as a crucial aspect of that very process, thus reclaiming utopianism as vital to Marxism. Writing in *Archaeologies of the Future* (2005) about utopian, future-oriented SF, Jameson's notion of the "future as disruption" acts as an indirect rebuttal to Trotsky's essay 'What Is Proletarian Culture, and Is It possible?' (1923). Here, Trotsky famously outlined his argument that it is impossible to imagine and map the classless society that follows a successful revolution with any real sense of authenticity until such a society actually exists: essentially, utopia cannot be imagined until it has been achieved. As the development of a society's culture is so intrinsically meshed with its economic foundations, and the relationship between art and the society in which it was produced is so organic, any such visions made pre-socialism would inevitably reflect little more than the bourgeois, capitalist reality in which they were produced. The new social conditions sought through Marxism, his argument goes, are simply too radically different to the present to be conceived of until they become reality.[115] Jameson accepts that artists can therefore inevitably provide only incomplete and fragmentary visions of a post-revolutionary society, necessarily leaving areas indistinct and vague. But he argues that "this increasing inability to imagine a different future *enhances* rather than diminishes the appeal and also the function of Utopia."[116] To Jameson, visions of the future act not as blueprints but as *disruption*, "the name for a new discursive strategy, and Utopia is the form such disruption necessarily takes."[117]

While Jameson's study does not mention Banks, being largely restricted to American examples, the importance of his ideas to the Culture series is clear. The value of utopian fiction texts lies less in the details that they provide for explaining *how* the transition to a radically new future society might be achieved, and more in the ability such visions provide to *challenge a conservative narrative of history*. With his famous declaration that, following the collapse of the Soviet Union, "the universalization of Western liberal democracy" is "the final form of human government", "the end point of mankind's ideological evolution", and therefore the "end of history",[118] Frances Fukuyama cut off entirely any imaginative space in which to conceive of radical alternatives to our

---

[115] Leon Trotsky, 'What Is Proletarian Culture, and Is It Possible?' Marxists.org, [1923]. www.marxists.org/archive/trotsky/1923/art/tia23c.htm.
[116] Fredric Jameson, *Archaeologies of the Future* (London: Verso, 2005), 232. Emphasis added.
[117] Jameson, *Archaeologies*, 231.
[118] Francis Fukuyama, 'The End of History?' *National Interest* 16 (Summer 1989): 3–18.

current political system.[119] The notion encourages us simply to accept the present as fundamentally unchanging and unchangeable, to the extent that it becomes less and less acceptable or even possible to consider an alternative in the first place. Therefore, "the Utopian form itself", Jameson argues, "is the answer to the universal ideological conviction that no alternative is possible, that there is no alternative to the system."[120] Through this disruptive potential, utopia forces us to "think the break *itself*, and not by offering a more traditional picture of what things would look like *after* the break."[121] While readers of Banks's series do glean a stronger picture of the inner places of utopia than many critics acknowledge, it is certainly incomplete: the Culture is often far from the star of its own series, visible in the background if never entirely absent. Banks's series, then, does provide tantalising glimpses of what utopia might be like, but, most importantly, develops a unique form of utopian writing that inspires the radical patterns of thinking necessary to *think the break* from the dystopian, Neoliberal present.

While the Culture remains spatially and temporally disconnected from Earth for much of its existence (the Culture is therefore not us), the original societies from which it was formed are perhaps similar to our own (the Culture used to be something like us), and they each had their own conservative narratives of history. Therefore, it is implied by the general logic of the series that the Culture can only exist as it does in its current form as the result of a radical break from the other, initially non-utopian societies from which it is now formed (we would need a radical break to ever become like the Culture). Thus, the Culture provides a means by which we can begin to imagine *something like* the kind of society that could result from the removal of our current socio-political, economic, and technological restraints. As such, R.C. Elliott could have been referring to the Culture specifically when, in 1970, he wrote the following for his preface to *The Shape of Utopia*: "In utopia it is easier to specify what has been avoided than what has been achieved."[122] Rather than simply illustrating the complexities of defining the term, Elliott provides a way of seeing the utopian process itself: a method of positive negation, a denial of the dystopian in pursuit of its opposite. In one sense, More's original understanding of the term "Utopia" as

---

[119] See also Frances Fukuyama, *The End of History and the Last Man* (Free Press, 1992).
[120] Jameson, *Archaeologies*, 232.
[121] Jameson, *Archaeologies*, 232. Emphasis added.
[122] Robert C. Elliott, *The Shape of Utopia: Studies in a Literary Genre* (London: University of Chicago Press, 1970).

"no place" contains within it a similar logic: somewhere that does not exist – or does not *yet* exist – in lived history. Jameson explains Theodor Adorno's argument that "the mark of violence, whose absence, if that were possible or even conceivable, would at once constitute Utopia".[123] Following a similar logic, Jameson identifies "the absence of money" as both the "fundamental principle" in More's Utopia and "the precondition for this enclave utopia".[124] These two utopian negations are related, with the removal of the need for money relieving society of the burden of economic inequality, and therefore also removing the root cause of violence. In exactly the same manner, the absence of money is the radical break that allows the Culture to exist as utopia, as I explore in Chapter Two.

This book focuses on these different "positive negations" in the Culture series, discussing the different inhibiting factors or blockages to the establishment of utopia that our current, non-utopian society upholds. Wegner and Bruno Bosteel connect Jameson's break with what Alain Badiou describes as the Event: "the very possibility of a radical new beginning, the inauguration of that which was unexpected, unknown, and uncounted",[125] the "shattering of the constraints of the world".[126] Jameson reminds us of the necessity of such an event in any project of radical change, due to the complexity and interconnectedness of any social system:

> A reform which singles out this or that vice, or this or that flaw or error in the system, with a view towards modifying that feature alone, quickly discovers that any given feature entertains a multitude of unexpected yet constitutive links with all the other features in the system [...] Thus, in order adequately to represent such changes, the modification of reality must be absolute and totalizing; and this impulsion of the Utopian text is one with a revolutionary and systemic concept of change rather than a reformist one.[127]

The event that enables utopian transformation, then, must address the *root cause* of a society's problems first and foremost, an *absolute*

---

[123] Fredric Jameson, *Late Marxism: Adorno, or, The Persistence of the Dialectic* (London & New York: Verso, 1990), 109.
[124] Jameson, *Archaeologies*, 18.
[125] Phillip E. Wegner, *Shockwaves of Possibility: Essays on Science Fiction, Globalization, and Utopia* (Bern, Switzerland: Peter Lang AG, 2014), 51.
[126] Wegner, *Shockwaves*, 55.
[127] Jameson, *Archaeologies*, 39.

modification of reality, and the implied order of the Culture's development – its process of transformation from pre-existing, non-utopian societies – reads as follows. First, the technological Singularity enables the Minds to exist, which in turn enables the establishment of a post-money, postscarcity society. In the radically new space that has been opened by this techno-economic revolution (what Csicsery-Ronay calls the *technologiade*), a wave of socio-political and technological reforms (shifts) can occur, radiating outwards from the central event, such as moving beyond class and gender inequality and the limitations of human biology. Each chapter of this book focuses on a different cluster of related themes in the Culture series, inspired by the event and subsequent reforms that Banks's civilisation is implied to have undergone, and locating them in the relevant historical contexts of the Post-Cold War era.

While the Culture's formative context of Britain in the 1970s is frequently perceived as a period of turmoil, others argue that "the approaching disintegration that many saw or simply accepted was apocalyptic in the creative sense, in that the end of one order heralded the start of the new", noting the "political and cultural gains made by the Women's Movement in the 1970s" by way of example.[128] This notion of being "apocalyptic in the creative sense" has been expounded by Wegner (in *Shockwaves*) and Evan Calder Williams (in *Combined and Uneven Apocalypse* [2011]) who challenge the conservatism they see as inherent in the popular sub-genre of "post-apocalyptic" SF. The term "apocalypse" is rooted in the Biblical sense of "the complete final destruction of the world."[129] Yet Wegner and Williams emphasise the ancient Greek translation of the term as revelation, the "lifting of the veil", an "uncovering".[130] Rather than simply an end point, then, apocalypse suggests a new beginning, with radical potential, as in Badiou's event. Yet Wegner contends that "Very often the post-apocalyptic world presented is simply a return to the past, trapping humanity in an endless circular history", with any of the apocalypse's radical potential denied as a "pseudo-event".[131] What we find in more radical fiction such as Banks's, then, is a sense of apocalypse reformulated as the "authentic event: not the end of *the* world, but the end of *a* world, that of the

---

[128] Hubble, McLeod, and Tew, eds., *The 1970s*, 9.
[129] Oxford Dictionaries, 'Apocalypse', Oxford University Press. www.oxford-dictionaries.com/definition/english/apocalypse.
[130] Oxford Dictionaries, 'Apocalypse'.
[131] Wegner, *Shockwaves*, 94.

current socio-political or symbolic order we call global or neo-liberal capitalism."[132] As Williams explains,

> The sense we pursue [...] is the end of a totality, here meaning not the sum of all things but *the ordering of those things in a particular historical shape* [...] this doesn't mean total destruction but rather *a destruction of totalizing structures*, of those universal notions that do not just describe "how things are" but serve to prescribe and insist that "this is how things must be." What is revealed is what has been hidden in plain sight all along. Previously only caught askance from the corner of our eye.[133]

The end of a "totalizing structure", such as Neoliberalism or patriarchy, reveals the flaws, contradictions, and failures of such a system as well as the new, utopian possibilities that arise in its wake.

Operating within a space-opera framework, and through the Culture's radically utopian Event and subsequent technoscientific shifts, Banks's series narrates the *technologiade* as outlined by Csicsery-Ronay in the penultimate chapter of *The Seven Beauties of Science Fiction*: humankind's process of wielding control over the "natural" universe through the mastery of artificial, technological tools, with the creation of a "techno-utopia" like the Culture as its zenith. As such, the *technologiade* process is the point at which the forms of space opera and utopian fiction meet in the Culture series. It is this fundamental process that drives the Culture itself, and on the fundamental ethical and ideological trajectory of its specific *technologiade* that an effective definition of the Culture relies.

This book provides a thematic, critical analysis of the Culture series, with each of the six chapters that follow focusing on a different set of related themes from within Banks's work: ultimately, each chapter identifies and examines a radical shift from the non-utopian, real-world present that the Culture seems to have achieved. The first chapter considers the Culture's expansionist tendencies in the light of critics who see Banks's creation as following a logic of imperialism, concluding that the series utilises the dialectic of utopia and empire as part of the process of critical utopia, as outlined by Tom Moylan.

---

[132] Wegner, *Shockwaves*, 94.
[133] Evan Calder Williams, *Combined and Uneven Apocalypse* (Zero Books: Winchester, 2011), 5. Emphases added.

Chapter 1

World Systems
Imperialism, Interventions, the Technologiade

"Utopia spawns few warriors," "Don't fuck with the Culture"
– Iain M. Banks

How far should a developed society go to help others? When does humanitarian intervention stop and imperial conquest begin? The Culture's desire to offer itself as a model to others throughout the galaxy threatens to turn its utopianism into the very imperialism it claims to oppose: enclaves becoming empire, and egalitarian utopia becoming totalitarian dystopia. The Culture series was written against a background of near-continuous military intervention by Western governments: the Vietnam War (1954–1975); NATO in Bosnia and Herzegovina (1992–2004); the Gulf War (1990–1991); the Iraq War (2003–2011); the War in Afghanistan (2001–present); and Libya (2011). In turn, Michael Hardt and Antonio Negri argue that Neoliberal globalism (Globalisation) – with its network of supranational companies, so-called free trade, and the exploitation of developing-world workers for the profit of the developed world – continues the modern phenomenon of Western imperialism (empire) in a postmodern guise (distinguished using their term, Empire).[1] As a socialist, then, Banks can be broadly aligned with "Alter globalism", various clusters of social justice, environmental, and anti-Globalisation movements linked by opposition to Globalisation if not globalism per se. The Culture series begins with the Culture at war with the Idirans, religious zealots who parallel the spread of a third loose movement, that of jihadist, terror-oriented globalism which has spread throughout the late twentieth and early twenty-first centuries. The loose group of Neo-Nazis, conspiracy theorists, white nationalists and Holocaust deniers known as the "Alt Right", which

---

[1] Michael Hardt and Antonio Negri, *Empire* (United States of America: Harvard University Press, 2000).

developed in response to the election of President Barack Obama in 2009 and gained prominence with the election of President Donald Trump in 2017, also poses a threat to democracy and the current global order. A similar logic of the physical and ideological conflict between these four types of global worldview permeates Banks's series.

But it is not always easy to recognise the Culture as the socialist, anti-imperial alternative to Empire/empire. If the Culture's idyllic, egalitarian habitats seem motivated by utopianism, its meddling in the development of other societies seems, like the military interventions enacted by Western, Neoliberal governments, motivated by imperialism. Rather than socialism within, anarchism without, as Banks intended, some critics argue for the Culture as effectively *socialism within, imperialism without*.

This chapter demonstrates the ways in which the metanarrative of Banks's series provides an important example of Csicsery-Ronay's notion of the *technologiade*, and explores the links between this idea and notions of global/galactic dominance. I explore the Culture series in relation to notions of imperialism and various understandings of empire, including the traditional, centralised model, Kerslake's notion of meta-empire, and Hardt and Negri's conception of Empire, asking to which of these – if any – the Culture might conform. I explore the extent to which the Culture itself is representative of a system that has passed beyond imperialism altogether, or whether such practices remain. Finally, I provide a close reading of *Inversions*, focussing on the ways in which the text demonstrates the practices of the Culture's SC division from within societies with whom Contact has established relations. Ultimately, one of the Culture series' key innovations is to use intervention in the name of peace as a part of the process of the critical utopia.

Space Opera, World Systems, and the *Technologiade*

Space opera presupposes the expansion of human life beyond the Earth and out into the solar system, tracing either a pan- or inter-galactic diaspora of Earth humans, or – as in Banks's series – postulating a pre-existing yet undiscovered plethora of human cultures across the galaxy, alongside those of alien life. Wherever humans exist, we bring politics with us. As Csicsery-Ronay observes, "space opera finds it hard to resist the trope of the world-system [...] turning the cosmos into a scene of political conflict between competing interests".[2] Indeed all space opera – both old and new – is replete with such systems, with different

---

[2] Csicsery-Ronay, *Seven Beauties*, 224.

authors developing huge networks of interlinked planets, moons, ships, and other habitats arranged according to different political, social, and economic frameworks.

In constructing such systems, traditional space opera often failed to look far beyond the familiar politics and economics of Earth. E.E. "Doc" Smith's Lensman series, for example, amongst the earliest examples of the sub-genre (*Triplanetary* was first published in serialised form in *Amazing Stories* in 1934) offers a vision of Globalisation in macrocosm. While the galaxy it depicts is linked by a supposedly harmonious "fellowship of free, independent, and co-operative worlds,"[3] it is overseen by the Galactic Patrol, consisting of military fighters and law-enforcement officers known as the Lensmen, which operates according to a binary moral framework of "Good" and "Evil". Discussing their primary law-enforcement tool, the Lens – an alien amulet that provides them with powerful abilities – Jerome Winter identifies "neoliberal ideology" in the series, for the ways in which the Galactic Patrol "polices all national borders and collectivities in an elite cosmopolitan pose", under the mandate that "the galaxy will have to change their thinking from a National to a Galactic viewpoint."[4] On the other hand, Le Guin's Ekumen sought to overturn the triumphant imperialism and capitalism of traditional space opera, existing as "not a kingdom, but a coordinator, a clearing-house for trade and knowledge."[5] Featuring "three thousand nations on eighty-three habitable worlds", the Ekumen are motivated by "Material profit. Increase of knowledge. The augmentation of the complexity and intensity of the field of intelligent life. The enrichment of harmony and the greater glory of God. Curiosity. Adventure, Delight."[6] Similarly, *Star Trek*'s United Federation of Planets depicts a post-capitalist, egalitarian, and humanitarian galactic collective, albeit one that incongruously retains formal elements of military structures.

Describing the "microworlds" that constitute SF's world systems, Brian McHale explains that "domed space colonies, orbiting space-stations, subterranean cities, 'cities in flight'" appear "throughout the genre's history", but "recur yet again in cyberpunk SF, but with a new intensity of emphasis, sharpness of focus, and functional centrality."[7] Such

---

[3] E.E. "Doc." Smith, *First Lensman* (St Albans: Granada Publishing Ltd, 1971), 242.
[4] E.E. Smith, *First Lensman*, 36.
[5] Ursula Le Guin, *The Left Hand of Darkness* (London: Orbit, 1992), 28–29.
[6] Le Guin, *The Left Hand of Darkness*, 28–29.
[7] Brian McHale, 'Towards a Poetics of Cyberpunk', in *Beyond Cyberpunk: New Critical Perspectives*, Graham J. Murphy and Sherryl Vint, eds. (New York: Routledge, 2012), 7.

microworlds are ultimately "derived from the castles, forests and bowers of medieval romance".[8] But "Where space-stations and space-colonies of traditional SF are glamorous showcases of high technology [...] those of cyberpunk are likely to be orbiting slums – shabby, neglected, unsuccessful, technologically outdated".[9] Alongside the Culture's practical yet marvellous Os and GSVs, *Phlebas*, for example, describes two grim, heterotopic spaces akin to those from cyberpunk – Schar's World, a long-abandoned, politically neutral safe zone, with its huge, dangerous tunnel complex (309), and the Culture Orbital Vavatch, which, preceding its imminent destruction, experiences "the breakdown of law and order" (186), and plays host to the decadent game of Damage for an audience of "hyper-rich dead-beats" (185) – established from the outset as part of Banks's critical-utopian method (see Chapter Three).

So world systems in space opera come in many different forms, but, according to Csicsery-Ronay, there is a broader impulse often at work in the background that provides shape to the narratives of space opera. Csicsery-Ronay acknowledges the antecedents of SF in ancient writings, and heroic and chivalric romance, and traces its modern development through "the class of narrative models" that he calls "the *modern adventure cluster*, consisting of the modern colonial adventure tale [...], the Gothic, and the utopia".[10] Viewing SF as essentially about the relationship between human beings, technology, and the natural world, Csicsery-Ronay argues that the trajectory of generic development is underpinned by a metanarrative known as the *technologiade*, described as "the epic of the struggle surrounding the transformation of the cosmos into a technological regime".[11] Csicsery-Ronay coins and expounds the term *technologiade* in response to critics who argue that SF has no "distinctive myth or storytelling formula", but merely combines elements of other pre-existing "host plots", and colours them with different varieties of nova.[12] Following a Suvinian conception of SF as fundamentally rational, Csicsery-Ronay sees this process of mastering the biosphere through the application of technoscience – the natural world of First Nature replaced by, or coexisting with, an artificial Second Nature – as science fiction's quintessential narrative element.

Whether this process is inherent to all SF is open to debate, but that it is integral to space opera seems an uncontroversial notion.

[8] McHale, 'Towards a Poetics of Cyberpunk', 7.
[9] McHale, 'Towards a Poetics of Cyberpunk', 8.
[10] Csicsery-Ronay, *Seven Beauties*, 217.
[11] Csicsery-Ronay, *Seven Beauties*, 217.
[12] Csicsery-Ronay, *Seven Beauties*, 216.

Csicsery-Ronay identifies space opera alongside the *"techno-Robinsonade"* as the two prominent "dialectically related forms" of the *technologiade*. The *techno-Robinsonade* clearly refers to science fictional updates of Defoe's *Robinson Crusoe* (1719) in which an individual or a small group's attempt to bring technoscience to, and effectively colonise, isolated, "uncivilised" planets often mirrors the imperialistic impulses of the original narrative. After *Crusoe*, the *technologiade* developed in the modern adventure cluster and other works of proto-SF. If Smith's *The Skylark of Space* instigated the interplanetary politics of the space opera, then Clarke's *Rendezvous with Rama* (1973) is probably the earliest *techno-Robinsonade*, recasting Crusoe himself as an isolated group of explorers, the island as a planet-sized enigmatic structure, and the native Friday as the extraterrestrial Ramans.

Csicsery-Ronay's six key tropes of *technologiade* fiction – the Handy Man, the Fertile Corpse, the Willing Slave, the Shadow Mage, the Wife at Home, the Tool Text – provide an analytical toolkit that is especially relevant to space opera, the huge scale of which provides ample opportunities for these tropes to be utilised and developed. "Handiness" is an attribute of the traditional protagonist of *technologiade* fiction because it describes the ability to wield the technoscientific tools that are intrinsic to the mode; such protagonists are almost exclusively male in early examples because such mastery of technoscience is seen to embody masculine attributes of rational logic, assertiveness, and power in an essentialist understanding of gender. Traditional Handy Men are therefore generally scientists, inventors, explorers, ambassadors, pilots, and/or soldiers. Antagonists are often Shadow Mages: ideological inversions of the Handy Man from a society that is equal or near-equal in terms of technological development, but portrayed as socially and politically stilted. Traditional space opera often imbues its Shadow Mages with the qualities of political scapegoats of the era, complete with the associated trappings of racism and xenophobia: the Yellow Peril, the Red Terror, the Jihadist Arab.

Robots, androids, and other AIs provide the quintessential Willing Slave in SF, equivalent to the hero's side-kick in adventure fiction: an assistant on the Handy Man's mission that is a slave because the machine exists to serve, but willing in that its programming exempts it from exploitation. The Handy Man may cling to a "Wife at Home" figure, a far-away source of comfort and potential refuge, which is as likely to be a human being as it is a home planet or culture.[13] The Tool Text refers to the technological apparatus, gadgets, computer code, spacecraft, weaponry, and so forth with which the Handy Man, and

[13] Csicsery-Ronay, *Seven Beauties*, 255.

the Shadow Mage, masterfully manipulates their environments. The space opera often portrays an environment so saturated with advanced technology – a Second Nature – that its presence feels commonplace and goes unnoticed. This Second Nature draws power from the "Fertile Corpse", that is fertile because it is pregnant with exploitable energy, yet a corpse because it is ultimately non-conscious.

The Culture texts work to critically reimagine and subvert these tropes, underpinned by a complex and ambiguous *technologiade* metanarrative. The Culture – as a collective of planet-sized habitats, linked through information and communications networks – is one world system among many and a primary concern of Banks's texts is the political relations between the Culture and other civilisations in the galaxy. According to Banks's authorial intentions and its own self-conception, the Culture is motivated by a humanist, rationalist drive to spread utopianism throughout the galaxy, offering and enabling technoscientific transformation: this need not – in theory – constitute the imposition of one culture upon another, but merely the provision of that culture with the means by which it may develop itself in its own image, unencumbered by lack of access to resources or information. The Culture is part of a world system, the Involved, "space-faring species beyond a certain technological level which are willing and able to interact with each other," (*Windward*, 71) represented as the high point of civilisation to which others should aspire. The Involved have often achieved such status through the missions of Contact and SC, yet technological sophistication does not necessarily lead directly to utopianism, as demonstrated by the various Shadow Mages in Banks's texts, such as the Idirans, a cruel, warrior empire from *Consider Phlebas*, the fascistic Empire of Azad from *The Player of Games*, or the Affront warrior culture from *Excession*.

As such, the Culture sees itself as a techno-utopia, what Csicsery-Ronay calls "the city of handiness, for the ways in which it represents the successful result of social and political planning, actualised mainly by the use of technology, and mechanical engineering."[14] In this manner, the Culture sees itself as the zenith of civilisation, providing an aspirational example of the utopian success to which other societies are entitled. But what Banks's Culture series provides is a complex parallax perspective on the *technologiade*, which, following Jameson, simultaneously reflects its context of Western intervention *as well as* a utopian alternative, as we will see in this chapter and that which follows.

[14] Csicsery-Ronay, *Seven Beauties*, 249.

The Problem of Intervention

If the series concentrated on the internal workings of the Culture, as we see briefly at the start of *Player*, it would be more straightforward to classify its world system as a utopia. Yet Banks's books rarely follow the "visitor to utopia" narrative of utopian fiction, being primarily concerned with the Culture's broader political engagements with other societies through the missions of Contact and SC, through which he subverted the imperialistic conventions of traditional space opera. Yet his approach was not straightforward. Roddenberry's *The Next Generation*, for example, subverted colonial space opera using the Federation's famous 'Prime Directive', a policy which expressly forbids them from interfering in the development of other civilisations, according to a philosophy of cultural relativism. Under the command of Captain Jean-Luc Picard, the USS *Enterprise*-D encounters other cultures and races, and the struggle between wanting to learn and evolve from these cultures, and wanting to help them whilst upholding the Directive, provides the basic conflict of the series. Banks could have imagined the Culture adopting a similar policy, but he deliberately chose an exactly opposite procedure: "when in doubt, intervene."[15] Contact is an intergalactic-relations division maintaining friendly and mutually beneficial relationships, while SC enacts interventions, often without the full or unambiguous consent of those involved. The basic conflict of the Culture, however, is similar to that of the *Enterprise*: the struggle to enact its desire to spread utopia without undermining the nature of other societies through coercion, violence, or the exercise of totalitarian/authoritarian power in the process.

Focusing on SC's policy of intervention, the series runs as follows. The Idiran–Culture war, which provides the background for the events of *Phlebas*, is the largest and most deadly conflict in the Culture's history. While war on any scale goes against the Culture's fundamental values, to leave the religious fundamentalism of the Idirans to expand unchecked would be far worse than engaging in conflict. In *Player*, the Culture persuades its Handy Man, Gurgeh, to hasten the downfall of the Empire of Azad, another cruel Shadow Mage. *Weapons* concerns the mercenary Zakalwe, who turns rogue and uses his Culture training to effect personal vendettas. In 'State', the Culture considers affecting the course of Earth's history, following the violent wars of the twentieth century. *Excession* concerns the emergence of a huge and mysterious alien artefact, the power of which seems to outstrip all of the Involved,

---

[15] David Smith, 'A Conversation with Iain (M.) Banks', in Hubble, Norman, and MacCallum-Stuart, eds., *The Science Fiction of Iain M. Banks*, 38.

potentially placing the Culture within an even greater *technologiade* process. *Inversions* provides a perspective of SC intervention written from *within* the other, non-Culture (Contacted) societies. *Windward* concerns the repercussions of a failed SC intervention and the ways in which this forces the organisation to reconsider its own practices. In *Matter*, the Culture is dragged into a personal and political feud by the former society, elsewhere in the galaxy, of one of its Handy Women. *Surface Detail* challenges the cruel CEO of a barbaric, intergalactic company that practises abuse, slavery, and torture in both physical and virtual environments. Finally, in *Hydrogen*, the Culture exposes a plot to cover up fundamental information about the religion of the Gzilt civilisation, former Contacts of the Culture, which affects their decision to Sublime en masse.

In each of these narratives, the Culture is convinced that such interventions are morally correct and completed with the utmost care, with the exception of the Chelgrian society, with whose caste system it interfered in *Windward*, a mistake from which it has learned and for which it has atoned. Utopia and empire, however, are not necessarily mutually exclusive, as Vint suggests in 'Iain M. Banks: the Culture-al Body': "the seductive danger of any utopia is the desire to convert others and the risk of imperialism that accompanies the evangelical impulse. The central tension in Banks's work between benevolent imperialism and its inevitable discontents is linked to this rejection of utopianism."[16] Clearly, postcolonial theory and history teach us that imperialism, from ancient Egypt to the British Empire, leads to oppression and violence, even genocide, and fascism. Kerslake, too, propounds the argument that "the most common attraction of empire is not through dystopia [...] but through utopia [...] where everyone is free to explore and colonise at will, and where even the colonized subjects appear happy about their condition."[17] Vint and Kerslake's thinking in this regard, then, clearly challenges the project of utopian expansion, even questioning utopianism itself. In *Archaeologies*, Jameson examines a similar issue in what he calls post-revolutionary communist utopias, contrasting "the closure and international secession of that enclave called 'socialism in one country'" with "a Utopian imperialism of further worlds to conquer, both geographically and scientifically".[18] His phrase "Utopian imperialism"

---

[16] Sherryl Vint, 'Iain M. Banks: The Culture-al Body', in *Bodies of Tomorrow: Technology, Subjectivity, Science Fiction* (London: University of Toronto Press Ltd, 2007), 86.
[17] Kerslake, *Science Fiction and Empire*, 132.
[18] Jameson, *Archaeologies*, 20.

neatly encapsulates the contradictions present in Banks's work, as well as in related real-world systems. Essentially, Vint and Jameson suggest the same paradox at the heart of much utopian/dystopian fiction: that within utopia lie the potential seeds of dystopia, and vice versa;[19] and Jameson adopts this principle as a utopian method in *Valences of the Dialectic*, arguing that some of Globalisation's dystopian aspects could theoretically be radically re-functioned for the benefit of the utopian Left.[20]

Similarly, Michal Kulbicki identifies "moral black holes" in Banks's series, produced when utopia contradicts its own intentions and intervenes into other societies using violence. Writing in 'Iain M. Banks, Ernst Bloch and Utopian Interventions', Kulbicki argues that the Culture ultimately resists "a totalizing vision" of imperial hegemony due to its fundamental multiplicity, openness and continual state of flux.[21] David Farnell interprets the Azadian intervention in *Player* as "Pre-emptive Regime Change", and reaches the ambivalent conclusion that the Culture, "in its ongoing struggle to survive as a utopia among other civilizations, is forced into morally difficult positions" that sometimes "violate its own internal moral precepts of individual freedom from interference."[22] In '"Special Circumstances": Intervention by a Liberal Utopia', Chris Brown argues that SC's missions are simultaneously similar to and different from the real-world West.[23] Robert Duggan also draws parallels between the Culture's interventions and those of the United States, reading *Phlebas* and *Windward* in the context of "the aftermath of the first Gulf war" and "looking ahead to terrorism in the post-9/11 world."[24]

As Banks explains in 'A Few Notes on the Culture', "Contact is the part of the Culture concerned with discovering, cataloguing, investigating, evaluating and – if thought prudent – interacting with other civilisations".[25] Contact seems distinct from SC, representing the Culture neutrally through ambassadors, and maintaining ongoing peaceful

---

[19] Margaret Atwood identifies this phenomenon as "Ustopia" in her book *In Other Worlds: SF and the Human Imagination* (London: Virago, 2011).
[20] See Fredric Jameson, 'Utopia as Replication', in *Valences of the Dialectic* (London: Verso, 2009), 410–435.
[21] Michal Kulbicki, 'Iain M. Banks, Ernst Bloch and Utopian Interventions', *Colloquy: Text, Theory, Crtitique* 17 (August 2009): 34–43.
[22] Farnell, 'Preemptive Regime Change in Iain M. Banks's *The Player of Games*', 1,505.
[23] Brown, '"Special Circumstances": Intervention by a Liberal Utopia'.
[24] Robert Duggan, 'Iain M. Banks, Postmodernism and the Gulf War', *Extrapolation: A Journal of Science Fiction and Fantasy* 48, no. 33 (Winter 2007): 558–577.
[25] Banks, 'A Few Notes on the Culture'. Web.

political relations; it is a "relatively small part of the whole Culture" and the "average Culture citizen will rarely encounter a GSV or other Contact ship in person."[26] The fact that Contact is necessary demonstrates that the Culture refuses to exist as an enclave or system of enclaves cut off from other civilisations, and disconnected from wider politics, instead interacting with other societies, races, and organisations.

The key concerns that must be addressed in order to ascertain the extent to which SC/Contact can be considered imperial are: how can a utopia that feels a responsibility to other, non-utopian societies end the suffering and exploitation of others without actually resorting to manipulation and subterfuge to achieve its goal? Is it acceptable to risk war and domination in the name of achieving peace and freedom? At what point do the Culture's interventions stop being benign and utopian, and start being malicious and imperialistic? How can utopia avoid using its success as seduction for empire building?

Traditional Empire

Before the breakdown of traditional imperial structures following World War Two, the term "empire" was defined as follows: "a large political body which rules over territories outside its original borders. It has a central power or core territory – whose inhabitants usually continue to form the dominant ethnic or national group in the entire system – and an extensive periphery of dominated areas."[27] Superficially, the Culture has some parallels with such a system. It is a body of habitats, many of which are associated with it from outside its original borders, and some of which operate in a peripheral relationship. Also, the Culture's inhabitants are predominantly human or humanoid, therefore operating effectively as a dominant "ethnic" group.[28] There are crucial differences, however. As I explore in Chapter Two, the Culture has no central core territory, being spread equally across many habitats, and the Minds are too limited and unaffected by human citizens to be called a power as such, and too dispersed and lacking in consistent organisation to be considered centralised. Given that they must have core and periphery territory, "empires, then must by definition be big, and they must be

---

[26] Banks, 'A Few Notes on the Culture'. Web.
[27] Stephen Howe, *Empire: A Very Short Introduction* (Oxford: Oxford University Press, 2002), 15.
[28] "The Culture is a group-civilisation formed from seven or eight humanoid species" – Banks, 'A Few Notes on the Cultre'. Web.

composite entities, formed out of previously separate units. Diversity – ethnic, national, cultural, often religious – is their essence."[29] Placed within the expansive galactic scope of Banks's series, it is easy to assume that the Culture is a very large system, occupying a huge amount of physical space – yet this is not the case. As Banks explains in *Excession*, the spread of the Culture is quite small in relation to the size of the galaxy and in comparison with other civilisational groups, occupying approximately five per cent of each galactic region (59). The Culture *is* composed from entities that were previously separate, and its many habitats *do* seem to be diverse; yet "in many observers' understanding", empire "cannot be a diversity of equals".[30] If such a system features "no relation of domination between 'core' and 'periphery'" as seems to be the case with the Culture, "then the system is not an empire but deserves a title such as 'commonwealth'" – a "free association of equals."[31]

Writing in *Player*, Banks offers a similar definition of empire, especially through his emphasis on dominance and centralisation: "Empires are synonymous with centralised – if occasionally schematised – hierarchical power structures in which influence is restricted to an economically privileged class retaining its advantages through – usually – a judicious use of oppression and skilled manipulation... In short it's all about dominance" (*Player*, 74). Banks argued that the Culture could only be considered an example of such a structure if the term "empire" was used in a problematically broad and vague manner: the term empire,

> at its widest definition [...] becomes so wide and so loose it really starts to lose any genuine utility. You could call [the Culture] an empire but it doesn't really work that way. It's too intrinsically self-contained and of course [...] empires exist because a group, a state [...] with power, is able to go out and basically take over and enslave and exploit [...] I think... if you insist on calling [the Culture] an empire, it can be, but I think it's kind of pointless. [...] You might as well call it an agrarian commune or something. That makes about as much sense.[32]

He goes on to reassert his conviction that exploitation and enslavement are fundamental to empire and therefore anathema to the Culture,

---

[29] Howe, *Empire: A Very Short Introduction*, 15.
[30] Howe, *Empire: A Very Short Introduction*, 15.
[31] Howe, *Empire: A Very Short Introduction*, 15.
[32] Smith, 'A Conversation with Iain (M.) Banks'.

which intends to "lift the yoke of oppression" from others rather than impose it.[33] *Player* provides fictional examples of societies that conform much more clearly to Banks's definition of empire – the Idirans and the Azadians respectively – which sharply contrast with the nature of the Culture. It seems clear then that however we choose to classify the Culture, it is not an empire in the traditional sense of the term.

Meta-empire

Empire has acquired a much more complex meaning following World War Two, when the various imperial structures of old eventually collapsed, at least in their traditional, centralised forms, and we entered what has become known as the postcolonial era. Writing in *Science Fiction and Empire*, Kerslake argues that the Culture novels "offer the clearest concept yet [in science fiction] of a postcolonial future".[34] But as Stuart Hall explains,

> postcolonial is not the end of colonisation. It is after a certain kind of colonialism, after a certain moment of high imperialism and colonial occupation – in the wake of it, in the shadow of it, inflected by it – it is what it is because something else has happened before, but it is also something new.[35]

Kerslake, then, considers the Culture within this context, as part of the broader literary project that unpicks the threads of traditional models of empire and colonialism as they were woven in previous centuries. Crucially, she emphasises the Culture series as a somewhat unique vision in SF, taking us "*beyond* an awareness of our own imperial history" into what she calls the realm of "*metaempire*: an unknown place where options of both neo-empire and political atrophy are eschewed and a new form of political structure is embraced".[36] Here, Kerslake affirms Banks's place at the vanguard of SF, identifying the Culture as a radically different vision to the standard options resulting from the fall of traditional empire.

---

[33] Smith, 'A Conversation with Iain (M.) Banks'.
[34] Kerslake, *Science Fiction and Empire*, 7.
[35] Julie Drew, 'Cultural Composition: Stuart Hall on Ethnicity and the Discursive Turn', in *Race, Rhetoric, and the Postcolonial*, Gary A. Olson and Lynn Worsham, eds. (Albany: State University of New York Press, 1999), 230.
[36] Kerslake, *Science Fiction and Empire*, 169.

Yet Kerslake also emphasises the complexities and contradictions faced when defining Banks's vision, and her own analysis contains ambiguities. Initially Kerslake argues that "Banks's Culture books are utopian" because of the ways that the needs of everyone are met in this decentralised, postscarcity society, and because "everyone is as physically and intellectually perfect or imperfect as they want to be."[37] Banks's texts, too, "share common ground with anarchism and socialism", and illustrate a "utopianist form of anarchy".[38] Kerslake assures us that, "in Banks's novels, empire has finally become obsolete" and "imperialism of any form is redundant".[39] Yet later in the book, Kerslake's argument shifts, appearing to contradict her previous statements. She now describes the Culture as "far from utopian",[40] then, more emphatically, "non-utopian",[41] and, through its intention to "sacrifice individuality for the benefits of assimilation", the Culture is "the metaphorical embodiment of a deeply imperialist rationale, in that its very elitism and superiority render it supremely attractive to 'lesser' groups".[42] Kerslake sees the Culture as having achieved, or at least of being capable of achieving, an imperialist, galactic hegemony – different from more familiar models of empire, as its power is achieved, not through force or the active coercions of SC, but through the persuasive force of its status as an achieved utopia "which does not need to flaunt its ideological superiority over others; it simply exists in such a manner that all competition and all competitors are outranked before they begin. The only way to 'win' in a confrontation with such ideology is to become one of 'them'."[43] According to this understanding, the Culture participates in a galactic struggle of ideology and power where it could eventually rise to dominate as a uniform *mono*Culture, absorbing and assimilating all others, simply because its success is so supreme and self-evident that none would fail to succumb to its attractions. Banks's utopia poses the danger of becoming not just *a* culture amongst many others, but *the only* Culture, as all others eventually sacrifice their identities to become part of it. Vint, too, discusses the Culture as a kind of imperialism of the body, where physical differences are ultimately effaced as part of a homogenous conformist project.[44]

---

[37] Kerslake, *Science Fiction and Empire*, 175.
[38] Kerslake, *Science Fiction and Empire*, 175.
[39] Kerslake, *Science Fiction and Empire*, 175.
[40] Kerslake, *Science Fiction and Empire*, 169.
[41] Kerslake, *Science Fiction and Empire*, 170.
[42] Kerslake, *Science Fiction and Empire*, 47.
[43] Kerslake, *Science Fiction and Empire*, 45.
[44] See Vint, 'The Culture-al Body'; and Chapter Three of this book.

Unpacking this argument, it is necessary to consider the extent to which the Culture achieves galactic hegemony in such a manner. Smug, self-satisfied, and pompous it may seem at times, but the examples provided in the series demonstrate that the Culture only actively affects the development of a "lesser" group if the continued existence of that group would inhibit the freedom or the very existence of others to a significant extent. If the Culture does act like an empire and achieve "the suppression of one culture by another",[45] as Kerslake suggests, it focuses exclusively on those cultures practising violence, intolerance, slavery, genocide, fascism, and so forth – an important distinction – and even then prefers to suppress those specifically negative traits, rather than that culture in its entirety. The extent of any subsequent assimilation becomes therefore entirely voluntary.

In *Phlebas*, for example, the Idirans essentially lost their conflict with the Culture, although they "technically never surrendered" (462). In the aftermath, the Idirans' computer network became "a Culture Mind in all but name", suggesting that they would be capable of achieving a postscarcity society similar to the Culture. While much of the Idiran Empire was destroyed or broken up, only "a few" of those who remained actually joined the Culture; many went into exile, escaped to other planets, or even established "independent, nominally non-military habitats within other spheres of influence (under the Culture's eye)" (462), in a relationship perhaps similar to the Commonwealth of Nations. In *Hydrogen*, the hidden knowledge which the Culture makes available to the Gzilt society – essentially debunking their holy book (111) – has little ultimate effect on their decision to Sublime, and the Culture makes no attempt to stop 99.9 per cent of the Gzilt population doing so (515). Following such a revelation, an imperially oriented society might use the resulting turmoil as the basis for a secular transformation and cultural assimilation. Instead, however, the Culture does very little in response – seeing this revelation as part of their duty to uncover an important truth to those affected by it, who would otherwise remain ignorant – and the Gzilt continue to Sublime as intended, as their religion dictates, at the end of the novel.

Kerslake's conception of the Culture as imperialistic arises from her understanding of the terms "empire" and "imperialism" themselves, which directly contrast with Banks's, and those of other politically Left-oriented and postcolonialist thinkers. As quoted in full above, Banks understood empire to be an innately flawed and negative political system because of its focus on the dominance of one class

---

[45] Kerslake, *Science Fiction and Empire*, 132.

over another, use of "skilled manipulation", and suppression of dissent and non-hegemonic cultures. Kerslake argues, however, that "empire" is a neutral term, and "not intrinsically wrong; it is outward evidence of the social needs of the human species to develop, progress and grow".[46] She argues that "empire is not itself an evil thing, yet our histories demonstrate that those who have created empires do not do so in order to produce a state of peace and beauty."[47] Clearly, Kerslake's understanding of empires as potentially contributing towards human progress and development clashes dramatically with Banks's, and is "politically revealing".[48]

The Culture as "Empire"

Hardt and Negri consider the future of imperialism following the collapse of traditional empires around the world in their influential book *Empire*, focusing upon the nature of twenty-first-century Globalisation (Neoliberal globalism). It is important to examine the Culture in relation to their concept of Empire with which it has important parallels, as Vint has begun to do in her two essays on Banks's work.[49] In *Empire*, Hardt and Negri suggest that, rather than fading completely, past imperialisms persist in a different, subtler form as Globalisation, where a new form of sovereignty has emerged, "composed of a series of national and supranational organisms united under a single logic of rule. This new global form of sovereignty is what we call Empire."[50] Hardt and Negri contrast Empire with traditional imperialism, stating that: "Empire establishes no territorial centre of power and does not rely on fixed boundaries or barriers. It is a decentred and deterritorializing apparatus of rule that progressively incorporates the entire global realm within its open, expanding frontiers."[51] Empire, therefore, boundaryless and limitless, refers to a regime "that effectively encompasses the spatial totality", that "effectively suspends history and thereby fixes the existing state of affairs for eternity", and aims to rule "social life in its entirety" by seeking "directly to rule over human nature."[52]

---

[46] Kerslake, *Science Fiction and Empire*, 164.
[47] Kerslake, *Science Fiction and Empire*, 171.
[48] Kerslake, *Science Fiction and Empire*, 70.
[49] See Vint, 'The Culture-al Body', 2007; and 'Cultural Imperialism and the Ends of Empire', 2008.
[50] Hardt and Negri, *Empire*, xii.
[51] Hardt and Negri, *Empire*, xii.
[52] Hardt and Negri, *Empire*, xv.

Following these descriptions, there are clear parallels between the Culture and Empire: just as "Empire is characterised fundamentally by a lack of boundaries",[53] Fal N'geestra observes "no clear boundaries to the Culture, then; it just fades away at the edges, both fraying and spreading" (*Phlebas*, 26). Furthermore, Hardt and Negri explain that, with Empire, "no subjectivity is outside, and all places have been subsumed in a general *"non-place"*,[54] just as the etymological root of "utopia" contains the Greek words *ou* ("not") and *topos* ("place").[55] The artificial environments of Culture citizens are spread across the galaxy in a largely autonomous relationship yet are interconnected by a communications web. Echoing this notion, Mendlesohn compares the Culture directly with the real-world West, stating that "the Culture has become McDonaldised",[56] drawing upon George Ritzer's term for "the imposition of uniform standards that eclipse human creativity and dehumanize social relations," resulting from the wide-spread adoption of "socio-cultural processes by which the principles of the fast-food chain are coming to dominate more and more sectors of American society as well as the rest of the world."[57] Mendlesohn compares the structure of Banks's civilisation to global capitalism, then, asking readers to liken the Culture's GSVs, for example, with the blandness and banality of corporate franchises, due to their self-sufficient, self-replicating nature.[58]

Vint, too, portrays the Culture as a monoculture that strives "to be a utopia, offering consolidation, rather than the more challenging heterotopia that disturbs the given orders of things."[59] Referring to Michel Foucault's concept from *The Order of Things* (1971) and 'Des Espace Autres' (1986), Vint implies that the Culture's purpose is to offer comfort by assimilating disparate elements into sameness, rather than productive discomfort through difference and separation: a utopian yet hegemonic space free from "undesirable" elements that operate outside the accepted order.

---

[53] Hardt and Negri, *Empire*, 363.
[54] Hardt and Negri, *Empire*, 363.
[55] Oxford Dictionaries, 'Utopia', Oxford University Press, 12 February 2015. www.oxforddictionaries.com/definition/english/utopia.
[56] Mendlesohn, 'The Dialectic of Decadence'.
[57] Manfred B. Steger, *A Very Short Introduction to Globalization* (Oxford: Oxford University Press, 2003), 73.
[58] Hardt and Negri, *Empire*, 85.
[59] Vint, 'The Culture-al Body', 86.

Banks on SC and Contact

While he acknowledges that many narratives within the series address potential problems arising from the Culture's interventions, Banks condoned the activities of SC from the outset, regularly reaffirming his view that the Culture – in both its structure and actions – is not an empire, that it should not and cannot be described as imperialist in any regard, and that any attempt to do so would be pointless.[60] Banks justified the Culture's *technologiade*-through-intervention because of its motivation to ensure that as many beings as possible are allowed to experience the freedoms it has achieved for its own citizens and he argued that the interventions are carried out in as peaceful a manner as possible, in order to end suffering and exploitation, and spread its utopian message, with no subsequent attempt to reassert a system of control or power. As Banks explains, the Culture "can prove statistically that interfering is the right thing, the morally right thing, to do"[61] – suggesting that SC's missions are planned and enacted according to rational analysis based on numerical data and a utilitarian ethical framework.

Banks saw SC's missions as solving the problem of boredom in utopia (explored in Chapter Three) by providing Culture citizens with a sense of moral obligation and purpose, to make them

> feel good about themselves. I mean, there's nothing in a sense for them to strive for personally. In a sense at any given level, whatever fractal scale you look at of the society, it's kind of done it all. It's got everything. So what is left? What is left is looking out into the rest of the galaxy and seeing mayhem, anarchy, disease, warfare and bad behaviour in general. So they are going on saying "Well, we can help affect this, we can do something."[62]

Intervention, then, is a moral duty to extend the freedom and peace the Culture has achieved for itself as a utopia to other, non-utopian societies – it would be irresponsible and morally wrong, in fact, to enjoy peace passively while others suffer. Therefore, the Culture operates according to the philosophy that – when absolutely necessary, and conducted in the least harmful, exploitative, or imperialistic manner possible – it has a responsibility to intervene in the development of other civilisations, offering political, intellectual, and material support throughout the

---

[60] Smith, 'A Conversation with Iain (M.) Banks', 49.
[61] Smith, 'A Conversation with Iain (M.) Banks', 49.
[62] Smith, 'A Conversation with Iain (M.) Banks', 49.

process, and in the future. The Culture aims to be a key force that drives the *technologiade*'s technoscientific transformation of the galaxy without breaking its own fundamental axiom that nothing and nobody is exploited.[63]

The Culture and Utopian Globalism

The importance of considering the Culture series as a multi-volume form of the critical utopia cannot be overstated: with each text in the series, Banks found new ways to critique the Culture, fresh perspectives that would continually complicate and extend his civilisation. Banks's whole series developed from the *Weapons* character Zakalwe, whose existence and behaviour threaten to undermine the values of the Culture, and even its very ability to exist. The decision to introduce his readers to the Culture from Horza's perspective in *Phlebas* ensured that all of its problems would be foregrounded from the outset. The devastating failure of Culture intervention is most pronounced in *Windward*, making its *technologiade* seem indistinguishable from imperialism. The Interesting Times Gang in *Excession* shows the first indication that the Minds' benevolence may have limitations, and seems to demonstrate how their system may provide the template for totalitarianism.

Yet other texts render intervention in a more complex light, and Banks provocatively suggests that there may be ways in which deliberately affecting the development of other cultures does not have to constitute a form of colonialism or imperialism:

> part of the idea of the Culture is that they're not trying to turn everyone deliberately into, you know, little versions of themselves. I think this is probably what's going to happen anyway at the higher end of civilisation. They're not trying to [...] impose their own sort of *brand of utopia* on [...] everybody else. They just want to get on with their own lives basically and having the freedom to do it. They don't want to impose another sort of, you know, imperial or even philosophical sort of template on the people that they are attempting to free.[64]

Farnell, however, sees this process differently, arguing that part of the Culture's modus operandi whilst affecting a system of "regime change"

---

[63] See Banks, 'A Few Notes on the Culture'. Web.
[64] Smith, 'A Conversation with Iain (M.) Banks', 49.

is to "discredit the cultural basis of its negative hierarchical structure".[65] Yet, as demonstrated by the analysis of *Inversions* that follows below, it is far from clear that the Culture does in fact police the universe, as Vint suggests. Also, Farnell does not suggest that the discredited culture must necessarily be replaced with that of the Culture itself, making it clear that this would only be the case when dealing with an especially oppressive regime.[66]

It seems, therefore, that – similar to Kerslake's discussion of the Culture and (meta-)empire – the discussion here is really to do with the similarities between the Culture and the notion of Globalisation itself, as broadly defined, rather than the specific Neoliberal manifestation of it, known as Empire. Manfred B. Steger offers a more neutral definition of Globalisation, or what he calls globalism: "a multidimensional set of social processes that create, multiply, stretch, and intensify worldwide social interdependencies and exchanges while at the same time fostering in people a growing awareness of deepening connections between the local and the distant."[67] Through this definition, Steger emphasises that the basis of globalism is fundamentally *cultural* – a "set of *social* processes" – rather than being in economics or politics. As such we can see that Empire (imperialism in the form of globalism), fundamentally enacts economic exploitation; and the definitions of Empire (and empire) provided by Kerslake, Vint, and Mendlesohn seem to make the deeply postmodern assumption that imperialism is first and foremost a matter of culture and hegemony, rather than economic exploitation and political oppression.[68]

The Culture Series as *Technologiade*

Csicsery-Ronay links Empire to his notion of the *technologiade*, arguing that the goal of the "ruling orders" is a "technological empire, whose systems of communication, commodification and control infiltrate, and indeed saturate, all formerly 'natural' relationships, from the institutional to the biological."[69] So the *technologiade* in SF, which aims to transform the cosmos into a technological system, articulates the same fundamental

---

[65] Farnell, 'Preemptive Regime Change', 1,517.
[66] Farnell, 'Preemptive Regime Change', 1,517.
[67] Steger, *A Very Short Introduction to Globalization*, 13.
[68] See Jameson's distinction between economic expoitation and political oppression, outlined in the final chapter of *Representing Capital: A Reading of Volume One* (London: Verso, 2011).
[69] Istvan Csicsery-Ronay Jr., 'Empire', in *The Routledge Companion to Science Fiction*, Bould et al., eds. (Oxon: Routledge, 2009), 362–372.

deterritorialising, decentralising impulse as Globalisation but extrapolated beyond planetary limits, and continuing into outer space; and it therefore has the potential to take the form of a hierarchical, imperial project or enable an egalitarian, utopian system.

In *Phlebas*, Banks pits the Culture against an empire of equivalent power, that of the Idirans – who aim to transform the universe into a fundamentalist religious, militaristic regime, obliterating all other forms of life and culture. While ultimately the Idirans seem "bad" and the Culture "good", the clear-cut morality of traditional space opera is made grey through protagonist Horza's perspective, which highlights the Culture's limitations from the outset. We are left with a generally positive impression of the Culture's utopian globalism, but only as preferable to the jihadist globalism of the Idirans or the libertarian, social Darwinism of Horza and the crew of the *Clear Air Turbulence*.

In *Player*, Culture protagonist Gurgeh facilitates the last stage in the structural implosion of the cruel, fascistic Empire of Azad by literally beating them at their own game, in a narrative that comes closer to the intensely focussed scale of the *techno-Robinsonade* than the "wide-screen baroque" of space opera, with no other sub-narratives focussed on the outer galaxy and its politics. Thus, *Player* portrays the Culture's intervention as a very carefully managed and timed procedure, instigated only when it has collected relevant information and which is committed to finding alternatives to violence.

In *Weapons*, Culture Handy Man and outsider Zakalwe makes a career of bringing the Culture's technoscience to remote corners of the galaxy, yet exploits his position to accomplish personal vendettas. In 'State', the Culture considers altering the Earth's development, which – portrayed as complex and beautiful yet also violent and illogical – is positioned alongside the other galactic "backwater" locations discussed in the series, before deciding ultimately to leave "us" as a control experiment for the *technologiade* campaign. In *Excession*, the Culture and other civilisations in the galaxy, all with differing views about the process of galactic redevelopment, come to understand that the Excession – an entity from beyond the known universe – may be part of a process similar to the *technologiade*, but on an even grander scale, and conducted by entities of previously unimagined power. As suggested by its title, *Inversions* flips the standard perspective of the *technologiade*, presenting two personal narratives from *inside* two very different civilisations that are slowly, without their knowledge, being transformed into more scientific societies, as implicitly instigated by the Culture. *Windward* is concerned with the failure of the Culture's *technologiade* and the grief, violence, and deep-seated hatred that can result, as well as with the Culture's atonement. In *Matter* Banks contrasts the development of a feudal society, Sarl, with the galactic-scale machinations and rivalries of warring civilisations and species. Following the uncovering of deep corruption within Sarl's monarchical system, a Culture Handy Woman sacrifices herself to avoid the destruction of the planet, and a new political leader from within the Sarl is implicitly appointed to begin a positive transformation. In *Surface Detail*, the Culture brings down Veppers, the CEO of a very powerful business empire – and known murderer, slave owner, and rapist – and ends a network of environments that Veppers maintained, which equated to something like a barbaric, digital inversion of the *technologiade*. Finally, *Hydrogen* examines the relationship between the Culture and a civilisation, the Gzilt, who have embraced technoscience to develop their society to a similar level, yet, for religious reasons, choose to enter a different part of the universe, the Sublime, where technoscience seems to be irrelevant.

Viewing the narrative of the whole series through this lens of techno-transformation, therefore, reveals the interplay of opposing themes: the barbaric and the civilised; the scientific and the superstitious; the personal and the political; the dominant and the submissive; freedom and control; peace and war. To continue examining the ideological character of the Culture's *technologiade* in further detail, then, it is pertinent to begin with the text in which Banks shows how such a process operates from within the society being transformed rather than from without.

Inversions as Planetary Romance

Inversions, published on 27 May 1998, is technically the sixth Culture text yet remains something of an anomaly for several reasons. Firstly, Banks intended for the novel to have a different relationship to the rest of the sequence than the others, stating that "*Inversions* was an attempt to write a Culture novel that wasn't."[70] While *Inversions* was published as an "M. Banks" book, it was the first not to feature "A new Culture novel" printed on the cover, and its narrative does not explicitly reference the Culture. The novel does work as a stand-alone novel, although, as Kincaid points out, small plot details would then be unclear, thus not "playing fair" with the reader.[71] Yet, through a process of oblique allusion and intertextual games, readers in-the-know can draw connections between *Inversions* and Banks's Culture universe.

---

[70] Nick Gevers, 'Cultured futurist Iain M. Banks creates an ornate utopia', *Science Fiction Weekly*, 15 May 2008. archive.is/FgDHg.
[71] Kincaid, *Iain M. Banks*, 86–87.

58   THE CULTURE OF "THE CULTURE"

The novel is set on an unnamed planet resembling Europe in the Early Modern period in terms of culture, as well as technological and social development. Prior to the events of the novel, an empire that had dominated the planet for many years fell apart, leaving the remaining societies in a state of constant war. One narrative is concerned with Doctor Vosill, who serves King Quience of Haspidus, while another focuses on the story of DeWar, bodyguard to General Urleyn, the Prime Protector of the Protectorate of Tasassen. Haspidus is a feudal nation, with a monarch appointed by Providence, "the name of the mystical, divinely inhuman Court before which we wish our actions to be judged" (Prologue, 2) and organised according to martial and patriarchal values, similar in these respects to Sursamen from *Matter*. Tasassen is a secular society, established following the murder and supersession of the Emperor by the General Urleyn. Reading between the lines, Vossil and DeWar are cousins, originating from the Culture, but have become separated from each other and their home for ideological reasons. Vossil, aligned with the Culture's values, is an SC agent working undercover to bring scientific knowledge to Haspidus, while DeWar, having becoming dissatisfied with Culture life, lives in exile on Tasassen, trying to fit in.

Inversions achieves its perspective of "intervention from within" through another anomalous aspect, relating to the text's genre/sub-genre. The narratives of *Inversions* are confined to the cultures of a single planet, and only the Culture characters demonstrate awareness of a universe beyond it. It is therefore the only text in the series – with the possible exception of *Player* – that achieves the smaller scale of the planetary (or *inter*planetary) romance rather than the epic, universe-spanning scope of space opera.[72] Gary K. Wolfe defines "interplanetary romances" as "broadly, an adventure tale set on another, usually primitive, planet".[73] As Hubble explains of *Inversions*, "The presentation of the alternative stories – neither of which are narrated by their principal characters – generates a stereoscopic depth that enables the novel to work simultaneously as an actual planetary romance as well as a narrative containing future perspectives."[74] So the planetary romance enables Banks to

---

[72] As explored in Tony Keen's paper given at 'The State of the Culture: a One-day Symposium on Iain M. Banks's "Culture" series', Brunel University London, 11 September 2013.

[73] John Clute and David Langford, 'Planetary Romance', in *The Encyclopedia of Science Fiction*, Clute et al., eds. (London: Gollancz), updated 4 December 2013. http://www.sf-encyclopedia.com/entry/planetary_romance.

[74] Hubble, Norman, and MacCallum-Stuart, eds., *The Science Fiction of Iain M. Banks*, 75.

provide an account of the quasi-medievalism of Haspidus and Tasassen while still incorporating potential comparison with the far-advanced Culture.

Inversions, the *Technologiade* and Clarke's Third Law

In this manner – focusing upon a "primitive" planet that is known to exist within a galaxy of many others at different levels of social and technological development – the planetary romance operates as a text-length illustration and exploration of Clarke's Third Law: to the people of Haspidus and Tasassen, the technoculture of the Culture is indistinguishable from magic. Doctor Vosill's narrative explores the effects of introducing very advanced medical science into a relatively primitive society whose medical practice is largely based on folklore and superstition. As the Culture exists at the extreme end of the developmental scale (Csicsery-Ronay's utopian "city of handiness") compared with Haspidus, most of Vossil's methods, knowledge, and equipment (her "handiness", the Tool Text she introduces) are easily attributed to the supernatural. The most prominent example of this is the emergence of a knife missile – a militaristic drone – which Vosill uses to save herself from rape, torture, and death. As Martingale notes, "Banks's voice-activated knife-missiles are pure magic".[75]

Doctor Vosill is very aware of how this is interpreted, and uses it to her advantage, choosing to communicate scientific ideas in quasi-magical terms to King Quience so as to bridge the gap between her advanced knowledge and his relatively primitive views. Vosill asks the king to use an ointment, in order to treat a wound on his leg; unconvinced, yet trusting of the Doctor, he acquiesces. "As you feel, sir, it dulls the pain," Vosill states; "also it fights the particles of ill humour which infest the air, and it aids the healing process" (50–51). Similarly, Vosill corrects Oelph for wearing a bandanna around his mouth to fend off "ill humours" and instructs him that "infectious agents are transmitted in breath or bodily fluids, even if they are in bodily fluids [...] A bad smell by itself will not make you ill" (84). Vosill deliberately uses the antiquated phrase "ill humour", drawing on the term from Greco-Roman medicine, to get her point across. "Humours", and "humoral theory", refers to four distinct bodily fluids – blood, phlegm, black bile, and yellow bile – believed to cause illness when insufficiently balanced in

---

[75] Moira Martingale, *Gothic Dimensions: Iain Banks – Time Lord* (Quetzalcoatl Publishing, 2013), 26.

the body,[76] and Vosill uses it instead of the modern term "bacteria" that would be unfamiliar to King Quience.

Later in the novel, Vossil gradually introduces more accurate, contemporary terminology, replacing pseudo-scientific magical phrases with the language of biology and physics. Describing the neck wound of a murder victim, Vosill says, "It severed all the major blood vessels, the larynx" – but is cut off by a rival, Doctor Skelim: "The what?" Following her scientific explanation, Vosill is written off as a "quack" who deliberately obscures her lack of knowledge with "foreign words" (189). Continuing to compare Vosill to "priests of old" who read entrails "to find the murderer's name" (189), Skelim's response is ironic in this context because, to Banks's readers, that is exactly how the rival doctor himself appears.

At points, Vosill tries to challenge superstitious beliefs. When King Quience talks of "old stories" about giant kings tearing strange creatures in half with their bare hands in order to smite their enemies, Vosill asks "Might these not be simply legends, sir?" (52) The king circumvents her by accusing Vosill of rudely interrupting him, and her question is forgotten. Vosill, demonstrating her characteristic calmness and patience, answers: "I will try never to interrupt you again" (52) – yet she continues to do so. While at first her deeds seem motivated by personal and professional concerns, the reader comes to suspect her involvement with Contact and/or the Culture: it becomes clear that Doctor Vosill acts in accordance with its broad aims, providing culturally and politically neutral information. In the first chapter, Vosill is called to the chief torturer's chamber to attend to a victim; she carefully challenges the legality of the interrogation – *"does* the King know?" (13) – before exercising compassion and putting the victim out of his misery, easily fooling the guards into thinking this death their own doing. Doctor Vosill's behaviour – her unfailing moral responsibility for the health of all people regardless of background – challenges much of that which those around her have grown up to believe. The chapters concerned with Vosill are narrated in first person by her assistant Oelph, who is quickly revealed to be spying on her for his unnamed "Master". Clearly deeply in love with this strangely assertive, intelligent, and beautiful doctor, Oelph's account reveals the extent to which Vosill's progressive tendencies affect him. In the second chapter, Oelph becomes shocked, indignant, and derogatory when Vosill responds to a cry for help by a child from a poor district: "The King's physician was about to pay a

---

[76] Science Museum, 'Humours'. www.sciencemuseum.org.uk/broughttolife/techniques/humours.aspx.

call in a storm, not on anyone noble, likely to be ennobled or indeed even respectable, but on a family of slack-witted all-runt ne'er-do-wells, a tribe of contagiously flea'd happen-ills" (43). Having grown up in this rigidly hierarchical, monarchical society, it takes a long time for Oelph to succumb to Vosill's patient wisdom and parental scolding, and to overcome his class prejudice. Similarly, Oelph lives in a rigidly patriarchal society, describing "the facts of life which dictate the accepted and patent preeminence of the male," (9) and Vosill who – with her advanced Culture knowledge, quick thinking, and wit – is the only woman who can convince him otherwise. The narrative makes it explicit that Oelph – after the doctor moves on to practise elsewhere – continues developing his medical skills: in the epilogue, Oelph reveals that he has been appointed a doctor, and finally as Royal Physician.

Vosill still affects and maintains her influence due to her close relationship with the king: no matter how suspicious she seems, Vossil's maintenance of Quience's health ensures that her actions are generally seen as eccentric rather than untrustworthy. The fact that Vosill's treatments and medicines – replacing crude, pre-scientific techniques such as leeches and "burn-glass veining" (45) – are effective ensures that the king keeps her in his service, and allows her leverage in his thoughts and decision making.

Detective Fiction and the *Technologiade*

Alongside the planetary romance form in *Inversions*, Banks incorporates tropes from detective fiction that also further the *technologiade* narrative. A key development in Vosill's story is the death of Nolieti, the king's chief torturer, with Vosill effectively assuming the role of detective. First, Banks establishes the *sjuzet*: the known facts of the crime as they are presented to the "detective" in a jumbled order.[77] Gathered around Nolieti's corpse, most of the key players within the Haspidus court, including King Quience, Doctor Vosill, Doctor Skelim, Guard Commander Polchiek, and Oelph, discuss the details of the crime in an attempt to solve it. The murder proves difficult to solve, however, as Banks incorporates the device of a "locked room mystery", familiar from many works of crime fiction.[78] Following inaccurate and biased

---

[77] Scott McCracken, *Pulp: Reading Popular Fiction* (Manchester: Manchester University Press, 1998), 54.

[78] There are numerous examples across media, including 'The Murders in the Rue Morgue' (1841) by Edgar Allen Poe; *The Sign of the Four* (1890)

suggestions made by Doctor Skelim and Polchiek – mostly based upon facile observation, guesswork, and flimsy logic, guided by prejudice and self-interest – Doctor Vossil eventually solves the crime using an objective process of deduction, estimates based upon empirical evidence and logic; and the *fabula*, or the chronological order of events, is eventually revealed to the investigators. Discussing detective fiction, Scott McCracken observes that

> the history of the contemporary genre is closely linked with the history of the modern legal process. One of the characteristics of modernity is the use of the law instead of arbitrary power. The detective narrative emerged at a time when the collection of evidence and the presentation of a case were replacing the extraction of confession by torture.[79]

Following this, it is easy to see how, using the Nolieti murder story, *Inversions* directly plays out the replacement of the "extraction of confession by torture" by the "collection of evidence and the presentation of a case". This is emphasised by the fact that the chief torturer is the victim this time, his case ironically solved without the methods for which he is so enthusiastic. At one stage, Banks makes the arguments for and against the use of torture explicit: Doctor Vossil argues emphatically that "the barbaric custom" of torture "produces not the truth but rather whatever those commanding the questioner wish to hear", while King Quience, describing people as "lying beasts", argues that "the only way to get the truth out of them sometimes is to wring it out of them" (195–196). It also becomes clear, therefore, that Vosill brings the potential for the development of such a "modern legal process" with her, in order to replace the current system of Haspidus, which clearly adheres to the "arbitrary power" of the pre-Enlightenment medieval period. While Vosill (and therefore the Culture) represents the overturning of arbitrary power, she brings with her the potential for another kind of power: as McCracken argues, "the judicial process plays an important part in establishing the consent for hegemony" in "societies governed by the rule of law."[80]

---

by Arthur Conan Doyle; and more recently *The Girl with the Dragon Tattoo* (2005) by Stieg Larsson. For a more detailed outline of the trope, see 'The Locked Room', Donald E. Westlake, *Murderous Schemes: An Anthology of Classic Detective Stories* (Oxford: Oxford University Press, 1996).

[79] McCracken, *Pulp*, 51.
[80] McCracken, *Pulp*, 51.

By incorporating the rationalism and empiricism of crime-fiction tropes into SF, Banks makes explicit his ongoing intention to write within a Suvinian framework; and *Inversions* co-opts Doctor Vossil as detective into the Culture's covert *technologiade* process, effecting a gradual and careful transition from belief in magic to understanding of science.

The Utopian *Technologiade*

Inversions dramatises a Culture intervention that is deemed successful by the Culture and is not challenged. The Culture's justification for intervention emerges in coded form through a kind of fairy tale which DeWar and his friend, court concubine Perrund, improvise to entertain a child. Set in the land of Lavishia, where everybody was "as happy as they could be", informed readers of Banks's series start to recognise a familiar pattern. In Lavishia lived

> two friends, a boy and a girl [...] They were the best of friends but they disagreed on many things. One of the most important things they disagreed about was what to do when Lavishia chanced upon [...] tribes of poor people. Was it better to leave them alone or was it better to try and make life better for them? Even if you decided it was the right thing to do to make life better for them, which way did you do this? Did you say, Come and join us and be like us? Did you say, Give up all your own ways of doing things, the gods that you worship, the beliefs you hold most dear, the traditions that make you who you are? Or do you say, We have decided you should stay roughly as you are and we will treat you like children and give you toys that might make your life better? (*Inversions*, 104)

Hubble argues that, when such stories appear in the series, Banks subverts the politically conservative and patriarchal norms of fairy tale as well as enabling the consideration of ethics with which fairy and folk tales are associated, but in a more progressive form.[81] Such tales work well within the planetary romance, serving as a familiar vehicle through which advanced cultures can communicate complex ideas to

---

[81] Nick Hubble, '"Once upon a time, over the gravity well and far away...": Fairy-Tales Narratives in Banks's Science Fiction', in Hubble, Norman, and MacCallum-Stuart, eds., *The Science Fiction of Iain M. Banks*, 61–79.

those relatively less developed. Using this moralistic tale, DeWar outlines debates surrounding intervention and cultural relativism in a simplified manner appropriate to a children's story, which obliquely serve to explain the Culture's justification for its interventions.

The boy and the girl in the tale clearly represent DeWar and Vossil, and the two arguments regarding intervention that are outlined – "leave them alone" or "do the right thing" – align with the characters' attitudes in the novel: DeWar largely goes along with the society of Tasassen, while Vossil tries to change that of Haspidus. Vossil, as metonym for the Culture, justifies her actions according to the fairy tale: rather than the imperialism of forcing other cultures to give up "the traditions that make you who you are", the Culture sees itself as merely providing the "toys that might make your life better". Vint argues that "Empire is a useful model for understanding Banks's Culture," as the expansion of both is effected far more often through their "way of life" than through sheer military might.[82] In this sense, the two loosely intertwined narratives of *Inversions* dramatise the effect that the Culture's way of life – its culture, embodied by both the rational Handiness and the sympathetic kindness of Vossill – has on its intervention. The Culture rarely engages in armed conflict: while the series opens with the Idiran–Culture war taking place in the background of *Phlebas*, it is an occurrence so unique and abhorrent that it shapes the Culture's history, ultimately resulting in a commitment against entering into war again. Instead, *Inversions* narrates the Culture's soft power, portrayed as providing less-developed societies with the means by which they may become *something like* the Culture – potentially leading a *similarly utopian* way of life, enabled by Contact's instigation of technoscientific understanding – but without the other society necessarily becoming fully assimilated or eventually forming a clone-like version of the Culture.

In fact it seems likely that Haspidus may never even come to know the truth about Vossil and DeWar, and the Culture may never need to re-establish Contact. In the 'Epilogue', Oelph reveals the ways in which Haspidus has developed post-Contact. When Oelph becomes a successful doctor, building upon Vossil's training, he demonstrates awareness of his part in the process that led to the establishment of a new era: "The Kingdom is at peace, we prosper." (Epilogue) Yet Haspidus's development remains modest. It has not become a utopia, for example, and certainly not a *techno*-utopia or member of the galactic Involved like the Culture; but it does indeed seem oriented toward "what the good Doctor would have termed in that vague, generalizing way of hers

---

[82] Vint, 'Cultural Imperialism'.

'progress'." (Prologue) While it remains a regal system, its monarchy is now open to those of "low birth"; there is less war, although struggles between empires remain. Even Vossil's lie about her origins works to support the *technologiade* because it encourages Oelph to research her past, which, while futile, provides the impetus to foster a positive alliance between Haspidus and the relatively more developed republic of Drezen. So, as Kincaid argues, "Both Vossill and DeWar act as irritants in the conservative societies slowly and painfully emerging into what we would recognize as the modern world. Their very irritation has a progressive effect upon the world: for once, Culture interference works."[83]

Yet the representation of the Culture's benign, utopian *technologiade* in *Inversions* remains open to debate, with questions remaining regarding the efficacy, ethics and politics of Vossil and DeWar's influence specifically.

The *Technologiade* from Within

The most convincing way in which *Inversions* works to justify the Culture's interventions is by potentially offering a perspective that inverts that usually provided within the series: instead of providing the Culture's view of its interventions, *Inversion* describes intervention from *within* the society affected, from its own point of view. Oelph's narrative of his time with Doctor Vossill provides an account of a Culture intervention, the consequences of which – while he remains unaware of the full truth – he describes in positive terms. That Vossil herself seems unaware that Oelph documents her actions in his journal works to authenticate the narrative, which is seemingly free from the bias of direct Culture influence.

The final of *Inversions'* anomalies relates to both the identity of the individuals who narrate the stories as well as the manner in which they are conveyed, and so is therefore perhaps the most important, as it draws the truth of the accounts into question. It becomes clear in the epilogue that the two narratives of the doctor and the bodyguard, presented alongside each other in *Inversions*, have been compiled and edited by Oelph, with the prologue and epilogue themselves providing a brief frame narrative of this editorial process. The doctor's tale is described as a "Closed Chronicle, in which [...] one has to guess the identity of the person telling the tale" (22), in a similar manner to the narrative of *Player*. While Oelph himself wrote the doctor's tale, that

---

[83] Kincaid, *Iain M. Banks*, 92.

of the bodyguard is eventually revealed to have been written by the concubine Perrund, although existing in multiple versions. "One part of my tale is presented as something I can vouch for," states Oelph, "for I was there. As to the other part, I cannot confirm its veracity." (Prologue) If the tale of the bodyguard was indeed written by DeWar's concubine, then it must be viewed with her potential bias, or her naïveté regarding DeWar's history in the Culture, in mind.

Furthermore, Oelph explains that there is more to DeWar's story than is written in the bodyguard's final chapter, which ends with the bodyguard confronting Perrund for having killed the king, and moving toward her with his sword. DeWar's tale also exists "in the form of a play which I discovered in another bibliophile's library here in Haspide." This version, "in the guise of a drama in three acts", describes DeWar killing Perrund to revenge the dead king, and reveals the bodyguard as having been a prince all along, eventually becoming king himself. Oelph regards this as the "more morally satisfying version." The ending of Perrund's version, "which she claimed she only committed to paper to counter the sensationalised untruths of the dramatic edition" (Epilogue), sees the bodyguard and the concubine make a dramatic escape together, eventually forming a financial bank in a far-away kingdom. Despite his belief in cultural relativism – his "leave them alone" approach – DeWar's actions clearly affect the course of Tasassen to some extent, whether intentional or otherwise; yet Banks's playful metafictional approach, and postmodern use of alternative endings, ultimately leaves the extent and nature of DeWar's influence ambiguous.

In turn, the identity of Oelph's Master, for whom his account of the doctor is written, is not made explicit in the novel, so again we are left questioning the extent to which his anticipated readership has affected his account of his time with Doctor Vossil. Oelph ruminates on the subjectivity of historical accounts, and the difficulty of ascertaining objective truth: "The past, then? Surely there we can find certainty because once something has happened it cannot unhappen, it cannot be said to change. [...] And yet how little historians agree. Read the account of a war from one side and then from the other." (Prologue) The subjective process of interpreting historical events, of course, relates to interpretation of the novel, and we are left to question how Oelph's positive account of the Culture's *technologiade* in Haspidus would have been different had he known the full truth. Here Banks highlights the importance of perspective – of seeing intervention from inside as he offers through *Inversions* – and offers a warning about interpretation of the rest of the series, reminding us that the Culture's view of its actions is merely one amongst many.

Hubble offers an interpretation of how the novel itself, with its insightful if potentially problematic view of intervention from within, or narratives like it, may perform a valuable role in the decisions surrounding intervention. Speculating that "it is possible to imagine another layer to his narrative," Hubble postulates an extra-textual eventuality where "the Culture subsequently recover these texts and present them in this format".[84] Here, with the volume that Oelph compiled and edited, "*Inversions* might be thought of as another Culture fairy tale or adventure that provides not only entertainment but also a means of allowing Culture citizens to think through the ethics of intervention."[85]

Inversions, then, suggests that a process of soft intervention can have progressive effects; yet it works to highlights the value of a postcolonial perspective and to ensure that the success of progressive actions – no matter how well intended – is never taken for granted.

Conclusion

Space opera – premised on an interlinked galaxy, populated by human diaspora – assumes that a globalised future is inevitable; and Csicsery-Ronay has identified an increased acceptance of SF more generally as "a cultural mediation for the regime of globalizing hypermodernism."[86] Yet with the Culture series, Banks suggests that the *politics* of Globalisation, with its thinly veiled economic imperialism, rather than the *form* itself, is at fault. Hardt and Negri's conception of Empire has undeniable overlaps with Banks's conception of the Culture, providing the possibility for a reading of the series as a reflection of the political status quo of Neoliberalism; yet *Empire* is positioned against capitalism and not necessarily against the particular, globalised form which it currently inhabits per se. If *Empire* begins to offer ways of thinking beyond the Neoliberal order as the End of History, then Banks's Culture can be viewed as a system that inverts the political ideology underpinning that order, but drawing upon the fundamentally interlinked and decentralised nature of Globalisation to the advantage of the Left. What Banks does, effectively, is narrate a possible result of

---

[84] Hubble, Norman, and MacCallum-Stuart, eds., *The Science Fiction of Iain M. Banks*, 76.
[85] Hubble, Norman, and MacCallum-Stuart, eds., *The Science Fiction of Iain M. Banks*, 76.
[86] Csicsery-Ronay, 'Empire', 362.

the "Utopian 'method'" that Jameson outlines in *Valences of the Dialectic*, arguing that "what is meant by utopian here" is that "that what is currently negative can also be imagined as positive in that immense changing of the valences which is the Utopian future."[87]

Therefore, in the following chapter of this current book, it is necessary to shift focus from the peripheries of Banks's civilisation to the internal nature of its habitats, its political, social, and economic structures, which appear to have been shaped in radically utopian form by the absence of material scarcity, any unit of financial exchange, and of class boundaries, as well as the presence of AIs vastly superior in intellect to its human citizens.

As a form of critical utopia, the Culture series works to critique as well as advocate the utopianism it describes and embodies. Whilst there is an ever-present danger that the Culture's tactics may fail or that the possibilities for power and domination may prove too great, the potential of the Culture's utopianism should not be overlooked. By providing a comprehensive critique of all forms of imperialist, fundamentalist, totalitarian, hierarchical, and authoritarian social structures, and providing a fragmentary yet powerful vision of the society that could be formed in their wake, Banks's Culture series provides one of the most effective fictional methods of "thinking the break" from the Neoliberal status quo.

---

[87] Jameson, *Valences of the Dialectic*, 423.

Chapter 2

Thinking the Break
The Culture as Postscarcity Utopia

"Money is a sign of poverty" – 'A Gift from the Culture'

Often physically disconnected from broader galactic politics, Culture citizens enjoy lifestyles of freedom and abundance – Banks's vision of a pan-galactic, utopian civilisation. Writing at a time when the monetarist, market-driven philosophy of Neoliberalism was reshaping Britain, this chapter explores Banks's counterproposal: the Culture as an antithetical vision of Alter Globalism, an egalitarian society without any need for money whatsoever, replacing financial with informational exchange. The moneyless nature of the Culture is the boldest disruption that Banks's series details, which is necessarily the first to occur, providing the impetus for, and the possibility of, those that follow. The Culture's move beyond material scarcity is the fundamental political break or event, enabled by the technological break of the Singularity. The Culture is an unapologetic vision of a centralised, state-run political system written and developed during the post-Cold War era, when such ideas have fallen into disrepute. This chapter explores the political structure of Banks's civilisation in terms of liberalism, libertarianism, socialism, communism, and totalitarianism. I read the second Culture book published, *The Player of Games*, as an example of Moylan's critical utopia, contrasting the Culture's postscarcity techno-utopia with the fascist, capitalist Empire of Azad, within the historical–political context of Thatcher, Pinochet, and Cuba in the 1980s.

Banks, Utopias, and Utopianism

That Banks should envision his personal utopia during the 1970s was, in many ways, unsurprising, given the key developments in the history of the idea which occurred in that decade. The academic field of utopian studies first emerged during this time, with the Society for Utopian Studies founded in 1975, and holding the first of its ongoing annual conferences in New York the following year. As Levitas explains, "An upsurge of political activism in the 1970s stimulated utopian thought, and the very nature of those policies altered both its content and its form."[1] Moving beyond utopia-as-blueprint, utopian thinkers and practitioners re-conceived the term as "a dialectic of openness and closure, transcending the binary through an implicit though not yet conscious treatment of utopia as method."[2] Levitas highlights "the feminist turn", which had a "transformative impact" on utopian writing and thinking. By introducing more utopian texts by women writers into the canon, arguing for the intrinsic utopianism in feminism's desire to replace the "unnatural state" of patriarchy with an equal alternative, and reinvigorating utopia-as-fantasy into "a force that moves and shapes history", feminist thinkers provided writers of New Wave SF with the intellectual backbone to support their creative ideas. This followed the broader "Cultural Turn" at this time amongst humanities and social sciences scholars towards *culture* itself as the focus of critical debate, emphasising "the causal and socially constitutive role of cultural processes and systems of signification".[3]

Moylan's seminal *Demand the Impossible* was one of the most important books in the field of utopian studies concerned with this period in history, and which discusses key works from the New Wave. Like *Phlebas*, Moylan's book was published in the mid-1980s but "written from inside the oppositional political culture of the 1970s."[4] As such, *Demand* provides one of the most important contexts in which the Culture series should be considered, documenting radical innovations to utopian fictions published following the "dystopian turn" of the 1950s and theorised as the "critical utopia". Moylan argues for a break "with previous utopias by presenting in much greater, almost balanced, detail both the utopian society and the original society against which the utopia is pitted as a revolutionary alternative."[5] Similar to Levitas's "dialectic of openness and closedness", the critical utopia allows for a rigorous examination of the utopian society, exposing its faults, ambiguities, and problems. Critical utopias tend to provide deeper characterisation and narrative

---

[1] Ruth Levitas, *Utopia as Method*, 103.
[2] Ruth Levitas, *Utopia as Method*, 103.
[3] George Steinmetz, *State/Culture: State-Formation after the Cultural Turn* (Ithaca, NY: Cornell University Press, 1999), 1–2.
[4] Tom Moylan, *Demand the Impossible*: *Science Fiction and the Utopian Imagination* (Germany: Peter Lang AG, Internationaler Verlag der Wissenschaften, 2014), back cover.
[5] Moylan, *Demand*, 43.

than the traditional form, and to better account for the transition from non-utopia to utopia. Moylan himself acknowledges Banks's series as operating within this tradition in the expanded edition of *Demand* from 2014, following Simon Guerrier and Michal Kulbucki.[6] As explored in the preceding chapter, Banks's narratives allow for nuanced discussion of anti-utopian arguments relating to the problems of boredom, totalitarianism, and intervention, with this process of critique often working to strengthen rather than undermine his powerful vision of a utopian, alter globalism enabled by the spread of the culture of technoscience.

Just as Banks wrote space opera during the New Wave, a time when the sub-genre was often seen as unpopular, he continued writing the Culture books into the 1990s and the twenty-first century. While utopian fiction is often portrayed as relatively scarce during this period, Wegner argues that "there appear in the 1990s a number of major new utopian fictions", including works by Kim Stanley Robinson, Ken MacLeod, and Philip Pullman.[7] Yet, as Fredric Jameson explains, following the "moment of convulsive transition" from modernism into the period of late capitalism or postmodernism, characterised by Globalisation and the spread of Neoliberal economic policy, "traditional Utopian production seems to have come to a halt."[8] Therefore, Banks is one of a minority of SF authors who continued to publish and innovate within the field of utopian fiction during this time.

Second Nature

The Culture is predicated upon a philosophy of nurture over nature, the artificial over the preordained, culture over commerce. The notion of the *technologiade* suggests a spectrum with First Nature at one end and Second Nature at the other, with the Culture's near-total mastery of its environments and all human lives within them enabling it to shape its own nature into a utopia through the application of technoscience: a successful techno-utopia.

As a network of interlinked, technological environments, the Culture's system of Second Nature necessarily requires a great deal of power to run. As such, it relies upon the Fertile Corpse trope that Csicsery-Ronay identifies in "classic techno-adventure" as the "exploitable body, material

---

[6] See Guerrier, 'Culture Theory', 36; and Kulbicki, 'Iain M. Banks, Ernst Bloch and Utopian Interventions', 34.
[7] Wegner, *Life Between Two Deaths*, 35.
[8] Jameson, *Archaeologies*, 216.

to the degree that it is productive and without consciousness",[9] and usually taking the form of a planet's natural resources. Beginning with Smith's *The Skylark of Space*, which opens with an account of the accidental discovery of "'X', an unknown metal" that is eventually combined with copper, producing a space drive that powers the book's titular spacecraft to other worlds,[10] the trope continues in parodic form in the quest for control of "Unobtanium" at the heart of James Cameron's *Avatar* (2009). The Culture's Fertile Corpse is the Energy Grid, a highly fecund source of pure energy located between universes in Banks's fictional cosmology.[11] Banks's Fertile Corpse is notable for the fact that its fecundity seems in fact endless, a detail that not only ensures – in theory – that the Culture could continue in its current state indefinitely, but that also ensures that the Culture does not break its central axiom: "nothing and nobody in the Culture is exploited".[12] The Culture refuses to use natural resources in the development of its Second Nature, seeing terraforming – the SF trope of artificially altering the terrain and atmosphere of a planet so that it is habitable for humans – as exploitative: terraforming is "ecologically unsound", Banks explains: "the wilderness should be left as it is, when it is so easy to build paradise in space from so little".[13] This extends, presumably, to a kind of culture-wide veganism, suggested by the Culture's use of synthesised meat in 'The State of the Art', as discussed in Chapter Six. Instead, the Culture builds entirely artificial habitats – separate from those that exist in First Nature – for its inhabitants: grand feats of mechanical and social engineering that do not rely upon the finite resources of the natural world, but instead draw only from the Grid's infinite energy. In this way, Banks's series provides an example of a "major turn" in the Fertile Corpse archetype, as identified by Csicsery-Ronay, where the Handy Man (or his home culture) refuses "to exploit the source, or bring it to consciousness";[14] instead, Banks posits the Energy Grid as a second kind of source, the unlimited fruitfulness of which renders it beyond exploitation. However fantastical Banks's system may be, it serves as a reminder that we need to adopt a similar strategy in order to avert the very real potential for immanent, catastrophic climate change.[15]

[9] Csicsery-Ronay, *Seven Beauties*, 249–250.
[10] E.E. "Doc" Smith, *The Skylark of Space* (Sussex: Granada Publishing Limited, 1974), 5.
[11] Banks, 'A Few Notes on the Culture'. Web.
[12] Banks, 'A Few Notes on the Culture'. Web.
[13] Banks, 'A Few Notes on the Culture'. Web.
[14] Csicsery-Ronay, *Seven Beauties*, 250.
[15] See Naomi Klein, *No Is Not Enough* (St Ives: Penguin Books, 2017), especially 'The Climate Clock Strikes Midnight', 69–82.

The Minds of 'The Minds': The Culture as PostSingularity Utopia

While the Grid's energy seems unlimited and powerful, it must first be processed before it can be used as matter. It would be impossible for the Culture to exist in the form described in Banks's series, therefore, were it not for the existence of the Minds (although, while their existence is certainly *necessary* to achieve utopia, it is not a single, *sufficient* condition, as I explore below). Not only do these AIs have a capacity for thought and memory vastly superior to our own, they also provide the means through which the Culture is able to access limitless resources. In Banks's fictional cosmology, the universe is underpinned by a grid of pure energy that – like a kind of cosmic alchemy or an extrapolated version of material state changes, such as water boiling into steam – the Minds can convert into raw matter and then fashion into any item they require.[16] Similarly, in *Skylark*, protagonist Richard Seaton uses the metal X to create a machine that enables "pure and total conversion of matter to controllable energy".[17] Later chapters involve a search for deposits of copper and X in order to fuel further exploration of space, and the novel ends with Seaton returning to Earth laden with an abundance of these, and many other resources. Following the central role of the Minds in the conversion process, it seems that the Culture's resources are also distributed throughout the Os and GSVs via the Minds and drones, in a process that resembles the functions of a state, as I will soon discuss.

Futurists, scientists, economists, and SF authors alike have discussed the theoretical possibility of AI advanced enough to outsmart humanity occurring in our lifetime, in the event known as the Technological Singularity. It is likely that the Minds and Drones exist following such an event, making the Culture an example of a PostSingularity utopia, and the series PostSingularity fiction. The idea was first pioneered in the mid-1960s, most notably by futurists such as Ray Kurzweil and SF author and mathematics professor Vernor Vinge. The Singularity is understood as a threshold moment – a spike – in the rate of a society's technological progress, following which development will vastly and unpredictably accelerate, until the capabilities of technology become almost unimaginable. The outcomes of this generally cluster around the transition from a human to a posthuman mode of existence. While this transition is sometimes effected by biological or pharmaceutical changes,

---

[16] Banks, 'A Few Notes on the Culture'. Web.
[17] E.E. Smith, *The Skylark of Space*, 17.

as we will see in Chapter Two, it is often a result of the emergence of AI that is vastly greater than ourselves, irrevocably changing both the nature of ourselves and the ways in which we live.[18] As David Chalmers describes: "What happens when machines become more intelligent than humans? One view is that this event will be followed by an explosion to ever-greater levels of intelligence, as each generation of machines creates more intelligent machines in turn."[19] As such, an integral aspect of the Singularity is the idea of a self-developing computer, a generation of machines focused upon developing superior versions of themselves:

> The key idea is that a machine that is more intelligent than humans will be better than humans at designing machines. So it will be capable of designing a machine more intelligent than the most intelligent machine that humans can design. So if it is itself designed by humans, it will be capable of designing a machine more intelligent than itself. By similar reasoning, this next machine will also be capable of designing a machine more intelligent than itself. If every machine in turn does what it is capable of, we should expect a sequence of ever more intelligent machines.[20]

To Chalmers, these intelligent machines would inevitably leave mankind intellectually "far behind."[21]

The narrative voice of *Look to Windward* explains the Singularity in the Culture, when its early AIs "underwent their own form of evolution and began to design their own successors – with or without the help, and sometimes the knowledge, of their creators" – and eventually became the Minds. The narrator continues, explaining that "creating such intelligences was not particularly challenging once you could build AIs in the first place" (126). These AIs were proto-Minds, continuing the development of successively more intelligent versions of themselves, until this development peaked and the mind of the first Mind blinked into existence.

The scientific plausibility of the Singularity is a matter of debate, yet it remains a popular trope in recent SF (especially in the work of

---

[18] See Ray Kurzweil, *The Singularity is Near* (New York: Viking, 2005) and also: http://www.singularity.com/; and David Langford, 'Singularity', in *The Encyclopedia of Science Fiction*, Clute et al., eds. (London: Gollancz, 2018), 25 October 2018. http://www.sf-encyclopedia.com/entry/singularity.
[19] David Chalmers, 'The Singularity: a philosophical analysis' (Singularity Institute, 2010), 1. http://consc.net/papers/singularity.pdf.
[20] Chalmers, 'The Singularity: a philosophical analysis'. Web.
[21] Chalmers, 'The Singularity: a philosophical analysis'. Web.

MacLeod, Alastair Reynolds, and Charles Strauss). While Csicsery-Ronay recognises that the "vision of convergence appears plausible, given the world-historical explosion of technologies of digital computation and interlock"[22], he sees it ultimately as "the quintessential myth of contemporary techno-culture".[23] The Singularity posits one of the most radical outcomes of the *technologiade* process, if perhaps one of the most unlikely. Questioned about AI in 2011, Banks was similarly sceptical about the possibility of advanced digital intelligence emerging in such a manner, commenting that "As of the Singularity, I'll believe it when I see it."[24]

Banks as Pro-AI

> "worrying about AIs turning on us is about as productive as worrying that farm animals are going to revolt" – *Hyperion*, Dan Simmons

Iain Banks can be seen as "pro-AI", a firm advocate for its development in the service of humanity. Through this stance, Banks makes a radical break from the reoccurring cyberpunk narratives of AI effecting a totalitarian regime in a dystopian city-state. In the twenty-first century, AI has shifted from the province of SF narratives and into the broader public imagination through its increased impact upon daily life and scientific research. In January 2015, Musk, Stephen Hawking, and dozens of other experts signed an open letter entitled 'Research Priorities for Robust and Beneficial Artificial Intelligence' and published by the Future of Life Institute,[25] arguing that, given the steady progress in AI development, more research should be conducted into its potential social impacts, both positive and negative:

> The potential benefits are huge, since everything that civilisation has to offer is a product of human intelligence; we cannot predict what we might achieve when this intelligence is magnified by the tools AI may provide, but the eradication of disease and poverty

---

[22] Csicsery-Ronay, *Seven Beauties*, 263.
[23] Csicsery-Ronay, *Seven Beauties*, 262.
[24] *Guardian*, 'Live webchat: Iain Banks', 6 July 2011. www.guardian.co.uk/books/booksblog/2011/jul/06/live-webchat-iain-banks.
[25] Matthew Sparks, 'Top Scientists Call for Caution Over Artificial Intelligence', *Telegraph*, 13 January 2015. https://www.telegraph.co.uk/technology/news/11342200/Top-scientists-call-for-caution-over-artificial-intelligence.html.

are not unfathomable. Because of the great potential of AI, it is important to research how to reap its benefits while avoiding potential pitfalls.[26]

The ethics of the rise in autonomous weapons in modern warfare, such as airstrikes via drone technology, are a key point of concern, and the authors warn that it "'may be desirable to retain some form of meaningful human control' over intelligent machines designed to kill."[27] As in contemporary history, drones are a significant feature in the Culture series, acting as either domestic servants to the Culture's citizens or, in the quasi-military guise of knife missiles, as discussed with regard to *Inversions* in Chapter Two, deadly bodyguards to SC agents. Banks was editing the first Culture books around the time that modern drone warfare "began in earnest in 1982, when Israel coordinated the use of battlefield UAVs alongside manned aircraft to wipe out the Syrian fleet with very minimal losses";[28] and the series was 20 years old by the time that the first commercial, non-military drones became widely available.[29] So, while Banks's choice of name may have been coincidental, the term's usage in the series is allowed to accrue extra resonance when read in a contemporary context.

But it is for peace that AI is most widely used within the Culture. Like Banks and the Future of Life Institute's letter, the World Futurist Association (WFA) asserts that technology will play a crucial role in the establishment and maintenance of a postscarcity system: "the evolution toward free goods and a lack of scarcity is, in fact, already under way, thanks primarily to technologies (such as computers and the Internet) that have enabled and driven the growth of digitization over the last 20 years."[30] These advances, the WFA notes, will also contribute towards the abolition of money within a postscarcity society through financial evolution, rather than political revolution: "In the post-scarcity world, technological advances will facilitate decreasing costs until conceivably almost everything is free to the consumer [...] Scarcity will no longer exist in this world, and, without scarcity, the concept of charging a price

---

[26] Sparks, 'Top Scientists'. Web.
[27] Sparks, 'Top Scientists'. Web.
[28] Justin F, 'The History Of Drones (Drone History Timeline From 1849 To 2019)', *Drone Enthusiast*. https://www.dronethusiast.com/history-of-drones/.
[29] Justin F, 'The History Of Drones'. Web.
[30] Stephen Aguillar-Millan, Ann Feeny, Amy Oberg, and Elizabeth Rudd, 'The Post-scarcity World of 2050–2075', *Futurist* 44, no. 1 (January 2010): 36. https://www.researchgate.net/.../216807965_The_Post-Scarcity_World_of_2050-2075.

to consumers as a means of generating revenue will be unworkable."[31] However this society beyond economics is established, commentators across the political spectrum highlight the crucial role of technology in its establishment and maintenance.

A Postscarcity Utopia

While the Minds clearly play an integral role in the existence of the Culture, then, Banks's vision is not one of a reductionist determinism wherein technology is allowed to provide all of society's values: there are other essential conditions which are able to exist, following the emergence of the AIs, that are of equal – perhaps greater – importance to utopia. Despite its modern form as space opera, the Culture series should be considered part of a long-established literary tradition: beginning with Thomas More, Jameson describes "the abolition of money and poverty" which "runs through the Utopian tradition like a red thread".[32] Edward Bellamy's *Looking Backward 2000–1887* (1888) describes a place where money and private enterprise does not exist, property is equally distributed, and people work motivated by pride, and William Morris's *News from Nowhere* (1890) imagines a society where money has been abolished and "wage slavery" replaced by craftwork. The thread continues through the radical SF of the twentieth and twenty-first centuries, especially in the work of Kim Stanley Robinson and Ken MacLeod.

While contemporary futurologists view the term "postscarcity" as referring to a period of economic stability and material abundance – a temporary state always capable of returning to deficiency – immediately following an era of scarcity[33] (such as that which seemed briefly plausible in the Soviet Union during the 1950s),[34] Banks uses the term in his novels to refer to a society "where material scarcity is unknown",[35] suggesting a more permanent basis,[36] which the World Futurist Society

---

[31] Aguillar-Millan et al., 'The Post-scarcity World', 36. Web.
[32] Jameson, *Archaeologies*, 18.
[33] Aguillar-Millan et al., 'The Post-scarcity World'. Web.
[34] G.I. Khanin, 'The 1950s – the Triumph of the Soviet Economy', *Europe-Asia Studies* 55, no. 8 (December 2003): 1,187–1,211.
[35] See Iain Banks, 'A Few Notes on the Culture'; and David Smith, 'A Conversation with Iain (M.) Banks'.
[36] See the following interview for one of the many occasions on which Banks used the term to describe the Culture; in this case as "the most apt way": Marc Aplin, 'Fantasy Fiction; Iain M. Banks Interview – Part One', 26 October 2012. fantasy-faction.com/2012/iain-m-banks-interview-part-one

argues may have the possibility of achievement in reality, towards the middle of the twenty-first century.[37] As such, the Culture reflects the *human* decision to found a society from which money and exploitation have been abolished through the use of technoscience, rather than a society determined entirely by the influence of its technology.

Due to the absence of scarcity in the Culture, therefore, there is no need for controlling measures to be placed upon its production or distribution of goods, no need to withhold certain resources from certain groups of people, at certain times, whatever the motivations. Consequently, in theory, everyone in the Culture has access to everything that they could possibly want or need at any time; all material human needs and wants are fulfilled. This fundamental abundance is at the heart of Banks's utopia.

Such a radically limitless society, Banks argues, is only possible once money has been abolished, due to the exploitation inherent in the unalienated labour of capitalism:

> It's a post-scarcity society [...] They've got enough of everything. There's a phrase in the Culture, a saying that goes "money is a sign of poverty". The idea being that if you've got enough of everything to go round, there's no need to ration it. That's all that money really is. Your cheque book is actually a ration book.[38]

As such, Banks recalls one of the central tenants of the Declaration of the Socialist International, First Congress, held in Frankfort-on-Main, 30 June to 3 July 1951:

> Although the world contains resources which could be made to provide a decent life for everyone, capitalism has been incapable of satisfying the elementary needs of the world's population. It proved unable to function without devastating crises and mass unemployment. It produced social insecurity and glaring contrasts between rich and poor.[39]

---

[37] Aguillar-Millan et al., 'The Post-scarcity World'. Web.
[38] Smith, 'A Conversation with Iain (M.) Banks'.
[39] The Socialist International, 'The Declaration of the Socialist International', 30 June to 3 July 1951. http://www.socialistinternational.org/viewArticle.cfm?ArticleID=39.

Information as a Commodity

In a society like the Culture, then, which is not ordered and arranged according to the exchange of money or any other physical unit, meaning and value are free to be attributed more fairly to other commodities, according to their "real", innate usefulness, rather than arbitrarily as an unfair system of rationing. As far as the Culture has any medium of exchange whatsoever, "information or data", as Farah Mendlesohn has argued, are "the only kind of 'currency' the Culture values."[40] In *Use of Weapons*, Banks dramatically illustrates this point through a fairy tale. The novel's protagonist, Zakalwe – an important example of Csicsery-Ronay's Handy Man – is a former SC operative who has turned renegade, supposedly continuing their good deeds, but really carrying out acts of vigilante justice. Zakalwe holds a corrupt politician at gunpoint and torments him with an ominous story – which works as a Culture fable like Vossil's story in *Inversions* – before shooting him. Referring to an unnamed society, which Banks's readers recognise as the Culture itself, Zakalwe details the history and nature of this society, noting that "they always tried to bring with them the thing they saw as the most precious gift of all: knowledge; information; and as wide a spread of that information as possible" (*Weapons*, 29). Zakalwe highlights the role of information in Banks's *technologiade* metanarrative, with SC providing less-developed societies with, amongst other things, the knowledge of scientific and technological development, and hoping it will orient them toward progress, as seen in *Inversions*.

The narrative thrust of many of the texts in the series relies upon the (re-)acquisition by the Culture of crucial information, often in the form of digital data. In *Consider Phlebas*, for example, SC hunts for an estranged, endangered Mind with first-hand experience of an important event relating to the Idiran–Culture conflict. In *The Player of Games*, SC hides the existence of the Empire of Azad from the majority of Culture citizens, and details are strategically drip-fed to Gurgeh in order to convince him to accept their mission. Upon discovering the Earth in 'The State of the Art', Contact acquires huge volumes of information about our societies and cultures in order to make an educated decision about establishing contact. The titular entity of *Excession*, a trans-dimensional being of great power, seems to bring with it new knowledge so unprecedented in the Culture's history that it would constitute apocalyptic proportions, its own Event. In *Surface Detail*, SC seeks the physical substrate containing

---

[40] Farah Mendlesohn, 'Iain M. Banks: *Excession*', in *A Companion to Science Fiction*, David Seed, ed. (Oxford: Blackwell Publishing, 2005), 599, 562.

a digital system of virtual "hells", in order to shut down what it sees as a barbaric practice. Finally, one sub-narrative of *The Hydrogen Sonata* concerns the Culture's hunt for its oldest citizen, who has adapted his body to store vast reams of digital information within it, including historical data on the Gzilt civilisation's sacred text, the Book of Truth, which will potentially undermine its entire religious system.

Free and open access to information is a central concern of real-world postscarcity advocates who support current trends towards open-source software and open-access publishing. A 2009 report by the World Future Society argues that the seeds of a postscarcity future have already been planted: "the evolution toward free goods and a lack of scarcity is, in fact, already under way, thanks primarily to technologies (such as computers and the Internet) that have enabled and driven the growth of digitization over the last 20 years."[41] The current availability of some information, products, services, and communications channels freely and easily online – news, books, open-source software, social media, and so forth – could theoretically result in a completely open and free world-wide network, undermining the need for monetary exchange of any kind. Similarly, the Culture features a vast arrangement of information banks, potentially accessible to everyone at any time:

> This contained as a matter of course almost every even moderately important or significant or useful piece of information the Culture had ever accumulated; a near infinite ocean of fact and sensation and theory and artwork which the Culture's information net was adding to at a torrential rate every second of the day. [...] The Culture had theoretical total freedom of information; the catch was that consciousness was private, and information held in a Mind – as opposed to an unconscious system, like the Hub's memory-banks – was regarded a part of the Mind's being, and as sacrosanct as the contents of the human brain. (*Player*, 65)

AIs access this network automatically as an intrinsic part of their digital consciousness, while non-AI Culture citizens are provided with access through terminals, devices similar to a highly advanced smartphone, and sometimes neural-lace devices that enable human thought and consciousness to be converted into digital information (as detailed in Chapter Five). As well as allowing the transfer of knowledge for its own sake, this network also allows communications – often near instantaneous – with other areas of the Culture, and 'The State of the Art'

[41] Aguillar-Millan et al., 'The Post-scarcity World', 36. Web.

depicts Diziet Sma attempting to save her friend's life using a terminal, as we will see in Chapter Three. Given that the Culture's information nets, terminals and neural laces provide clear SF extrapolations from current technology, we can perhaps start to understand why Facebook CEO Mark Zuckerberg is also interested in Banks's fiction, given his key role in the development of social media, alongside Elon Musk. The World Wide Web has long been seen as intrinsic to the liberal project of progressive reform through increased knowledge production, ultimately leading to empathy, truth, and peace. Yet at the time of its fiftieth anniversary in 2019, the continued value of the Internet has been sharply challenged by discussions on the role that social media might play in enabling electoral and political manipulation, the spread of extremist ideology and terrorism, as well as bullying, suicide, and self-harm.

The Political Structure of the Culture

"Strength in depth" – Contact motto

As a socialist, Banks conceived of his personal utopia as an entirely egalitarian, classless society. "Succinctly", Banks states, the Culture reflects "socialism within, anarchy without".[42] George Woodcock states the following about anarchy: "What we are concerned with, in terms of a definition, is a cluster of words which in turn represents a cluster of doctrines and attitudes whose principal uniting feature is the belief that government is harmful and unnecessary [...] *anarchy* means the state of being without a ruler."[43] This the Culture can achieve in outer space, Banks argues, when viewed in spatial terms as a collection of environments – GSVs, ships, Orbitals, and so forth – that are "deliberately and self-consciously very widely distributed through the galaxy, with no centre, no nexus, no home planet" (*Surface*, 198). They would choose to be dispersed "very widely", Banks argues,

> as the nature of life in space [...] would mean that while ships and habitats might more easily become independent from each other and from their legally progenitative hegemonies, their crew – or inhabitants – would always be aware of their reliance on each other, and on the technology which allowed them to live in space.[44]

---

[42] Banks, 'A Few Notes on the Culture'. Web.
[43] George Woodcock, ed., *The Anarchist Reader* (Fontana: Glasgow, 1980), 11.
[44] Banks, 'A Few Notes on the Culture'. Web.

Life in outer space, then, provides the freedom to exist without a centralised authority, and their highly sophisticated technoscience allows them to operate according to "a closely-knit fabric of voluntary relationships"[45] rather than a national/federal legal system. The Culture, then, perhaps conforms to certain philosophies of Confucius, which Woodcock describes as proto-anarchist for the former's belief that such systems "impoverished" countries. Instead, according to Confucius, "the wise man says: 'I will design nothing, and the people will shape themselves.'"[46] Yet, as I will soon discuss, it is difficult to establish the extent to which the Culture has a central government-like authority.

At the heart of the Culture's ability to remain dispersed yet connected are its most powerful and most quintessential environments, the General Systems Vehicles (GSVs), moving habitats on an immense scale. Existing as completely autonomous entities, GSVs are "individually quite capable of rebuilding the entire Culture from scratch", a function that operates as both "security mechanism" and preferred way of living (*Surface*, 198). Culture citizens can travel between these and other environments freely and easily, arranging this through their established communications networks. The Culture's internal environments certainly seem socialist, "The most fundamental characteristic" of which, as Michael Newman explains, "is its commitment to the creation of an egalitarian society".[47] With limitless abundance, no-one needs to be poor and everyone in the Culture has equal access to the same publically owned resources in equal measure.

Newman states that: "The most obvious common feature in the utopian socialists' transformative projects was the belief that a society based on harmony, association, and cooperation could be established through communal living and working."[48] Here, Newman discusses figures such as Plato, Etienne Cabet, and Henri Saint-Simon as early socialists, noting that Marx and Engels described these figures as "utopian" but in a pejorative sense, and he challenges this view by emphasising the impulse toward utopianism necessary for and integral to socialism. While the Culture has alleviated the need for mandatory employment, its environments clearly display similar values of social co-operation and collective responsibility, as demonstrated in its de facto system of local democracy, as I will return to shortly.

---

[45] Woodcock, ed., *The Anarchist Reader*, 12.
[46] Woodcock, ed., *The Anarchist Reader*, 17.
[47] Michael Newman, *Socialism: A Very Short Introduction* (Gosfort: Oxford University Press, 2005), 2.
[48] Newman, *Socialism*, 7.

Despite the ability of individuals in the Culture to participate in democracy in this manner, Gurgeh (the protagonist of *Player*) questions the ability of individuals to have impact within the Culture in any significant way, whether this impact be social, political, artistic, or something else. Banks's narrative is concerned with Culture citizen Gurgeh, who – disillusioned with his life as an academic in the field of game-playing – becomes embroiled in a mission for SC. Before he leaves for his mission, Gurgeh questions life in the Culture, bemoaning the fact that "this is not a heroic age," to his friend, drone Chamlis Amalk-ney, and that "the individual is obsolete. That's why life is so comfortable for us all. We don't matter, so we're safe. No one person can have a real effect anymore" (*Player*, 22). Yet it is exactly the loss of individuality, in this specific sense, that defines Banks's utopia: "The Culture was every single individual human and machine in it, not one thing" (*Phlebas*, 149). It is not, in fact, the case that individuals "don't matter" in the Culture, and that a person cannot "have a real effect" any longer: the Culture has removed the contexts – capitalism – which unbalance the relationship between individual rights and social responsibility; due to its unique nature, individuals are in fact free to do almost anything, apart from commit murder.[49] While some citizens, such as Sma or Doctor Vossil, seem conscientious about the rights of their fellow citizens,[50] regarded as a whole, most people in the Culture seem largely unconcerned, preferring to live their lives as they choose, but safe in the knowledge that various unique aspects of the Culture's societies combine to ensure that individuals' life choices do not seriously impede upon those of others. What emerges, then, given that it couples social ownership of the means of production with the democratic process, is a picture of the Culture as democratic socialism, or perhaps as exemplifying Hardt and Negri's concept of the "Multitude" proposed in their eponymous book (2005): "the creation of a truly pluralistic democracy for all mankind", an Alter Globalism opposed to Empire.[51]

---

[49] In 'A Few Notes on the Culture', Banks argues that A: the chances of this happening are almost impossible due to the combination of an abundant society removing many criminal motives, and the Culture's genetic manipulation to improve human nature; and B: that, even if a murder were attempted – which could really only really be a "crime" of passion – the murderer would be "slap droned", to ensure that they would behave.

[50] Sma regularly expresses concern about the personal and political lives of her fellow Culture citizens, while Vossil's role as doctor – which is clearly core to her being – clearly expresses a high level of social responsibility.

[51] Thomas N. Hale and Anne-Marie Slaughter, 'Hardt and Negri's Multitude: The Worst of Both Worlds', *Open Democracy*, 25 May 2005. https://www.opendemocracy.net/en/marx_2549jsp/.

Liberalism, Libertarianism, Minarchism

Yet several critics such as Vint, Patrick Thaddeus Jackson, James Heilman, Alan Jacobs,[52] and Chris Brown view the Culture quite differently, associating it with political philosophies such as liberalism and libertarianism that are founded upon core beliefs of individual autonomy taking a degree of precedence over state control. In order to disambiguate such contradictory readings, it is important to focus upon the nuances, complexities, and contexts of such terminology, for, as with empire and imperialism, terms such as "liberalism" and "libertarianism" are loaded with baggage. In a European political context, for example, the classical liberalism of the nineteenth century, advocating "individual liberty, free trade, and moderate political and social reform",[53] is often casually conflated with Neoliberal economic policy, characterised by the total dominance of unregulated, lasses-fair market forces and the withering of the welfare state. Banks often described himself as "a liberal, on the Left, a socialist",[54] for example, a combination of terms that, in some contexts, would be contradictory. It is most likely that Banks uses the word "liberal", in a general context, to convey his fundamental beliefs in tolerance, compassion, and a "willingness to respect or accept behaviour or opinions different from one's own",[55] a position that does not indicate an economic stance on achieving such an end. Banks's position is also perhaps closer to being liberal in the understanding of the term in American politics, where liberals are commonly associated with the Democratic Party, and conservatives with Republicanism.

Jackson and Heilman read the Culture in terms of classical liberalism, arguing for it as an "ideal-typical liberal society" and "perfect liberal utopia" that has achieved liberalism's "three central tenets" of "individual liberty, equality, and reason."[56] Jackson and Heilman agree with Brown on the above, but clearly disagree on the exact manner in which the Culture has achieved them. While Jackson and Heilman do acknowledge the importance of the Culture's postscarcity environment to its freedom and egalitarianism – acknowledging that its "distribution of productive capabilities" means that "everyone has the same claim on basically

---

[52] "The philosophy of Banks's Culture is that of Liberalism" – Jacobs, 'The Ambiguous Utopia', 47.
[53] Jacobs, 'The Ambiguous Utopia', 47.
[54] Scott Beauchamp, 'The Future Might Be a Hoot'.
[55] Oxford Dictionaries, 'Liberal', Oxford University Press, 14 March 2016. www.oxforddictionaries.com/definition/english/liberal.
[56] Jackson and Heilman, 'Outside Context Problems', 239, 242.

every object produced"[57] – they do not acknowledge the problems that identifying such a society as liberal present. As Vint argues, capitalism is "the economic form of liberal humanist democracies",[58] and she quotes Katherine Hayles' assertion that "the liberal self is produced by market relations and does not predate them."[59] Capitalism creates and maintains a system of stark class inequality, and – in its Neoliberal form – means that such a system can never truly achieve the equality and freedom it claims to represent. So it is clearly problematic to ignore the radically postscarcity and postmoney nature of the Culture, even if it does share superficial similarities with classical liberal society. Vint rectifies this problem in one sense by reading the Culture as Empire, which places the focus upon the role of liberal societies in spreading "cultural imperialism", motivated by a desire for establishing global/galactic domination.[60] Yet I wish to suggest that the issue relates more closely to Jameson's parallax notion of reading SF, simultaneously presenting a vision of the future and a reflection of the present.

Pushing the philosophy of individualism further, Kerslake has argued for the Culture's advocacy of an "extreme form of libertarianism",[61] while Jude Roberts notes that "many critics and reviewers have claimed that the Culture represents the American Libertarian ideal."[62] The views of such critics are supported by the influence that figures such as Elon Musk and Mark Zuckerberg take from Banks's work. Banks, however, stated that "I pretty much despise American Libertarianism", reasserting his "deep distrust of both Marketology and Greedism".[63] He clearly became frustrated when commentators ignored the fundamental, radical notion of the Culture as a postmoney society. Yet the term "Libertarian" has not always referred to such ideals of individual over government responsibility, private charity and support for a free market.[64] As Colin Ward explains: "For a century, anarchists have used the word 'libertarian' as a synonym for 'anarchist', both as a noun and an adjective. The celebrated

---

[57] Jackson and Heilman, 'Outside Context Problems', 239, 242.
[58] Vint, 'Cultural Imperialism'.
[59] Katherine N. Hayles, *How We Became Posthuman: Virtual Bodies in Cybernetics, Literature and Information* (Chicago: Chicago University Press, 1999), quoted in Vint, 'Cultural Imperialism'.
[60] Vint, 'Cultural Imperialism'.
[61] Kerslake, *Science Fiction and Empire*, 175.
[62] Jude Roberts, 'A Few Questions about the Culture', in *Modern Masters of Science Fiction: Iain M. Banks*, Paul Kincaid, (Oxfordshire: University of Illinois Press, 2017), 159.
[63] Roberts, 'A Few Questions about the Culture', 160.
[64] The Libertarian Party, 'Libertarian Party 2010 Platform', May 2010, 1.

anarchist journal *Le Libertaire* was founded in 1896. However, much more recently the word has been appropriated by various American free-market philosophers."[65]

Ken MacLeod was certainly aware of this distinction, and was more willing to consider a libertarian position in his thought and writing, with debate on this issue between himself and Banks continuing throughout their friendship. As MacLeod explains, "I could never persuade him that libertarianism was anything but a shill for corporate interests: a common misconception, and one that many libertarians have worked hard to confirm."[66] Again, this debate centres on the complexity of the term, with "libertarianism" potentially describing political positions as varied as libertarian socialism, anarcho-communism, anarcho-capitalism, and monarchism, which stretch across the political spectrum. If libertarianism never represented anything other than a "shill for corporate interests", then it seems that Banks struggled to see such philosophies outside of a market system. This debate becomes reified in the three Prometheus awards – given to SF that is "nominally Libertarian or attempts to 'examine the meaning of freedom'"[67] – that MacLeod won for his fiction, an acknowledgement that Banks was not to experience.

Therefore, the Culture can also be read as an example of a Left-libertarian society, in a manner that resolves its individualism with its anarchism: as Mendlesohn has argued, "the Culture, although Utopian, is not a planned society but a neo-anarchist collection of individuals".[68] The extent of the personal freedom from state intervention experienced by the Culture's citizens is indeed great, perhaps "extreme" as Kerslake suggests. As Banks outlines in 'A Few Notes on the Culture', in fact technically murder – "the very worst crime (to use our terminology)" – is the only action that would cause the Minds to intervene in the actions of a citizen operating outside of Contact or SC:

> the result – punishment, if you will – is the offer of treatment, and what is known as a slap-drone. All a slap-drone does is follow the murderer around for the rest of their life to make sure they

---

[65] Colin Ward, *Anarchism: A Very Short Introduction* (Oxford: Oxford University Press, 2004), 62.

[66] Ken MacLeod, 'Use of Calculators', *The Early Days of a Better Nation*, 26 July 2013. http://kenmacleod.blogspot.com/2013/07/use-of-calculators.html.

[67] The Star Fraction in 1995, Stone Canal in 1996, and Leaving the World in 2005. See *The Encyclopedia of Science Fiction* entry on 'Prometheus Award'.

[68] Mendlesohn, 'Iain M. Banks: *Excession*', 557.

never murder again. There are less severe variations on this theme to deal with people who are simply violent.[69]

For others whose actions or desires fall outside the acceptable conventions of its society – Banks gives the example of megalomaniacs – the Culture sometimes creates virtual-reality environments into which they can be "diverted successfully", or even allows them to pursue their interests on a non-virtual, "backwood planet" so long as they cause no harm. The postscarcity nature of the Culture, as discussed above, combined with certain physiological and psychological adjustments often adopted by Culture citizens, as discussed in Chapter Three, greatly reduces the necessity for slap-drones or these other forms of punishment, diversion, or therapy. Echoing this, Brown has asserted that the Culture is a "liberal anarchic utopia."[70] The Culture is liberal, Brown states, "in so far as it is individualist and committed to the autonomy of all sentient beings", yet this is "not inconsistent with its anarchism" because, "as Marxists used to say, anarchism is liberalism without a police force".[71] Brown emphasises how the Culture's postscarcity nature makes the need for law and law enforcement all but redundant, therefore identifying this as the enabler for a form of anarchism.

Yet the Culture is not an entirely Libertarian society in this manner, as the Minds do in fact perform the functions of a state to some extent, even if – in certain texts – they seem very minimal. *Look to Windward* provides an example of how the Mind's bureaucratic role in the Culture seems to operate in practice, on a minimalistic, ad hoc basis. An avatar takes a newcomer to the Culture, Ziller, on a tour of the Masaq' Orbital, and explains how a local dispute over use of land was resolved. One Culture citizen, Bregan Latrey, decides that a system of cable cars should be built over an area of wilderness to help people cross the land (*Windward*, 196). In an illustration of the extent of the Culture's freedom and its postscarcity economy, the only formal procedure Latrey needs to go through in order to begin is to speak to the Orbital's hub Mind. While the hub refuses to build them itself because "this place was designed as a wilderness" – suggesting that the hub does at least have an opinion on the matter, even if it cannot or will not interfere in an official capacity – it merely tells Latrey to "do it himself", while providing Latrey with the required "manufacturing capacity and design time", and does not restrict him amassing some

---

[69] Banks, 'A Few Notes on the Culture'. Web.
[70] Brown, '"Special Circumstances": Intervention by a Liberal Utopia', 628.
[71] Brown, '"Special Circumstances": Intervention by a Liberal Utopia', 628.

volunteers to help with the project (197). With no formal system of laws or regulations in place to mediate this project, the hub is involved only as is required in its role as facilitator of the means of production. It plays no other part in the process until other Culture citizens who are opposed to the project form a protest group, the Preservationeers, who begin to undo Latrey's work, and it becomes clear that it is necessary for the hub to arbitrate the dispute. Further demonstrating the ad hoc nature of the system, and the infrequency of such situations, the avatar explains that "they had lots of votes", in "one of those rolling campaigns where they had to vote on who would be allowed to vote" (198). In the end, after several stages of voting, confined to those living on Masaq', Latrey was allowed to complete his project, building miles of pylons across the area, but upon the condition that he agree not to repeat the process elsewhere (199).

This example works to lightly satirise the mechanisms of a democratic state, recalling the sometimes long-winded bureaucratic processes of real-world local governments; as the avatar states, "Believe me; democracy in action can be an unpretty sight" (198). Yet it also provides an insight into the ways in which a system like the Culture might settle disputes when they do arise. The Mind in question does fulfil something like several different state functions – arbitrator of disputes, law-enforcement officer, etc. – but in specific response to the individual situation, as proves necessary given that a dispute arises, rather than in a general manner as a matter of course. If no-one had objected to Latrey's project then the hub would have allowed him to continue without interfering, even though it personally considered the project to be problematic.

The Culture, then, considering the huge degree of personal freedom afforded to its citizens, and the seemingly minimalistic role of the Minds as a state-like function, could perhaps most effectively be characterised as a form of minarchy – defined as "Minimal government; specifically a (hypothetical) form of government that does not interfere with individual rights and civil liberties"[72] – as David Farnell has argued.[73] This definition, therefore, allows for a degree of anarchy, but underpinned by a fundamentally socialist economic philosophy. Yet it still does not fully encompass the true extent of the Culture's complexity.

---

[72] Oxford Dictionaries, 'Minarchy', Oxford University Press. www.oxforddictionaries.com/definition/english/minarchy.

[73] "'The Culture' is a post-scarcity spacefaring socialist minarchy" – Farnell, 'Preemeptive Regime Change', 2.

The Minds as State

The Culture's state system is actually more comprehensive than it may first appear. For example, along with the political and democratic functions discussed above, the Culture has a higher-education system, evidenced by the university in which part of *The Player of Games* is set, as we will see shortly; an agricultural system – the Minds have artificially created the Culture's habitats, including 'natural' features, such as mountains, rocks, and grass, which it is their responsibility to maintain (*Phlebas*, 85); internal security, in the form of the slap-drones who monitor violent individuals (*Surface*, 154); military defence, as provided by SC in the absolute direst of circumstances (*Hydrogen*, 137); and an extremely effective health-care system, as explored in Chapter Three. Furthermore, the Culture has its total surveillance system covering all of its habitats, for the purposes of safety and security. The Minds are able to view all Culture areas at all times, and they can communicate with citizens extremely effectively through their terminal devices (*Phlebas*, 87; *Surface*, 164–167), or even more directly through neural-lace devices (*Surface*, 447–448). The reason that this state structure may be easily overlooked is to do with the extent of the Culture's technoscientific mastery. The system of Second Nature that constitutes the Culture is underpinned by technoscience that is so complex and so ubiquitous that it renders this state apparatus almost invisible. As Csicsery-Ronay explains, in space opera the Tool Text becomes so advanced – having passed through the ages of stone, iron, and bronze, mechanical, analogue, digital, and beyond – it reaches the culmination of the *technologiade*, saturating "the ground of reality itself, creating barriers between human beings and first nature [...] With technoscience and sf, tool and text cease to be merely occasional objects, dormant or ready for use; they become the dominant means of reality production."[74] Every part of life in the Culture is enabled by the combination of the Tools that form the physical environment and the virtual Text of computer code that enables them to function. The Minds perform their state functions, then, but these functions are seamlessly integrated into the Culture's all-encompassing Second Nature, forming the fabric of life for its people. The state may seem minimal, yet only because its functions have become so "naturalised" that they are easily overlooked. Furthermore, in this postscarcity environment, no citizen has any need or responsibility to give anything in return for these services – in the form of tax, for example – as all can be provided endlessly and effortlessly. This fact,

---

[74] Csicsery-Ronay, *Seven Beauties*, 259.

therefore, means that the Culture still conveys the impression of being a liberal/libertarian society in that individuals may live seemingly without being encumbered – as libertarian thought sees it – by state interference. Yet they still automatically receive the benefit from state functions, with little obligation to do anything in return.

From an anti-utopian perspective, state functions – no matter how benevolent they seem – always have the potential for totalitarianism. Referring to early utopian writers, Elliott points out that "Thomas More, [Tommaso] Campanella, [Étienne] Cabet, and others all fail to provide for individual freedom",[75] and therefore their works, such as Campanella's *The City of the Sun* (1463) and Cabet's *The Voyage to Icaria* (1840), are frequently seen as totalitarian. He reminds us of the writings of Nikolai Berdyaev, to whom, following his experience of the October Revolution of 1917, "utopia is always totalitarian, and totalitarianism, in the conditions of our world, is always utopian."[76] Cyberpunk, too, decades later, would provide a significant site for criticism of centralised economic and political systems as a slippery slope to total state control. Yet Banks was resolute, acknowledging and challenging the warnings of anti-utopian and dystopian fiction, which suggest that such a surveillance system could potentially enable a more repressive, totalitarian regime, if used with such intent.[77] So much of the Culture as positive utopia rests upon the Minds, and Banks even informs us that "a trace of some sort of bias, some element of moral or other partiality must be present in the Culture's Minds [...] a dark, wild weed of spite in the endless soughing golden fields of their charity" (*Excession*, 127). Simone Caroti describes the conspiracy of Minds who appear in *Excession* (a nameless group within that known as the Interesting Times Gang) as "one of the bad dreams nestling inside the hopeful good works of the Contact and Special Circumstances sections, because any single ship of the power of, say the *Sleeper Service* could ravage entire star systems if left to its own devices", and asks if such a conspiracy could ultimately "change the Culture's shape [...] through the kind of overpoweringly skilful manipulation god-like AIs are capable of", and bring "that change about without anyone else noticing".[78] It is exactly this kind of potentiality that has convinced Kincaid that Banks's Culture series is, at points, anti-utopian. Yet, while Banks acknowledges and explores

---

[75] Elliott, *The Shape of Utopia*, 90.
[76] Elliott, *The Shape of Utopia*, 90.
[77] See Raffaella Baccolini and Tom Moylan, eds., *Dark Horizons: Science Fiction and the Dystopian Imagination* (London: Routledge Publishing, 2003).
[78] Caroti, *The Culture Series of Iain M. Banks*, 133.

such anti-utopian warnings, I suggest that this works to strengthen the Culture texts as a critical utopian series rather than as one that works against the utopian project per se.

AIs as Willing Slaves

There is an inverse reading of the Culture's AIs which also seems to threaten the utopian status of Banks's civilisation by suggesting that they, especially the drones, occupy a subordinate position in relation to human beings. As Simon Guerrier notes, "what the Minds essentially seem to operate is the bureaucracy of the Culture [...] handling the administration of the utopia [while] all the humans have to do is get on with enjoying themselves."[79] Frequently providing the role of central, mainframe computer (Hub Minds) for the Culture's Orbitals and ships, for example, the Minds are responsible for fulfilling the needs of Culture citizens, generally on a long-term basis, as well as maintaining general communications and information networks, and of course underpinning SC and Contact. The drones, also, contribute directly to the freedoms provided for Culture citizens. As demonstrated above through the relationship between Gurgeh and various drones in *The Player of Games*, these less-advanced AIs often provide day-to-day support for individuals, in a role seemingly akin to that of servant or butler. As allegedly "nothing and nobody in the Culture is exploited", therefore, the exact status of the Minds and Drones within it must be addressed: how can such entities, ostensibly afforded citizenship alongside all other Culture citizens, also be considered free and equal if the liberty of non-AIs seems to be dependent upon the exploitation of their labour?

In this manner, the Minds and Drones fulfil the "science-fictional archetype of the Willing Slave" as outlined by Csicsery-Ronay, which initially developed in proto-SF such as colonial adventure narratives, propagating the "myth of the colonized subaltern" that was "unreservedly appreciative of its colonization".[80] A slave therefore but, supposedly, a willing one. Once the genre of SF had fully developed, this human slave figure of "proletarian and colonial labor" was eventually replaced by that of a machine.[81] Csicsery-Ronay continues, observing that "one might assume that the transition from adventure to sf would have been

---

[79] Guerrier, 'Culture Theory', 31.
[80] Csicsery-Ronay, *Seven Beauties*, 229.
[81] Csicsery-Ronay, *Seven Beauties*, 252.

unproblematic in terms of the Willing Slave function", as such a figure "should cease to be both willing (a machine is no longer a sentient being), and a slave (a machine has no inherent claims to freedom)."[82] But, as the complexities of Banks's series demonstrate, "things have turned out differently."[83]

Banks formulated the Culture in such a way as to ensure that the relationship between AIs and the humans whom they support does not simply recreate such conditions of colonial subordination or the class-based hierarchy of capitalism, maintaining that artificial life in the Culture falls within its egalitarian system. Banks explains the AIs' position as follows: "machines have no capacity to suffer – that's what it's all about. If they can't suffer, they can't be exploited. You can't exploit a calculator."[84] Therefore, if the Minds are categorically incapable of experiencing torment of any kind, perhaps they cannot be considered sentient; if they are not sentient, then they have no inherent claim to freedom, and perform their function automatically as they are programmed to do. This line of reasoning is problematic, of course, because it would be extremely difficult to prove definitively that a machine of sufficiently developed intelligence is not sentient, with Csicsery-Ronay citing *Star Trek: The Next Generation* and *Aliens* as examples of SF that effectively problemetise this issue.[85]

Despite Banks's comments above, and regardless of the extent to which the Minds and Drones can be considered sentient, their function as Willing Slaves can be justified for other reasons. Firstly, they seem to act out of a *genuine* willingness different to that of the colonised subaltern because they are free to fulfil an entirely different function, or – more importantly – are free to fulfil no specific Culture function whatsoever, adopting the uninhibited lifestyle enjoyed by non-AI Culture citizens. Some Minds are deemed "Eccentric", for example, for their unusual lifestyle choices, such as the Mind that inhabits the GSV *Sense Amid Madness, Wit Amongst Folly* in *Surface Detail*. Many choose to operate as part of SC or Contact, whose roles may not necessarily directly benefit other Culture citizens, as may be the case with Mawhrin-Skel-Flere-Imsaho in *The Player of Games*. The drone Hassipura Plyn-Frie in *The Hydrogen Sonata* chooses to spend centuries in a remote desert, building elaborate sand sculptures. Also, even those AIs who do chose to assist with the Culture's bureaucratic functions need only give up a very small

---

[82] Csicsery-Ronay, *Seven Beauties*, 252.
[83] Csicsery-Ronay, *Seven Beauties*, 252.
[84] Nolan, 'Iain Banks and Kim Stanley Robinson in Conversation', 71.
[85] Csicsery-Ronay, *Seven Beauties*, 252.

amount of their processing power for such tasks. In *Look to Windward*, for example, referring to the Mind at the centre of the Chiark Orbital, Banks explains that

> The Hub has millions of human-form representative entities called avatars with which it deals on a one-to-one basis with its inhabitants. It is theoretically capable of running each of those and every other system on the Orbital directly while communicating individually with every human and drone present on the world, plus a number of other ships and Minds. (275)

The Minds are so intelligent, their capacity so broad, that they can potentially live rich personal lives that are entirely separate from their function as Willing Slave; such voluntary duties simply do not impact their lives to any real degree. The Drones, also, are never likely to suffer or become dissatisfied with their function, even if they were not free to desist at any time. As explained by Tersono in *Windward*:

> We drones are perfectly used to being patient while human thoughts and meaningful actions take place. We possess an entire suite of procedures specifically evolved over the millennia to cope with such moments. We are actually considerably less boreable, if I may create a neologism, than the average human. (337)

Because human beings think and act so sluggishly slowly in relation to AIs, Tersono explains, drones have become used to passing the time in the spaces between human beings starting to form thoughts and consider actions, and the moment when they finally speak or act; the implication being that there is a private world of thought and communication occurring behind the interactions between Willing Slave and Handy Man "master".

Perhaps most importantly, the Culture's AIs share the same citizen status as its human beings. As Unaha-Closp explains in *Phlebas*, the drones have something like an equivalent of the Human Rights Act for AIs: "I am an Accredited Free Construct, certified Sentient under the Free Will Acts by the Greater Vavatch United Moral Standards Administration and with full citizenship of the Vavatch Heterocracy" (260). Closp asserts that, "I am not just a computer, I am a drone. I am conscious and I have an individual identity. Therefore I have a name" (264).

The Problem of Hierarchy

Egalitarianism is at the core of any socialist project, even in certain understandings of classical liberalism, as it is core to the Culture; so it is necessary to ask whether it has in fact been achieved. The Culture does not have classes in a Marxist understanding of the term as private ownership of capital does not exist, meaning in turn that a capitalist class does not exist, and therefore neither does an exploited, alienated proletariat. Yet, despite such concerted attempts to eradicate inequality and hierarchy, the question of the extent to which the Culture is truly egalitarian is still complex. Two issues that must be addressed in this regard relate to the nature of Contact and SC – members of which appear to have a certain level of power over other citizens of the Culture in a way that most do not – and the existence and nature of universities in the Culture, which potentially demonstrate the presence of hierarchical arrangements, as discussed below.

In some ways, the organisations Contact and SC seem intrinsically hierarchical and perhaps could be considered elitist. These organisations – responsible respectively for establishing and maintaining communication with other societies, and for, when deemed absolutely necessary, affecting change in Contacted societies – require highly trained and disciplined individuals in order to ensure that their protocols are maintained and their missions accomplished effectively. When SC is first described in the series, the reader is introduced to it through the perspective of *Consider Phlebas* protagonist, Bora Horza Gobuchul:

> Special Circumstances had always been the Contact section's moral espionage weapon, the very cutting edge of the Culture's interfering diplomatic policy, the élite of the élite, in a society which abhorred elitism. Even before the war, its standing and its image within the Culture had been roguish sexiness – there was no other word for it – which implied predation, seduction, even violation. (30)

This description tends towards the pejorative, of course, as Horza is known to hate the Culture; yet SC does seem elitist to a certain extent, and its reputation for excellence and intrigue is spoken about with a certain seductive quality – a "sexiness" – as exemplified by Banks's novels.

As with *Inversions*, *The Player of Games* is an example of what Banks calls a "closed chronicle", in which the identity of the narrator is not revealed until the conclusion. At the start of the novel, protagonist Gurgeh is blackmailed into joining SC by the drone Mawhrin-Skel.

This blackmail is motivated by the fact that the drone was rejected by SC shortly after joining, and intends to exploit Gurgeh to assure its reinstalment. Initially created especially to work in SC, Mawhrin-Skel was designed as a superior drone: "effectively a military machine with a variety of sophisticated, hardened sensory and weapons systems which would have been quite unnecessary on the majority of drones" (14). The drone's character was left to develop of its own accord; it was subsequently deemed "rogue" and therefore unsuitable for SC (14). These details, suggesting a highly demanding and competitive recruitment process, seem to highlight the division's superior attitude towards the rest of the Culture. At the end of *Player*, however, much of the narrative's accuracy is implicitly called into question once the identity of the narrator is revealed in the final chapter to be another drone, Flere-Imsaho, making it difficult to verify several aspects of the novel, including those relating to the nature of SC. Flere-Imsaho explains that he was in fact posing as Mawhrin-Skel all along, creating and adopting this false identity and back-story in order to aid SC's manipulation of Gurgeh into overthrowing Azad. When Flere-Imsaho asks at the novel's conclusion "would I lie to you?" (309) the reader is made to reconsider many aspects of the proceeding narrative and the drone's identity. Who was the original drone and which identity was invented? Perhaps rogue SC agent Mawhrin-Skel was the original drone, all along, and it was in fact Flere-Imsaho – supposedly the more respectable of the two – that was invented, achieving a double bluff in a manner similar to the "double agent" trope of Cold War spy fiction. Following this reading, Mawhrin-Skel exploited SC's interest in Gurgeh to allow the drone's own clandestine return to SC, and not vice versa. The narrative's unreliable narrator leaves the exact extent of SC's hierarchies ambiguous, although serving to exemplify its secretive, seductive nature, regardless of which version of events is believed.

It is not just SC drones that are customised to be superior or especially shaped in this manner, and examples of the extent to which SC's human operatives are similarly privileged can be found in almost every text in the series. While the majority of Culture people choose to have their bodies and minds enhanced to a certain extent – granted longer, healthier life, cranially implanted "drug glands" free from side-effects and so forth, as I explore in Chapter Four – SC operatives have access to potentially more powerful and more dangerous tools, such as knife missiles, poisoned fingers tips, and other weapons. Yet, in *Phlebas*, Contact admits that it sometimes picks its operatives at random because it knows it seems the fairest method given that there are too many potential recruits for the job (271–272). Given that knowledge is treated as a commodity within the Culture, as explained above, it is important to note that Contact is described as having "the best Minds, the most information" (22), which could potentially be used to acquire leverage and power. In an information economy, Contact and SC are indeed "wealthy".

The fact that Gurgeh is an academic, who teaches at the University of Chiark, also has interesting implications for the egalitarian nature of the Culture. Universities are often conceived of as an intrinsically meritocratic concept – at least traditionally – as progress within them is judged upon the acquisition of knowledge and intellectual achievement, rather than upon class privilege or wealth. At the time of writing in 2019, increased tuition fees and other higher-education reforms are topical subjects, with many arguing that entry into some of the more esteemed universities – Russell Group institutions such as University of Cambridge, Oxford, and London, or Ivy League universities such as Brown or Yale, for example – is biased towards those from privileged backgrounds, and threatens the traditional meritocracy of university education. Arguing that the post-war Robbins report is being implicitly challenged by the current Conservative government, Peter Scott states that "the increasing weight placed on attending 'good universities', which just happen to be those with the most privileged student intakes, shows what is really happening. Social connections now trump academic aspirations and achievements."[86] This situation is clearly impossible in the Culture universities, however, as class privilege does not and cannot exist – yet that does not mean that they operate according to a completely different system with no aspect of hierarchy whatsoever. Judging by Gurgeh's title ("itinerant guest lecturer" [11]) and those of his colleagues (*Professor* Boruelal for example), the University of Chiark is structured according to a familiar hierarchy of academic attainment – Reader, Lecturer, Professor, etc. – which in turn suggests that it also follows something akin to the traditional quasi-regal university managerial structure – Dean, Pro-Vice-Chancellor, Vice-Chancellor, and so forth. Banks's texts offer no further detail on such structures, yet their use of academic positions does demonstrate that the Culture's higher-education system cannot be said to be *completely* flat and free from hierarchy, perhaps demonstrating the difference between hierarchy, suggesting inequality and autocracy, and organisation, suggesting meritocracy and egalitarianism.

---

[86] Peter Scott, 'Meritocracy is in retreat in twenty first century higher education', *Guardian*, 1 September 2015. www.theguardian.com/education/2015/sep/01/higher-education-class-degree-university-inequality.

The key point here is that this potentially unequal aspect scarcely seems to matter in such an advanced society: the fact that citizens can live for essentially as long as they wish means that, in theory, anyone could achieve such positions within academia through applying themselves for as long as was necessary, with no economic, geographic, or social barriers withholding them. Titles such as "doctor" or "professor" would exist purely as markers of intellectual achievement and profession, attracting a kind of prestige perhaps, but not allowing the bearer any serious privileges that would lead to fundamental social inequality. In this respect, universities represent the core values of the Culture: the spirit of discovery and open-minded inquiry; the quest for mutual understanding and mutual tolerance between peoples and races across the galaxy; and a desire to encourage the best qualities in human beings.

Postscarcity and Human Behaviour

One of the most significant benefits that Banks postulates to have arisen from the Culture's move beyond scarcity is the way in which this shift affects human behaviour, maybe even the human condition itself, and encourages our more positive instincts. By removing inequality and the class system entirely from a society, the argument goes, the individuals within that society will also be radically reshaped, with negative attributes such as jealousy, snobbery, greed, and aggression becoming less and less necessary, and therefore less and less prevalent. Right-wing and/ or anti-utopian critics have stressed the fundamental selfishness, greed, or war-like tendencies of *homo sapiens*, and the inescapable and insidious nature of Darwinian survival of the fittest, which supposedly ensures that we will never achieve or maintain such an end;[87] whereas more progressive schools of thought have challenged the basis of this notion, arguing for a fundamental re-conception of human evolution, and our understanding of humanity. Woodcock discusses Russian anarchist Peter Kropotkin's argument that even humankind's

> intellectual faculty is "eminently social", since it is nurtured by communication – mainly in the form of language, by imitation, and by the accumulated experience of the race. He [Kropotkin]

---

[87] See Francis Fukuyama, *Our Posthuman Future: Consequences of the Biotechnology Revolution* (Farrar, Straus and Giroux, 2002); *John Grey, Black Mass: Apocalyptic Religion and the Death of Utopia* (St Ives: Penguin Books, 2007) and *Straw Dogs: Thoughts on Humans and Other Animals* (London: Granta Books, 2002).

admitted that the struggle of existence, of which evolutionists such as Thomas Huxley made a great deal, was indeed important, but he saw it as a struggle against adverse circumstances, rather than between individuals of the same species.[88]

Human beings, Kropotkin's argument goes, evolve according to the ways in which we respond to our surroundings, as much as we react to each other. We will naturally group together for shared protection and support, a concept he called "mutual aid", and which Hardt and Negri bring up-to-date for a globalised era in their notion of Multitude. The central logic of the Culture series does seem to support this idea, even though in interviews Banks often stated his significantly more pessimistic view of humanity writ large.[89] So effective is Banks's conception of the Culture, however, that regardless of whether one views humankind as fundamentally selfish and violent, or social and caring, the eradication of our worse tendencies can be explained by a social response to the changes incurred in a postscarcity society, to genetic manipulation of human beings, or a complex mixture of both.

One fundamental change undergone by the Culture is directly related to the postscarcity nature of their society: they have a slightly reconfigured sense of personal ownership and possession, and no sense of private property. When Gurgeh is guided around Azad by the drone Flere-Imsaho, it is necessary to explain such concepts at a basic level, in order for Gurgeh to understand fundamental aspects of the society into which he has been introduced:

> The thing to remember, Gurgeh [...] is that their society is based on ownership. Everything that you see and touch, everything you come into contact with, will belong to somebody or to an institution; it will be theirs, they will own it. In the same way, everyone you meet will be conscious of both their position in society and their relationship to others around them. (114)

This description, given from the perspective of a Culture drone who has never experienced scarcity, serves to estrange the basic nature of capitalism, and reveals the fundamental economic inequality present on

---

[88] Woodcock, ed., *The Anarchist Reader*, 19.
[89] At the event 'Iain Banks and Kim Stanley Robinson in Conversation', held at the British Library, London, on 9 June 2012, Banks aired his opinion that humankind is prone to being violent, as well as towards various "isms" – racism, sexism, etc.

Earth. With ownership and social position absent in the Culture, due to the fact that acquisition of anything at all is an entirely easy, fluid, and frequently instantaneous process, any instinct to possess material items for oneself in order to ensure that an individual retains ownership has dimmed or vanished, as the item could be replaced perfectly and instantly. The consequences for society would be considerable, especially relating to criminal or anti-social behaviour; as Banks notes: "In a society where material scarcity is unknown and the only real value is sentimental value, there is little motive or opportunity for the sort of action we would class as a crime against property."[90]

The Player of Games: Private Property, Sentimentality, Possession

Originally drafted in 1979, and re-drafted in the years preceding its publication in 1988, the period in which *The Player of Games* was written roughly aligns with Margaret Thatcher's term as prime minister of the United Kingdom (from 4 May 1979 until 28 November 1990). Written within this context, as Thatcher's programmes began to be enforced, it is possible to draw parallels between the ideologies underpinning her policies and those of Azad, especially considering the much-documented relationship between Thatcher and the Chilean dictator General Augusto Pinochet, who implemented a free-market, Neoliberal economic system in Chile, inspired by Thatcher as well as economists such as Milton Friedman.[91]

While money does not exist in the Culture, nor the concept of private property in a Marxist sense, and its citizens have to have the concept of ownership explained to them as in the preceding quotation, some of its citizens still display an understanding of ownership and possession even if it is in a general, more abstract sense, in relation to personal possessions. Again in *The Player of Games*, throughout Gurgeh's narrative there are instances when this character displays a sense of attachment to personal effects for sentimental or symbolic reasons. Banks's second-published Culture text is perhaps uniquely suited to revealing such details as it is the only text in the series that portrays the life of a Culture

---

[90] Banks, 'A Few Notes on the Culture'. Web.
[91] See the full text of Margaret Thatcher's speech to the Blackpool fringe in 1999 (www.theguardian.com/world/1999/oct/06/pinochet.chile) and *Sunday Times* economics editor David Smith's article on this relationship (www.economicsuk.com/blog/000406.html).

citizen (the male protagonist Jernau Morat Gurgeh) living in their home environment (the Orbital Chiark) for a substantial portion of the text. In this respect, Gurgeh acts as a kind of bridge character, allowing a contemporary audience to understand the nature of the Culture by experiencing it through a character to whom they are more likely to be able to relate, given his somewhat ambiguous positioning in relation to his home. The other Culture texts detail the exploits of individuals who exist in a complex and ambiguous relationship with the Culture, and live on its fringes. The plot of *Player* follows Gurgeh, the Culture's best game-player, who is blackmailed by an ex-SC drone into accepting a mission to visit the Empire of Azad, in order literally to beat them at their own game, instigate an intervention, and overturn the regime.

At the beginning, the reader experiences Gurgeh's working life as an academic in the field of game-playing, as well as snippets from his personal relationships, before he is unwillingly drafted into SC, leaving Chiark to begin his mission to the Empire of Azad. It is during the transition period, before Gurgeh boards a ship to leave Chiark, when notions of ownership are acknowledged. Wondering what Gurgeh will need to pack for his journey, the drone Chamlis asks: "What about personal possessions? It could be awkward if you want to take anything larger than a small module, say, or livestock larger than human size." Gurgeh shook his head. "Nothing remotely that large. A few cases of clothes... perhaps one or two ornaments... nothing more" (90). Gurgeh's somewhat sparse travelling habits could suggest the somewhat stereotypical image of an academic who lives an ascetic lifestyle, more concerned with intellectual pursuits than material possessions. It is Gurgeh's inclusion of "perhaps one or two ornaments", however, which is of more interest in this context. On two occasions in *Player*, physical objects presented to an individual explicitly as a gift are mentioned in relation to Gurgeh. In both instances they reveal the residual presence of the feeling of sentimentality. Slightly after Chamlis asks after Gurgeh's possessions, for example, while Gurgeh sorts through his quarters, selecting items to bring with him on his mission, Gurgeh's friend Yay interrupts this process, communicating with him remotely through a screen. Viewing Gurgeh sat in his home, Yay notices one such object: "a rusting piece of ironware beside the bench; a present from an old lover he'd almost forgotten about" (90). "What is that you're sitting beside?" asks Yay. "Gurgeh looked at the piece of ironware by the side of the bench. 'That's a cannon,' he told her. 'That's what I thought.' 'It was a present from a lady friend,' Gurgeh explained. [...] 'I see'" (85). In this verbal exchange, the cannon may operate at least partly as a joke drawing upon the gun's clear phallic symbolism, yet it plays a more important function later on in the text. Similarly, before Gurgeh departs for Azad, apparently without Chamlis, the drone hands Gurgeh a "small parcel; paper tied up with ribbon." "'Just an old tradition,' Chamlis explained" (93). Preoccupied with his study of Azad onboard the ship, Gurgeh forgets to open this gift until much later on. When he does unwrap it, Gurgeh pulls out what appears to be "a thin bracelet" (116–117), the significance of which he does not understand at the time. (Banks's more informed readers at this point would probably pick up the hint offered here to its real nature – a model of Gurgeh's home Orbital – by the description's use of the word "bracelet", which Banks often uses to describe Orbitals.)

Gurgeh's decision to bring the bracelet and a photo of the cannon with him on his journey (only his second away from Chiark) suggests his sentimental attachment to the objects, just as Chamlis offering Gurgeh a gift places a special kind of value upon the mysterious object. While Gurgeh could clearly ask a drone or Mind to produce a replica of the cannon, which would be technically perfect in every way, this would not be enough for him. Implicitly, there is a special significance, a special value, in bringing *that particular* object along with him, which could not be acquired by bringing even a perfect replica. Perhaps the fact that Gurgeh's former lover fashioned the object herself, crafted it through human endeavour, and presumably would have touched the final object with her hands, gives the gift a meaning that cannot – for Gurgeh – be achieved in any other way. Similarly, at first, the gift Chamlis offers Gurgeh seems like a personal gesture – a personal token of friendship, which – as an object crafted from metal – has a similarly tactile and physical presence, even if Gurgeh views the purpose for which he assumes it to be used – a bracelet – as trivial.

Eventually, Gurgeh realises Chamlis's gift is not a bracelet as such, but in fact represents a Culture Orbital, such as that on which he was born. Described as "bright in the darkness, lighting up his fingers and the covers of the bed", and with "microscopic whorls of weather systems over blue sea and dun-coloured land" (145), the model is clearly a highly detailed object of great beauty and aesthetic value. As with Gurgeh's model cannon, however, the Orbital is allowed to develop a somewhat grander meaning in the novel. Necessarily immersed in the alien world of Azad, Gurgeh faces the threat of assimilation, potentially abandoning the values of the Culture (of which he is openly sceptical) where life is but a game, and succumbing to the lure of Azad, which, with its cruelty and violence, represents the dangerous thrills of gambling that he desires. The bracelet, then, far from a mere decoration, represents Gurgeh's home literally, but also signifies the Culture's values symbolically.

The gift given to Gurgeh by his former lover performs a similar function. Gurgeh explains that the metal item is shaped like a cannon because his friend "was very keen on forging and casting. She graduated from pokers and fire grates to cannons. She thought it might be amusing to fire large metal spheres at the fjord" (85). Despite the military connotations of the item, the gift still represents a link between Gurgeh and the fjords of his home, Chiark, as well as to a significant past relationship. Even the drone Chamlis displays a similar inclination towards sentimentality at the very end of the novel, by mounting on the wall the physical shell of the drone whose identity it assumes during Gurgeh's journey – that of Mawhrin-Skel (306) – behind glass, and admitting that "this means a great deal to me" (306).

Alongside this literal discussion of sentimentality for personal artefacts, Banks's discussion of the theme of possession within a postscarcity society is allowed to achieve a more metaphorical significance within *Player*: Gurgeh's game-playing is symbolic of his general outlook, which marks him as unusual within the Culture, especially regarding his relationships with women. At the start of the text, Gurgeh has become disillusioned with his game-playing career essentially due to the postscarcity nature of the Culture itself. To Gurgeh, playing games in this environment eventually loses its enjoyment and meaning: "With no money, no possessions, a large part of the enjoyment the people who invented this game experienced when they played it just... disappears" (21). In a society where no-one actually owns anything for themselves (at least in theory), it is impossible to gamble anything, to maintain an element of genuine risk, as it is impossible to lose something that cannot be easily and quickly re-obtained. In retort to this, Chamlis defends the Culture's stance:

> You call it enjoyment to lose your house, your titles, your estates; your children maybe; to be expected to walk out onto the balcony and blow your brains out? That's enjoyment? We're free of that. You want something you can't have, Gurgeh. You enjoy your life in the Culture, but it can't provide you with sufficient threats; the true gambler needs the excitement of potential loss, even ruin, to feel wholly Alive. (21)

Arguing that such logic is absurd, Chamlis challenges the notion that one must face the threat of danger in order to experience joy and pleasure. He states that "you called yourself 'Morat' when you completed your name, but perhaps you aren't the perfect game-player after all; perhaps you should have called yourself 'Shequi'; gambler" (21). The

Culture's outlook, implies Chamlis, is that of a game-player, a professional playing for the intellectual pleasure of the game itself, and not the glory of winning or losing, the latter of which should be accepted in a sportsman-like manner of mutual respect and appreciation. The attitude of a gambler, by contrast, belongs to the older, backwards society through which the Culture has passed, where pleasure derives from self-interest, insecurity, and even a form of sadism: "To glory in the defeat of another," states Chamlis, "to need that purchased pride, is to show that you are incomplete and inadequate to start with" (21).

So Gurgeh's dissatisfaction with his life in utopia shows that his general values and worldview clash with those of the Culture; yet his attitude toward game-playing also demonstrates an uncomfortable view in relation to sexual relationships. The novel's early scenes in which Gurgeh and Yay discuss the model cannon develop the pair's relationship, characterised by tension caused by opposing worldviews and unresolved sexual attraction; and, reading between the lines of this conversation, Yay's affection for Gurgeh is clear. Before leaving for Azad, Gurgeh "took a few photographs" of the cannon present, to which he is clearly sentimentally attached (84). Yay's brief yet loaded response to Gurgeh's continued interest in the gift – "I see" (85) – speaks volumes, suggesting perhaps jealousy on her part at his continued interest in the former relationship from which the gift originated. In fact, Gurgeh has been making sexual advances toward Yay for some time, with Yay politely turning him down. While Yay is attracted to Gurgeh, and has strongly considered acquiescing to his advances, she is concerned about several of his attitudes towards sexuality and sexual relationships, which reveal a great deal about Gurgeh's general character, as well as the subtle devices Banks uses to develop the reader's understanding of the Culture. Yay's ambivalence about Gurgeh arguably stems from the fact that Banks portrays him as a person who, despite being born in the Culture and only leaving it on one occasion, displays views and adheres to values that more typical Culture individuals deem to be old-fashioned – indeed, he is referred to at one stage as "primitive", and at another as a "throwback" (29).

Yay identifies concepts derived from Gurgeh's game-playing in his treatment of women: "'I feel you want to... take me,' Yay said, 'like a piece, like an area. To be had; to be... possessed'" (24). Here, Gurgeh implicitly reflects views from an archaic patriarchal order, which sees woman as an inferior sex, and therefore as the "property" of men. Here Banks cleverly has Yay draw upon Gurgeh's game-playing terminology to subtly indicate the fact that she seems unfamiliar with the concept of possession from anywhere other than the games that Gurgeh has explained to her. (At one stage, Gurgeh plays a game entitled 'Possession', which requires pieces to be taken, implying an ownership that can change hands [24].) These notions are also reflected by Gurgeh's reactions when pitted against a very young but talented female game-player, who attempts an especially audacious move known as a "Full Web": "simultaneous capture of every remaining point in the game-space" (48). The age and gender of his opponent cause Gurgeh anger, yet it is seemingly the nature of the Full Web itself that irks him most. If possession of gamepieces stands metaphorically for patriarchal male "possession" of a female, then his opponent is not only using such tactics against him, but attempting total "patriarchal" domination in this manner.

This fact, that Gurgeh is developed initially as an old-fashioned man from the perspective of the Culture – displaying gendered-male traits that it has supposedly left behind – has several important implications for this text. Firstly, Gurgeh's mission to the dystopian Azad is portrayed as a kind of katabatic descent, with his subsequent return to Chiark indicating that he has been significantly changed by his experience. In one of the text's deliberate ironies, Gurgeh's mission to Azad succeeds, resulting in this society becoming "Culture-ised", implicitly because Gurgeh – as a Culture "relic" – is more accepted by the relatively primitive people of Azad. In turn, by experiencing the extreme contrasts between these two societies, Gurgeh finally grows to fully understand and appreciate the nature of his home. Secondly, it lies at the heart of Yay's reluctance to take him as a lover, and reveals important details about attitudes towards gender roles in the Culture (which are discussed in Chapter Four).

The Player of Games: the Empire of Azad as Capitalist Dystopia

Race Matthews has argued that: "The major preoccupation of [Banks's] science fiction is with whether – and, if so, on what terms – societies characterized respectively by abundance and scarcity can coexist."[92] While *Player* does contrast the Culture's abundance with Azad's scarcity, as occurs in a similar manner in other Culture texts, Banks's preoccupations are much more radical than merely negotiating a mutually beneficial compromise between these two modes of society: Banks's

---

[92] Race Matthews, 'Iain M. Banks: The "Culture" Science-Fiction Novels and the Economics and politics of Scarcity and Abundance', *Metaphysical Review* 28/29 (August 1998): 9.

series depicts nothing short of attempts to fundamentally transform less-advanced societies, such as the unambiguously cruel and sadistic Empire of Azad, into postscarcity environments, which are therefore capable of becoming something more like the Culture. In *Player*, Banks first establishes the abundance of the Culture, with the novel's first sections providing a "tour" of utopia and insight into the daily lives of Culture citizens, and then provides a contrasting view of the Empire of Azad as a society mired by scarcity. In this fashion, Banks establishes a dialectic between utopia and dystopia – a device used in earlier examples of classic utopian SF such as Ursula Le Guin's *The Dispossessed* (1974) or Marge Piercy's *Woman on the Edge of Time* (1976), which it is very likely that Banks read.

The Empire of Azad is an imperial bureaucracy ruled by a single emperor, Nicosar. It is notable for the extreme inequality and sadism of its laws, and also for the unusual manner in which all of its decisions are made, its socio-political and economic systems arranged, and its hierarchies established. In the text's major innovation, Azad is also the name of a complex, large-scale game, the playing of which determines everything in the Empire: Azad the empire and Azad the game are literally one and the same: "Whoever succeeds at the game succeeds in life; the same qualities are required in each to ensure dominance" (76–77). The reader gleans the majority of detail regarding the Empire through several paragraphs of exposition in discussions between Gurgeh and the various Culture drones who brief him on his mission. The startling cruelty and oppression of the Empire – brutal deaths and torture as standard legal punishment; a semi-fascist eugenics programme; reported genocide, sterilisation, and mass deportation (79–80) – which are detailed at length, suggest that through it Banks is overtly targeting the various empires on Earth, which developed from antiquity and peaked at the end of the modern era.

Following Jameson's insight that SF, and by extension utopian fiction, whilst often appearing to deal with the future, also sends back "reliable information about the contemporary world",[93] Banks uses the Culture's rival societies, not just to establish the utopian nature of the Culture by contrast, but also to satirise and critique elements of the

---

[93] "In any case, the representational apparatus of Science Fiction, having gone through innumerable generations of technological development and well-nigh viral mutation since the onset of that movement, is sending back more reliable information about the contemporary world than an exhausted realism (or an exhausted modernism either)" – in Jameson, *Archaeologies*, 384.

capitalist, post-Globalisation context in which the series was written, using techniques of defamiliarisation and estrangement.

The Player of Games: Class Inequality in Azad

The Empire of Azad, located on the "home planet" entitled "Ëa",[94] resembles a capitalist system characterised by rigid class boundaries and divisions. As the Contact drone Worthil explains, the Empire features "hierarchical power structures", with influence "restricted to an economically privileged class" (74–75). Whilst reading about its history and politics, Gurgeh notes that Azad is both "fabulously rich and grindingly poor" (106). The drone continues: "It looks perverse and wasteful to us, but then one thing that empires are not about is the efficient use of resources and the spread of happiness; both are typically accomplished despite the economic short-circuiting – corruption and favouritism, mostly – endemic to the system" (75).

Azad, therefore, is characterised by its inequality, its power structures, and scarcity, in the same way that the Culture is by its classlessness and its abundance; also Azad relies upon money in order to "ration" its resources, as did the civilisations from which the Culture was formed hundreds of thousands of years ago. Exploring Azad on foot, Mawhrin-Skel describes the area through which they walk:

> that's called a shantytown, and it's where the city draws its surplus unskilled labor from. [...] That is where people who have left the countryside for the bright lights of the big city often end up. Unfortunately many of them are just loafers [driven off the land by an ingeniously unfair property-tax system and the opportunistic top-down reorganization of the agricultural production apparatus]. (122)

Here, the drone defamiliarises the fringes of cities in the capitalist West, drawing attention to the crumbling, derelict zones about which conservatives would wish to forget. In this damning critique, we see the result of the concept of a "property owning democracy", developed

---

[94] This is probably a reference to the word for "universe" in the fictional cosmology created by J.R.R. Tolkien for his Middle-earth legendarium (also "Ëa"). The fact that Tolkien insisted that Middle-earth was conceived as existing in fact on the Earth that we know, in the distant past, would seem to strengthen connections between Azad and Earth society.

by Anthony Eden following World War Two, and adopted by Margaret Thatcher in her first speech as party leader in 1975.[95] Through this lens, the society of Azad, which places importance upon the values associated with the ownership of personal property – the prestige of owning one's own house and associated consumer items, and the glamour of rich celebrities – begins to seem uncomfortably like our own, despite its more glaringly fascist elements. Drawing its "surplus unskilled labour" from such areas, Azadian society echoes the exploitation perpetrated by many Western countries in the current era of Globalisation, which rely upon the desperation of workers from overseas, and their subsequent willingness to work for low pay and with few rights, in order to produce cheap products and services.[96]

Azad as Game

As outlined above, the Empire of Azad and the game of Azad are in fact synonymous – therefore an analysis of one would not be complete without analysis of the other. As Mawhrin-Skel explains to Gurgeh, the results of the game's various stages equate to social and political changes in the larger society, including economics: "The game of Azad is used not so much to determine which person will rule, but which tendency within the empire's ruling class will have the upper hand, which branch of economic theory will be followed" (76). In this manner, therefore, the tactics and strategy used by the game's winner reflect the fundamental ideologies of the final socio-economic conditions that they enforce. By having the Azadian economic system also determined by the outcome of a game, Banks invites the reader to compare this notion with that of the free-market, Neoliberal economic system that Margaret Thatcher helped to usher in, through her deregulation of financial markets – known as the "Big Bang" – in 1986. Banks once described the Market as

> a good example of evolution in action; the try-everything-and-see-what-works approach. This might provide a perfectly morally

[95] "In the footsteps of Anthony Eden, who set us the goal of a property-owning democracy – a goal we still pursue today; of Harold Macmillan whose leadership brought so many ambitions within the grasp of every citizen" – full speech at: www.britishpoliticalspeech.org/speech-archive.htm?speech=121.
[96] See Felicity Lawrence, 'Sweatshop campaigners demand Gap boycott', *Guardian*, 2 November 2002. https://www.theguardian.com/uk/2002/nov/22/clothes.globalisation.

satisfactory resource-management system so long as there was absolutely no question of any sentient creature ever being treated purely as one of those resources. The market, for all its (profoundly inelegant) complexities, remains a crude and essentially blind system.[97]

Instead of a deregulated market, then, Banks advocated a planned economy, by way of contrast, as "more productive" and "more morally desirable",[98] as there was much less chance of people being treated as mere "resources", a form of exploitation detailed in classic Marxist theory as reification. The "try-everything-and-see-what-works approach" of Neoliberal economics – in which as little control as possible is exerted over the financial systems, instead leaving the balance of wealth up to the whims of the market system – can be regarded as similar to game-playing, or more accurately gambling, as real losses are at stake.

Whilst undertaking one of several "tours" of Azad, the drone Flere-Imsaho, explains to Gurgeh the nature of private property ownership, as well as the related notion of possession, which it implies are deep-rooted in a capitalist society, affecting more than just finance:

> It is especially important to remember that the ownership of humans is possible too; not only in terms of actual slavery, which they are proud to have abolished, but in the sense that, according to which sex and class one belongs to, one may be partially owned by another or others by having to sell one's labor or talents to somebody with the means to buy them. In the case of males, they give themselves most totally when they become soldiers; the personnel in their armed forces are like slaves, with little personal freedom, and under threat of death if they disobey. Females sell their bodies, usually, entering them into the legal contract of "marriage". (114)

Gurgeh is a relatively naive protagonist who has lived his whole life within the safe and abundant realms of the Culture: "the longest he'd spent away from Chiark had been when he'd gone on a cruise once, thirty years earlier" (32). Without visiting other societies, Gurgeh would not have encountered the various forms of exploitation outlined here; and, by having the drone explain such fundamental social concepts to the reader, Banks achieves estrangement of a patriarchal, capitalist society

---

[97] Banks, 'A Few Notes on the Culture'. Web.
[98] Banks, 'A Few Notes on the Culture'. Web.

with a state-run military. This passage, therefore, shows how Banks uses the game of Azad to develop his metaphorical use of possession in game-playing to refer to various kinds of possession and ownership in a capitalist society – ownership of private property; patriarchal "ownership" of women; the financial exploitation of human beings as "wage slaves" and their "ownership" by private companies, institutions, and corporations; the military "ownership" of soldiers; and in fact any facet of society that requires a relationship of the master and the subjugated.

As outlined above, the Culture has no need to play the "game" of free-market economics as it operates within a kind of controlled economy where goods and services are fairly distributed within the various habitats that make up the Culture network. In order for this limitless abundance of resources to exist, the pure output of the Energy Grid must be converted into matter before it can be utilised and organised – a process that can only be conducted by the Minds. Moving beyond a money-based economic system such as capitalism, then, is not the only shift through which the Culture must pass in order to establish an egalitarian system.

Conclusion

As explored above, many of the problems that must be overcome in order to achieve a utopia stem from economic, social, and political issues. As Banks explores with his Culture series, moving beyond an economic system based on monetary exchange would constitute nothing less than a radical change in the fabric of a society and its citizens. As an example of Jameson's future as disruption, Banks's Culture appears already fully developed, with scant attention paid to its history: a powerful means by which we can once again begin to consider how life might appear beyond inequality, exploitation, violence, and greed. There are other potential barriers to Utopia, however, which the removal of scarcity cannot address, as they exist within human beings ourselves. Culture people are still affected by universal aspects of the human condition, such as declining health and limited lifespan, that seem to be unavoidable; yet the Culture uses its advanced technology to allow its human citizens to shape themselves, perhaps even altering fundamental aspects of their very nature.

Chapter 3

Posthuman Culture
Senescence, Rejuvenescence, (Im)mortality

"Virtually everyone in the Culture carries the results of genetic manipulation in every cell of their bodies" – Iain M. Banks

At the core of the Culture is a web of human beings dispersed widely across the galaxy, many living for hundreds of years with seemingly superhuman characteristics. While people elsewhere grow old, inhabiting fragile bodies with vulnerable minds, and remain uncertain of everything about death except its inevitability, most in the Culture live eternally young in idealised, embellished bodies, and control the parameters of their own death. Some are reborn, following death, in new bodies, or allow for their individual, inner essence to inhabit other vessels, other realms. Most experiment with their body and their mind over a lifetime, potentially becoming open and fluid beings, changing their sex, altering their perceptions and their emotions, even adopting the form of radically different, alien life they encounter or choosing to return to a less-altered state of humanity. Culture humans live closely with radically new digital and alien forms of intelligence – other forms of *being* – many of which surpass our own capabilities and call our understanding of human being itself into question. Following the Culture's interventions into other societies in the name of enabling other techno-utopias, this chapter explores the technoscientific interventions (biological, psychological, and pharmaceutical) that the Culture offers its citizens into their own bodies and minds: a kind of *technologiade* of the individual, which provide the potential for a similarly utopian transformation of human existence. Banks's utopia poses answers to fundamental human questions – how best to live? how to cope with death? – through technoscience. Focusing on four areas that these interventions affect most profoundly – senescence, rejuvenescence, mortality, and immortality – I provide close analysis of *Use of Weapons*, 'The State of the Art', and *Surface Detail* to interrogate the complex political, ethical, and philosophical questions that Banks's series raises. I consider how Banks's interventions into human being relate to current debates about posthuman and transhuman philosophy, and how this shapes his representation of the Culture.

The Problem of Human Nature

For all of its implied diversity, the Culture series seems quite human-centric. As Ken MacLeod observes,[1] a core premise of the Culture stories draws upon a prominent trope of Golden Age SF: the assumption that the galaxy in which the stories are set (*our* galaxy) is populated by a vast diaspora of human – or at least *humanoid* – beings,[2] and, according to figures stated in *Consider Phlebas*, the Culture's population numbers "in excess of eighteen trillion people" (87). Whether this constitutes a majority is difficult to say but, as with many aspects of the Culture's origins, Banks is not especially concerned with providing detailed explanation of this diaspora: in 'A Few Notes on the Culture', he asks "why were there all those so-similar humanoid species scattered around the galaxy in the first place?" before deciding that the answer is "too complicated to relate here."[3] We know that this galaxy is teeming with life – machine and alien, as well as human – and that all three are welcomed into the Culture. All life in the Culture is literally extraterrestrial as human beings indigenous to Earth are not Contacted, but few of its citizens seem to be of alien origin. The character Kabe from *Look to Windward*, a Culture ambassador from the Homomdan race, is a rare example of a Culture citizen with alien biology. Most humans in the Culture, we know, choose to look broadly similar. Kabe stands out due to his alien physical form, eliciting a mild sense of unease amongst the Culture's legendarily tolerant humans: at one stage, a messenger "appears surprised" upon catching sight of Kabe. "This happened fairly often," Kabe explains; "a function of scale and stillness, basically. It was one hazard of being a glisteningly black three-and-a-bit-metre-tall pyramidal triped in a society of slim, matte skinned two-metre-tall bipeds" (*Windward*, 16). This example suggests that alien Culture citizens are less well integrated into utopia than humans and AIs – at least on the Chiark Orbital where the novel is set. Reviewers of *Windward* criticised Banks's portrayal of the Homomdans and other aliens in that text as

---

[1] Ken MacLeod, 'Phlebas Reconsidered', in *The True Knowledge of Ken MacLeod*, 1.
[2] See Banks, 'A Few Notes on the Culture'. Web.
[3] Banks, 'A Few Notes on the Culture'. Web.

merely "humans in fancy dress,"[4] with the Pavuleans from *Surface Detail* receiving similar comments, while earlier examples such as the Idirans and the Azadians were better received.

The Culture, then, as a functioning utopia with trillions of humans, must have overcome the supposed "problem of human nature", which anti-utopians argue forms an irreconcilable hurdle in the practical establishment of a society characterised by universal peace and egalitarianism, arguing that human beings have a natural predisposition towards greed, selfishness, tribalism, intolerance, and aggression, which combine to ensure that inequality and conflict will always eventually and inevitably reassert themselves. Francis Fukuyama, for example, writing in *Our Posthuman Future*, argues that almost all of the various revolutions, utopian social experiments, and movements of the twentieth century have failed based upon a false belief that human behaviour is infinitely malleable, when in reality "at a certain point deeply rooted natural instincts and patterns of behaviour reassert themselves to undermine the social engineer's best-laid plans."[5] Such comments often disguise a dogmatic and self-serving fatalism as straightforward realism. Yet Banks himself did accept a degree of truth to such views, acknowledging that human nature provides obstacles along the path to achieving the Culture or something like it: "We as a species are too prone to 'isms'," Banks stated, "racism, anti-Semitism, homophobia, xenophobia. It would be impossible to have a utopia with people like this."[6]

Addressing this issue, Lyman Tower Sargent asks "whether a better social order allows people to become better or better people create a better social order."[7] We have seen that the Culture adopts the former approach in the previous chapter: the Culture's network of postscarcity utopian environments, the Second Nature in which its citizens enjoy an equal distribution of abundance, may yield a potentially radical social transformation, ending internal conflict by removing the motivations for greed and jealousy, and therefore theft and violence. Yet Banks also adopts the latter approach: the Culture applies its technoscientific mastery – its *technologiade* process – to its citizens themselves, providing both technological and biological developments. These new, hybridised beings may overcome the problem of human nature by constituting a

---

[4] Phil Daoust, 'Brushes with Doom', *Guardian*, 2 September 2000. www.theguardian.com/books/2000/sep/02/sciencefictionfantasyandhorror.iainbanks.

[5] Fukuyama, *Our Posthuman Future*, 13–14.

[6] Banks's comments at: 'Iain M. Banks and Kim Stanley Robinson in Conversation', British Library, London, 9 July 2012.

[7] Lyman Tower Sargent, *Utopianism: A Very Short Introduction* (New York: Oxford University Press, 2010), 111.

Second *Human* Nature, an oxymoron that indicates a radical shift within people to accompany their radically new environments (and that also enacts a dialectical overcoming of another fundamental antinomy, that of culture as human and changeable, and nature as beyond human and fixed). Banks's approach, therefore, is to adopt all possible aspects of technoculture in the radical reconstitution of society.

The Culture's amendments are biological, pharmaceutical, and psychological; therefore, in this regard, they conform to the bio-engineering techniques of "biopunk" rather than the electronic and bio-mechanical augmentations more familiar from cyberpunk (although Culture citizens do use mind–computer interfacing, as we will see in Chapter Five).[8] As Banks explains, "virtually everyone in the Culture carries the results of genetic manipulation in every cell of their bodies; it is arguably the most reliable signifier of Culture status."[9] Banks imagines that, in the future, it will be possible and desirable to target specific unwanted negative character traits – racism, anti-Semitism, homophobia, and so forth, as previously mentioned – by identifying specific genes and simply switching them off. Banks began developing the Culture during a period of advances in genetic engineering, including the first recombinant DNA in a living organism, achieved at the University of California in 1973.[10] This continued alongside the series, with the infamous cloning of Dolly the Sheep in 1996 achieved a few miles away from Banks's house in South Queensferry at the University of Edinburgh, which provoked controversy for the ethical issues it raised, especially relating to the possibility for human cloning and genetic engineering. In this manner, Banks ignores the scepticism of commentators like Fukuyama who maintain that the ability to control behaviour through genetics in such a specific manner is very unlikely.[11] While other SF authors have explored such possibilities in the sub-genres of biopunk and cyberpunk, Banks's approach in the Culture series is to completely eschew such arguments against human genetic engineering that abound in dystopian fiction and media scare tactics.[12] The ethical difficulties relating to this

---

[8] For a full discussion of biopunk and cyberpunk, see Brian McHale's chapter 'Towards a Poetics of Cyberpunk' in *Beyond Cyberpunk*, 13–16.
[9] Banks, 'A Few Notes on the Culture'. Web.
[10] Genome News Network, 'Genetics and Genomics Timeline: 1973', accessed 29 March 2019. http://www.genomenewsnetwork.org/resources/timeline/1973_Boyer.php.
[11] Fukuyama, *Our Posthuman Future*, 77.
[12] For a concise discussion of the issues from a libertarian perspective (which surprisingly, in some respects, seems to align with Banks's stance as implied by the Culture's genofixing) see Henry Miller I, 'Designing Improved

are eased, to some extent at least, because the Culture seems able to offer such possibilities directly to people *whilst alive*, rather than to those with control over them prior to birth, as "designer babies", and can guarantee complete "success" in their attempts. The Culture's genetic manipulation is therefore framed as a genuine choice, and not forced upon individuals or coerced. Banks assumes that many, perhaps most, people would at least be interested in the potentials that such "tinkering" would provide for their own bodies and lives.

Secondly, Culture people have mastered the science of neuropharmacology, with most citizens choosing to adopt special drug glands that secrete a variety of side-effect-free drugs, ranging from the pharmaceutical to the psychedelic, at will, in order to regulate their emotions according to their situation. At one tense stage in *Games*, for example, Gurgeh glands *Sharp Blue*, "an abstraction-modifier", to aid his game-playing (8–9), while Djan Seriy Anaplian glands *quickcalm* during an especially traumatic event in *Matter*, in order to postpone her emotional response until she is clear from danger (75). Everyone in the Culture has the option of receiving genetic manipulation and drug glands, limited to within a degree deemed reasonable and safe, while those in SC are allowed more radical changes and access to stronger drugs, becoming in effect the Handy People that Csicsery-Ronay identifies as agents of space opera's technoscientific transformation. As such, there can be nothing that demonstrates the Culture's agenda of promoting the radical alteration of that which is deemed "natural" than the freedom to alter one's own physique and body chemistry at will. As Antonia Leach argues, the bodies of Culture citizens have been "augmented for comfort. In this way the posthuman body appears to have become a vehicle for promoting the political and social structure of the Culture itself."[13]

Overall, the assumption in the Culture novels is that, given the choice, humans would overwhelmingly choose to intervene into the human condition and improve themselves using whatever means available. While this possibility might potentially facilitate a fair amount of selfish behaviour – individuals adapting their bodies, experiences, emotional responses, and so on with no consideration of other people – the nature of selfishness itself would operate differently within a utopia such as the Culture, where problems such as greed and conflict have been removed. As Gurgeh tells Chamlis in *The Player of Games*: "'this is not a heroic

---

Humans: Playing Cat and Mouse with Genetic "Enhancement"', *Genetic Engineering News* 28, no. 6 (5 March 2008). Web.

[13] Antonia Leach, 'Iain M. Banks – Human, Posthuman and Beyond Human', *Elope* 15, no. 1 (June 2018): 73. revije.ff.uni-lj.so/elope.

age,' [...] 'the individual is obsolete. That's why life is so comfortable for us all. We don't matter, so we're safe. No one person can have a real effect any more" (22). Therefore, the manner in which individuals live their lives – whether self-indulgent or socially conscious – no longer matters, as their society will continue to function regardless of their actions, and the selfishness of individuals will not be able to inhibit the freedom of their fellow citizens.

The cumulative effect of these augmentations and the idea of a Second Human Nature raise fundamental questions about the category of the human being: at what point in this process of change should a being stop being considered human? Should the Culture be considered a culture of *post*humans? In Nick Bostrum's use of term, "posthuman" refers to "possible future beings whose basic capacities so radically exceed those of present humans as to be no longer unambiguously human by our current standards", through "cumulatively profound augmentations to a biological human".[14] The augmentations that Bostrum suggests clearly align closely with Banks's vision: "genetic engineering, psychopharmacology, anti-aging therapies, neural interfaces, advanced information management tools, memory enhancing drugs, wearable computers, and cognitive techniques."[15] This list of augmentations – covering the physical, psychological, neurological, and technological – could easily describe the comprehensive array of modifications available to Culture citizens, demonstrating the scientific developments and theories from which Banks extrapolated some of his ideas for the series. Yet the citizens of the Culture are far from "no longer unambiguously human", no matter how far they may distance themselves from "our current standards", known as human basic.

In *The Posthuman*, Rosi Braidotti calls for a radical re-conception of the Renaissance philosophy of humanism, as well as for a fresh understanding and reinterpretation of what it means to be human, given our relations with animals and with technology. Careful to acknowledge the continued value in many aspects of traditional humanism, however, Braidotti calls posthumanism "the historical moment that [...] traces a different discursive framework, looking more affirmatively towards new alternatives".[16] While she sees herself as a student of anti-humanism, or discourse critical to humanism, Braidotti

---

[14] Nick Bostrum, 'The Transhumanist FAQ', in *Readings in the Philosophy of Technology*, David Caplan, ed. (Maryland: Rowman and Littleford Publishers, Inc., 2009), 346.
[15] Bostrum, 'The Transhumanist FAQ', 346.
[16] Rosi Braidotti, *The Posthuman* (Cambridge: Polity Press, 2013), 37.

concludes that "humanism is not fundamentally flawed but sort of warped or infected by Eurocentrism."[17]

Braidotti argues for scientific advances (which would include the possibility of the augmentations listed above) as one major factor in contemporary society – alongside market Globalisation – that necessitate her major deconstruction of humanism, which she calls posthuman.[18] She argues that the Renaissance conception of humanism "historically developed into a civilisational model, which shaped the idea of Europe as coinciding with the universalizing powers of human reason", and was used to justify European forms of imperialism and the branding of various "others" as inferior – due to humanism's problematically restricted definition of humanity.[19]

Sherryl Vint has discussed the Culture specifically in the context of posthumanism, following an understanding of the term similar to Braidotti's. Discussing the Culture's customisation of its citizens' bodies, Vint argues that the Culture's attitude in this regard amounts to a form of imperialism of the body – an effacement of all difference, a homogenisation – in a subtler internal form, no less problematic than other external forms.[20] Vint argues for this as a demonstration of one of humanism's worst flaws: a dangerous universal understanding of an essential humanness that erases difference. She gives considerable space to critiquing Banks's Cartesian conception of subjectivity, using examples from *Phlebas*, *Windward* and *Weapons* to argue that "the body is a risk" for subjectivity understood in this way.[21] Ultimately, Vint sees the Culture expanding the conceptual horizon of posthumanism by redefining it, from a supersession of humanness, to meaning "something beyond or after," and "new categories of identity rather than new appendages".[22]

Yet, in her PhD thesis 'Culture-al Subjectivities: the Constitution of the Self in Iain M. Banks's Culture Texts', Jude Roberts challenges Vint's essay, arguing that, in the Culture series, Banks conceptualises his masculine subjects as fundamentally and foundationally vulnerable, according to theories developed by Donna Harroway and Judith Butler. Banks's vulnerable subjects, then, such as Gurgeh and Zakalwe, can therefore be seen to work at undermining the centralised, rational

---

[17] Dave Shaw, 'Summary of Rosi Braidotti's *The Posthuman* (Part 1)', 14 June 2015. https://medium.com/open-objects/summary-of-rosi-braidotti-s-the-posthuman-part-1-12e79316940f.
[18] Braidotti, *The Posthuman*.
[19] Braidotti, *The Posthuman*, 13–16.
[20] Vint, 'The Culture-al Body'.
[21] Vint, 'The Culture-al Body'.
[22] Vint, 'The Culture-al Body'.

subject assumed in the tradition of secular humanism following the Enlightenment, after all.[23]

Senescence and Rejuvenescence in SF

The precise understanding of what it means to be human has been debated for centuries, as has the notion of an essential, universal set of characteristics that constitute a nature common to all humans throughout all space and time. Few, however, would dispute the inevitability of both the biological ageing process and of mortality itself as central facets in our attempts to understand ourselves and our place in the universe: as fundamental aspects of the human condition. In turn, the quest for immortality as eternal youth – through halting or reversing senescence, and overcoming death – is the oldest theme of literature. Introduced in our earliest known long-form narrative, *The Epic of Gilgamesh* (circa 1800 BC), the eponymous protagonist undertakes a quest for the wisdom of immortality known by survivors of the Great Flood. Life expectancy began to increase rapidly during the Enlightenment, continuing in industrialised countries during the nineteenth century through rapid developments in technoscience. The nineteenth-century colonial adventure narratives and Gothic fiction from which space opera was ultimately derived, such as H. Rider Haggard's *She* (1886), *The Picture of Dorian Gray* (1890) or *Dracula* (1897), largely issued warnings about, and terrifying visions of, old age and immortality. Space opera produced during the pulp era of the 1920s and '30s, and during the Golden Age, was largely enthusiastic about, and optimistic for, the potential of life-extension technologies. Due to the inherent inter-galactic/interstellar scope of the sub-genre, it necessarily requires a novum to explain the ability of humans to cross such distances, given the limits maintained under the special theory of relativity, including: faster-than-light travel (especially through "hyperspace"); the use of an Einstein–Rosen bridge ("wormholes"); forms of cryogenic freezing; generation starships;[24] or methods of dramatically extending human lifespans. For his *Cities in Flight* series (1950–1962), James Blish imagines anti-agathic drugs, which stop the ageing process; in *Cure for Death* (1960), Victor Valentine employs a kind of ray gun that cures cancer and ageing; and Philip K. Dick's *Ubik* (1969) describes the physiological and psychological effects of ageing

---

[23] Roberts, 'Culture-al Subjectivities'.
[24] See Simone Caroti, *The Generation Starship in Science Fiction: A Critical History, 1934–2001* (North Carolina: MacFarland & Co, 2011).

as a result of the universe's tendency toward entropy. Brian Aldiss's *Greybeard* (1964) and Thomas Disch's *334* (1972) both explore dystopian societies struggling to cope with a rapidly increasing, ageing population. During the 1980s and '90s the bio-mechanical and bio-engineering augmentations of biopunk and cyberpunk provided new opportunities for human life extension such as mind–computer interfacing, cloning and "human–machine symbiosis or fusion",[25] whilst the sub-genres also highlighted the dangers and failures of such processes.

In New Space Opera, all life-extension nova are available for use. In Robinson's "Mars" trilogy (*Red Mars* [1992], *Green Mars* [1993], *Blue Mars* [1996]), the scientist–colonist protagonists delay the onset of biological ageing in humans through genetic engineering, dramatically increasing their lifespan, which is a major factor in their ability to colonise the red planet successfully. Martin Silenus, the drunken poet from Dan Simmons's *Hyperion Cantos*, eventually recovers from brain damage resulting from a long journey under cryogenic fugue, and later undergoes "Poulsen Treatments" enable him to reach his 150th birthday, with blue-tinted skin as a side-effect, while Louis Gridley Wu from Niven's *Ringworld* celebrates his 200th birthday in perfect physical condition due to the longevity drug "boosterspice". More recently, a form of "cryosleep" or suspended animation depicted by Alastair Reynolds in *Chasm City* (2001) allows Tanner Mirabel to live the length of several standard lifetimes, accumulating traumatic memories, while in Tobais Buckell's *Crystal Rain* (2006), John DeBrun is implied to be one of the "old fathers", the original settlers of the Nanaganda colony "hundreds of years ago, near immortal due to strange, tiny machines in him", thusly introducing the motif of extended senescence via nanotechnology.[26]

Senescence in the Culture

During the approximately 40-year period in which Banks developed and published the Culture series, Britain underwent significant social changes: between 1976 and 2013, the proportion of the UK population over 65 years old increased from 14.2 per cent to around 18 per cent, of an overall population total of 56,216,121 and 65,648,054 in those years respectively.[27] Following centuries of human speculation, recent

---

[25] McHale, 'Towards a Poetics of Cyberpunk', 16.
[26] Tobias Buckell, *Crystal Rain* (Tor Books, 2006), 171. Ebook.
[27] Office for National Statistics, 'Overview of the UK Population', 21 July 2017. Web.

research into rare conditions such as Hutchinson–Gifford Progeria syndrome can potentially provide valuable insights into the mysteries of human ageing,[28] and scientists can actually "confront the question of whether it is possible to postpone, or even reverse, the process of biological aging."[29] Banks extrapolates from this with the Culture, imagining this mystery to have been firmly solved, and its citizens to be able both to postpone and to reverse this process through genetic engineering. Members of the Culture choose to adapt themselves in many different ways,[30] most of which are focused upon improving overall health, longevity, and quality of life. Due to their genetic manipulation, Culture citizens are generally born "whole and healthy and of significantly (though not immensely) greater intelligence than their basic human genetic inheritance might imply"[31]; their immune systems have been improved; they have full control over their nervous systems: in effect, pain can be "switched off"; illness, disease, birth defects, and so forth are no longer a threat.[32]

The cumulative effect of these modifications on the human body results in the extension of the average lifespan way beyond the maximum 122-year limit currently verified in 2016:[33] as Banks states, "humans in the Culture normally live about three-and-a-half to four centuries."[34] During this greatly extended lifespan, Culture inhabitants are able to fully control and tailor their body's biological ageing process:

[28] See BBC News, 'Ageing Gene Discovered', 17 April 2003.
[29] See *Aging: Concepts and Controversies* (Los Angeles: Pine Forge Press, 2010) by Harry R. Moody, in which the author outlines the key reasons why ageing remains such a mystery, arguing that different parts of the body age in different ways, and at different rates, making it difficult or impossible to identify a single, unifying cause (16–19).
[30] Banks, 'A Few Notes on the Culture': "There are thousands of alterations to that human-basic inheritance – blister-free callusing and a clot-filter protecting the brain are two of the less important ones mentioned in the stories."
[31] Banks, 'A Few Notes on the Culture'. Web.
[32] Banks, 'A Few Notes on the Culture': "The major changes the standard Culture person would expect to be born with would include an optimized immune system and enhanced senses, freedom from inheritable diseases or defects, the ability to control their autonomic processes and nervous system (pain can, in effect, be switched off), and to survive and fully recover from wounds which would either kill or permanently mutilate without such genetic tinkering."
[33] Guinness World Records, 'Oldest Person Ever'. www.guinnessworldrecords.com/world-records/oldest-person.
[34] Banks, 'A Few Notes on the Culture'. Web.

The majority of their lives consist of a three-century plateau which they reach in what we would compare to our mid-twenties, after a relatively normal pace of maturation during childhood, adolescence and early adulthood. They age very slowly during those three hundred years, then begin to age more quickly, then they die.[35]

So after a Culture child is born, their body is allowed to grow older and develop in a natural way; usually in their mid-twenties their ageing is genofixed: meaning not quite fully halted, but slowed down substantially. Recent research into the human biological ageing process may offer reasons for why Banks imagines that Culture people choose to genofix at this age: once a person reaches 30 years of age, their body meets a significant milestone. In *Aging: Concepts and Controversies*, Harry R. Moody discusses studies that employ a cross-sectional methodology: "that is, [...] look[ing] at physical functions of people at different chronological ages, but at a different point in time. The general conclusion from such studies of human beings suggests that most physiological functions decline after age 30, with some individual variations."[36]

An individual in their mid-twenties has reached full physical maturity, then, and is capable of a sophisticated level of emotional and social development. It is fair to assume that, by beginning this "three-century plateau" in their mid-twenties, most Culture citizens (and, presumably, Banks himself) adhere to the notion that, at this stage of early adulthood, the human body has reached a biological peak. However, while the physical development of a Culture inhabitant is suspended, the individual's psychological development will continue, shaped by the responsibilities taken on, and the experiences undergone. In this way, Culture citizens can achieve an arguably desirable balance between the vigour of youth and the experience of older age.

Banks is careful to ensure, however, that this mass genofixing at a young age does not constitute a monotonous "cult of youth" society featuring only people who appear outwardly young. While it is true that the vast majority of Culture citizens are said to have undergone the treatment, choosing to keep a body that is biologically young, they adopt a multitude of different appearances, some of which might be suggestive of older age. For example, in *Player*, Banks describes a Culture woman who is "well into her second century, but still tall and handsome and striking... her hair was white, as it always had been" (11), and in *Surface* Hvel Costrile is described as "an elderly looking gent with dark

---

[35] Banks, 'A Few Notes on the Culture'. Web.
[36] Moody, *Aging*, 17.

skin, long blonde hair, and a bare chest" (37). When SC agent Tefwe from *Hydrogen* locates the whereabouts of the Culture's oldest person, Ngaroe QiRia, he retains visible indications of his age: appearing "smaller, reduced; like something boiled down to its essence. His skin, visible on his face and hands and feet, had gone a dark red-brown, again like something undergoing a reduction in the bottom of a pan" (331). While Banks's simile here, comparing QiRia's appearance with that of food as it is cooked on a stove, is unflattering, his earlier similar description, "something boiled down to its essence", has more positive connotations, suggesting a removal of anything extraneous, a concentration of vital matter, an affirmation of purpose. Furthermore, the existence of such individuals who have chosen to retain features representing biological old age challenges Vint's assertion that the Culture's practices lead to the effacement of individual physical difference, leading to a society of strikingly similar citizens, equal yet bland and homogenous, as discussed above.[37]

Use of Weapons: Senescence, Extended Life, Gene Fixing

Use of Weapons, the third-published book in Banks's Culture sequence, is the text in which the trope of extended life is incorporated into its narrative most significantly, and in which the theme of senescence is explored most thoroughly. In the narrative present of the novel, the protagonist Zakalwe is a retired employee of SC, who is living a life of luxurious hedonism on a secluded island. Two current employees of SC – Diziet Sma and Skaffen-Amtiskaw – are trying to track him down and coerce him into returning to work for SC for one final mission. Zakalwe has, without their knowledge, gone renegade and exploited his SC background to gain personal revenge. The novel has a complex and innovative narrative structure: these present-time events of finding and persuading Zakalwe, and the subsequent completion of his mission, are told in conventional chapters: arranged in chronological order, marked with corresponding standard Arabic numerals running forwards. Alternating with these are episodes from Zakalwe's past, told in reverse chronological order, and marked by Roman numerals running backwards. As the present-day events unfold, and events from his past are traced back, unpleasant secrets and a major twist about Zakalwe's life and identity are revealed. As we shall see shortly, Zakalwe is an example of the postmodern, fractured subjectivity that McHale describes as the

---

[37] See Vint, 'The Culture-al Body'.

"centrifugal self";[38] and, as a depiction of character that seems to have lost access to large sections of his life memories, Zakalwe shares strong parallels with Reynolds's Tanner Mirabel and Buckell's John DeBrun.

While the secretive and morally suspect nature of his work requires him to remain an outsider living independently from the Culture, Zakalwe has been rewarded by SC with access to the Culture's genofixing treatment and retro-ageing drugs, in return for carrying out their missions. The full effects of this treatment are revealed during a scene set in the novel's present time, when Zakalwe states that "I was born two hundred and twenty years ago… and physically I'm about thirty" (114). Outsider or not, this renders Zakalwe's lifecycle and biological ageing process similar to that of a typical Culture inhabitant. In *Weapons*, Banks places his 220-year-old protagonist alongside other characters whose bodies are older than his, such as the Ethnarch Kerian and Tsoldrin Beychae. Through Zakalwe's relationship and interactions with these characters, Banks's novel provides a thorough analysis of the different representations of ageing in the novel.

The Ethnarch Kerian, a former political ally of the Culture, is introduced in Chapter XIII when Zakalwe breaches his security compound and confronts the Ethnarch at gunpoint about alleged crimes of political corruption and mass murder. Contact had made the Ethnarch a deal in the past, offering him access to their life-extension technologies if he agreed to end his regime of tyranny and genocide, trying to resolve the situation by offering rewards instead of further violence. This offering of a very tangible "fountain of youth" is just one example of Contact's humanitarian role as doer of self-perceived good deeds. As Zakalwe outlines: "Another thing [the Culture…] do[es…], another way they deal in life rather than death, is they offer leaders of certain societies below a certain technological level the one thing all the wealth and power those leaders command cannot buy them; a cure for death. A return to youth." (30) These instances of bribery by Contact are calculated acts of political engineering that operate on a very practical level; but they are also symbolic acts that reaffirm the Culture's hegemonic status in the galaxy. The message seems clear: join the Culture, and you could live forever. Zakalwe, however, believes that the Culture's policies are too soft, that the bribe is not incentive enough, and that the Ethnarch has continued committing atrocities: "You promised to stop the killings in Youricam, remember? […] the death trains" (30). Operating outside the remit of Contact and the Culture, though, Zakalwe is indulging in a spree of vigilante justice, inflicting violent revenge upon some of the

---

[38] McHale, 'Towards a Poetics of Cyberpunk', 13–15.

Culture's political contacts, who are corrupt and dangerous individuals in positions of great power.

Zakalwe himself stands as a warning against the dangers of wielding such powerful technological advancements: working independently from SC, he murders the Ethnarch and exploits his Culture experience, training, and resources for his own selfish ends. He steals and sells the Culture's anti-ageing treatments for financial gain: "And what is the core of his business empire? Genetechnology... there are five elderly autocrats on this planet, in competing hegemonies. *They are all getting healthier.* They are all getting, in fact, younger. Zakalwe's corporation... is receiving crazy money from each of these five people" (83). However benign and well-intentioned the methods of SC may be, and how much they achieve with their vast power and influence, the possibilities for misuse if their advanced technologies were to fall into the wrong hands may arguably, if not outweigh the benefits of their intended use, at least raise serious moral concerns. Zakalwe, who chooses to exact revenge upon the corrupt and murderous politicians that SC failed to deal with effectively, is an individual with an ambiguous sense of morality, even if it is decidedly misplaced; but in carrying out this revenge, he contradicts and undoes much of the Culture's commitment to life rather than death.

While the Ethnarch's age is never made explicit, Zakalwe describes him as an "old pisshead" (129); in return, the Ethnarch describes Zakalwe as a "young man" (26–29). These descriptions are ironic because, of course, Zakalwe has lived for at least twice as long as the Ethnarch, but his physical appearance does not make this initially seem to be the case. The Ethnarch's descriptions of Zakalwe highlight the uncanniness of seeing a man who not only looks much younger than he really is, but has lived for an exceptionally long time; the most obvious aspect being Zakalwe's voice: "The young man's voice was slow and measured. It sounded, somehow, like the voice of someone much older; older enough to make the Ethnarch feel suddenly young in comparison. It chilled him" (27). This implies that Zakalwe's tone – calm, confident, and measured – is indicative of an older person: one who conveys the relaxed confidence gained from years of experience, rather than the implied arrogance and impetuousness of youth.

It is through the Ethnarch's physical descriptions of Zakalwe, however, once he examines him more closely, that a deeper understanding of Banks's protagonist is revealed: "The man looked young; he had a broad, tanned face and black hair tied back behind his head, but thoughts of spirits and the dead came into his head not because of that. It was something about the dark, pit-like eyes, and the alien set of that face" (26–27). Somehow, Zakalwe's decades of life and experience seem to be revealed through his facial features and expression, even though his appearance otherwise – tanned face and long black hair – suggests vitality and youth. Banks's choice of language is interesting, as it suggests that more than mere experience and memory are conveyed through Zakalwe's face: the "dark, pit-like eyes" that inspire "thoughts of spirits and the dead" suggest a monstrous or supernatural apparition, "like having a dream, or seeing a ghost" (26). The implication is that Zakalwe's wealth of lived time – the colossal amount of thoughts, memories, and experiences that he has amassed in his 220 years of life – is eating away at him instead of filling him with joy, leaving him hollow: "a slightly skewed projection" (26). In effect, in a manner reminiscent of Wilde's Dorian Gray, the more Zakalwe lives, the more part of him seems to die.

This disturbing reading of the protagonist foreshadows the huge revelation at the novel's conclusion that Zakalwe is not who he says he is. The calm, poetically inclined Cheradenine Zakalwe actually killed himself some years prior, enabling his sadistic foster brother Elethiomel to assume his identity, and therefore forcing the reader to reconsider the nature of the preceding narrative. (Replying to an attentive fan's letter in 1994, Banks took the time to briefly clarify some of the nuances and ambiguities – the "fancy footwork" – he undertook to effectively withhold this revelation until the last moment without undermining the integrity of the text, which can further help us to accurately understand the identity of *Weapons*' protagonist at various stages in the novel.)[39] Therefore, the young-yet-old man who stands before the Ethnarch is consumed and made hollow: by the sheer weight of his long life's experiences; by the "spectre" of his foster brother (Cheradenine) whose identity coexists within him, alongside his own

[39] The fan refers to a seeming anomaly in a passage on pages 340–342 where the narrator directly refers to Zakalwe by name. Banks replies, explaining that: "The central character in the book is never referred to by the name Zakalwe in the text, only by other characters. The real Zakalwe is referred to by name in the bit you mention, when he orders Swaels out of the staff car; he dies sometime after shooting himself. He is referred to by name in the summerhouse bit, again because he is the real guy." This confirms that the individual referred to in this section is Cheradenine. Banks continues: "The same applies to the section when they're all children, when Zakalwe, Elethiomel, Liveuta and Darckcense are present and referred to by their correct names. There is a bit of fancy footwork on page 183 of the paperback edition where, in the bit between the line breaks, the 'he' referred to is Elethiomel. The point is that Zakalwe doesn't know what happened in the staff car or the summerhouse but the book does; this is omniscient narration, not a memoir." Letter dated Friday, 23 September 1994, Archive of Iain Banks, University of Stirling.

original identity (Elethiomel); and by implied guilt and trauma relating to Elethiomel's lifetime of barbarism, especially the grizzly act of murdering Cheradenine's sister and assembling her bones into a chair.

Another "old" character in the novel with whom Zakalwe is compared is Tsoldrin Beychae, a former political leader of the planet Voerenhutz, which has descended into chaos. Again, as with the Ethnarch, Beychae's exact age is not stated, but it becomes apparent that he has not been rewarded with access to the Culture's life-extension technologies; Beychae has lived nowhere near as long as Zakalwe, but still appears older. In the present time of the novel, two members of SC, Diziet Sma and a drone named Skaffen-Amtiskaw, are appointed with the task of finding Zakalwe in order to persuade him to locate Beychae: in short, one "older" man, Zakalwe, must be found and brought out of retirement, so that he may in turn perform a similar task regarding another retired "old" man, Beychae.

As Skaffen-Amtiskaw explains, Beychae "became president of the cluster following our [SC's] involvement. While he was in power he held the political system together, but he retired eight years ago, long before he had to, to pursue a life of study and contemplation" (21). Banks's descriptions of Beychae contrast starkly with his youthful descriptions of Zakalwe:

> The old man – bald, face deeply lined, dressed in robes which hid the modest paunch he'd developed since he'd devoted himself to study – blinked as she tapped at it and opened the door. His eyes were still bright. [...] Tsoldrin Beychae put on some glasses – he was old fashioned enough to wear his age rather than try to disguise it – and peered at the man. (216)

Through this traditional, and fairly stereotypical, depiction of an older, male scholar, Beychae becomes instantly familiar; recognisable in him are all of the negative attributes that are often associated with older people: hair loss, wrinkles, and failing eyesight. Here, Beychae is doubly contrasted with Zakalwe, both as scholar and older man: Beychae's "modest paunch" indicates a lack of physical exercise, while his glasses have associations of excessive reading in dim rooms – both stereotypical attributes of a scholar or academic. Both men may choose to live in relative isolation (Zakalwe is indicated to be living a reclusive existence on an obscure island), but Beychae's quiet dedication to study contrasts sharply with Zakalwe's hedonism and dangerous SC missions. Also, Beychae is not merely just recognisable as biologically old through his aged appearance, but also in terms of attitude and values: he is described as "old-fashioned" because he refuses to hide his failing eyesight with contact lenses, or have it improved using scientific methods, in order to appear younger. At one stage, Beychae draws himself up because "he'd noticed that he was stooping more these days, but he was still vain enough to want to greet people straight-backed" (217). Beychae's concern with his own posture seems suggestive of more than mere vanity, however, possibly also indicating pride at his own self-perceived morally "upstanding" social position as an esteemed scholar.

Later in the novel it is revealed that Beychae's female assistant, Ms Ubrel Shiol, is employed on a mission as a spy and assassin, feigning friendship with him in order to collect information about his research, and initially intending to murder him. When Zakalwe reveals this deceit to him, Beychae indicates that he hopes the friendship he maintained with Ms Shiol was – despite her occupation – not entirely false. Through his dejected comment, "I hope [...] that is not the only way the old can be made happy... through deceit" (248), Beychae suggests that, had he been younger, he would have considered it more likely that Ms Shiol would have genuinely enjoyed his company at points, despite her mission. As he considers himself old, though, it is more likely to him that she would have needed to fake their friendship. Zakalwe tries to console him, saying that "Maybe it wasn't all deceit [...] And anyway, being old isn't what it used to be; I'm *old*" (248) in order to remind the scholar that perceptions of old age are very subjective, particularly when the parameters of senescence can be changed freely and readily. This conversation acts as a clear exposition of the two positions in the age-related debate explored in *Weapons*: the natural process of ageing without interference from genetics, pharmaceuticals or transplants as represented by Beychae; and the Culture's artificial interventions and extensions as represented by Zakalwe. Natural ageing, although often complete with deeply unfortunate consequences, can be seen as simpler and more honest; however, the example of Ms Shiol's feigned friendship shows how natural ageing has provided a context for deceit. Life extension by intervention, by comparison, is more controlled and relaxed; the Culture's anti-ageing treatments remove or certainly reduce the need to feign youth, yet they carry with them a whole new range of unique problems.

By genofixing himself at the age of "about thirty", Zakalwe has prolonged his biological ageing process, but cannot (or perhaps will not) halt his mental development, therefore continuing to age psychologically. While his body will remain fit and healthy – if physical damage does occur, the relevant part can be replaced reasonably simply and very effectively – Zakalwe's mind will accumulate memories and experiences at the normal rate. This means that the longer he lives, the more information he will store, amassing far more experiences and memories in his extended lifetime than the average (i.e. human basic) person. The effects of this upon someone's emotional development, amongst other things, could be potentially problematic, even devastating, especially – as indicated above – when combined with particularly traumatic memories. Not only is a person such as Elethiomel Zakalwe repressing his most harrowing memories, something that has damaging repercussions for anyone, but he is doing so for potentially much longer, with effects potentially exacerbated by being repressed for such an unprecedented period of time.

The Problem of Boredom

Writing in *Childhood's End* (1953), Arthur C. Clarke referred to boredom as "the supreme enemy of all Utopias",[40] identifying a now-familiar criticism. As Jameson explains, "the reproach of boredom so often addressed to Utopias envelops both form and content: the former on the grounds that by definition nothing but the guided tour can really happen in these books, the latter owing precisely to our own existential reluctance imaginatively to embrace such a life."[41] In *Childhood's End*, Clarke depicts the invasion of Earth by a peaceful alien race called the Overlords who transform the planet into a kind of utopia. Some human groups feel the need to establish creative, arts-based colonies in order to avoid the perceived stagnation of their lives. Following the emigration of many humans to the "Overmind" – essentially mass transcendence to a kind of meta-civilisation – many of the remaining humans, denied access to the Overmind, chose to commit suicide as their lives seemed to have lost all meaning. In Clarke's utopia, therefore, finding purpose and fulfilment for its citizens is a serious and persistent problem. It is an issue that Banks too addressed, both in his conception of the Culture itself as well as regularly throughout the series. As has been established above, Banks overcame the potential problem of utopian form – restricting narratives to the "boring" form of guided tours – by focusing upon the Culture's relations with other cultures, and by exploring individuals in a liminal relationship with his utopia. The latter notion – that life would be boring in a utopia – is a potential problem that Zakalwe and the Culture inhabitants face, especially given the large amount of extra time

---

[40] Arthur C. Clarke. *Childhood's End* (London: Pan Books Ltd, [1954] 1956), 64.
[41] Jameson, *Archaeologies*, 190.

generated by life extension. With fear of illness and disease removed, fear of death greatly reduced, and employment rendered entirely optional, it might seem that Culture citizens are left with no general direction or purpose, leading to a frivolous or futile lifestyle. How then should one occupy a life that continues for three entire centuries or more? How does extending life affect the *quality* of life?

Banks, alongside fellow utopian author Kim Stanley Robinson, has recently spoken out against the so-called problem of boredom, with both authors agreeing that it is often used as an anti-utopian attack from the political Right.[42] Using the Culture series, Banks directly challenges this argument, offering essentially three general life-course options for the average, non-AI Culture citizen, which give their lives some kind of meaning and purpose: 1) hope to be selected for Contact or SC and gain fulfilment knowing that you have contributed to the continuation of the Culture's benign *technologiade*; 2) choose to become employed in a different role – despite the lack of obligation due to the presence of the Minds and drones – often as an academic, teacher, or philosopher; and 3) indulge in a somewhat casual, lackadaisical, or hedonistic lifestyle, exploiting the limitless nature of the Culture environments to their full advantage. Despite assertions by critics, such as Christopher Palmer and Bruce Gillespie, that the Culture's "leisure and pursuit of pleasure" make it "an essentially decadent society", it can be argued that this is in fact positive: as Farah Mendlesohn has asserted, "the headlong flight into hedonism and away from 'reality' is the Culture's *raison d'être*, not an indication of its decline."[43] The sheer breadth of options available in this limitless environment should not be underestimated: in the Culture, virtually any kind of lifestyle can be maintained, from safe, parochial, and austere, to wild, adventurous, and opulent. For many Culture citizens, life is only limited by the extent of their imagination.

In 'The State of the Art', Banks playfully satirises the so-called problem of boredom in utopia, having the character Li start a Boredom Society in the Culture, before changing its title to the Ennui League (145–146). As with those Culture citizens in *Weapons* who chose to catch a common cold in order to see what the experience is like (53–54), Li is fascinated by the idea of boredom, calling it "an underrated facet of existence in our pseudo-civilisation", because it is something he and others in the Culture are suggested never to have experienced. The point is that, in the Culture, virtually any lifestyle choice is possible: one would actually *struggle* to be bored in such a limitless environment, having in

---

[42] Nolan, 'Utopia is a way of saying we can do better', 69.
[43] Mendlesohn, 'The Dialectic of Decadence', 116.

fact to artificially engineer a state of boredom in order to experience it. Here, with heavy irony, Banks reverses the problem of boredom as levelled at utopia, instead turning it around onto Earth society: "Earth is a deeply boring planet," argues Li; "What is the *point* of a planet where you can hardly set foot without tripping over somebody killing somebody else, or painting something or making music or pushing back the frontier of science" (146–147). Here Banks's satire is a little heavier, challenging those who see utopia as boring to confront the violent reality of life in the alternative system of Earth: aren't you fed up of struggle, implies Li's argument, and wouldn't you chose to end it if you could?

Even so, despite providing near-limitless possibilities for the lives of its citizens, the Culture does acknowledge that boredom may become a problem for some. As Banks explains in *Excession*, Storage is a kind of hibernation in cyberspace "where people went when they had reached a certain age, or if they had just grown tired of living [...] with whatever revival criterion they desired" (81). People often chose to go into Storage out of boredom, with their revival criterion revolving around the desire to witness the changes that society has undergone, desiring "to come back when something especially interesting was happening", or to be awoken after "one hundred years", to live "for a single day before returning to their undreaming, unageing slumbers" (83). Again, the sheer scale of the possibilities offered by the Culture seems to provide an option for every lifestyle choice, even if they contradict the values generally favoured. For people living somewhere like the Culture, Banks suggests, boredom seems very unlikely, but if it does occur, and that is the utopia's biggest problem, then surely it is indicative of its success. Radical changes to a broader social and political structure would remove the conditions for most conflict, but that does not mean that people's personal relationships would have to be perfect and unchanging. As Banks points out, there might not be conflict on a grand scale *inside* utopia, but there could still be unrequited love,[44] as we will see with the complex, intense, and vicious relationship between Genar-Hofoen and Dajeil in Chapter Four. This provides an example of the ways in which Mendlesohn and Kincaid argue that Banks used *Excession* to subvert the space-opera form, using several narrative threads, each focused upon geographically separated characters, which may be related tangentially to one another, but do not dramatically coalesce or contribute significantly to the central, political plot.[45]

---

[44] Nolan, 'Utopia is a way of saying we can do better', 68.
[45] See Mendlesohn, 'Iain M. Banks: *Excession*', 562; and Kincaid, *Iain M. Banks*, 72–73.

Mortality: The Final Frontier

In McHale's words, "The ultimate ontological boundary, the one that no one can help but cross, is of course the boundary between life and death, between being and non-being," and he notes Thomas Pynchon's view of SF as immature based upon the genre's perceived lack of concern with the subject.[46] While McHale notes that "no generation or group of SF writers has made the exploration of death its special province until the emergence of the cyberpunk 'wave' in the 1980s," he offers the prevalence of SF writing on "the theme of nuclear holocaust" as rebuff, and argues for Philip K. Dick and Thomas Disch as notable exceptions.[47] While mortality may not constitute a special province in Banks's oeuvre (although this is perhaps the case with his mainstream fiction) it is a topic that is seriously considered in the Culture series.

Despite the extended senescence available to them, Banks explains that most Culture citizens choose to cross this boundary eventually, generally limiting their lives to no more than 400 years, and conceding that in the end – despite the freedom and abundance of their habitats – they would ultimately "get bored with it. People will want to have an end."[48] As well as boredom, centuries of memory may weigh heavily on a person – as seems to be the case with Zakalwe – and contribute to their final decision to pass on. Despite its manifold commitments to extending and improving life, then, the Culture is not against death per se, and death is not absent from the Culture. In effect, most Culture citizens still chose to die, eventually – a fact that may seem surprising for people living in utopia. In 'A Few Notes on the Culture', Banks explains the Culture's general philosophy on death: "death is regarded as part of life, and nothing, including the universe, lasts forever. It is seen as bad manners to try and pretend that death is somehow not natural; instead death is seen as giving shape to life."[49] Expressed in this manner, it would seem that the Culture's attitude towards death is sensible, rational, and pragmatic. There are probably few people who would wish to live literally forever, Banks implies (apart from *Hydrogen*'s QiRia, perhaps), but most would opt for a longer lifespan in good health if the possibility existed. This is essentially the view that the Culture takes also, except that its inhabitants have the luxury of controlling their lives, as well as their deaths. When they feel the time

---

[46] McHale, 'Towards a Poetics of Cyberpunk', 20.
[47] McHale, 'Towards a Poetics of Cyberpunk', 20.
[48] Iain M. Banks, Q&A session, The Roundhouse, London, 6 October 2012.
[49] Banks, 'A Few Notes on the Culure'. Web.

is right, they can choose to stop the various life-extension treatments and courses of drugs, effectively ending their "plateau period", causing their body thereafter to age naturally and to begin the processes of fatal decline, or to eschew the ageing process altogether and simply choose the appropriate time and circumstances for their life to end. For this eventuality, Banks imagined a suitably beautiful and poetic return to the stars: as indicated in 'A Few Notes on the Culture', while forms of body disposal such as burial and cremation are sometimes requested, most commonly the corpse is deposited in the "core of the relevant system's sun, from where the component particles of the cadaver start a million-year migration to the star's surface, to shine – possibly – long after the Culture itself is history."[50] Boredom is not the great problem of utopia, then, but merely the final end state over which utopians – as with every other aspect of their lives – are provided with control.

A Culture inhabitant could, of course, still technically die from a violent incident, by unfortunate accident or murder. Their heightened immune systems, drug-induced resistance to pain, and generally improved and toughened physiques, resulting from genetic engineering, may make this eventuality more difficult, but not impossible. So peaceful are the Culture's internal habitats, though, that this would be very unlikely, unless resulting from an attack by a force from outside. Therefore, deaths that are depicted in the series generally affect members of SC, who, due to the nature of their work, are more at risk of danger and violence due to their interaction with those from outside of the Culture.

Banks's novella, 'The State of the Art', published in 1991, provides further engagement with many of the issues raised in *Weapons*. This story marks the return of SC employee, Diziet Sma, this time on a mission to Earth in the 1970s to find her friend, former SC colleague and former-lover, Dervley Linter, who is part of a team that clandestinely landed on Earth in order to perform research. The results of this research are to determine if Earth should be Contacted by the Culture in the future. Linter once benefitted from the Culture's anti-ageing treatments and life-extension and enhancement technologies, but has now chosen to have these alterations almost entirely removed or reversed, so that he can pass for an Earth-human – human basic – and live on Earth. Therefore, he has had to come to terms with the return to natural, gradual biological ageing, and a drastically reduced lifespan.

In a similar manner to Zakalwe and Beychae in *Use of Weapons*, Banks uses the opposing views of Sma and Linter to rehearse the arguments for

---

[50] Banks, 'A Few Notes on the Culture'. Web.

and against intervention into senescence. In this way, Banks reconfigures the relationship between visitor and guide of classic utopian fiction: traditionally, a visitor from outside stumbles upon a utopia, and is shown around by one of its inhabitants – the guide – who reveals the details of their peaceful realm; then the visitor returns to their homeland, to share the virtues of the utopia with their people. Instead, Sma, an altered human citizen of the Culture, can be regarded as an outsider on Earth due to both her physical enhancements far beyond the level of the human-basic people on Earth, as well as her extraterrestrial origins; Linter is her guide, but, as he is also originally an outsider who has adapted to Earth's conventions, he is not a true native of the visited land. The voice and opinions of a true Earth human are not heard, as Contact decides that the Culture's presence upon the Earth should not be made known.

Sma views Linter's decision to stay on Earth initially as unusual and, eventually, as outrightly offensive: to her, the Culture is a symbol of radical progress and advancement, and Linter's decision to reject, not just the life-extension methods it offers, but the Culture as a whole is seen as foolish, rebellious, and regressive; choosing a human-basic life of comparatively rapid decline is surely madness. Over the course of several months, Sma visits her friend and notices the ways in which Linter's physiology changes: a stooped posture; a wrinkled and lined forehead; shaking and clumsy hands – all sure signs of the natural biological ageing process.

When Linter states that: "I'm staying here on Earth. Regardless of what else might happen," Sma replies: "Any particular reason?" Linter's reply is simple:

> Yes. I like the place... I feel alive for a change... I want to live here. I don't know how to explain it. It's alive. I'm alive. If I did die tomorrow it would have been worth it just for these last few months. I know I'm taking a risk in staying, but that's the whole point. ('State', 129)

So Linter chooses to stay on Earth as a human basic, with all the imperfections and uncertainties that this entails; he favours a comparatively short life, with inevitable decline in later years exactly because of these imperfections and uncertainties: his constantly blissful life in the Culture never changes; it has no urgency and no importance. Life on Earth has ugliness as well as beauty, and by experiencing this contrast Linter is able to truly appreciate his life. While human existence on Earth is ephemeral, it means more to him, as he knows it will end sooner.

The transient nature of life on Earth is made apparent when – with a heavy irony that is typical of Banks – during Sma's last day on Earth, several men attempt to mug Linter, fatally wounding him. After stabbing Linter, his attackers flee, leaving him with Sma, who is anxious to persuade Linter to allow her, or some Culture drones who have been monitoring the situation, to intervene to attempt to save his life: "Linter spun around, letting go of my elbow, I turned quickly. Linter held up one hand and said – did not shout – something I didn't catch" (196). Linter's actions imply that, when he becomes aware that his death is immanent, he accepts his fate stoically. The gesture of raising his hand would seem to indicate a "stop" motion, signalling that he does not want her or the Culture drones to intervene. Sma indicates that it would be simple for her or the drones to save him by swiftly returning him to a Culture spacecraft; but Linter stands by his decision to live as naturally as possible, choosing to die a final, absolute death, rather than be resuscitated – "revented" – by the Culture; a process that implicitly could be performed endlessly.

Using Sma's and Linter's opposite positions, then, Banks establishes a dialectic between an "artificial" death (and life) in the Culture and a "natural" death as human basic. 'The State of the Art' is narrated by Sma herself in the first person, allowing for an extended meditation on the significance of the episodes documented in the novella, especially surrounding Linter's death. She discusses her guilt about the incident, which she decides stems not from her "complicity in what Linter was trying to do" but in what she calls "the generality of transferred myth" that Earth people "accepted as reality" (201). Sma denounces the notion that a life lived with suffering and pain provides a more authentic experience than one lived in Utopia, because when Culture people worry about their lives, and "carp on about Having To Suffer [...] we are indulging in our usual trick of synthesizing something to worry about" but "we should really be thanking ourselves that we live the life that we do" (201). Worrying that one doesn't suffer, her logic goes, is a self-defeating attempt to bring that suffering about. Anyone who claims that pleasure can only be understood through pain, or peace through conflict, then, is merely regurgitating a "set of rules largely culled from the most hoary fictional clichés, the most familiar and received nonsense" (201). Here Sma renders such notions as kinds of fairy tale, mythology as coping mechanism invented by those forced to suffer, which become meaningless as soon as the possibility of cruelty, torment, and unplanned death has been ended. In the Culture, it is the *absence* rather than the presence of suffering that provides for an authentic, meaningful existence, a life emancipated.

Immortality

"There's dying, then there's dying" – William Gibson, *Mona Lisa Overdrive*

As R.C. Elliott explains in *The Shape of Utopia*, "it is a rare utopia that does not broach the theme of immortality or greatly increased longevity in one form or another, from elixirs in Bacon's *New Atlantis* to application of evolutionary theory in twentieth-century utopias."[51] While the Culture may believe ultimately in the importance of death as an available end state, there are nevertheless several ways in which an individual may live a kind of life that is potentially immortal, both within Banks's fictional universe. As John M. Fischer and Ruth Curl explain, conceptions of immortality can be divided into two main categories: nonserial immortality, where "the individual simply leads an indefinitely long single life," and serial immortality, where "the individual in question in some ways lives a series of lives".[52] There are potentially two options for both serial and nonserial immortality in Banks's series. In terms of the nonserial category, firstly, in the Culture and other equally advanced societies, one may chose never to allow one's body to die: by replacing cells, tissues, organs and other physical components vital for life as necessary; continually halting the biological ageing process; and avoiding fatal conflicts of any kind. This is an option technically open to any Culture citizen, although only two prominent individuals in the series – Zakalwe and QiRia – seem intent upon living longer than the average Culture lifespan, perhaps indefinitely. Secondly, one may choose to perform the act of Subliming, as explored in Chapter Five of this book. This process – becoming a powerful, energy-based being in a different dimension – would very probably allow one to live indefinitely, although it is impossible to qualitatively determine the nature of life in the Sublime due to the fundamental mystery associated with this aspect of Banks's series.

There are two options for serial immortality also: the biopunk motif of repeated rebirth into a physical body, or repeated rebirth into virtual space *à la* cyberpunk, as McHale explains.[53] As explored in

---

[51] Elliott, *The Shape of Utopia*, 10.
[52] John Martin Fischer and Ruth Curl, 'Philosophical Models of Immortality in Science Fiction', in *Immortal Engines: Life Extension and Immortality in Science Fiction and Fantasy*, George Slusser, Gary Westfahl, and Eric S. Rabkin, eds. (London: University of Georgia Press, 1996), 6.
[53] See Murphy and Vint, *Beyond Cyberpunk*, 23.

detail in Chapter Five, mind–computer interfacing has been mastered by the Culture to the extent that an individual can have their entire consciousness – personality, memories, etc. – perfectly captured and saved as digital information in an automatic process.[54] If a person dies, then their consciousness can be simply and efficiently revived, ready for reinsertion wherever and whenever they choose (a similar process to that described in Greg Bear's biopunk classic *Blood Music* [1985]). In both *Weapons* and *Surface* the protagonists – Zakalwe and Lededje, respectively – are killed, only for their saved consciousnesses to be reinserted into fresh physical bodies. This digital consciousness can also be inserted into one of the virtual reality (VR) environments that various civilisations, including the Culture, have developed to perfectly mimic consensus physical reality (*Windward*, 351). Another character from *Surface*, Vatueil – a soldier fighting in a virtual war, continually killed in action only to be resurrected for another mission – is the most prominent example from the series of someone whose life comes close to serial immortality, and enacts a similar cycle to the cyberpunk "death addiction" experienced by one character in Pat Cadigan's *Synners* (1991), albeit in a less extreme form.

The question of in what *manner* one might live an immortal life, however, is not as important as establishing the *quality* of such a life. To this end, Fischer and Curl outline an analytical framework for establishing the quality of an immortal life, as first developed by Bernard Williams.[55] According to this framework, the life in question would need to meet both of the following criteria in order to be considered appealing: the "identity condition" stipulates that "there must be a future in which an individual can recognize himself or herself – someone genuinely *identical* to the individual, not just qualitatively similar or with identical properties"; while the "attractiveness condition" stipulates that "the future life of the individual must be *appealing* (in some way) to that individual; it cannot involve constant torture, hard labour, tedium, or the like."[56] Zakalwe's extended, nonserial existence does not seem to meet either criterion. As established above, his life has caused him psychological and existential trauma: being continually reborn, both literally in a new body following physical death and symbolically following the assumption of his murdered brother's identity, causes disruption of his personality and seems to render his existence torturous to some extent. In turn, reading Zakalwe through the lens of material developed by

---

[54] See Banks, *Look to Windward*, 166.
[55] Fischer and Curl, 'Philosophical Models of Immortality in Science Fiction', 3.
[56] Fischer and Curl, 'Philosophical Models of Immortality in Science Fiction', 3.

Judith Butler, Jude Roberts has argued that Zakalwe's revenge missions constitute an "excessive performance of traditional masculinity", which is "shown to be founded on a fundamental vulnerability."[57] Therefore, as with each increasingly violent mission, so with each of his serial lives, "each repetition brings the protagonist closer to the realization that beneath his performance of Zakalwe, invincible action hero, lies Elethiomel: a vulnerable human being."[58]

QiRia – the Culture's oldest-known citizen, who has dedicated his long life to music – on the other hand, seems best placed to continue his life in an indefinite manner as he appears to meet both criteria in Williams's framework. SC agent Tefwe, an old acquaintance of QiRia's, meets up with the old man again after many years. Despite the fact that he has lived a period of time equivalent to Tefwe's lifetime several times over, there is no reason to doubt that QiRia's identity remains consistent, judging by Tefwe's reactions to meeting with her friend after such a long time: she never has cause to question his identity. QiRia also meets the attractiveness condition, for his vocation as a musician provides him with a purpose: this artistic passion has fuelled his long existence so far, and shows every sign of continuing to do so indefinitely. Rather than his greatly extended life becoming an ordeal, leading to boredom and despair, in fact it enables QiRia to continue his life's purpose in a more successful manner – it is suggested that it has uniquely enriched his knowledge of sound and music, enabling him to gain a deeper understanding of the subject in a manner that would not have been possible in just one lifetime of a more average length. For QiRia, nonserial immortality may prove to be a very attractive option.

Vatueil's potentially serially immortal existence, however, does not seem to meet either criterion. It is clear that Vatueil's life does not meet the attractiveness condition. One of his lives involves long gruelling shifts of hard labour, digging tunnels underground (*Surface*, 17–29) and resulting in capture and torture (144). At other times, as a soldier, he fights to the death in a disastrous laser battle (142–143) or barely survives the inhospitable conditions of a volatile water planet (246–252). There is evidence in *Surface Detail* to suggest that Vatueil's life also does not fit the identity condition. His succession of lives – starting a mission, repeatedly dying and being reborn for a new goal in the war effort – clearly makes for a deeply confusing and unsettling experience: dying in pain and shock, only to re-emerge in an unfamiliar yet equally

---

[57] Roberts, 'Iain M. Banks' Culture of Vulnerable Masculinities', *Foundation* 43, no. 117 (Spring 2014): 53.
[58] Roberts, 'Iain M. Banks' Culture of Vulnerable Masculinities', 53.

dangerous location. Sometimes, Vatueil's virtual rebirth goes wrong: during one mission, "he had not even been his complete self" due to an "all-too-believable glitch within the re-created scenario meaning that his download into the combat unit had been only partial" (144). It seems clear, therefore, that this version of Vatueil cannot be considered truly whole – he is the equivalent of a corrupted computer file. Throughout these continual lives, Vatueil recognises places and faces from his past, though struggles to retain a complete image of his personal history; he is frequently bewildered about the purpose of his mission and for whom he is fighting. As Banks makes explicit about Vatueil, "it had been so long since he was really alive" that he can no longer tell virtual from material reality (145). Making the unpleasantness of his situation clear, a young doctor – presumably from SC – asks Vatueil, "'do you feel you're being punished?' 'Borderline,' he told her. 'It depends how long this goes on for'" (315). His reply, then, makes it apparent that the quality of his life in this form is a feat of endurance, which he does not wish to continue indefinitely. Once his serial ordeal is over and all his missions completed, Vatueil is rewarded by revention, rebirth into a new body back in the physical world, and his sense of relief is clear (625–627).

The nature of Vatueil's life is made even more complex, however, when – through the very last word of *Surface* – Banks suggests that "Vatueil" is actually a pseudonym for Zakalwe himself, once again working for SC. While Banks's readers are left to speculate about which version of Zakalwe this may be, *Surface Detail* is set in 2970 AD,[59] much later than *Weapons*, the present-time narrative of which is set in 2092 AD; this makes it clear, then, that the Zakalwe formerly known as "Vatueil" must very likely be the Zakalwe from the present time of *Weapons*.[60] In this manner, Banks brings back the character around which the whole series grew, casting him as a kind of eternal mercenary, who has experienced both serial and nonserial models of immortality. Given that both his long, single life as Zakalwe in physical space and his succession of virtual lives as Vatueil seem to have provided him

[59] Michael Parsons, 'Interview: Iain M Banks talks "Surface Detail" with Wired', *Wired*, 14 October 2010. www.wired.co.uk/news/archive/2010-10/14/iain-m-banks-interview.

[60] In the final scene of the novel, Zakalwe is awaiting the arrival of a poet friend; whilst waiting, he ponders the poetic qualities of some of his own thoughts. This may seem to imply that he is therefore Cheradenine and not Elethiomel, although it is suggested in *Use of Weapons* that Cheradenine was killed long before his contact with the Culture, and therefore he would probably not have the possibility of revention. See Banks, *Surface Detail*, 626–627.

with more punishment than pleasure, immortality perhaps functions as a kind of penance or atonement for this character's immoral behaviour rather than some kind of utopian reward. Ultimately, Banks's (and therefore the Culture's) stance seems to be anti-immortality, arguing that, "In the Culture you can live forever, if you want to, but do you really want to? Living forever you take up a lot of real estate – people end for ecological reasons."[61]

Conclusion

The Culture series is posthuman in that human beings are not the most advanced beings in this fictional universe – the Minds, the powerful extradimensional Excession, and the Sublimed clearly supersede our intelligence – and perhaps we never were. With the Culture itself, Banks created an environment designed to bring out the very best attributes in human beings, based on the principle that people would want to use all the tools available to adapt and improve themselves. Yet, despite the possibilities for radical self-transformation in such an environment, the Culture's citizens overwhelmingly choose to remain recognisably human; they are therefore not posthuman in the sense that they have transcended this fundamental category, moving *beyond* humanity to become another kind of being altogether. In the Culture, the wish to become *more* than human is seen as a kind of hubris, an insult to those who have fought hard for a utopia that brings out the best in humanity. Biological ageing is controlled because it limits life's utopian possibilities, whilst retaining physical signs of ageing can display positive difference and diversity. Immortality is generally discouraged as a life that eventually decreases in quality as it increases in quantity, while death on one's own terms is the final necessity of a life lived in freedom. Perhaps the Culture's citizens, therefore, should be considered more as transhuman: individuals whose capabilities have been extended, expanded, and improved, but still remaining identifiably human.[62]

As Vint has argued, Banks's thinking in this regard is essentially rooted in a Renaissance model of humanism, which emphasises the problematic notion of a common "essence" to humankind. I think it is clear that Banks's conception of the human does not result in the complete effacement of physical and cultural differences within the

---

[61] Banks, Q&A, The Roundhouse, 6 October 2012.
[62] See 'What is Transhumanism?', whatistranshumanism.org/ and humanityplus.org/philosophy/transhumanist-faq/.

Culture, as Vint argues.[63] Throughout Zakalwe's greatly extended life, *Use of Weapons* forms an extended commentary on the subjectivity of the ageing process, demonstrating the various understandings of ageing itself as psychological and social as well as biological. Linter is clearly a plot function for 'The State of the Art', illustrating the differences between the Earth and the Culture, as well as a means by which Banks could expound philosophical arguments key to the series. The dialogue between Sma and Linter forms a dialectic between two different approaches to life: respectively the belief in a body produced by Culture, and by nature. Linter's desire to return to human basic is motivated by a yearning for his life to have meaning, in a tragic, poetic sense, which he feels is not possible in an environment where all conflict has been ended. Fundamentally, it is this yearning for deeper meaning that is problematic as it is antithetical to all that for which the Culture stands: Sma's view is that life lived under the threat of conflict and tragedy is demeaning to the lives of all; a life emancipated from pain becomes meaning in itself. It's no surprise, then, that when Banks was asked by *New Humanist* magazine "isn't it the messy struggle, in which scarcity, crime and bad things are inevitable, that makes life worthwhile?" he replied – with amusing and confident brevity – simply "No."[64] For Banks, humans find meaning in the pursuit of a life of freedom, peace, creativity, and equality. As I have been demonstrating, the Culture strives to achieve equality in its relations with other civilisations, and has created an egalitarian society within its own environments by eradicating class differences; it must too, therefore, ensure that its habitats are equal in terms of gender. The next chapter of this book expands upon the ways that Culture citizens adapt themselves, as discussed above, analysing the ways in which Banks imagined that the physical and psychological changes the Culture offers its humans would help it to achieve and maintain its goal of gender equality.

---

[63] Vint, 'The Culture-al Body'.
[64] *New Humanist*, 'Iain Banks: Q&A', 127, no. 4 (July/August 2012): 36. https://newhumanist.org.uk/articles/2832/qa-iain-banks.

Chapter 4

The Handy Wo/Man
Feminism, Space Opera, Ambisexuality

"Did IQs just drop sharply while I was away?" – Lieutenant Ellen Ripley, *Alien*

Spanning almost four decades, Banks's Culture series was written alongside key developments in the history of feminist thought and activism, and in the rights of women and LGBTQ+ people worldwide. Beginning in the 1960s in the United States, Second Wave feminism – with its focus on sexuality, the family, reproductive rights, and legal inequality – continued throughout the Western world until the Third Wave in the 1990s redefined understandings of the term and broadened discussion to the intersectionality of gender, race, and class. Space opera, born decades earlier in the US, was from the outset hampered by the problematic, sexist, and heteronormative gender dynamics that would shape the sub-genre through the Pulp era and into the Golden Age. In response, inspired by the radical feminism of the New Wave of SF, Banks envisioned his personal utopia as a place in which all structures of inequality, especially patriarchy, were non-existent, and he worked to ensure that the representation of women characters, in particular, was appropriate and positive, given the near absence of such in early classics of the form.

Through close attention to *The Player of Games, Matter, Excession*, and *Surface Detail*, this chapter explores the extent to which Banks was successful in his critical-feminist reimagining of the space-opera sub-genre through the Culture series and how this affects our understanding of the Culture itself. I explore how the Culture works to subvert the militaristic, masculine aggression of the traditional space-opera world system through its adherence to feminine traits of empathy and compassion. Focusing on the role of the Handy Man and the Wife at Home, I demonstrate the critical deconstruction of the traditional, male space-opera protagonist that Banks achieves through the characters Gurgeh, Linter, and Genar-Hofoen, as well as the trope's critical-feminist reimagination as the Handy Woman. I examine the methods Banks developed for achieving gender equality within his utopia, gender relations within the Culture, and the extent to which Banks successfully imagines a radical system beyond patriarchal and essentialist thinking.

Women and Representation in Space Opera

In her essay 'The Image of Women in Science Fiction' (1970) Joanna Russ observed that "There are plenty of images of women in science fiction. There are hardly any women".[1] Here Russ refers to the small minority of women publishing SF, the almost total lack of female protagonists, and the numerous stereotypes which abound, prior to the radical impact of feminism and the New Wave. Lisa Tuttle lists some of the key stereotypes – the Timorous Virgin, the Amazon Queen, the Frustrated Spinster Scientist, the Good Wife, the Tomboy Kid Sister[2] – and reminds us how long it would take for improved representation to start to occur: "It would be hard for even the most ardent fan to list a dozen Genre SF novels written before 1970 which feature female protagonists".[3] The space captain Rydra Wong from Samuel Delaney's *Babel-17* (1966) is one of the very few exceptions in space opera, whilst Heinlein's teenage Podkayne "Poddy" Fries from *Podkayne of Mars* (1963) is an earlier example in planetary romance.

The problematic gender relations with which space opera in particular would be associated were present from the outset in *The Skylark in Space*. Whilst E.E. "Doc" Smith is usually remembered as the book's sole author, it was in fact co-written by Lee Hawkins Garby, the wife of Smith's school friend, chemist Dr. Carl Garby, near to whom he was living at the time; and the nature of their collaboration was to be stereotypically gendered. While Smith felt comfortable writing adventure and the scientific elements, Lee's contribution – subsequently excised from the 1958 revision of the text[4] – was, "according to Smith focused on dialogue

---

[1] Nick Hubble and Aris Mousoutzanis, *The Science Fiction Handbook* (London: Bloomsbury Academic, 2013), 87.
[2] Lisa Tuttle, 'Women in SF', in *The Encyclopedia of Science Fiction*, Clute et al., eds. (London: Gollancz, 2018). http://www.sf-encyclopedia.com/entry/women_in_sf.
[3] Tuttle, 'Women in SF'. Web.
[4] John Clute, 'Smith, E E', in *The Encyclopedia of Science Fiction*, Clute et al., eds. (London: Gollancz, 2018). http://www.sf-encyclopedia.com/entry/smith_e_e.

and other people issues",[5] while Smith's biographer Sam Moskowitz adds that she wrote the novel's romantic elements.[6] The protagonist of *Skylark*, scientist Dick Seaton, fits firmly within the modern adventurer archetype of the Handy Man, with his technological mastery, intellectual rigor, and upbringing as a rugged outdoorsman. In turn, Seaton's fiancée, Dorothy Vaneman, fits with Clute's description of "the chummy, clammy idiocy" of Smith's women characters.[7] While Dorothy is involved in the action of the story, discounting her as a Wife at Home figure, her kidnapping at the hands of antagonist Marc "Blackie" DuQuesne establishes her as the hackneyed "damsel in distress", which Smith would continue with Clio Marsden in *Triplanetary*, who is in constant need of rescue, consolation, and rationalisation throughout the book. Smith would further deny all but one of his female characters the agency and power provided by the series' titular Lens device itself because "Women's minds and Lenses don't fit. There's a sex-based incompatibility."[8] Written between 1916 and 1920 whilst Smith and the Garbys were living in Washington DC, then, the gender relations of *Skylark* prove Russ's point that "many far future sf works imagine societies that are socially analogous to contemporaneous civilization": "despite being set *'very* far in the future' (206) even the most intelligent fictional texts can carry 'today's values and standards into future Galactic Empires' (206)."[9] As such, and as with many works from the Golden Age that followed, we can see that *Skylark* portrays "the relations between the sexes as those of present-day, white, middle-class suburbia [...] In short, the American middle class with a little window dressing."[10] It was a pattern that would continue beyond Smith's work, long into the Pulp era and Golden Age, inscribing itself deeply into the sub-genre, and which would contribute to the dissatisfaction and animosity that would be directed toward space opera in the New Wave and in the transformation of the sub-genre that followed.

Banks and Feminist Representation

As a leading figure in New Space Opera, Banks was well aware of his responsibility to correct this pattern. Banks told Jude Roberts in 2010 that

---

[5] John Clute, 'Smith, E E'. Web.
[6] Sam Moskowitz, *Seekers of Tomorrow* (United States: World Publishing Co., 1966), 14.
[7] John Clute, 'Smith, E E'. Web.
[8] E.E. Smith, *First Lensman*, 39.
[9] Hubble and Mousoutzanis, *The Science Fiction Handbook*, 87.
[10] Hubble and Mousoutzanis, *The Science Fiction Handbook*, 87.

he was very concerned with the way he represented female characters in his writing, and always made an "attempt to redress the (im)balance" he found "in so much other fiction or other fictive media."[11] Furthermore, Banks intended the Culture itself to be a "post-sexist" society that has eradicated gender inequality and patriarchy.[12] Early space opera transposed the patriarchal "rule of the father"[13] out beyond the Earth, recreating "a system ruled over by men," or at least systems upheld by masculine authority, and "enforced through social, political, economic and religious institutions"[14] – or, as the non-Culture Oelph has been lead to believe in *Inversions*, "the facts of life which dictate the accepted and patent preeminence of the male" (9). So Banks's aspirations help locate the Culture series within what Pat Wheeler identifies as "the major project of feminist science fiction": "to call attention to the 'constructedness' of gender and to question those patriarchal ideologies that posit the pervasive belief in 'essential' differences which permanently distinguish men from women and which invariably render women as passive and inferior."[15] Asked about influential feminist SF writers, Banks expressed admiration for Le Guin, C.J. Cherryh, Octavia Butler, James Tiptree Jr. (Alice Sheldon), Gwyneth Jones, and Joanna Russ, although noted that "probably only Le Guin could have been any sort of influence on me".[16] Le Guin's Hainish Cycle, for example, bears strong thematic, political, and stylistic comparison, as do Cherryh's Alliance–Union series, both of which were published contemporaneously with Banks's development of the Culture.

The Wasp Factory remains the text from Banks's oeuvre most widely recognized for its contribution to the feminist cause as outlined above by Wheeler, even if it is not recognised as SF. The book was praised for its conclusion which works to shatter the notion of a gender identity naturally linked to biological sex through the revelation that protagonist Frank was born biologically female but raised to believe she was a boy, forcing a striking re-evaluation of Frank/Frances's aggressive behaviour

---

[11] Roberts, 'A Few Questions about the Culture'.
[12] Channel 4, 'Iain Banks', *The English Programme: Scottish Writers* (Warwick: Channel 4, 1996).
[13] Kathy E. Ferguson, 'Patriarchy', in *Women's Studies Encyclopedia* 2, Helen Tierney, ed. (Westport, CT: Greenwood Publishing, 2009), 1,048.
[14] Sarah Gamble, 'Patriarchy', in *The Routledge Companion to Feminism and Postfeminism* (New York: Routledge, 2006), 271.
[15] Pat Wheeler, 'Issues of Gender, Sexuality and Ethnicity', in *The Science Fiction Handbook*, Nick Hubble and Aris Mousoutzanis, eds. (London: Bloomsbury Academic, 2013), 213.
[16] Roberts, 'A Few Questions about the Culture', 157.

throughout the preceding text. As Berthold Scoene-Harwood explains: "The ending of *The Wasp Factory* hints at a remedial reassemblage of human subjectivity. Injurious distinctions between femininity and masculinity, madness and sanity, have collapsed into a vision of restorative unity beyond the systemic inscription of woman's congenital lack in opposition to man's phallic plenitude."[17] To date, some critics have also acknowledged the similar contribution made in Banks's SF. Janice M. Bogstad recognises a similar "remedial reassemblage" of Golden Age tropes at work in Banks's Culture stories, a shift that, as in *The Wasp Factory*, "comes from the understanding that gender is socially constructed rather than historically fixed or biologically grounded in the individual."[18] Moira Martingale affirms Banks's commitment to positive representation, arguing that Banks "creates strong female protagonists, and even secondary female characters are, in the main, assertive, smart, sexually uninhibited and in control of their lives – frequently more in control than their male counterparts."[19] Sarah Falcus notes that, while Banks's work may feature unreconstructed male characters, it highlights the "repression and dangers of patriarchal masculinity" and "exposes female sublimation" into a patriarchal system.[20] Jude Roberts implicitly affirms the views of Martingale and Falcus, and, by positioning "the vulnerability of the masculine body" as "the foundation of the masculine subject" in his fiction, Banks works to critique patriarchal and toxic modes of masculinity – an approach that, as demonstrated below, allows for the development of more progressive, feminist modes of masculinity.[21]

Yet other critics have challenged the feminist potential of Banks's fiction. Sheryl Vint argues that a strong essentialist tendency underpins his conception of the Culture, drawing attention to its sex-changing procedure (explored below) which she sees as displaying a continued attachment to "the notion of the body as natural, rather than as cultural."[22] While Falcus praises much of the feminist content of Banks's work, she offers caveats about his writing of female characters, worrying that – while seeming to challenge patriarchy – they also seem to run "perilously close at times to the traditional portrayal of women as little

---

[17] Berthold Schoene-Harwood, 'Dams Burst: Devolving Gender in Iain Banks's *The Wasp Factory*', *Ariel* 30, no. 1 (1999): 146.
[18] Janice M. Bogstad, 'Men Writing Women', *Women in Science Fiction and Fantasy* 1 (2009): 171.
[19] Martingale, *Gothic Dimensions*, 330–331.
[20] Sarah Falcus, 'Gender in *The Wasp Factory*, *Whit* and *The Business*', in *The Transgressive Iain Banks*, Martyn Colebrook and Katharine Cox, eds., 124.
[21] Roberts, 'Iain M. Banks' Culture of Vulnerable Masculinities', 60.
[22] Vint, 'The Culture-al Body', 89.

more than sexual objects"[23] – a view also held by Gwyneth Jones.[24] Such issues of representation, essentialism versus social constructionism and gender role/identity in Banks's fiction form the subject of the present chapter, in relation to the Culture series.

The Culture and the Gendered World System

The world systems of early space opera, such as Smith's Galactic Patrol or Heinlein's Terran Federation from *Starship Troopers*, embody "conventionally masculine qualities (such as vigour, courage, rationality, authority, mastery, independence)"[25] through their version of the *technologiade*, based respectively upon values of economic free-market competition and government bureaucracy, as well as colonialism, imperialism, and military rule. Similarly, Banks would frequently describe the Culture as a whole, or as a group of people en masse, in gendered terms. "The kind of future the Culture represents," Banks wrote in 1998, "is more female than male in its demeanour".[26] He would reiterate the point in 2010: "I've always thought of the Culture as being more feminine than male, at least as far as we as a species would react to it if we were ever exposed to it."[27] Here we experience a reoccurring issue in Banks's writing and explanation where the terms "sex" and "gender" are used casually, without necessarily considering the distinction between biological sex and a culturally developed gender identity. Making sense of his comments, then, it is fair to assume that by referring to the Culture's *demeanour* as female, it seems much more likely that Banks refers to *femininity* and *masculinity* understood as "the distinct sets of characteristics culturally ascribed to maleness and femaleness",[28] rather than to sex or biological differences. Writing in *Sex and Gender* (1968), for example, Robert Stoller made an important, early acknowledgement of the difference between biological sex and cultural gender, explaining that "one can speak of the male sex or female sex, but one can also talk about masculinity and femininity and not necessarily be implying anything about anatomy or physiology."[29] Banks, then, developed the

---

[23] Falcus, 'Gender in *The Wasp Factory, Whit* and *The Business*', 124.
[24] Gwyneth Jones, 'Review of *Matter*', *Strange Horizons*, 14 April 2008. http://strangehorizons.com/non-fiction/reviews/matter-by-iain-m-banks/.
[25] Anna Tripp, *Gender* (London: Palgrave, 2007), 11.
[26] *Dillons Review*, 'Inversions: An Interview', *Dillons Review* 16 (May–June 1998).
[27] Roberts, 'A Few Questions about the Culture', 166.
[28] Tripp, *Gender*, 3.
[29] Robert Stollers, *Sex and Gender* (1968), in Tripp, *Gender*, 4.

outlook of the Culture not merely as femin*ist* but also as fundamentally femin*ine* in that sense, in a further attempt to create politically radical space opera. As Holly Devor explains, a "description of the social qualities subsumed by femininity and masculinity might be to label masculinity as generally concerned with egoistic dominance and femininity as striving for cooperation or communion".[30] Banks saw the Culture as feminine in similar if more essentialist terms, arguing that "women are, compared to men, generally more caring, less aggressive, and more open to using discussion as a way of resolving disputes".[31] Describing "a certain manic wildness" and "a refusal to be constrained" in space opera generally, Banks saw the Culture as a society that celebrates different values, including "empathy", "altruism", and the "alleviation of suffering", to which we could also add emotion, tolerance, self-reflection, and communality: in other words, the "feminine" values missing from the classic world systems in the field. In this regard, Gavin Miller has described Banks's approach as a "feminine mythology".[32]

Comments made by non-Culture characters in the series seem to support such an approach. In *Surface Detail*, Lededje visits the Culture for the first time: "one of the few things that she could recall having heard about the Culture back in Sichult: its people were hopelessly effeminate, or unnaturally aggressive females" (157). Lededje, then, views Culture people in fairly pejorative and essentialist terms and possibly does not understand the importance and/or existence of the sex–gender distinction. This is not surprising given that Lededje grew up outside of the Culture in the Sichultian Enablement, a series of planets which – heavily market-driven, patriarchal, and still practising slavery – are ideologically opposite to the Culture in almost every way. As patriarchies, societies such as the Sichultian Enablement are thrown into sharp relief by the Culture. As Anna Tripp explains, quoting Devor, "in patriarchally organised societies, masculine values become the ideological structure of the society as a whole. Masculinity thus becomes 'innately' valuable and femininity serves as a contrapuntal function to delineate and magnify the hierarchical dominance of the masculine."[33] In Banks's utopia, this logic is inverted. The Culture, as the focus of the series, where feminine

---

[30] Holly Devor, 'Gender Role Behaviors and Attitudes', in *The Lesbian and Gay Studies Reader*, H. Abelove, M.A. Barale, and D. Halperin, eds. (New York: Routledge, 1993), 484–488.
[31] Roberts, 'A Few Questions about the Culture', 166.
[32] Gavin Miller, 'Iain (M.) Banks: Utopia, Nationalism and the Posthuman', in *The Edinburgh Companion to Contemporary Scottish Literature*, Berthold Schoene, ed. (Edinburgh: Edinburgh University Press, 2007), 207.
[33] Tripp, *Gender*, 11.

values become the ideological structure of the society as a whole, serves to highlight the "egoistic dominance" of more masculine, traditional space-opera world systems – often the Culture's antagonists in the series, such as the Idirans or the Affront in *Excession* – and to magnify their frequently oppressive, authoritarian nature. If any aspect of the Culture is masculine in this way, it is in the interventionist tendencies of Special Circumstances which – when all other possibilities have been exhausted – force them to rely upon self-motivated and violent mercenaries such as Zakalwe, who remain relatively unaffected by the internally peaceful and "feminised" culture of the Culture proper.

Sex-swapping or Ambisexuality

For the Os and GSVs of the Culture to be utopian, they must represent what Banks called a "post-sexist society". The key to the success of this fundamental shift, Banks argues, lies in the success of the Culture's system whereby all citizens can transition perfectly from one biological sex to another as part of their altered human condition, through a complex mixture of genetic engineering and hormonal secretions by drug gland.[34] This process is described in 'A Few Notes on the Culture' as "an elaborate thought-code, self-administered in a trance-like state (or simply a consistent desire, even if not conscious) [that] will lead, over the course of about a year, to what amounts to a viral change from one sex into the other."[35] In describing the logic of this process, then, Banks clearly maintains the traditional gender binary. Though the Culture series rarely touches on issues relating to trans identity explicitly, Banks's conception of this sex-swapping process affirms the potential existence of a "dissonance between 'felt body' and the external appearance of the body" as explored, for example, in Gayle Salamon's work on the phenomenology of trans experience,[36] and there is a similar dissonance at

---

[34] The similarities between the Culture's long-lived, sex-changing inhabitants and the titular hero of Virginia Woolf's modernist classic *Orlando: A Biography* (1928) are clear. Published during the original era of space opera, the forward-looking nature of Woolf's writing is thrown into sharp perspective by the conservative and reactionary politics displayed in many examples of the sub-genre. Sally Potter's film adaptation of Woolf's novel was released in 1992, between the release of *The State of the Art* and *Excession*, to critical acclaim.

[35] Banks, 'A Few Notes on the Culture'. Web.

[36] See Gayle Salamon, *Assuming a Body: Transgender and Rhetorics of Materiality* (New York: Columbia University Press, 2010).

work in Genar-Hofoen's desire for an alien body in *Excession*, as detailed below. When someone experiences such a dissonance in the Culture to a powerful enough extent, then the body will automatically adjust itself in accordance with the individual's consistent desire for a "felt body". Importantly, Culture society *encourages* each individual to perform this change at least once during their lifetimes, for the purpose of empathising with the "opposite sex", perhaps with the implicit suggestion that almost everyone will, at some stage, feel such a dissonance. Banks goes on to argue that this ease of sex-swapping has allowed the Culture to achieve a system of gender equality:

> A society in which it is so easy to change sex will rapidly find out if it is treating one gender better than the other; within the population, over time, there will gradually be greater and greater numbers of the sex it is more rewarding to be, and so pressure for change – within society rather than the individuals – will presumably build up until some form of sexual equality and hence numerical parity is established.[37]

Despite the "feminine mythology" surrounding the Culture, and an emphasis on active women and problematic men for protagonists which we will soon explore, then, Banks is clear that men and women exist in roughly equal numbers in his utopia. Again the description quoted above assumes a traditional gender binary rather than a spectrum of morphologies and conflates the sex–gender distinction. Yime, a temporarily androgynous Handy Person from *Surface*, is the closest Banks's series comes to portraying non-binary characters, as explored below, and such individuals clearly problematise Banks's system for gender parity which relies upon a clear gender binary.

Yet, despite its flaws, the logic of Banks's system of sex-swapping is nevertheless fundamental to his conception of utopia. According to this rationale, in such a society, the quantity of members of one sex is directly related to the quality of life experienced by individuals of that sex: significantly larger numbers of Culture citizens choosing to live as a man for long periods of time would seem to indicate a patriarchal order or at least an androcentric system; an abundance of women would perhaps indicate a more gynocentric arrangement. The logic behind this rationale suggests that prejudice and inequality could be minimised or removed altogether if all could directly experience life from the perspective of individuals in different circumstances. As such,

---

[37] Banks, 'A Few Notes on the Culture'. Web.

it is a fundamental belief in the social importance of empathy, which cuts through patriarchal conceptions of gender and sex, placing values of mutual understanding and respect at the heart of a healthy culture. The details and significance of this process are seldom described until *Matter*, the eighth text in the series, when SC agent Djan Seriy Anaplain becomes a man for a year and documents the experience.

The Ambisexual Handy Person in *Matter*

Originating in the highly conservative and patriarchal society of Sursamen, Djan was exiled from her home at a young age, which enabled her to achieve her secret dream of joining the Culture and becoming an operative for SC. Djan's transition from biologically female to biologically male is detailed in several chapters of *Matter* concerned with Djan's adjustment to life in the Culture, which is radically different in many ways to the militaristic and monarchical society of her home. As Banks explains, Djan "had been a man for a year. That had been different. Everything had been different. She had learned so much: about herself, about people, about civilizations" (163). Djan compares her change with other adjustments that she has experienced – temporal and gravitational adjustment to her new physical environment; social adjustment to a postscarcity society; and a kind of aesthetic adjustment regarding the appearance of her fellow Culture citizens, who appear as almost unanimously perfect in their beauty and health (164) – suggesting that she regards her experience of sex change as similarly radical, and demonstrating the deep connections between sex and gender identity in social development. When Djan focuses on the experience of becoming biologically male, the transition causes her both amazement and shock:

> Over most of the year, she grew slightly, bulked out further, grew hair in strange places, and watched, fascinated, as her genitals went from fissure to spire. She did wake up a couple of nights covered in sweat, appalled at what was happening to her, feeling herself, wondering if this was all some enormously laboured joke and she was being made a freak of deliberately, for sport, but there were always people to talk to who had been through the same experience – both in person and via screens and sims – and no shortage of archived material to explain and reassure. (170)

The above description works to suggest the biological simplicity with which one sex may become as the other, emphasising the relative lack of significant physical difference between male and female bodies: the changes amount to slight adjustments in size and weight, the placement and amount of hair growth, and differences in genitalia; and includes a healthy, fully functional reproductive system, as explored below in *Excession*. Djan's transition, therefore, suggests the fundamental fluidity of the human form and emphasises the similar aspects of human bodies regardless of biological sex. The nature of the archived material she mentions suggests that, as in our society, trans people in the Culture are also good at documenting their experiences and transitions, just as the Culture itself makes use of such material to help normalise the process.

Alongside these progressive notions, however, this description also portrays Djan's physical transition as a traumatic and frightening ordeal to be endured, rather than a positive cultural development, almost certainly due to her status as a relative newcomer to the Culture. By viewing the process as a "joke" and her altering physical form as a "freak", Djan emphasises the radical nature of such a change – especially considering its relative ease and complete effectiveness – from the perspective of a patriarchal society. Djan's physical body, at this stage situated somewhere between biologically male and female, can also be read as highlighting the trauma and prejudice endured by intersex individuals in contemporary society, whose naturally "queered" bodies disrupt the values of binary, essentialist culture. Even so, the process that Djan undergoes seems designed purely to allow binary adjustment from one rigid, normative conception of biological sex to another, with Djan's liminal, intersex state rendered as a purely temporary stage in this process rather than suggesting a potential variety of different sexes across a spectrum.

As with Banks's outline of the Culture's sex-swapping in 'A Few Notes on the Culture', this description in *Matter* focuses entirely on biological sex and does not mention gender identity in relation to Djan, who – given the nature of her background – would presumably also need to have this distinction explained to her. This may perhaps indicate, however, that if Djan retained her gender identity at the same time as becoming biologically male, her resulting queer identity – as we understand it – was accepted without question or comment, suggesting that gender discrimination *has* been ended within the Culture with understanding and acceptance of the sex–gender distinction being so widespread that it need not be frequently acknowledged.

As well as detailing Djan's transition, Banks discusses the sexual encounters that she undertakes around this time, which provide further insight into how gender and sexuality are represented in the Culture. As Banks states, Djan "took a couple of intermittent, unbothered lovers even as she changed, then, as a man, took many more, mostly female" (170). These comments, then, leave the identity of her pre- and mid-change lovers unspecified, although Banks does explicitly note that, after completing the transition to a biologically male body, Djan takes significantly more female lovers, and more in general. The suggestion here, that in male form, Djan's interest in sexual relations increases and that he is more interested in those who are biologically female, implicitly perpetuates the stereotype that men are more promiscuous than women and more inclined to heterosexuality, or at least that men are less open-minded regarding homosexuality than women. The passing comment that Djan's experimentation includes sexual encounters "even as she changed", confirms that Djan was sexually active during the intersexual, liminal stage of her biological transition from one sex to another; and her comment that her lovers were "unbothered" about this suggests the Culture's success in establishing a sexually open society.[38]

At one stage Djan contemplates returning to "Sursamen as a man, [to] see what they made of him then" (170). While jesting about returning in *his* new male physique and claiming the throne, as he would now technically be entitled to do, Djan also mentions that "apart from anything else, there had been a couple of ladies at the court he had always been fond of, and *now* felt something for" (170, emphasis added). This statement is a little ambiguous. On the one hand, Banks could be saying that, whilst living in a society in which homosexuality was viewed as a crime and with abhorrence – at one stage, Sursamen Prince Oramen uses the homophobic insult "man-fucker" (245) – Djan would not and could not accept that the feelings she harboured for other women were anything other than platonic. Therefore, if she were to return to such a society having lived in an inclusive and diverse Culture habitat where homosexuality is accepted and celebrated, Djan would understand the true nature of her feelings. On the other hand, the statement could also be read as suggesting that, now *she* has become physically *he*, Djan's prior affections will inevitably adjust along with these bodily changes: whereas her prior feelings towards other women *were* only platonic, a "fondness", they will inevitably become a more physical, sexual attraction now that Djan inhabits a man's body. Seemingly, then, one's sexual orientation

---

[38] "Work by John Money, Joan Hampson, and John Hampson on intersexuality (the state of having both female and male biological characteristics) led to the introduction of the technical term gender (1955)." – Talia Bettcher, 'Feminist Perspectives on Trans Issues', *Stanford Encyclopedia of Philosophy*, Edward N. Zalta, ed. (Spring, 2014). plato.stanford.edu/entries/feminism-trans/#PhenTransEmb.

is directly related to one's biology, in an affirmation of heteronormative values, which seems problematic for Banks's representation of the Culture's attitudes, especially given Vint's assertion that an essentialist tendency runs throughout his work.

During other scenes in *Matter*, Banks parodies the tropes of romance fiction to demonstrate Djan's conflicted views regarding her sexuality, resulting from her combined Sursamen–Culture background. As in *Player* regarding Gurgeh and Yay, Banks depicts a woman from the Culture being sexually propositioned by a man, only to turn him down. In this instance, Djan is propositioned by a Culture avatoid – "a ship's avatar of such exquisite bio-mimicry it could pass for fully human" (*Matter*, 377) – Quike, originally part of the Culture, but who has "Absconded", in a manner that is compared with the GSV *Sleeper Service* from *Excession* (see Chapter Six). Quike sends Djan a long transmission, written in an elaborately polite and suggestive manner, the underlying sexual proposal of which is quickly interpreted and rejected by Djan, to amusing effect. "I think your trick does not work on me, sir," replies Djan. "Quike smiled. 'Well, it doesn't work with everybody [...] Perhaps I might be permitted to try again some other time?'" (*Matter*, 379) Djan does further consider Quike's proposal, however, and almost succumbs to his seduction routine:

> She looked into his languidly beautiful eyes and saw in them – well, being cold about it, more precisely in the exact set of his facial features and muscle state – hint of real need, even genuine hunger [...] she was only experiencing what untold generations of females had experienced throughout the ages. (383)

In many ways, these scenes are allowed to develop into parodies of depictions of seduction from stereotypical romantic fiction, which reproduce heteronormative values of active male and passive female, of which both implied reader and fictional couple are aware. When Djan is described as "experiencing what untold generations of females had experienced throughout the ages", Banks knowingly reproduces the romance trope of a woman protagonist falling for a man who appears initially to be proudly strong and assertive in temperament, but who eventually reveals an underlying sensitivity that belies his true nature, perhaps best known from Mr. Darcy in Austen's *Pride & Prejudice* (1813). The parodic effect is enhanced by the fact that the relationship crosses boundaries of "species", as Djan is being wooed by a person who is not human: "She was thinking, Dear shafted Worldgod, all my potential bedfellows are machines. How depressing" (379).

This exchange shows further comparison between the sexual standards represented by the Culture and Sarsuman. Djan ultimately does reject Quike, in a manner not dissimilar to Yay's initial rebuff of Gurgeh: "She thought, a real Culture girl would definitely say yes at this point. She sighed regretfully. However, I am still – deep down, and for my sins – both my father's daughter and a Sarl" (383). A "real Culture girl", as Djan describes herself, who lives in a society with no socio-political, familial, patriarchal, or religious influences affecting her personal freedom, would be entirely free to make this decision according to her own desires at the moment in time. Yet, no matter how hard she tries – in a similar manner to Gurgeh who is a somewhat unreconstructed man at the start of *Player* – Djan cannot fully shake off the trappings of the conservative and patriarchal society in which she was raised. (In turn, her background on Sarl, a deeply religious community, is perhaps further exemplified by her continued reference to the "Worldgod" in the previous quotation.) Acquiescing to a sexual encounter so soon upon meeting her partner, while socially acceptable in the Culture, would bring shame upon her and her Sarl family. Here, Banks illustrates how deep the influence of a repressive, orthodox society such as the Sarl runs, given that Djan has lived in the Culture for most of her life; she is in the process of "Culturing out" the negative, unwanted elements of her heritage.

SC Agents and Unreconstructed Handy Men

As well as enabling Banks to demonstrate the Culture's attitude toward sexuality and gender roles, Djan – as an SC operative and active, nuanced woman protagonist – is a prominent example of Banks's successful critical subversion of Csicsery-Ronay's Handy Man, a space-opera archetype. The Handy Man is the archetypal protagonist in such a narrative, derived from early modes of SF such as colonial adventure stories, and is therefore an archetype that is almost always automatically gendered. Csicsery-Ronay describes the Handy Man as follows:

> a figure, usually male, who possesses skill in the handling of tools [...] his many ideas and plans are almost exclusively devoted to technical problem-solving. The Handy Man is able to manipulate tools, to fashion new ones [...] and, most important, to extend his power over the environment through technological control.[39]

[39] Csicsery-Ronay, *Seven Beauties*, 227.

The origins of this archetype can be traced back to characters such as Homer's Odysseus, Daniel Defoe's Robinson Crusoe, and Jules Verne's adventurer heroes, then later protagonists such as Clarke's Dr. Carlisle Perera or H.G. Wells's Dr. Moreau.[40] As McHale explains, such figures would later develop into "Space-travelling versions of the knight-errant or cowboy" which "abound in cyberpunk", whom William Gibson calls "sundogs", probably after rugged "seadogs" such as Melville's Captain Ahab.[41]

In the Culture novels, it is straightforward to identify the agents of Contact and SC as versions of the Handy Man archetype: posthuman, tech-savvy agents of the Culture's expansion. Banks's Handy Men are adventurers "induced or forced out of a culturally comfortable, predictable home environment, to exotic and undeveloped regions".[42] They either "solve a fundamental problem", allowing them to function as an "entrepreneurial hero" for their original c/Culture, or they "establish a base" for a "Cultural" transformation, or frequently both.[43]

While Banks is often concerned with constructing updated versions of the Handy Man, as I will demonstrate shortly, he does provide more traditional examples of the archetype for comparative and deconstructive purposes: for example, Gurgeh from *Player* is "an adventurer though not always a willing one,"[44] whose begrudging, yet ultimately successful, role in the political machinations of SC forms a unique kind of rational/technical and emotional/political problem solving. This notable scholar and practitioner of game-playing grows bored of his peaceful academic life on his home Orbital Chiark, and becomes embroiled in an SC mission to "solve the problem" of the "volatile and unstable" Empire of Azad (77). He helps the Culture defeat Azad at the eponymous game that forms the centre of their culture, resulting in the implosion of Azad's infrastructure, and helping to establish it as a base for a Cultural transformation. Gurgeh is a typical Handy Man because "he has an ambivalent relationship with his home"[45]: he leaves the safe, sanitised Culture to play dangerous games elsewhere for "real" stakes. The Culture is ambivalent to Gurgeh as it is simultaneously the site of what he regards as his stultifying *ennui*, but also of everything and everyone for which and for whom he cares. At

---

[40] See Homer, *The Odyssey* (8 BC); Daniel Defoe, *Robinson Crusoe* (1719); Arthur C. Clarke, *Rendezvous with Rama* (1973); and H.G. Wells's *The Island of Doctor Moreau* (1986).
[41] Murphy and Vint, *Beyond Cyberpunk*, 8–9.
[42] Csicsery-Ronay, *Seven Beauties*, 221.
[43] Csicsery-Ronay, *Seven Beauties*, 221.
[44] Csicsery-Ronay, *Seven Beauties*, 227.
[45] Csicsery-Ronay, *Seven Beauties*, 227.

the novel's conclusion, Gurgeh returns to Chiark and is reunited with his friends and colleagues; yet as his own character and relationship with his home have changed considerably, the text does achieves a critical/progressive rather than conservative narrative closure.

Gurgeh is a fairly traditional Handy Man for his gender role as well as for the political role that he performs for SC. Described initially as "primitive" and as a "throwback" (29), Gurgeh is marked as a man who – despite living on a Culture Orbital his entire life – has yet to fully embrace the ways of the Culture, and does not easily fit in, as made explicit in the following conversation between Gurgeh and his friend and potential lover Yay, in which they discuss Gurgeh's sexual proclivities:

> "There's something very... I don't know; primitive, perhaps, about you, Gurgeh. You've never changed sex have you?" He shook his head. "Or slept with a man?" Another shake. "I thought so," Yay said. "You're strange, Gurgeh." She drained her glass. "Because I don't find men attractive." "Yes; *you're* a man!" She laughed. "Should I be attracted to myself, then?" (24)

Yay's comments here suggest that the Culture encourages its citizens to practise not only sex-swapping but also bisexuality. Yay finds it genuinely odd – even disturbing – that Gurgeh has not changed sex (a detail that Banks altered from early drafts of the novel),[46] and is not attracted to men as well as women. By associating the fact that Gurgeh has never slept with a member of the same sex with primitivism, Yay associates heterosexuality with a bygone era, emphasising further that bisexuality is the Culture's norm, even associating heterosexuality with patriarchy. In fact, her question "Or slept with a man?" suggests that that she is surprised, and could potentially be accusing her friend of homophobia. Also, Yay's comment "you're a man" could be read as having a double meaning: on the one hand, wittily pointing out the perceived strangeness of heterosexuality, which, according to an individual from a post-patriarchal society, implicitly casts one's own self as unattractive; on

---

[46] In a typewritten draft of *Player*, marked "IB/6/1/1" by the University of Stirling archive, a roughly equivalent version of this scene states that Gurgeh had been in a relationship with the later-abandoned character Vossle Cho "for over fifty years", and that he *had* changed sex in the past. The reason for reverting to male again – that he "didn't want a child" – was wisely excised from subsequent versions, before the non-sex-changing version finally went to print. In this early draft, Banks experimented with Gurgeh as asexual, discussing his relative lack of sexual desire for Yay with the drone, Chamlis.

the other hand, by "man", Yay may refer to a traditional or "unreconstructed" man, therefore further confirming his identity as an oddity, a patriarchal man living in a post-patriarchal society.

Gurgeh's comments suggest that he has missed the wider, social role of sex-swapping in the Culture, reducing this practice to mere pandering to sexual preferences; while the fact that he is free *not* to do so reinforces the Culture's lack of a legal structure, operating according to a much looser de facto system of codes, manners and practices. The sexual chemistry and desire between the pair is clear from the outset, yet, at the start of the novel, Yay gently and consistently rejects Gurgeh's advances:

> "You're going to ask me to stay again, aren't you?" [...]
> "Oh," Gurgeh said, shaking his head and looking up at the ceiling, "I doubt it. I get bored going through the same old moves and responses."
> Yay smiled. "You never know," she said. "One day I might change my mind. You shouldn't let it bother you, Gurgeh." (24)

Judging from his responses here, while Gurgeh may be something of a throwback in Culture terms, he clearly does not respond to sexual rejection with anger or violence, and handles the situation by speaking with Yay and understanding her motivations. His response is more one of genuine bemusement, rather than frustration, and his process of seduction is not portrayed as one of aggressive persistence to pressure Yay into "giving in"; it is a playful process within a context of openness and consent, where Yay need not turn down desired casual sex for fear of shame and stereotyping. Her last comment, "One day I might change my mind", clearly indicates the fact that, in the Culture, Yay is entirely free to choose whom she takes as a lover, with none of the patriarchal pressure that maintains, at its most extreme, that women somehow have a responsibility – are obliged even – to please the men who are attracted to them, regardless of their own wishes. Yay continues:

> "It's almost an honour."
> "You mean to be an exception?" "Mmm." She drank. "I don't understand you," he told her.
> "Because I turn you down?"
> "Because you don't turn anybody else down."
> "Not so consistently." [...]
> "So; why not?" There he'd finally said it. Yay pursed her lips.
> "Because," she said, looking up at him, "it matters to you". (24)

Here, Yay's semi-sarcastic quip that Gurgeh is an "exception" indicates that it is rare for her to turn down sleeping with someone to whom she is genuinely attracted. Perhaps, too, Yay's comments show that her behaviour is exemplary of Culture relationships: it seems that she only engages in sexual relations that are not meaningful on a long-term basis, merely enjoyable in the short term; as Banks notes in *Excession*, in the Culture, "life-long monogamy was not utterly unknown, but it was exceptionally unusual" (321). By patriarchal standards she would seem promiscuous, yet – in the Culture – individuals are encouraged to be free with their sexuality, as it is regarded as an integral part of their personal identity and humanity; also, in many ways, Culture citizens might perhaps feel it natural to do so, as arguably the whole point of the Culture is to fight for the existence and maintenance of such freedoms.

Yay gives her reason for turning Gurgeh down as the fact that their relationship clearly "matters" to Gurgeh: it seems that he feels very strongly about her, and wants their relationship to be more than a series of casual sexual encounters, as seems to be more common practice for both of them. (While Banks could perhaps be construed here as portraying monogamy as undesirable in the Culture, he may simply regard a *life-long* commitment to one other individual as impractical when lifetimes span centuries, and when postscarcity environments radically re-function issues of economic and emotional support.) Yet Yay has further concerns about Gurgeh's slightly hidebound nature: her turning down of Gurgeh may also matter to him for more unsettling reasons. As previously explained in Chapter Two of this book in relation to the Culture's postscarcity nature, Yay believes that Gurgeh sees the act of becoming her lover merely as a form of conquest – the essence of his worldview as a professional game-player: "'I feel you want to... take me,' Yay said, 'like a piece, like an area. To be had; to be... possessed'" (24). Here Yay identifies in Gurgeh further "residual" views from an archaic patriarchal order, which sees women as an inferior sex, and therefore as the "property" of men. These patriarchal views are, in turn, directly reflected in the Empire of Azad, to which Gurgeh is sent on his SC mission.

As with *Phlebas*, where Banks's space-opera tropes mixed the traditional with the subverted, Gurgeh – as initially unreconstructed Handy Man – provides something like a traditional protagonist of the sub-genre that readers would recognise. Gurgeh is only able to defeat Azad when he acknowledges its inherent cruelty, troubling the sympathy for its culture that he feels initially, and Yay will only accept him as her lover – which she eventually does at the text's conclusion – when Gurgeh returns home to Chiark changed by his experiences, with a fuller understanding of the Culture's society and his own nature. Ultimately, Banks deconstructs Gurgeh using this trajectory and, in the final sections of the novel, begins to rebuild him as an ideological subversion of the Handy Man: a more emotional, empathetic, and open-minded individual who is more likely to thrive in the Culture.

As discussed in the previous chapter, Banks's novella 'The State of the Art' provides another complex example of a man, Dervley Linter, who – like Gurgeh – does not sit comfortably within the Culture; yet unlike *Player*, the narrative is ultimately concerned with the Culture's *failure* to reconstruct Linter as one of its own. Before the events of the text, Linter worked in SC, and is suggested to have fitted comfortably within Culture society for several years, but, in 'State', Linter is deliberately "reverting" to an unadorned, human basic form: being stripped of all physical enhancements, including SC privileges, and trying to un-learn his Culture characteristics in order to fit in with the cultures of 1970s' Earth. In discussion with Sma, Linter adopts a version of the anti-utopian attitude that Banks's readers first encountered via Horza in *Phlebas* and then through Gurgeh, which denigrates utopian life as artificial for its focus on culture rather than nature and boring for its lack of conflict and violence: in Linter's heavily romanticised view, the turbulent twentieth-century history of Earth provides authentic experience, precisely because of its imperfections, the threat of violence, and for a truly final death without the possibility of revention. It is clear that Linter conforms much more to the Culture's culture than does Gurgeh, and the strong, equal relations Linter maintains with Sma demonstrate that he is far from a "throwback" to a more primitive society. Yet, as with Gurgeh's relationship to Azad, Linter believes that he can relate better to a patriarchal society, and some of Linter's comments suggest that his quest for a human basic life is also intertwined with a kind of chivalric attitude toward gender relations. He describes his feelings to Sma, stating that: "Well… no, I guess you could say I've changed." He smiled uncertainly. "I'm not the *man* I was" (153, emphasis added). There are three possible interpretations of this comment, hinging on Linter's meaning of the term "man". Firstly, he may use it as a metonym for *hu*manity more generally, indicating that he is now human basic: no longer generally enhanced as a result of the Culture's genetic amendments. Secondly, the comment could be intended as a sexual innuendo, meaning that his genitalia in particular is now unenhanced, suggesting that he is a less-enticing prospect for a sexual partner. A third interpretation, however, reads the comment as suggesting that Linter sees himself as emasculated by the society of the Culture, and that he wishes to become "a real man" in patriarchal terms, perhaps desiring to exhibit an unreconstructed mode of masculinity, or even one of hypermasculinity. Linter's line echoes the kind of trite dialogue common to traditional space opera, with Clio from Smith's *Triplanetary* saying to the novel's hero, Conway Costigan: "You are very much a *man*, my Conway, a real, *real* man," following a scene in which he wins a brawl.[47] Despite Linter's views on the Culture, however, his respectful and equal relationship with Sma could not be further away from that of Clio and Conway, providing a clear example of how far gender roles have advanced in Banks's society.

Linter, then, to some extent exemplifies the more progressive Handy Man achieved by the Culture, yet clearly the fact that he has left SC, as well as his desire to revert to human basic, make his status as such more ambiguous. As with Gurgeh, Linter provides a prominent example of a Handy Man in the series, yet both are located on the Culture's margins in order to achieve a subversion of the archetype. If Gurgeh ultimately performs something of a heroic role in *The Player of Games*, overturning the Culture's enemy, his liminality in relation to the Culture ensures that the problems of such individualist heroism can be challenged and deconstructed. If Linter once represented a defining example of the ideologically reconstructed Handy Man, he comes to demonstrate Csicsery-Ronay's assertion that the Handy Man "may also have more complex, self-contradictory motivations complicating their heroism"[48] – in this case, a flawed desire for tragic, poetic meaning. It is no coincidence that, following her failed debates with Linter, Sma reads "Goethe's *Faust* in German" (163): while Linter's decision may not constitute a literal pact with the devil, Sma bitterly rebukes him because he seems to find Earth, "this... hellhole more fulfilling" (158), aligning him with the "evils" of inequality and violent conflict. Like Goethe's protagonist, Linter is driven by a flawed ambition – motivated by masculine insecurity and romantic illusion – for knowledge and experience of that which is forbidden or has been expelled.

In *Excession*, Banks provides a third unreconstructed male Handy Man, Byr Genar-Hofoen, who does not sit comfortably within the Culture yet is still employed by Contact. Contact is aware of Genar-Hofoen's nature, employing him in fact *because of* rather than *in spite of* his faults. The novel's various plot threads are loosely connected by the sudden appearance of the Excession, a Big Dumb Object in outer space, which – like Clarke's Monolith from 'The Sentinel' and *2001: A Space Odyssey*, or the enigmatic titular spacecraft from *Rendezvous with Rama* – remains largely impervious to understanding, yet seems to pose a potential threat

[47] E.E. "Doc" Smith, *Triplanetary* (St Albans: Granada Publishing Ltd, 1975), 122.
[48] Csicsery-Ronay, *Seven Beauties*, 247.

to the Culture and other Involved civilisations. Genar-Hofoen is similar to the Culture's mercenary Handy Men – Zakalwe for his tendency towards aggression, and Gurgeh for his ability to empathise closely with the Culture's antagonists – which therefore leaves him well-suited to gathering information about troublesome civilisations such as the deeply aggressive Affront, which intends to exploit the Excession for its own gain. And as with Linter, the Culture hopes that the mission process of Contact will work to reconstruct Genar-Hofoen, yet, on this occasion, it is largely unable to bring him around to its way of thinking.

It is a testament to the Culture's lack of social coercion that, upon joining Contact, Genar-Hofoen is able to act as a stereotypical male lothario. Even living in the Culture with its liberal sexual mores, where sexual openness is accepted and encouraged, Genar-Hofoen objectifies women and views them as conquests; he approaches the task of bedding as many women as possible "with a single-minded determination and dedication" (323). At the start of *Excession*, Genar-Hofoen attends a formal dinner with the Affront, the latter of which Mendlesohn describes as "reminiscent of satirical descriptions of the British gentry of the huntin', shootin' and fishin' sort",[49] and Banks clearly satirises their highly patriarchal, hypermasculine, and militaristic culture, through elaborate displays of competition, strength, and machismo. As Genar-Hofoen displays a number of these traits himself, he soon bonds with the Affront officers, acting comfortably at "an all-male gathering [...] therefore likely to be fairly boisterous even by Affronter standards" (33). As such, Genar-Hofoen is the clearest example of the unreconstructed Handy Man in Banks's series, and the character who would best fit into a traditional space opera written around the time of the Golden Age.

Genar-Hofoen's willingness to bond with the Affront affects more than just his attitude towards sex and ethics, however, as soon after the dinner he states that: "all I want is an Affronter body, one that I can just zap into and... well, just *be* an Affronter" (63). Genar-Hofoen indicates that this change would aid relations between the Culture and the Affront, therefore serving a professional purpose, seeing the ability to become like those with whom the Culture has alliance as key to understanding their society. Yet it becomes clear that Genar-Hofoen wishes to become like the Affront because he relates more to their culture than he does to his own. While Linter's casting aside of his augmented body ("arguably the most reliable signifier of Culture status") for that of a human basic signifies a rejection of the Culture for that of an older, romanticised humanity, Genar-Hofoen's denunciation of the Culture in

---

[49] Mendlesohn, 'Iain M. Banks: *Excession*', 561.

favour of the Affront is more severe: signifying reversion to a specific version of society characterised by extreme patriarchy. The Affront rely upon a "sub-class of oppressed females" and others deemed inferior, who are subjected regularly to rape and other practices of sexual torture (168) – all of which Genar-Hofoen is said to be aware of, yet able to write off as an unfortunate "degree of exploitation" deemed "necessary in a developing culture" (170); indeed, he seems opposed to Contact's processes of de-colonisation. Upon being shown the heads of three Affront adversaries mounted as trophies upon the wall, Genar-Hofoen "found himself laughing wryly" even though he was aware that this was "just the kind of attribute the Culture in general [...] found to be such a source of despair" (28), suggesting a degree of complicity with their cruelty, despite his prior justifications.

As with Gurgeh, *Excession* traces Genar-Hofoen's conflicted relationship with the Culture in a narrative of dissatisfaction, rejection, conflict, and a form of resolution; yet it is a personal, romantic relationship rather than a political, professional one that ultimately helps to mediate Genar-Hofoen's hypermasculinity. Against the background of political turmoil and galactic intrigue that occupies the major plot threads of the novel, Banks tells the story of the relations between Genar-Hofoen and his lover, former Contact agent Dajeil Gelian, who – at the start of *Excession* – have been estranged for many years, due to a violent, near-fatal incident between the pair. In this manner, as Mendlesohn observes: "*Excession* is a novel of romance, of the day to day of lives lived through great events,"[50] in which "Ruritanian romance gives way to the affectionate satire Jane Austen brought to military balls."[51] Dajeil and Genar-Hofoen's relationship is similar to that between Gurgeh and Yay in *Player*, with the woman attempting to change the man to a more progressive way of thinking and acting. Just as Yay was concerned that Gurgeh merely wished to "possess" her like a game piece, and Gurgeh initially exhibited such a tendency, Genar-Hofoen reacts to Dajeil's initial reluctance to sleep with him by deciding "he would *win* her" (323, emphasis added). While Dajeil does not object to her future partner's promiscuity in principle, she associates it with a fundamental childishness: "He could never grow and develop as a human being until he went beyond this infantile obsession with penetration and possession" (324). Eager to please Dajeil, Genar-Hofoen tries to overcome these problematic aspects of his identity, stating that "she was the still point in his life he needed [...] she was his lesson"

[50] Mendlesohn, 'Iain M. Banks: *Excession*', 559.
[51] Mendlesohn, 'Iain M. Banks: *Excession*', 562.

(324). In this manner, Dajeil's attitude represents the influence of the Culture more generally, as does this process of bringing Genar-Hofoen around to being considerate and equal in his treatment of his partner. Yet Genar-Hofoen has not changed: even though the pair decide to have children together, with both becoming simultaneously pregnant (as is possible through the process of Mutualling described below), Genar-Hofoen cheats on Dajeil leading to a violent incident, and the couple split up for many years. While the pair reconcile their differences at the end of the novel, Genar-Hofoen's mode of masculinity cannot be fully reconstructed through his relationship with Dajeil, as occurs with Gurgeh and Yay, and, like Linter, Genar-Hofoen is resolute about his decision to leave the Culture: at the end of *Excession*, Genar-Hofoen leaves the Culture for the Affront, and – adopting an Affronter body – finds love amongst this new community. When the Culture forces the Affront to surrender, Genar-Hofoen's assimilation is suggested to represent the beginning of a new era of peace between the two civilisations, as well as for Genar-Hofoen himself. Using three examples of male characters that struggle to adapt to the Culture's society, then, Banks provides examples of the Handy Man archetype, roughly commensurate with those from traditional space opera. These characters can then be deconstructed and remodelled in accordance with Banks's progressive agenda (as with Gurgeh), remodelled in a reverse process that demonstrates the Culture's reconstructed mode of masculinity (as with Linter), or demonstrate that, even if the Culture's utopian process may not work for all, none are forced to stay (as with Genar-Hofoen).

The Handy Woman

Gurgeh, Linter, and Genar-Hofoen, then, fulfil the Handy Man role, existing in an ambiguous relationship with the Culture. Yet it is more common for those fulfilling the role of Handy Men in the series who have less problematic relations with the Culture – current Contact/SC agents, for example – to be identified as women, as in the following six cases: Perosteck Balveda from *Phlebas*; Diziet Sma from *Weapons*, 'State', and briefly *Surface*; Doctor Vosill from *Inversions*; Djan Seriy Anaplain in *Matter*; Yime Nsokyi in *Surface*; and Tefwe in *Hydrogen*.[52] In

---

[52] Tefwe perhaps stands out from the others in this list as she occupies a very minor role in the novel – depicted across only a few pages – compared with other Handy Women in the series, who, even as minor characters, play a significant, sustained role.

'State', for example, Sma functions as a kind of ethnographic variant of the Handy Woman, who uses her research knowledge base, attuned observational skills, and social intuition as Tools with which she can help achieve her Contact mission to dissuade Linter from renouncing the Culture and its values. In this novella, Banks gives her a somewhat more personal and less dangerous role than in the earlier novel *Weapons*, in which Sma is required to perform a more traditional variant of the Handy Woman, in a mission of political intervention relying largely on technological Tools.

Csicsery-Ronay discusses the emergence of the Handy Women as "a variant that can bring with it enormous alterations in ideological import, supplanting a colonialist–patriarchal myth with a critical feminist one; or, alternatively, merely replacing an explicit male agent with a one-of-the-boys figure identified with phallocratic values."[53] Banks's series coincided with an increased appearance of Handy Women characters in space opera, especially in visual media, displaying both critical and conservative variation. Ellen Ripley from the original *Alien* trilogy provides by far the most widely discussed and well-regarded representations of the Handy Woman in space opera: "Ripley metamorphosizes from heroic survivor, to heroic surrogate mother, to tragically compromised carrier, to *Alien Resurrection*'s solo cyborg-dyke-warrior-leader-xenomorph-mother, the appropriator of every available form of power."[54] Lois McMaster Bujold's Captain Cordelia Naismith from the novel *Shards of Honour* (1986) is also one of the most fully realised women characters in the sub-genre, who has agency throughout instances of initial capture and subsequent command. Bujold refuses to allow Naismith to be defined solely by her relationship with Captain Lord Aral Vorkosigan, and the emotional depth of the former is most evident in scenes relating to the ill-health and complex birth of their son Miles in *Barrayar* (1991). Kara "Starbuck" Thrace from the *Battlestar Galactica* franchise (1978–2010) certainly acts as a one-of-the-boys figure in order to survive upon the Battlestar, but actress Katee Sackhoff's "take on the fleet's most mesmerizing fighter jock", as Hugh Hart argues, "doubtless continues to render gender utterly irrelevant",[55] making her "one of television's most complex, ever-evolving characters".[56] John

---

[53] Csicsery-Ronay, *Seven Beauties*, 248–249.
[54] Csicsery-Ronay, *Seven Beauties*, 208.
[55] Hugh Hart, 'Strong Women Steer Battlestar Galactica's Final Voyage', *Wired*, 15 January 2009. Web.
[56] Kat Angus, 'Katee Sackhoff returns to Earth', *Canwest News Service*, 2 September 2009. Web.

Clute describes Tabitha Jute, protagonist of Colin Greenland's *Take Back Plenty* (1990), as a "tough female space-tramp who runs her own ship and is in all sorts of trouble";[57] in this sense, she is the mercenary anti-hero typical of New Space Opera and cyberpunk, yet Greenland allows her greater depth of character through the complex friendship she maintains with the AI of her space barge, the Alice Liddell. In 1995, the *Star Trek* franchise introduced its first female lead protagonist, Kathryn Janeway, Captain of the USS *Voyager*, "as a role model to girls and women, an example of a future in which there was no gender bias, in which women could achieve anything they wanted".[58]

The issue of critical/conservative variation that Csicsery-Ronay raises is especially relevant to Banks's depictions of female SC operatives and characters, as critics have identified elements of both in his portrayals. On the one hand, Janice M. Bogstad has asserted that "A younger generation of Anglo-American and European writers, including Iain Banks [...] has done much to challenge the stereotypical constructions of Golden Age and cyberpunk texts," isolating the character Sharrow from Banks's non-Culture SF novel *Against a Dark Background* (1993) as a prime example.[59] On the other hand, in a review of the later novel *Matter*, Gwyneth Jones challenges Banks's portrayal of SC agent Djan Seriy Anaplian, and by implication those of other SC agents in the series, as "one of Iain M. Banks's trademark 'perfect girlfriend' tough females"[60]; while Jones does not develop this comment, she seems to suggest that Banks's characters offer mere male wish fulfilment, and that his depictions of people in a post-sexist society merely revert to clichéd tropes, rather than imagining the fresh gender identities made possible under such circumstances. Jones, by implication, suggests that Djan and other SC agents merely represent the trend identified by Csicsery-Ronay where Handy Men are replaced with ostensibly progressive, female operatives, who really represent "a one-of-the-boys figure identified with phallocratic values". Bogstad, however, praises the way Banks "uses female-viewpoint characters" and gives them "lives outside their sexuality", as well as the way "Banks is able to turn the classic space

---

[57] John Clute, 'Greenland, Colin', in *The Encyclopedia of Science Fiction*, Clute et al., eds. (London: Gollancz, 2018), updated 31 August 2018. http://www.sf-encyclopedia.com/entry/greenland_colin.

[58] M.A. Bowring, 'Resistance Is Not Futile: Liberating Captain Janeway from the Masculine–Feminine Dualism of Leadership', *Gender, Work & Organization* 11 (2004): 381–405. doi:10.1111/j.1468-0432.2004.00239.

[59] Bogstad, 'Men Writing Women', 176.

[60] Gwyneth Jones, 'Review of *Matter*', *Strange Horizons*, 14 April 2008. http://strangehorizons.com/non-fiction/reviews/matter-by-iain-m-banks.

opera SF theme into a true future vision of societies where all humans – male, female, and even robotic sentients as large as entire spaceships – enjoy positions of agency".[61] Yet challenging Jones's reading, Banks develops Djan Seriy Anaplain – one of several view-point characters in *Matter* – as a three-dimensional character throughout the narrative, providing her with narrative agency and an integral role in the political outcome of the novel, as well as a Handy Woman with a subtly fluid gender identity that subverts the archetype with feminist values.

Matter, the Handy Woman, and the Wife at Home

Matter, published in 2008, was the eighth text in the series, marking Banks's return to that universe after an eight-year break. As with *Inversions*, *Matter* concerns the Culture's relations with a significantly less technologically developed society, the Shellworld of Sursamen, as they become linked by Djan's turbulent personal history. Sursamen is a feudal, pre-industrial habitat, organised according to a divinely appointed monarchy which is as patriarchal as it is militaristic. Djan's father is King Hausk and her mother a woman named Anaplia; she has two brothers – Ferbin and Oramen – from different mothers. Djan's birth was marred by tragedy: Anaplia collapsed whilst pregnant and King Hausk had to choose between saving his wife and saving their child. As they were unsure of the baby's sex, King Hausk chose to save the baby over its mother, hoping it would be male, and therefore a suitable heir in this system of patrilineal descent (124). Disappointed that the child was a girl, and irrationally blaming Djan for her mother's death, King Hausk banishes his daughter while she is still a child: Djan, however, who had secretly hoped to escape the cruel, prejudiced society of Sursamen anyway, longing to join the Culture, eventually does so, achieving her dream of becoming an SC operative. Prince Ferbin, who has been wrongfully accused of treason and requires her help, eventually calls Djan back to Sursamen.

In this manner, the narrative of *Matter* reverses the gender expectations inherent in the archetypes of both Handy Man and Wife at Home: Djan is the Handy Woman, returning to her "home" – at least in an ancestral sense – in order to save her brother Ferbin. Yet, at one stage, Djan states that often she awakens "with a pang of homesickness, sometimes in tears" knowing that she has dreamed of the Culture: "The details of the dream itself were not important; what exercised her on waking was that it was the kind of dream she had

[61] Bogstad, 'Men Writing Women', 176.

always associated with *home*" (289). What Djan considers her home, then, is not where she was born but where she feels most free and most comfortable: Sursamen is now no longer her home but the site of her adventure as Handy Woman, and it is the place in which she has *chosen* to live, for which she longs. At the novel's conclusion, rather than a reunion of adventurer and partner to achieve the conventional *technologiade* closure, the narrative becomes similar to that of a classical tragedy, with Djan and Ferbin both performing acts of self-sacrifice, and all but one other character being killed. *Matter* provides a rare occasion when an SC operative actually dies, seemingly without the possibility of resurrection: at the end of the text, when Sursamen faces destruction from a monstrous machine created by a rival civilisation, the only way that Djan can save her home world is to sacrifice her own life by detonating a bomb that is part of her neural lace, leaving her with no possibility that her soul can be retrieved. Djan, then, provides a crucial example of a female character in the Culture series who is given narrative prominence and agency, and whom Banks develops as a Handy Woman, subverting the phallocratic expectations inherent in the original Handy Man archetype.

As with the Handy Man, the Wife at Home is another trope of *technologiade* fiction that is clearly gendered. As Csicsery-Ronay explains, in more conservative adventure narratives, even the most dedicated Handy Man often returns home eventually, however reluctantly, and they are almost always met there by their patient wife or female partner, in an affirmation of the norms of patriarchal society. At the conclusion of Verne's *Journey to the Centre of the Earth* (1864), for example, narrator Axel Lidenbrock becomes "the happiest of men, for my pretty Virland girl", Martha, who takes on "responsibilities in the house in Königstrasse as both wife and niece."[62] While largely absent from such narratives, it is the function of the Wife at Home to "secure the stability of domestic relations", representing "rooted tradition, the foot of the compass that does not move."[63] Regardless of the exotic people and locales that the Handy Man encounters on his journeys, the narrative logic of such stories almost always suggests a final return to "normality", and a reassertion of traditional values.

Banks's prominent inclusion of this trope is unusual, given Csicsery-Ronay's observation that – unlike other *technologiade* tropes – "the function of the Wife at Home becomes strikingly muted in sf, for

---

[62] Jules Verne, *Journey to the Centre of the Earth* (New York: Oxford University Press, 1992), 185.
[63] Csicsery-Ronay, *Seven Beauties*, 234.

clear-cut reasons. There is not much home in sf."[64] In a galaxy where interstellar travel and intergalactic communication are easy and commonplace, the notions of domestic stability and a nuclear family frequently become non-existent. Even though this is the case with the Culture's galaxy, Yay's function in *The Player of Games*, for example, is close to the traditional Wife at Home archetype: after Handy Man Gurgeh completes his mission, he returns to Yay, who finally acquiesces to sleeping with him, her doubts about his character overcome; this is similar to Verne's *Journey*, where Martha becomes betrothed to Axel only after the overcautious scholar has been changed by his journey. *Player* provides a progressive overhaul of the *technologiade* ending, however, as the wavering polarity of Gurgeh's political compass is already linked to a radically utopian environment by Yay, who, like Sma, embodies the Culture's values, and ultimately it is Yay who helps to ideologically re-root Gurgeh back in utopia after he had begun to identify with the dystopia of the Azadians.

Player's final image, before the Coda, is of Gurgeh observing the beautiful snow-covered fjords of Chiark, and finally allowing himself to cry (307) – these tears implicitly caused by his happiness at returning safely to a beautiful home, rather than in frustration at his adventures coming to an end. Here, Gurgeh's outpouring of emotion reveals characteristics strongly associated with femininity, an indication that his journey may have helped balance his otherwise prominently masculine traits of stoicism and egotistical dominance. Gurgeh's implicit final acceptance of the Culture gives the novel a conservative ending in strictly narrative terms, and perhaps in relation to Yay's role, although a more progressive one in terms of this particular Handy Man's overall ideological trajectory.

While Yay conforms to the Wife at Home in many ways, she is at least not portrayed as a passive figure, as exemplified by her freedom to turn down Gurgeh's advances in the first place – which he discusses with her but without appearing to pressurise her – and by the fact that Yay sets off travelling as Gurgeh does, and implicitly takes on other lovers as she chooses, in the meantime (85). Even though Yay is not a viewpoint character in the novel, Banks does portray her as having a separate life, living entirely independently from Gurgeh, disrupting the passive, obedient guardian of domestic stability inherent in the original trope.

---

[64] Csicsery-Ronay, *Seven Beauties*, 255.

Reproduction and Child-rearing

Banks's essay 'A Few Notes on the Culture' provides some details of the everyday lives of typical Culture citizens, including about social and familial living arrangements, and specifically the common practices in relation to the birth and nurturing of children:

> In terms of personal relations and family groupings, the Culture is, predictably, full of every possible permutation and possibility, but the most common life-style consists of groups of people of mixed generations linked by loose family ties living in a semi-communal dwelling or group of dwellings; to be a child in the Culture is to have a mother, perhaps a father, probably not a brother or sister, but large numbers of aunts and uncles, and various cousins.[65]

So the average Culture child grows up as part of a loose group (never depicted in detail in the series), living with a parent or parents and what we understand as their "extended family", probably in a very close-knit environment with a high level of participatory and shared experience, as suggested by the phrase "communal dwelling". Banks's reference to a "small-scale democratic process" that helps "supervise the child's subsequent development" in the "rare event of a parent maltreating a child" further substantiates the Mind's state role, as argued in Chapter One of this book, suggesting a social services function.

Children feature seldom in the series, specifically Culture children even less, and when they are depicted it is generally brief and circumstantial. As Banks explains through narration in *Look to Windward*:

> It was one of the effects of living in a society where people commonly lived for four centuries and on average bore just over one child each that there were very few of their young around, and – as these children tended to stick together in their own society – there seemed to be even fewer than there really were. (140)

Linter affirms this point in 'The State of the Art', when he compares the Culture to Earth, stating of the latter: "you see a lot more children on a planet like this" (194). Chomba from *Look to Windward* is one notable example of a Culture child depicted in the sequence, offering some insight into their life. Chomba explains some of the Culture's ways to the alien visitor Kabe, outlining the fitting of a neural implant, a device

---

[65] Banks, 'A Few Notes on the Culture'. Web.

that acts as a mind–computer interface, which "was about as close as some bits of the Culture got to a formal adult initiation rite" (*Windward*, 141). This detail suggests that the Culture reimagines and modernises tradition rather than simply abandoning it, wherever possible, so long as it does not breach its anti-exploitation commitment.

There is another aspect of this familial framework that Banks establishes, however, which has greater significance for his portrayal of gender and biological sex in an ostensibly post-patriarchal society. Considering the above long quotation from 'A Few Notes on the Culture', Sherryl Vint draws attention to Banks's use of the term "mother", arguing that it provides a further example of essentialism in his work: "This notion that the female sex is somehow essentially appropriate to motherhood – even within a social context of continually changing morphologies – again suggests an unacknowledged attachment to understanding our contemporary constructions of the body as 'natural'."[66] The term "mother", then, defined as "a female parent" by the Merriam-Webster dictionary[67] or more problematically as "a woman in relation to a child or children to whom she has given birth"[68] by the OED, is similar to that of "woman" itself, which is often used in a problematic manner, conflating biological sex with gender identity. Given that the Culture's technoscience makes it possible for the human body to be adapted into virtually any form, Vint asks implicitly, why would they still retain such a rigidly binary understanding of biological sex in relation to reproduction? Why must a body that is capable of giving birth still be regarded as innately female and/or feminine, when other physical options could be adopted that would make biology more fluid? Why could Banks not have used a more neutral term such as "parent" instead?

Banks seems to use the term here as shorthand to refer to anyone currently bearing the appropriate form for the *role* of birth-giver, regardless of their sex or gender, even though the term has such connotations. If a key guiding principle of the Culture is a lack of exploitation then its system for reproduction can be seen as justified: no-one is ever forced to have children or not, or stigmatised for their decision, and all combinations of biological makeup, sexual orientation, and gender identity are available freely to all, which makes the fact that only people who have chosen to bear a woman's body at that moment in time can

---

[66] Vint, 'The Culture-al Body', 89.
[67] Merriam-Webster, 'Mother'. www.merriam-webster.com/dictionary/mother.
[68] Oxford Dictionaries, 'Mother', Oxford University Press. www.oxforddictionaries.com/definition/english/mother.

give birth significantly less important. If Banks then does portray the *biology* of reproduction in essentialist terms, the *role* of mother can be freely chosen or rejected, which still seemingly enables the Culture to achieve a post-patriarchal and gender-equal society.

Banks published 'A Few Notes on the Culture' in 1994, based upon ideas that he began developing in the 1970s – a time when it seemed a biological and medical impossibility, even in theory, for cis men and trans women to bring a child to term within their own bodies. His thinking in this regard, then, reflects the time in which he was writing, for it was not until much more recently, in 2015, that successful uterus transplant surgery for cis women, and possibly for cis men and trans women, has been deemed theoretically possible, estimated to occur within the next decade.[69] Perhaps Banks's adherence to the notion of gender essentialism that retains links between women's bodies and giving birth, then, reflects the facts of the context in which he wrote, regardless of the broader intentions underpinning his writing. While society at present has clearly not achieved the "social context of continually changing morphologies" of the Culture, there are many scientific advances that allow physical sex to become fluid to an extent, although not yet with complete freedom. The continued adherence to the notion of women's essential motherhood in Banks's writing therefore also displays a further example of the ways in which his Culture novels fluctuate between depicting an imagined utopian society, and commenting upon the societies of his own lived experience.

However his use of the term is interpreted, Banks does at least affirm the Culture's general total openness to almost all eventualities, specifically in this regard, stating that "the Culture is, predictably, full of every possible permutation and possibility".[70] This could easily include the possibility of pregnant "fathers", or other child-bearing non-mothers, suggesting the only deciding factor is personal choice. Another possible method of reproducing in the Culture, known as Mutualling, is introduced in *Excession*.

---

[69] See Leah Samuel, 'With Womb Transplants a Reality, Transgender Women Dare to Dream of Pregnancy', *StatNews*, 7 March 2016, https://www.statnews.com/2016/03/07/uterine-transplant-transgender/; and Melissa Bailey, 'First Uterus Transplant in the US Gives 26-Year-Old Woman Chance at Pregnancy', *StatNews*, 25 February 2016. www.statnews.com/2016/02/25/uterus-transplant/.

[70] Banks, 'A Few Notes on the Culture'. Web.

Excession: Reproduction through Mutualling

The two lovers Genar-Hofoen (SC Handy Man, who begins the narrative as biologically male) and Dajeil (ex-Handy Woman, who begins the narrative biologically female) chose to reproduce by the process of Mutualling, a method that is complex and unusual, even by Culture standards. Mutualling enables a couple to have two children simultaneously by giving birth to one child each, which is clearly only possible through the Culture's practice of sex-swapping. As Banks explains, "a couple would have a child, then the man would become female and the woman would become male, and they would have another child" (*Excession*, 321–322). Explaining the process of Mutualling in more detail, Banks states that:

> It was possible for a Culture female to become pregnant, but then, before the fertilized egg had transferred from her ovary to the womb, begin the slow change to become a man. The fertilized egg did not develop any further, but neither was it necessarily flushed away or reabsorbed. It could be held, contained, put into a kind of suspended animation so that it did not divide any further, but waited, still inside the ovary. That ovary, of course, became a testicle, but – with a bit of cellular finessing and some intricate plumbing – the fertilized egg could remain safe, viable and unchanging in the testicle while that organ did its bit in fertilizing the woman who had been a man and whose sperm had done the original fertilizing. The man who had been a women then changed back again. If the woman who had been a man also delayed the development of her fertilised egg, then it was possible to synchronize the growth of the two fetuses and the birth of the babies. (*Excession*, 321–322)

So, through Mutualling, the biologically male Genar-Hofoen impregnates a biologically female Dajeil. Then, in the middle of that process, both Dajeil and Genar-Hofoen change sex. Dajeil, now biologically male, also impregnates Genar-Hofoen, who is now biologically female. If the process were to go according to plan, then both individuals would eventually give birth in synchronicity, and then change back to their original sex. Before they can both give birth, however, their relationship deteriorates into bitter argument and eventually violence, with Dajeil attacking the pregnant Genar-Hofoen and perhaps intentionally killing the foetus, after which the couple became estranged for a long time. At the start of the novel, Dajeil – still carrying the foetus created with her former lover – lives in isolation onboard the *Sleeper Service* whilst her personal circumstances can be resolved, pondering her fate and that of her child, about whom she feels deeply ambivalent, given the nature of her former lover.

The process of Mutualling is clearly intended to have a romantic purpose: "To some people in the Culture," Banks notes, this "process was quite simply the most beautiful and perfect way for two people to express their love for one another" (322). By synchronising pregnancies and births, this logic suggests, a couple develops a deeper empathy with each other, having undergone the same experience, and, as Dajeil states, "it seemed... I don't know; more romantic, I suppose, more symmetrical" (320). As such, it works again to highlight the Culture's values of empathy in all of its relationships. Yet Banks's depiction of Mutualling is not without problems. As Vint has noted, Banks retains the notion of two distinct biological sexes in human beings, even within a society that can easily adapt a citizen's biology in any manner they desire: in the Culture, all manner of other reproductive options would be possible, including for example parthenogenesis (as depicted in *Herland*) or another system relying upon a less rigidly binary understanding of biological sex (such as kemmer in Le Guin's *The Left Hand of Darkness*). Again, as with earlier descriptions of sex-swapping, Banks uses the word "mother", relating gender identity to biological process and parental roles: "Within a year a woman who had been capable of carrying a child – who, indeed, might have been a mother – would be a man fully capable of fathering a child" (*Excession*, 322). While these descriptions are still problematic, they again suggest Banks's need for convenient, shorthand, familiar terms in order to make his meaning clear for his readers, indicating the inadequacy of our already-gendered language. Here, it seems clear that the Culture's system seems to support a binary understanding of sex, or at least that the majority of people who live as part of the Culture choose to live this way. While Banks substantiates this to an extent, stating that "generally people eventually changed back to their congenital sex," he does acknowledge the existence of individuals whose sex exists somewhere in between, placing them on a spectrum nonetheless: "some people cycled back and forth between male and female all their lives, while some settled for an androgynous in-between state, finding there a comfortable equanimity" (321–322).

Surface Detail: **Yime as "Neuter"**

The most prominent example of such an individual is Yime Nsokyi from *Surface Detail* – an SC agent working for the secretive subdivision known as "Quietus" that concerns itself with the Sublimed. Yime was born biologically female, but has decided to have her body altered to become effectively "neuter", which Banks describes as "exactly poised between the two standard genders" (210), an androgynous position outside of the traditional gender binary that finds an SF precedent in the "nutes" or neutrals from Ian McDonald's *River of Gods* (2004). When Yime considers her alterations, she also touches herself, putting "one hand down between her legs, to feel the tiny slotted bud – like a third, bizarrely placed nipple – which was all that was left of her genitals. [...] She touched the little bud at her groin again. Just as much like a tiny penis as it was a relocated nipple, she supposed" (210–211).

It seems odd, in this context, for Yime's genitalia to be compared with a male sexual organ when her condition is apparently intended for the express purpose of removing her capacity for sexual pleasure. In this manner, while Banks uses the term "neuter" to describe Yime's body, his physical descriptions seem more akin to an intersexed body – which, as defined by the Intersex Society of North America, includes those: "born with genitals that seem to be in-between the usual male and female types."[71] The Society also specifically notes that "for example, a girl may be born with a noticeably large clitoris",[72] which may in fact be what Yime refers to as her "tiny penis". It is technically only the fact that Yime is left feeling no sexual desire that links the change she has undergone to the word "neuter", when the term is used as verb for the castration of animals.[73] Here, while the Culture often seems quite rigid in its binary understanding of sex, Banks's description suggests that biological sex be considered as a fluid spectrum, with Yime's clitoris seeming so much like a penis.

Yime's decision to alter her biological sex to become neuter in this manner is explicitly linked to her career in Quietus, and seems entirely unrelated to the way that she feels about her physical body. Trans people may choose to alter their sex in order to address "a lack of fit between felt sense of body and external appearance of the body".[74] Yet Yime is not motivated by a condition such as Body Dysmorphic Disorder, for example, perceiving "flaws" in her appearance that remain invisible to others, rather seeing the alteration as a way of dedicating herself to her role: "it had been her choice. A way of making real to herself her

---

[71] The Intersex Society of North America, 'What is Intersex?' 1993–2008. http://www.isna.org/faq/what_is_intersex.
[72] The Intersex Society of North America, 'What is Intersex?'
[73] Dictionary.com, 'Neuter', Random House, Inc. www.dictionary.com/browse/neuter.
[74] Bettcher, 'Feminist Perspectives on Trans Issues'. Web.

dedication to Quietus" (209). Yime's neuterism leaves her no longer feeling sexual desire: "she rubbed the little bud absently, remembering. There was no hint of pleasure in touching herself there any more; she might as well have caressed a knuckle or an ear lobe" (210). Neuterism, therefore, is portrayed as the result of a conscious decision on Yime's part – which activates the "elaborate thought code" of the Culture's sex-swap process – rather than something more innate like a sexual orientation, or a general inclination such as asexuality.[75] As such, Yime's decision is seen as contributing to her Handiness: her ability to function rationally and unemotionally under pressure whilst performing technical problem solving for SC, without emotion and desire interfering. Describing neuterism like taking a vow of "Nun-like" celibacy (209), Yime portrays it without enthusiasm, as something practical and working to a greater good, remaining sceptical about more extreme actions as taken by other members of Quietus – presumably adopting neuterism on a more permanent basis – referring to their "spirit of denial and asceticism" as "taking matters too far" (209). While Yime's neuterism could possibly be classified as a third gender, or exemplifying merely one of many potential genders, Yime suggests that it is only temporary: she "still thought of herself as female, always had," and "of course the decision was entirely reversible. She had wondered about changing back, becoming properly female again" (210).

Again, with Yime, Banks further suggests the Culture's fundamental need to reassert binary gender roles. The possibility of Yime remaining in her neuter or intersex condition on a more long-term or permanent basis does not seem to be considered. While Banks's fiction therefore portrays a position outside of the traditional gender binary as something temporary and unusual, it does not reproduce the problematic, sexist implications of gender swapping in John Varley's *Steel Beach* (1992), for example, where such individuals "find themselves turning into predetermined mirror versions of their inner selves, so that a red-blooded heterosexual male will turn immediately into a deeply "feminine" person obsessed with clothes and boyfriends".[76] The *SF Encyclopaedia* notes that "Characters in Iain M Banks's Culture universe routinely change gender

---

[75] Recent studies have categorised asexuality as a sexual identity alongside hetero- and homosexuality, emphasising the qualitative differences between identity and disorder. See Bella DePaulo, 'Asexuals: Who Are They And Why Are They Important?' 23 December 2009. www.psychologytoday.com/blog/living-single/200912/asexuals-who-are-they-and-why-are-they-important.

[76] John Clute, David Langford, and Cheryl Morgan, 'Transgender SF', in *The Encyclopedia of Science Fiction*, Clute et al., eds. (London: Gollancz, 2018). http://www.sf-encyclopedia.com/entry/transgender_sf.

at will but appear not to change personality much"[77], an observation that we have seen to be the case with Yime and Djan, and which actually works to support the sex–gender distinction in the series despite its more essentialist aspects: changing one's body need not drastically alter one's personality and associated gender identity.

Conclusion

The Culture series represents one of the most successful works of New Space Opera for the ways in which Banks extensively addresses the problematic traditions of the sub-genre, reworking classic narrative tropes into fresh and critical-feminist forms through the introduction of bold ideas drawn from utopian fiction and the New Wave. As such, the series plays with the gendered politics of the sub-genre, with the harmonious, inner-utopias of the Culture proper and the galactic-peacemakers of Contact often portrayed as feminine, while the actions of SC – variously portrayed as aggressive expansion or humanitarian intervention – trouble such distinctions. To reimagine the rugged and casually sexist, scientist/space-explorer Handy Men of E.E. "Doc" Smith or Heinlein's crude jingoistic military space warriors, Banks adopted two simultaneous approaches: deconstructing the vulnerable masculinities of his male SC officers whilst developing Handy Women as feminist/critical variations of the archetype. As Banks offers positive representations of vibrant and independent women protagonists in a sub-genre often regarded as a male-dominated sphere, with women demoted to minor or degrading roles or as occasional protagonists that promote sexist stereotypes, he provides male figures who demonstrate that masculinities are plural and are not fixed, with this state of flux offering the potential for progressive development. Furthermore, Banks's personal image of utopia provides a strong and engaging vision of a society in which patriarchy has been overcome and gender equality achieved through its progressive culture of empathy between genders and its radical advances in biotechnology. By developing his utopia as a place of almost infinitely varied and unconstrained morphology, he potentially places gender on a fluid spectrum, using his series to construct and examine the plethora of situations, bodies, identities, and relationships that may arise. Yet Banks's thinking in this regard suffers from limitations. While Banks began to explore the broader ramifications of a fluid conception of sex and gender with the Culture texts, as he

[77] Clute, Langford, and Morgan, 'Transgender SF'.

had in *The Wasp Factory*, this chapter has further demonstrated the vein of essentialist thought that Vint identifies in the series. As such, like earlier writers of space opera whose thinking often struggled to escape the confines of their immediate social environment, Banks's portrayal of a radically alternate, utopian culture is limited to a certain extent in its minimal and problematic consideration of queer and trans identity, for example, especially compared with canonical works by Le Guin and Russ. Despite this limitation, however, the Culture series undoubtedly provides a vital and, no doubt, long-lasting contribution to the feminist project of progressively re-conceptualising science fiction.

Chapter 5

Reason Shapes the Future
Atheism, Humanism, Quasi-Religion

"Reason shapes the future, but superstition infects the present"
– Iain M. Banks

R.C. Elliott recognised the utopian longings present in myths of the Golden Age and of millenarian visions of the Rapture, but argued that human beings must do more than merely dream of a harmonious society, describing utopia as "man's effort to work out imaginatively what happens – or what might happen – when the primal longings embodied in the myth confront the principle of reality".[1] When Elliott states that "in this effort man no longer merely dreams of a divine state in some remote time; he assumes the role of creator himself",[2] he articulates a call for human beings to actively seize the means of establishing utopia ourselves. So, as with many aspects of human culture, desire to live in a radically more harmonious society may originally derive from religious thought, but modern utopianism, following Elliott, describes humankind bringing such an eventuality about for ourselves, in this life, and in material reality. For Elliott, as for Csicsery-Ronay, "Utopia is the application of man's reason and his will to the myth",[3] and Banks also intended for the Culture to be a utopia founded upon entirely rational, scientific, and human terms. Following his adherence to the principles of Western humanism and the Enlightenment, the Culture claims to embody Banks's firm view that any and all religious beliefs and practices – but especially *institutions* – are fundamentally flawed, out-dated, and cannot provide the means for a happy and harmonious society. As such, the Culture, in its internal structuring and activity, is said to reject all forms of religious institution, all practice and application of theology, any

---

[1] Elliott, *The Shape of Utopia*, 9–10.
[2] Elliott, *The Shape of Utopia*, 9–10.
[3] Elliott, *The Shape of Utopia*, 8.

kind of religious ritual and tradition, and all beliefs based upon faith, superstition, and/or the supernatural – aspects of culture that Banks believed inhibit social progress. Instead, the Culture aims to provide its own material and rational alternatives within the limitless Second Nature of techno-utopia.

Nevertheless, as with much SF that makes similar claims, there are several integral aspects of the Culture – "souls", "gods", "afterlives", and "transcendence", as I identify and discuss below – that suggest the continuation of religious ideas, complicating Banks's thinking generally, and his personal vision of utopia specifically, as entirely secularist and atheistic. Through close readings of *Look to Windward*, *Surface Detail* and *The Hydrogen Sonata*, this chapter explores the complex significances of these "quasi-religious" elements, and the extent to which Banks has successfully recuperated them within his rational and materialist worldview, providing what he called "alternative angles" for looking at religious "dream fulfilment".[4] I argue that Banks was largely successful in this endeavour, and that the Culture is most accurately and most beneficially understood as a materialist, non-spiritual, and non-religious system, achieved using advanced technoscience.

Banks uses these "alternative angles" to provide a variety of different viewpoints on the beliefs and practices of religion. While there is perhaps an underlying degree of respect present in his exploration of the quasi-spiritual transcendence of the Sublime, for example, which he would develop in *Phlebas* and *Hydrogen*, Banks would more frequently use his series to critique, mock, and satirise various religious worldviews that he considered to be anti-rational and anti-scientific, and which he considered to be based upon magical, religious, or spiritual principles. Most significantly, though, Banks would focus the Culture series' critique upon the methods that religious *institutions* use to achieve and maintain positions of dominance (as he also does with the institutions of Neoliberalism and capitalism), especially the Catholic Church, rather than upon cultures that incorporate religious ethics, traditions, or practices per se.

---

[4] Orbit Books website, 'An Interview with Iain M. Banks on the 25th Anniversary of the Culture', 2012. www.orbitbooks.net/interview/iain-m-banks-on-the-25th-anniversary-of-the-culture/.

Banks as "Non-religious" Humanist

We have discussed some of the ways in which Banks's fictions engage with notions of humanism, with his conceptions of the human subject, of gender identity, and of the polymorphic body, often fluctuating between the humanism of the Enlightenment and that of the radically re-envisioned kind known as posthumanism. Yet humanism was not just one of many philosophies that Banks discussed in his fiction: he lived his life in accordance with a humanist worldview. As well as a distinguished supporter of the Humanist Society of Scotland (which reported 15,000 members in 2018),[5] Banks was an Honorary Associate of the National Secular Society, and he described himself as having been a "militant" and "evangelical" atheist for "over twenty years".[6] He would articulate his views on religion and philosophy in articles for publications from the Rationalist Association, such as *New Humanist* magazine, frequently throughout his career.[7] Banks married his second wife, Adele, in 2013 at a Humanist wedding at Inverlochy Castle Hotel, Scotland, and – when Banks unfortunately passed away shortly afterwards – his family and friends attended a Memorial Ceremony in Stirling led by a Humanist Celebrant.[8] Banks frequently spoke out publically against what he regarded as religious privilege in society, most notably when in 2009 he published letters in national newspapers, such as *The Times*, arguing that state funding for faith schools should be stopped as they "foster sectarianism".[9]

Banks would use both modes of his fiction to passionately explore this worldview, with the realism of his mainstream fiction often allowing for this message to be conveyed most directly. This is most notable in *The Wasp Factory* with its scathing satire of religious indoctrination and ritual,

---

[5] See Humanist Society Scotland website, 'About Humanist Society Scotland': www.humanism.scot/what-we-do/about-hss/; and Humanism, 'Tributes Pour In For Our Distinguished Supporter Iain Banks', June 2013. https://www.humanism.scot/what-we-do/news/tributes-pour-in-for-our-distinguished-supporter-iain-banks/.

[6] See author profile at: Secularism, 'Iain Banks (1954–2013)'. www.secularism.org.uk/iainbanks.html.

[7] For example, see *New Humanist*, 'Q&A: Iain Banks', *New Humanist* 127, no. 4 (July/August 2012). newhumanist.org.uk/articles/2832/qa-iain-banks.

[8] See Stephan McGinty, 'Iain Banks marries in his favourite place', *Scotsman*, 8 August 2013. www.scotsman.com/lifestyle/books/iain-banks-marries-in-his-favourite-place-1-2882190.

[9] John Robertson, 'Iain Banks: Stop Funding for Faith Schools', *Times*, 16 August 2009. www.thesundaytimes.co.uk/sto/news/uk_news/article182309.ece.

The Crow Road (1992) which uses the *bildungsroman* form to playfully and ironically explore the relationships between agnosticism, atheism, and more idiosyncratic personal belief systems,[10] and *Whit* (1995) in which Banks returned to the satirical mode, deconstructing the arcane rituals and illogical beliefs of a fictitious Scottish cult through a sympathetic portrayal of one of their naïve members, and exposing the cult's leader as a charlatan.[11] Similarly, Banks used the Culture series to critique and deconstruct religious worldviews, frequently drawing upon the techniques of defamiliarisation and estrangement that are core to the SF genre. The texts in the series most notable for their engagement with such themes are as follows. In *Consider Phlebas*, the uncompromising religious fundamentalism of the Idiran Empire is at the heart of a hugely destructive war between this civilisation and the atheistic Culture, which Rob Duggan reads as mirroring the "Clash of Civilisations" in the first Gulf War.[12] *Look to Windward* explores the results of a failed attempt by the Culture to reform Chelgrian society, built upon a draconian caste system and a Viking-esque belief that those who died in battle will earn their place in the afterlife. In both *Matter* and *The Hydrogen Sonata*, Banks establishes the elaborate cosmological and spiritual beliefs of a religious society, only to gradually undermine the principles upon which this belief is built, as well as the institutions that maintain them, in a similar manner to *The Wasp Factory* and *Whit*. In *Surface Detail*, Banks pits the Culture against various societies that use sadistic afterlives as both deterrent from and punishment for transgression in life.

So Banks's worldview was shaped significantly by his adherence to a form of humanism, which fed – often directly – into his fiction. But what exactly did he understand "humanism" to mean? Rosi Braidotti, for example, describes the progressive political creed of Enlightenment humanism as "the transformation of the Christian doctrine of salvation into a project of universal human emancipation",[13] yet Banks's understanding of humanism claims to reject ties with religion altogether. Asked how he understands the term, Banks explained to Jude Roberts that:

> I think I fit the dictionary definition of a Humanist pretty well: non-religious, non-superstitious, basing morality on shared human values of decency, tolerance, reason, justice, the search for truth,

---

[10] Iain Banks, *The Crow Road* (London: Abacus, 1992).
[11] Iain Banks, *Whit* (London: Abacus, 1995), 10.
[12] Duggan, 'Iain M. Banks, Postmodernism and the Gulf War'.
[13] Braidotti, *The Posthuman*, 31.

and so on. My personal take on this goes a little further – as any serious SF writer's would kind of have to unless they reject the very idea of both AI and aliens – to encompass the rights both of these (as it were, still potential) categories, but other than that I'm probably fairly typical.[14]

Speaking in 2012, Banks would further clarify his views as a "non-religious" humanist and atheist: "I think a lot of us were naïve and thought that religion would quietly slip away [...] Religion should have sloped off embarrassed by now."[15] Certainly Banks's native country can be closely associated with rapid secularisation, with national census statistics showing that the number of people identifying as atheist in Scotland rose by almost 10 per cent between 2001 and 2011, while those who identified as Christian fell by almost 12 per cent during this time period.[16] Yet, on a broader scale, as Braidotti observes, "The first cracks in the edifice of self-assured secularity appeared at the end of the 1970s," which helps to frame Banks's series in part as a secularist–atheist response to the "wave of conversions to a variety of conventional monotheistic or imported Eastern religions" that followed the "revolutionary zeal" of the 1960s.[17] Following this pattern, Banks conceded that, post-9/11, the progressive belief in inevitable religious decline had clearly waned, and he bemoaned the rise in religious fundamentalism. By continuing to value religion, Banks argued, humanity is rendered "embarrassing" and "gullible".[18]

Following this, then, we can easily see how Banks's personal views on religion fed into his development of the Culture. When Zakalwe observes the following in *Weapons*, "There are no Gods, we are told, so I must make my own salvation" (233), and he proposes a toast to the Culture's "total lack of respect for all things majestic" (259), we find another example of the Culture's attitude once again reflecting Banks's own. Similarly, *Phlebas* protagonist Horza explains how the Culture views monotheists:

---

[14] Roberts, 'A Few Questions about the Culture'.
[15] Parsons, 'Interview: Iain Banks'. Web.http://www.wired.com/underwire/2010/10/iain-banks/3/.
[16] The Scottish Government, 'Analysis of Religion in the 2011 Census', 17 May 2006, https://www.gov.scot/publications/analysis-religion-2001-census/pages/2/; and National Records of Scotland, 'Religion (detailed)', Scotland's Census 2011. https://www.scotlandscensus.gov.uk/documents/censusresults/release2a/rel2A_Religion_detailed_Scotland.pdf.
[17] Braidotti, *The Posthuman*, 31.
[18] Parsons, 'Interview: Iain Banks'. Web.

the Culture's attitude to somebody who believed in an omnipotent God was to pity them, and to take no more notice of the substance of their faith than one would take of the ramblings of somebody claiming to be Emperor of the Universe. The nature of belief wasn't totally irrelevant – along with the person's background and upbringing, it might tell you something about what had gone wrong with them – but you didn't take their views *seriously*. (*Phlebas*, 157)

Horza's views must be treated with caution due to his vocal hatred of the Culture, yet these comments still clearly chime with Banks's depiction of his utopia, and with his own views. But, despite his vehemence, Banks's attitude was not to "pity" religious people in the patronising manner that Horza suggests, and he certainly did not adopt the belligerent and aggressive tone sometimes associated with Dawkins or other New Atheists.[19] In an interview for BBC Radio 4 about *The Wasp Factory*, Banks was asked if he considered religion "a waste of time", to which he tactfully responded: "nothing that people believe in to that degree is entirely wrong or wasted". While religion is "technically wrong" he argued, "it tells us about ourselves, about what we want to believe, about what we wish to be the case. I don't want to denigrate anyone's belief in any particular religion because it means something to them."[20] To Banks, then, religious beliefs remain relevant to a certain extent – for an understanding of psychology and as a coping mechanism for individuals – but he clearly regards such views as antiquated and redundant. Perhaps, then, despite Horza's cynicism, the Culture's attitude towards faith could be similarly characterised as politely tolerant and respectful, but with the sense that they are humouring such views, and – as Horza notes – not taking them too seriously. For ultimately, the Culture itself – as the City of Handiness – is presented as the natural result of the increased rationalisation of humankind, directly commensurate with the decline of religious beliefs and institutions. The more we learn about the world through science and reason, Banks implies, the more we will become embarrassed by our supernatural interpretations and narrow understandings, until eventually we no longer see the need for such a way of thinking at

---

[19] See, for example, Sophie Elmhurst's article 'Is Richard Dawkins destroying his reputation?' *Guardian*, 9 June 2015. www.theguardian.com/science/2015/jun/09/is-richard-dawkins-destroying-his-reputation.

[20] BBC Radio 4, 'Iain Banks: *The Wasp Factory*', *Bookclub*, 10 November 2011. Quote, circa 15:00 in clip. www.bbc.co.uk/programmes/b016w0nf.

all. This suggests that, despite their tolerance of believers, becoming a Culture citizen is a kind of process that ultimately entails coming to view the universe in a more rational manner. Religion then is being, or may already have been, "Cultured out" of Banks's secular heaven: to be a religious Culture citizen, therefore, seems something of an oxymoron.

It has long been argued that the withdrawal of religion from society in this manner is essential for a form of utopia to exist, as A.C. Grayling explains, arguing for humanism as the natural replacement:

> Because humanism draws on 2,500 years of non-religious ethical thinking since Socrates, it is a deep, rich tradition of insight, wisdom and inspiration, and it is this without any supernaturalistic beliefs involved. That means that it offers the possibility of truly global ethics that everyone could live by. Consider a utopia in which people, having been liberated from religion at last, can agree to base their ethics on a generous view of human nature and needs.[21]

Here Grayling implies that humankind cannot live together in harmony and prosperity without a purely rational manner of thinking that unites us all through a shared sense of identity, drawn from our common heritage as the same species; and it seems an outline of both humanism and utopia that Banks would agree with.

Yet Stephen Law challenges this atheistic understanding of humanism supported by figures such as Banks and Grayling, arguing that "non-religious" humanism is merely one way of being a humanist. As Law states, "clearly, many humanists consider religion, not just false, but dangerous. Some even view religion as a great evil. But not all", and Law emphasises the fact that religious people may also identify as humanist, or collaborate with humanist projects.[22] Furthermore, Law also argues that "a humanist need not be a utopian, convinced that the application of science and reason will inevitably usher in a Brave New World of peace and contentment."[23] More specifically, therefore, we can locate Banks's particular understanding of humanism in accordance with the general stance of the British Humanist Association (BHA), an organisation

---

[21] A.C. Grayling, 'Humanism's faith in reason represents our best hope', *Guardian*, 3 March 2013. www.theguardian.com/commentisfree/2013/mar/03/humanism-religion-reason-our-best-hope.

[22] Stephen Law, *A Very Short Introduction to Humanism* (Oxford: Oxford University Press, 2011), 6–7.

[23] Law, *A Very Short Introduction to Humanism*, 4.

that regularly presents such views as "typical", with its promotion of a stridently anti-religious, and firmly atheistic/agnostic, message.[24]

Turning back to Banks's utopia, it is relatively easy to identify the Culture as an example of a humanist civilisation, in a very broad sense, following a neutral definition provided by Corliss Lamont: "one in which the principles of the Humanist philosophy are dominant and find practical embodiment in laws, institutions, economics, culture, and indeed all the most significant aspects of individual and social life".[25] The Culture's fundamentally socialist economic system, for example, geared towards equal treatment of human beings, is as rational and logical as it is profoundly moral; using extremely advanced computers to fulfil state functions seems to epitomise a rational approach; enabling citizens full control of their own bodies and lifespans demonstrates the "practical embodiment" of humanism in the most literal way; and SC's missions (such as in *Inversions*) often form a humanistic version of the *technologiade* metanarrative. Yet, as we have touched on already, the relationship between humanism and the Culture is more complex still and warrants closer inspection.

As discussed in Chapter Three, Sherryl Vint has clearly identified humanism as an integral aspect of Banks's conception of the Culture, as well as identifying important problems relating to this conception. Vint challenges Banks's humanist thinking for its essentialism, and argues that it amounts to a homogenisation of our varied human experiences, but she does not challenge the Culture's fundamental rationality and secularity. As we have heard, Banks intended the Culture as his "personal utopia" or "secular heaven", with every element, from terminal to Orbital, representing the zenith of technoscientific achievement. Yet, like the term "humanism", "secularism" can be understood variously, meaning more than simply *without* religion. According to Stephen Law, "secular" means that the "state takes a *neutral position* with respect to religion",[26] which has ramifications for our understanding of the Culture's structure. If the Minds are understood as a minarchy, then their role as state function is so minimal and ad hoc that it would scarcely seem to problematise their relationship with religion, as this understanding characterises them as largely neutral towards almost all

---

[24] See 'About Humanism' on the BHA website: https://humanism.org.uk/humanism/; for further discussion on this debate, see Tom Flynn, 'What is Religious Humanism – really?' *Center for Inquiry*, 23 August 2012. www.centerforinquiry.net/blogs/entry/what_is_religious_humanism_--_really/.

[25] Corliss Lamont, *The Philosophy of Humanism* (London: Pemberton Publishing Co Ltd, [1949] 1965), 273.

[26] Law, *A Very Short Introduction to Humanism*, 3. Emphasis added.

actions of Culture citizens anyway – regardless of their personal views. If the Culture is understood as fully anarchic, and the Minds do not perform the role of state, then the question of the relationship between "church and state", as it were, becomes moot. The Culture, however, clearly does fulfil state functions to some extent, as argued in Chapter One, so it would necessarily need to provide any citizen with the freedom "to follow and espouse, or reject and criticize, both religious and atheist beliefs."[27] Describing the Culture as secular, then, clearly becomes more complex in light of this definition and given the implications of the Culture's "total lack of respect for all things majestic" for its citizens.

Further complicating this issue, my discussion prompts the question: given the alleged pluralism and freedom of the Culture, could one of its citizens become religious in some manner if they wished, without engendering disharmony? Even if religion does eventually die out altogether in a purely rational and materialist society, it seems reasonable to assume that some citizens may wish to partake in, for example, something akin to the form of Quaker "worship", without ministers, creeds, hymns, or sermons, for quiet contemplation and meditation. Perhaps the closest Banks comes to depicting something like this is QiRia from *Hydrogen*, as explored in Chapter Six, who lives for many years experiencing strange sonic occurrences, one of which – known as 'The Sound' – he describes as "magisterial, bliss-making, overwhelming" (332). Yet, while "the locals treat it as a religious experience", QiRia does not, but still claims that "it is as important to me as it is to them" (332), suggesting that the powerful, sublime experiences provided by First Nature ('The Sound' is created by wind blowing through huge rock tunnels) can still be brought within a rational, materialist understanding. Along similar lines, we can also consider the issues raised by the fact that the Culture represents an accumulation of individuals who originate from various different cultural backgrounds, and, as we have seen with Ziller, the Culture does not pressure its new arrivals into conformity. Yet while this indicates the potential for those from religious cultural backgrounds to live amongst the Culture's more dyed-in-the-wool atheists, this eventuality is not depicted in the series.

Banks, however, does provide an example of the inverse, a Culture citizen choosing to "regress" into religion: as explored in Chapter Three of this book, Linter from 'The State of the Art' who, having "found Jesus", plans "to enter the Roman Catholic Church" at the end of the novella ('State', 191). Yet, Linter is in the process of reverting to the human basic form in order to live on Earth, and is therefore joining a society outside

---

[27] Law, *A Very Short Introduction to Humanism*, 3.

the Culture that continues to practise religion. While Linter has several reasons for wishing to leave the Culture, and he does not indicate that he has been persecuted for religious beliefs in any way whilst living there, the desire to live in a society which understands this way of thinking is one such reason for his desire to return to a human basic form – further indication that the practising of religion in the Culture is, at the very least, uncommon, if not actually completely absent.

The Problem of Quasi-Religious Imagery

While religion may not be recognised within Banks's utopia, there are several crucial aspects that fundamentally underpin the Culture, allowing it to exist in the form that it does, which appear to reproduce concepts originating in religious thought and tradition, or may be read as problematic in regards to a fully materialistic, rational conception of the universe. Several scholars have touched on such aspects. Victor Sage in 'The Politics of Petrifaction: Culture, Religion, History in the Fiction of Iain Banks and John Banville' mentions the politics of the Culture, but only deals with religious themes in Banks's mainstream fiction.[28] Timothy C. Baker and Moira Martingale both argue for the persistence of religious ideas in Banks's work, with particular emphasis on the "God-like" role that they see the Minds playing in the Culture series, touching upon aspects of this quasi-religious framework.[29] Jackson and Heilman have argued for Banks's concept of the Sublime – a form of retirement from normal galactic life – as a spiritual practice,[30] while Jim Clarke explores the Sublime in the context of the rich philosophical and aesthetic traditions from which Banks's term is derived.[31] By reading the roles of the Minds within the Culture as akin to the roles of gods in religious understandings of the universe, Baker and Martingale implicitly draw attention to other aspects of the Culture – digital capturing of personality and consciousness, and virtual afterlives, for example – which may suggest that elements of Banks's utopia reproduce religious concepts and philosophies.

[28] Victor Sage, 'The Politics of Petrification: Culture, Religion, History in the Fiction of Iain Banks and John Banville', in *Modern Gothic: A Reader*, Victor Sage and Allan Lloyd, eds. (Manchester: Manchester University Press, 1996).
[29] Timothy C. Baker, 'Scottish Utopian Fiction and the Invocation of God', *Utopian Studies* 21, no. 1 (2010); and Martingale, *Gothic Dimensions*.
[30] Jackson and Heilman, 'Outside Context Problems', 253–256.
[31] Jim Clarke, 'The Sublime in Iain M. Banks's "Culture" novels', *Vector* 281 (Winter 2015): 7–11.

Evangelical Atheism and Utopian Crusades

Public thinkers who propound strong atheistic views criticising religion, such as Christopher Hitchens, A.C. Grayling, and Richard Dawkins – sometimes referred to as the "New Atheists"[32] – with whom Banks could be broadly compared, frequently face the accusation that the vehemence of their opinions merely reproduces that of the institutions they oppose. Challenging the theological scholarship of the New Atheists, Brad Gregory argues that "Hitchens and [Sam] Harris, Dawkins and [Michel] Onfray proceed like fundamentalist doppelgangers of the untutored biblical literalists whom they deplore", while he criticises Dawkins's "fundamentalist atheism" for the unyielding certainty of his views, which Gregory suggests amounts to bigotry.[33] Writing in *The God Delusion* (2006), Dawkins expressed incredulity at such arguments, explaining that he is "often described as a deeply religious man", and, perhaps because he is a highly prominent spokesman for atheism, many feel that his work has turned into a crusade for a kind of atheist conversion.[34]

Following a similar logic, commentators have argued that the vehemence of the Culture's atheism, coupled with the practices of Contact and SC, also amounts to anti-religious crusades, attempting to impose their views and way of life upon others. Vint calls the "seductive danger" of utopia that desires to "convert others" an "evangelical impulse", and therefore potentially codes the actions of Contact and SC in quasi-religious terms.[35] Wrobik Sennkil, for example, the protagonist of 'A Gift from the Culture', leaves Contact initially and then the Culture entirely in part due to the "evangelical" nature of SC ('Gift', 17). Duggan compares the Culture with Jean Baudrillard's conception of the real-world West, for the way in which its expansion mimics that of "late capitalism's global 'progress'",[36] observing that the Culture replicates "Baudrillard's presentation of the West as a monolithic threat to diverse social formations, and especially Islam,"[37] so effectively characterising the Culture as an anti-religious crusade. Furthermore, even

---

[32] Brad S. Gregory, 'The Insights and Oversights of the "New Atheists"', *Logos* 12, no. 4 (Fall 2009): 17–55.
[33] Gregory, 'The Insights and Oversights of the "New Atheists"', 27, 37.
[34] Richard Dawkins, *The God Delusion* (London: Transworld Publishers, 2006), 33.
[35] Vint, 'The Culture-al Body', 86.
[36] Duggan, 'Iain M. Banks, Postmodernism and the Gulf War', 7.
[37] Duggan, 'Iain M. Banks, Postmodernism and the Gulf War', 7.

Banks described himself frequently using the tongue-in-cheek phrase "evangelical atheist".[38]

Following this, then, the Culture's utopianism is understood using religious concepts as metaphor, using the same logic underpinning Murray N. Rothbard's article 'Karl Marx: Communist as Religious Eschatologist', which argues that Marx's vision of communism, somewhat ironically, closely resembles core elements of Christian theology:

> In the same way as the return of the Messiah, in Christian theology, will put an end to history and establish a new heaven and a new earth, so the establishment of communism would put an end to human history. [...] for Marx and other schools of communists, mankind, led by a vanguard of secular saints, will establish a secularized Kingdom of Heaven on Earth.[39]

Yet Rothbard's formulation works to oversimplify Marx's ideas, and potentially the theology he describes also. Applied to the Culture, this would place the Handy (Wo)Men of SC as this "vanguard of secular saints" and the Culture itself as "a secularized Kingdom of Heaven on earth" – both of which are inherently problematic assertions, as is argued below. Furthermore, Marx never proclaims communism as the "end of history" in the manner that Rothbard asserts, rather describing the closure of the "social formation" of "the bourgeois mode of production" as the closure of the "prehistory of human society", after which real human history can begin.[40] In turn, the radical breaks through which the Culture may have passed, forming the basis of each chapter of this book, may be understood as apocalypses, as explained in the Introduction: a further example of this logic that applies religious concepts to secular ideas through metaphor.

Baker too introduces the notion that Banks relies upon "quasi-religious terminology" in the Culture series by drawing attention to the religious metaphors Banks uses to describe the Idiran–Culture war in *Consider Phlebas*: "the Culture *was* threatened, not with conquest, or loss of life, craft, resource of territory, but with something more important: the loss of its purpose and that clarity of conscience; the destruction of its spirit; the

---

[38] *Ontario Humanist Society*, 'In memoriam: Iain Banks, novelist, humanist, "evangelical atheist"'.

[39] Murray N. Rothbard, 'Karl Marx: Communist as Religious Eschatologist', *Review of Austrian Economics* 4, no. 1 (December 1990): 1.

[40] See 'Preface' in Karl Marx, *A Contribution to the Critique of Political Economy*, Marxists.org, [1859] 1999. https://www.marxists.org/archive/marx/works/1859/critique-pol-economy/.

surrender of its soul." (452) Here Baker suggests that the Culture places higher regard upon philosophical notions such as "purpose", "conscience", "spirit", and "soul" than upon material concerns like "craft", "resources", or "territory", even over ethical concerns like "loss of life". The words "spirit" and "soul" undeniably have religious connotations – suggesting an immaterial, transcendent essence – yet it seems very unlikely that Banks is suggesting that the Culture features these aspects in such a literal manner, as Baker's use of the prefix "quasi-" suggests he is aware. It is much more likely that Banks uses these terms metaphorically, drawing upon the gravitas granted to them through their religious connotations, but ultimately to convey an entirely secular concept: the Culture's essence, the core of its identity, purpose, and meaning.

Baker confirms that the Culture is "a completely irreligious society" in one sense;[41] yet he also argues that the Culture is in fact "presented as a society in which freedom from religion is itself a religion."[42] While he does not qualify this statement at length, Baker seems to suggest that the Culture practises a kind of fervent scientism that is merely another form of religion; through this logic, placing one's trust in evidence gained through the empirical method is the same as having faith in divine revelation and spiritual insight, which is clearly problematic. Banks was very clear in his view that "the world works in a certain way, and the way you find out about it is you do science, you do experiments, and you use reason", whereas "religion just doesn't do that [...] it doesn't describe reality".[43] The extent to which such views have actively become a crusade on the part of the New Atheists is debatable, but it seems clear that there is an important, fundamental difference between worldviews based on evidence obtained through scientific practice and those based on revelation. Furthermore, Banks argued that "the main reason that so many people are self-reportedly religious is because that's just the way they've been brought up".[44] If the Culture offers an environment in which citizens are not assigned to a religious belief system at birth, and – once they are old enough to comprehend such issues – can adopt or reject any kind of worldview as they see fit, then freedom from religion has not become a religion in itself, it is merely neutral freedom of choice.

In other respects, however, the notion of a quasi-religious element to the Culture is more convincing. Baker's analysis of the Culture draws exclusively on *Consider Phlebas* rather than the whole series, and therefore

---

[41] Rothbard, 'Karl Marx', 2.
[42] Baker, 'Scottish Utopian Fiction', 106.
[43] Parsons, 'Interview: Iain Banks'. Web.
[44] Parsons, 'Interview: Iain Banks'. Web.

reflects the differences in interpretation that are possible dependent upon which text(s) are selected. It is in a later book, *Surface Detail*, that Banks developed the notion that a Culture citizen, despite their lack of religious belief, might still have a kind of "soul"; but while Baker draws attention to Banks's usage of the term in *Phlebas*, Banks would allow the term to develop a different meaning in this later novel.

Secular Souls

Of all the quasi-religious elements I will discuss here, "soul" is perhaps the most important, as it is not only linked with some of the other elements, but it makes them possible. In the Culture universe, all forms of sentient life, including AIs, have what Banks calls a "soul". The term "soul" is somewhat slippery, creating a variety of different understandings and definitions in the fields of both theology and philosophy. According to the *Oxford Dictionary of Philosophy*, the soul is "the immaterial 'I' that possesses conscious experience, controls passion, desire, and action, and maintains a perfect identity from birth (or before) to death (or after)".[45] The *Encyclopaedia Britannica* adds that, "in theology, the soul is further defined as that part of the individual which partakes of divinity and often is considered to survive the death of the body".[46] Yet, despite the connotations of the term, souls in the Culture novels are quite different, being synonymous with mind–computer interfacing, what McHale calls "the most characteristic piece of cyberpunk iconography."[47] As described in *Surface*, souls are "mind-states [...] dynamic full-brain inventories" (66); the focus, therefore, is placed upon the contents of the mind, or the combination of personality and memories that Banks understands as consciousness. As we have seen in Chapter Three, perhaps the most important aspect of these fictional souls is the fact that they can be converted into or captured as *digital* information, effectively saved onto a computer in a similar manner to saving a file onto a USB stick or other data-storage device – the motif introduced in Gibson's *Neuromancer* (1984), when Case and Molly attempt to steal the saved consciousness of a former mentor, and Bruce Sterling's *Schismatrix* (1985) where the posthuman "Mechs" use "brain–computer interfacing to extend

---

[45] *Oxford Dictionary of Philosophy*, 'Soul' (Oxford: Oxford University Press, 2005), 346.
[46] *Encyclopedia Britannica*, 'Soul', Online Library Edition. www.britannica.com/topic/soul-religion-and-philosophy.
[47] Murphy and Vint, *Beyond Cyberpunk*, 16.

the mind, but with the side-effect of attenuating and dispersing it."[48] In Banks's fictional universe this saving can occur at any point in the soul-bearer's life without causing harm to the bearer, or to the soul-information itself; for most Culture citizens, the act of "backing up" one's soul is a routine part of daily life, and there are varieties of technology available with which to perform this action. Some Culture citizens, particularly those who work in SC, are fitted with a device called a neural lace – usually though not necessarily at a young age – that is similar to a soulkeeper, which merely stores a soul indefinitely, although in a much more sophisticated manner. The neural lace, a hybrid of organic and technological parts, "grows with the brain it's part of, it beds in over the years, gets very adept at mirroring every detail of the mind it interpenetrates and co-exists with" (*Surface*, 78); this makes the process of "soul-saving" automatic. Once they have been digitised, after the original body has died, these converted souls can even be transferred – "revented" – back into another physical body, or into a computer-generated virtual environment. This procedure means that one is potentially protected from the consequences of the effects of fatal or life-altering violence, and even, effectively, from death itself: once revented, all that they would lose would be the memory of what had happened between the time they last "backed-up" their soul, and the time of their revention.

The importance of souls in the Culture novels, including their resurrection potential, is best illustrated by *Surface*, in which the existence of souls allows various elements of the novel's complex narrative to converge. The novel's protagonist Lededje Y'breq tries and fails to escape her captor Joile Veppers, which results in her violent murder at his hands. Fortunately for Lededje, due to a favour that she granted an eccentric Culture Mind many years in the past, a neural lace has been planted in her brain, as its gift to her in return. Lededje, however, was unaware of this fact, and, when originally asked about compensation for her trouble, she had flippantly replied, "Whatever you think fit. Surprise me" (89). Lededje can therefore be subsequently resurrected by the Culture, and her soul revented, "brought back to life in a physical body in the Real" (91). Lededje's "new" life in the Real (used in Banks's novel to describe a material environment as opposed to a virtual one), motivated by gaining revenge on Veppers, forms the main narrative thrust of *Surface*.

Banks's dualistic conception of the relationship between the body and personality can be traced back to René Descartes's famous assertion that the soul exists in an entirely immaterial, non-physical state,

---

[48] Murphy and Vint, *Beyond Cyberpunk*, 15.

fundamentally distinct from the material physical state of the body.[49] Writing in *The Philosophy of Humanism*, Lamont associates monistic theory, where "the relationship between body and personality [is] so close and fundamental that they constitute an indissoluble unity",[50] with humanism, whereas dualistic theory, such as that which underpins Cartesian thought as well as Banks's, is associated with "the traditional religions of the world" because it leaves "a future life probable or at least possible."[51] If the idea of revention represents a logical if somewhat extreme extrapolation from the theory of dualism, then Banks's thinking in this regard does chime with religious ideas to a certain extent, but this particular extreme dualism is made possible through technoscience.

Lamont explains that "the issue of mortality versus immortality is crucial in the argument of Humanism against supernaturalism."[52] In religious understandings, it is important that the soul is entirely separate from the body so that it may continue after physical death and enable the individual to achieve immortal life in spiritual form. The Culture, however – while its fundamental belief in individual freedom means that it does not actually stop citizens from living endlessly – is generally opposed to immortal existence, as we have seen. So, while Banks's dualistic conception of the mind–body *relationship itself* is perhaps more in line with traditional religious rather than humanist thought, the actual philosophy underpinning the purpose of this relationship affirms its humanistic understanding within the Culture. Also, the fact that in the Culture's system the soul can only live on after death through technoscientific means makes it clear that this system is nothing more than the *material imitation* of a spiritual hypothesis, rather than any indication that the hypothesis is actually true.

Virtual Afterlives: Limbo/Purgatory

Another aspect of Banks's quasi-religious system explored in *Surface* occurs in the state that exists between Lededje's violent "death", and her subsequent revention. The clandestine nature of the neural lace that captured Lededje's soul, and the eccentric, ostracised nature of the

---

[49] Rene Descartes, 'Letter to Princess Elizabeth (28 June 1643)', in *Philosophy Then and Now*, N. Scott Arnold, Theodore M. Benditt, and George Graham, eds. (Oxford: Blackwell Publishing, 1998), 58.
[50] Lamont, *The Philosophy of Humanism*, 81.
[51] Lamont, *The Philosophy of Humanism*, 81.
[52] Lamont, *The Philosophy of Humanism*, 82.

Mind who implanted it in her, meant that her automatic revention had not been scheduled. For people who are *meant* to have neural laces, the device is registered, and therefore if anything happens to the person, the Minds will be notified and will begin the process of revention. As Lededje's is "unofficial", this has not occurred; she therefore awakens into what could be considered a kind of virtual limbo. Lededje's gradual coming to and awakening after her "death" is described in dream-like terms: "From somewhere came the idea that there were many different levels of sleeping, of unconsciousness, and therefore of awakening (58)". These thoughts emerge from "in the midst of [a...] pleasant woozy calm – warm, pleasantly swaddled, self-huggingly curled up, a sort of ruddy darkness behind the eyelids" (58). In this way, Lededje currently exists on the peripheries of consciousness, somewhere between the real world and the virtual. Eventually, Lededje awakens properly:

> She opened her eyes. She had the vague impression of a wide bed, pale sheets and a large, high-ceilinged room with tall open windows from which gauzy soft billowing white curtains waved out. [...] She noticed that there was some sort of fuzzy glow at the foot of the bed. It swam into focus and spelled out the word SIMULATION. (59)

The room in which she awakens, then, is comfortable and homely, suggesting a space for rest and relaxation. Soon a Culture Mind (in the form of a humanoid avatar) appears and speaks with her: Lededje learns that she is "presently, literally [...] in a computational substrate node of the General Systems Vehicle *Sense Amid Madness, Wit Amongst Folly*" (65). Essentially, her soul-information is resting temporarily inside a spaceship's computer awaiting further instructions.

As Lededje explores her new surroundings, she becomes aware, despite the implications of the message in her vision, that her environment is remarkably detailed on a sensory basis: "What she was looking at here – and feeling, and smelling – was effectively, uncannily flawless" (61). The environment of Lededje's virtual limbo is seemingly designed to be as comforting and reassuring as possible, partly to soften her inevitable initial disorientation, but also to help her deal with the traumatic memories of events leading up to, and including her physical death, which the Mind will slowly allow to re-emerge. As the Mind's avatar states: "I discovered that you've had a traumatic experience [...] which I've sort of held back, edited from your transferred memories, just for now, while you settle in" (67). This virtual limbo also serves as a neutral environment in which Lededje can choose what kind of body she is to be revented into subsequently: "I'll leave you with an image you can manipulate until you're happy with it, take a spec from that" (92).

Clearly, the state into which Lededje is transferred is different, both in form and function, from the limbo of Roman Catholic theology. Instead of a permanent place that grants Lededje freedom from eternal punishment in hell just as it denies her the joy of eternal existence, as in the understanding of the term in Catholicism,[53] the limbo provided by the Culture is a temporary environment given over to recovery, relaxation, and contemplation. Banks's virtual limbo is a kind of post-death "safe space" for souls prior to revention, rather than the religious model, with its emphasis on judgement and deprivation of pleasure. This space is located liminally, covering the thresholds between consciousness and unconsciousness, material and virtual environments, physical death and a form of rebirth. Here, referring to this phenomenon as limbo – even in a metaphorical sense – stretches the appropriateness of the term.

This space indeed proves to be temporary for Lededje. Due to her ties with the Culture, Lededje was given the choice to once again return to the Real, deciding upon revention into another physical body, and effectively continuing to live on again in the same manner as before; she chose this as it was necessary for her to achieve revenge. Yet there are spaces featured in the Culture series the purpose of which is closer to ideas associated with many religions. The souls of individuals from other races and civilisations in Banks's fictional universe, for example, may live on in virtual environments very close to religious notions of heaven.

Virtual Afterlives: Heavens

In describing the Culture as his "secular heaven", Banks conflates the notion of utopia with the idea of heaven in a casual way, in that both ostensibly offer a kind of idealised paradise. Frequently, Banks's descriptions of the various Culture habitats draw attention to their idyllic "natural" beauty, and strange, awe-inspiring surroundings:

---

[53] "Limbo, in Roman Catholic theology, the border place between heaven and hell where dwell those souls who, though not condemned to punishment, are deprived of the joy of eternal existence with God in heaven. The word is of Teutonic origin, meaning 'border' or 'anything joined on'". *Encyclopedia Britannica*, 'Limbo', Encyclopedia Britannica Inc., Online Library Edition. www.britannica.com/topic/limbo-Roman-Catholic-theology.

tumbling waters could be heard and tall, distant trees stood on gentle rolling hills. Dotted amongst the trees, long vertical bands of pale, almost transparent vegetation rose high into the air [...] surmounted by a dark ovoid [...] Dozens of these strange shapes swayed to and fro in the breeze, oscillating together like some vast seaweed forest. (*Surface*, 148)

These aesthetically pleasing surroundings, combined with the Culture's general ethos of peace, freedom, and pleasure, form an idealised environment, even if its beauty is not in fact natural at all: it may well have been *created* as part of the artificial system of Second Nature, rather than that of biologically formed First Nature.

Yet Banks's conflation of material paradise with spiritual heaven lacks nuance, and serves to muddy understandings of both terms. The Culture's paradise exists undeniably within material reality, and is therefore not the "abode of the gods", the "reward for a life well lived" or a "transcendent realm beyond" the reality known by humans, as heaven has been widely understood.[54] The Culture offers peaceful places available to all regardless of the manner in which their lives are led, and which exist physically in time and material space. A "heaven on Earth", therefore, can never be a heaven at all. Furthermore, as Mendlesohn argues, the fact that "the Culture proves that a paradise in the real world is possible" not only undermines its status as a heaven but also any need for belief in a spiritual heaven whatsoever.[55] Affirming Mendlesohn's point, Jim Clarke also argues that "the Culture is no afterlife", noting the ways in which it "facilitates and encompasses movement between life, virtual life and post-life states."[56]

As a realised techno-utopia, the zenith of rational, technoscientific achievement, the Culture is committed to providing everything that is needed for happiness in the material ontological plane. Yet, as McHale describes in relation to cyberpunk, Banks incorporates a "juxtaposed world", existing not in series "on a horizontal axis, but rather *in parallel*, on a *vertical* axis; that is, it is possible to juxtapose worlds, occupying *different* ontological planes".[57] Drawing on "the characteristic cyberpunk form of inset world" known as "cyberspace" (a term coined by William

---

[54] *Encyclopedia Britannica*, 'Heaven', Encyclopedia Britannica Inc., Online Library Edition. www.britannica.com/topic/heaven.
[55] Mendlesohn, 'The Dialectic of Decadence', 117.
[56] Clarke, 'The Sublime in Iain M. Banks's "Culture" novels', 11. I thank Jim for his discussion of this point.
[57] McHale, 'Towards a Poetics of Cyberpunk', 11.

Gibson) – "the computer-generated space mentally experienced by computer operators whose nervous systems are directly interfaced with the computer system"[58] – Banks provides a kind of digital "heaven" in the virtual plane, alongside the limbo that we have seen previously. This falls short of representing a virtual parallel of the Culture because the heavens are seemingly accessible only following physical death – they are truly *after*lives – and which can be tailored to the individual's particular pleasure: "Some Afterlives simply offered everlasting fun for the post-dead: infinite holiday resorts featuring boundless sex, adventure, sport, games, study, exploration, shopping, hunting or whatever other activities particularly tickled that species' fancy" (*Surface*, 127–128). The tone adopted by Banks for this paragraph seems irreverent and satirical. The list of activities he provides – variously hedonistic and materialistic – contrasts sharply with traditional Christian depictions of heaven as a space for purity, modesty, and spiritual fulfilment. Banks's phrase "tickled that species' fancy" seems to dismiss the pleasures of heaven as nothing more than whims, distractions, and follies, while describing them as "holiday resorts" suggests something short lived, frivolous, and perhaps mundane, a kind of commercialisation of the afterlife.

Challenging both the physical possibility of heavens and their role in religion, Johann Hari has argued that such ideas tell us more about the *lives* of believers than they do about the afterlives in which they believe.[59] "Heaven is constantly shifting shape," he argues, "because it is a history of subconscious human longings. Show me your heaven, and I'll show you what's lacking in your life."[60] To illustrate this thesis, Hari mentions the controversial issue of the *houri* (virgins) promised to Islamic men when they reach *Jannah* (paradise) in the Qur'an, and indulgences in Catholicism, sometimes characterised as buying one's way into heaven, as demonstrations of such a lack. Through this interpretation – which chimes with Banks's comments about the ways in which religious belief is useful as it reflects upon the believers themselves, as

[58] McHale, 'Towards a Poetics of Cyberpunk', 11.
[59] It must be acknowledged here that, in 2012, Hari left the *Independent* following accusations of plagiarism (See Conal Urquhart, 'Johann Hari leaves the Independent', 20 January 2012, www.theguardian.com/media/2012/jan/20/johann-hari-quits-the-independent). These allegations relate to a completely different article ("interviews with Gideon Levy, an Israeli journalist, and Hugo Chávez, the president of Venezuelato") than that from which I quote in this book ('Heaven: A Fool's Paradise'), and I have no reason to suspect that this latter piece was plagiarised in any way.
[60] Johann Hari, 'Heaven: A Fool's Paradise', *Independent*, 21 April 2010. www.independent.co.uk/opinion/faith/heaven-a-fools-paradise-1949399.html.

discussed above – heaven is easily deconstructed as nothing more than a kind of psychological urge, a symptom of a life restricted in certain ways by religious beliefs and institutions.

Banks's somewhat sarcastic characterisation of the Culture's afterlives, then, should reveal something about its nature. It is interesting to note that Banks mentions shopping and hunting as two possible activities in a Culture afterlife, as the former is perhaps impossible, or at least seems unnecessary, in a postscarcity environment that has no form of currency, while the latter is no doubt frowned upon in a society where "nothing and nobody is exploited" – which presumably includes animal life also – where violence is an absolute last resort, and where highly realistic meat can be simulated.[61] This perhaps shows that Culture citizens subconsciously perceive such activities – which they may encounter in other societies – as a lack, and may even indicate the start of a desire to live in a non-utopian society as human basic, as Linter experiences in 'State'. It also further expands the freedom offered by the Culture: seemingly allowing even those who wish to perform activities deemed old-fashioned, immoral, or unnecessary to do so in a fashion, within a kind of restricted environment where they are unable to do real harm to others.

Banks's portrayal of heaven is not all satirical and dismissive, however: other varieties of heaven that he describes are more focused on intellectual rather than just physical gratification, or "were of a more contemplative and philosophic nature" and therefore seem to offer a more genuinely fulfilling afterlife (*Surface*, 128). Furthermore, he balances his critique with this elegant and romantic image of the final moments of a soul's existence in a virtual heaven: "Some [...] featured a sort of gradual fading-away rather than genuine post-death VR immortality, with the personality of the deceased individual slowly [...] dissolving into the general mass of information and civilizational ethos held within the virtual environment" (*Surface*, 128). Ultimately, despite offering Afterlives to its citizens, the Culture still seems to encourage that an individual's consciousness – in whatever state – reach an end point eventually. Reiterating his argument for eventual bodily death, as discussed in Chapter Three, Banks states that: "those who had lived for a really long time in Afterlives were prone to becoming profoundly gravely bored, or going [...] mad" (*Surface*, 82).

As with souls, Banks's incorporation of heavens into his series clearly does not challenge the Culture as a rational, materialistic system. Furthermore, Banks uses the notion of a virtual paradise to satirise

[61] See Banks, 'State', 180–183.

religious belief in an afterlife, and to further undermine the notion that we need look beyond this life and the physical world for satisfaction. No discussion of heaven – whether in cyberspace or elsewhere – however, would be complete without its antithesis, and many of the various narrative threads of *Surface Detail* are also concerned with the existence of virtual hells.

Virtual Afterlives: Hells

In *Hell in Contemporary Culture* (2005), Rachel Falconer argues that religious imagery and ideas, specifically the idea of hell, have survived and proliferated in contemporary secular culture, in largely metaphoric and symbolic forms: "Many Westerners retain a vestigial or quasi-religious belief in hell: Hell as the absolutely horrific experience from which none escape unchanged".[62] While this symbolic notion of hell as a descent into horror and a traumatised return could undoubtedly be found in the Culture novels, the hells in *Surface Detail* are realms of eternal damnation in the classic sense, but again existing in virtual reality. In fact there are several different hells in cyberspace, which – like the circles of hell in Dante Alighieri's *Inferno* – are each allotted to the wrongdoing souls of every civilisation in the galaxy that condones their use, and each zone has been linked to form a vast virtual network of infernal realms.

While these cyber-hells recall the famous visions of Banks's literary and artistic predecessors, such as the vivid and imaginative realms of Milton, and the visceral and sadistic paintings of Bosch, they are more than mere revisions. Instead, Banks exploits the freedom that the nature of a virtual environment allows him. His descriptions certainly invoke some archetypal infernal images, such as vicious demons, rivers of blood, bleached bones, rotting corpses, and the emaciated, naked bodies of hell's denizens: "The wheel was constructed of many, many ancient bones, long bleached white by the action of the acid or alkali rains that fell every few days" (*Surface*, 46). But these images exist alongside more contemporary images, such as *cheval de frise*, a "giant X of crossed spikes laden with impaled, half-decaying bodies" (48); these were defensive obstacles, made from a wooden frame topped with broken glass or barbed wire, and used on the battlefields of World War One. When describing a demon, Banks also draws upon the technology of the Victorian era: "The thing had a lantern head, like an

---

[62] Rachel Falconer, *Hell in Contemporary Culture* (Edinburgh: Edinburgh University Press, 2005), 1.

enormous version of a four-paned, inward-sloping gas light from ancient history [...] At each of the four external corners of the lantern, a giant candle of tallow stood, each containing a hundred shrieking nervous systems intact and in burning agony within" (285). Also, when another character, Prin, who has become one of Hell's "dark angels", describes her surroundings, she draws attention to their computer-simulated nature: "it was as though everything about her had become pixelated, smoothed out" (580). The mention of a "pixelated" image is instantly recognisable as contemporary, and contrasts with Banks's more archaic imagery. In this way, the overall effect is of an omni-temporal zone: a kind of morbid, postmodern pastiche of infernal images.

In this virtual space, the strict laws of physics concerning the body and its surrounding environment need not necessarily apply: in "the Thrice Flayed Footprint district of the Pavulean Hell" (58) the limb of one of hell's sufferers – first flayed, and then amputated – can be enlarged to such a scale that it constitutes part of the physical environment; the limb's amputation from the body, while physically disconnecting the two parts, does not necessarily disconnect nerves from their endings, and the sufferer's pain is eternally amplified whenever someone passes over the ridge that the flayed limb forms in hell's landscape. Similarly, elsewhere in the region, fingernails decorate the roofs of buildings like tiles; bones form the structure of a mill wheel; and stretched skin lines the walls of the mill. So we can see that, in effect, Banks applies the central notion of Dante's Nine Circles of Hell depicted in *Inferno* to the dystopian virtual landscapes of cyberpunk works such as *Neuromancer* and Mamoru Oshii's *Ghost in the Shell* (1995), and pushes his creation to its extreme, creating an eternal network of fractal flesh that easily defies and manipulates the corporeal limits of the Real world.

Banks's descriptions of the hells in *Surface* form a vital link between many of the novel's narrative threads, and work to critique the fundamental ethical purpose of afterlives as used for deterrence and punishment. In the novel, only some races advocate the existence and use of hells, for any purpose. Those in favour, such as the Sichultians, argue that their existence has an important moral purpose similar to the function of hells in Catholicism: the souls of sinners will be cast into the virtual abyss to suffer eternally, the threat of unceasing damnation and punishment after death acting as a moral imperative for all to live a just and good life. For those opposed, these cyber-hells are simple sites of unspeakable barbarism: "The Culture took a particularly dim view of torture, either in the Real or in a Virtuality, and was quite prepared to damage its short-, and even – at least seemingly – long-term interests to stop it happening" (*Surface*, 133). These two clashing viewpoints have led to a war over the hells – both in the Real and the Virtual – and the Culture has vowed to end them once and for all by destroying the physical computer components, known as substrates, that enable them to exist. This war allows Banks to explicate and engage with the political and ethical debates surrounding the nature of hell, in both his fictional universe and our own. Also, the hells allow Banks to explicate the Culture's philosophy in a similar manner to the *Grey Area*'s torture museum in *Excession*, which we will discuss in the next chapter. In their most literal meaning, then, the virtual hells in *Surface* clearly serve as a bitter attack against religious systems that tyrannise their followers with threats of torture after death for transgression in life, yet they also achieve a grander symbolic meaning in the series. The Culture's fight to destroy the hells and permanently end their use is but one part of their overall utopian goal, their *technologiade*: as Zakalwe explains, "that's the way they prefer to work; offering life, you see, rather than dealing death" (*Weapons*, 30).

Yet Banks also uses the hells in *Surface* to further satirise the amorality of Neoliberalism, through the revelation that Veppers and his corporation are more connected to the sub-plots involving the hells than was apparent. In fact, it is Veppers who has been secretly storing the hardware on which the hells run at his country estate on Schilt all along, and some of his fortune was made from this morally dubious agreement. Furthermore, Veppers is planning to destroy the hells to free himself from the burden of this secret and to frame the Culture for the deed. Here we see the CEO of a vast galactic company, who clearly values profit over people, benefitting indirectly from widescale barbarism: living a nonchalant lifestyle with lavish wealth and power, Veppers remains entirely unconcerned about the blood money he spends, and seems used to covering up his actions through bribery and corruption.

The Minds as Gods

Just as the Culture series depicts souls and virtual afterlives as part of a quasi-religious system, it also features entities with power beyond that achieved by its human citizens: as Timothy Baker argues in his article 'Scottish Utopian Fiction and the Invocation of God', "even the most atheistic society cannot, finally, shake itself free of, if not gods, unfathomable and omnipotent beings."[63] The Culture's Minds are one example of such beings, which have been compared to gods by characters within

---

[63] Baker, 'Scottish Utopian Fiction', 106.

the series, Banks's critics, and even by Banks himself. For example: Fal 'Ngeestra describes their "near god-like power" (*Phlebas*, 87); Moira Martingale argues that "the Culture's AIs compare to mythic entities";[64] and Banks told *Wired* magazine that the Minds "play the part of Greek gods".[65] If these descriptions are accurate, then this is clearly a somewhat odd feature of a fundamentally atheistic society. In *Gothic Dimensions*, Martingale develops the Minds-as-gods interpretation and challenges the Culture's secularity, arguing that "Banks appears to create his 'gods' in the form of something he trusts: technology".[66] She goes on to emphasise the lack of technical detail that Banks provides in order to rationalise the Minds, arguing that they are in fact more similar to "guardian angels" that are "hiding behind pseudoscience".[67]

In Chapter Two we heard Csicsery-Ronay describe the Singularity – the autopoietic origins of the Minds – as a myth. And Arthur C. Clarke's most quoted Law of Predication ("any sufficiently advanced technology is indistinguishable from magic"[68]) could clearly be used to place the Minds on a spectrum between science and the supernatural, potentially supporting either argument. Yet Banks clearly believed that AI could theoretically advance to something like this level of power and self-awareness – fulfilling the Suvinian paradigm that something like the Minds is *not impossible* – and he emphasised that they are "constrained by the laws of physics."[69] The crew of the *Clear Air Turbulence* in *Phlebas* experiences awe upon seeing an Orbital, a technological marvel similar in complexity to that of the Minds, and again it is tempting to interpret Horza's views as those of Banks himself. Horza's ship-mate, Dorlow was

> struck by the beauty of the great Orbital, expressed the belief that even though it was a work of base creatures, no better than humans, it was still a triumphant testimony to the power of God, as God had made man, and all other souled creatures. Horza had disagreed, genuinely annoyed that the woman could use even something so obviously a testament to the power of intelligence and hard work, as an argument for her own system of irrational belief. (100)

[64] Martingale, *Gothic Dimensions*, 471.
[65] Parsons, 'Interview: Iain Banks'. Web.
[66] Martingale, *Gothic Dimensions*, 471.
[67] Martingale, *Gothic Dimensions*, 471.
[68] Arthur C. Clarke, 'Hazards of Prophecy: The Failure of Imagination', in *Profiles of the Future: An Enquiry into the Limits of the Possible* Profiles of the Future: An Enquiry into the Limits of the Possible(London: Harper and Row, [1962] rev. 1973), 36.
[69] Parsons, 'Interview: Iain Banks'. Web.

In turn, Yannick Rumpala, writing in 'Artificial Intelligences and Political Organization: an Exploration Based on the Science Fiction Work of Iain M. Banks', has argued for the rationality behind Banks's conception of the Minds: "The technical progress towards a growing presence of highly-evolved machines, more or less directly derived from computers and microprocessors, can have a certain level of plausibility."[70] Rumpala gives an overview of the widespread reliance upon highly sophisticated AI in the military, legal, financial, and aviation sectors, as well as the increasing automation of everyday life, to support Banks's extrapolations.[71]

Perhaps a more productive debate, however, should focus on the *role* of the Minds within the series, rather than just the rationality by which they are imagined. Baker also challenges Banks's vision of a truly secular society (among other secular Scottish authors of utopian fiction), but with a slightly different focus: through his reliance upon the *idea* of god-like beings, regardless of the form in which such a being actually comes to exist.[72] "The efficacy, or divinity in any common sense, of these Gods is irrelevant," Baker states; "what matters is that every society finds its own godlike being."[73] The Minds can be regarded as "god-like", Baker's argument goes, because they conform to the superlative powers attributed to the God of the New Testament: omnibenevolence, omniscience, and omniprescence. Even if they are entirely devoid of spiritual or supernatural elements, according to Baker, they fulfil a similar role to that of gods in the maintenance of the Culture and therefore – at least symbolically – make it a religious system.

Yet this is not the case. The Minds – with their ability to turn energy into matter, to access instant knowledge about the fringes of the galaxy, and to control huge habitats – clearly wield a high degree of power and knowledge. As they play a fundamental and highly successful role in the maintenance of a civilisation that seems utopian, and work to allow others access to that utopia, they are clearly benevolent to some degree. Also, their ability to manifest in humanoid form as avatars at any part of the Culture almost instantaneously, even in multiple locations simultaneously, is clearly impressive. But there are limits to their power, knowledge, righteousness, and technical ability. Banks explained that the Minds are

---

[70] Yannick Rumpala, 'Artificial Intelligences and Political Organization: an Exploration Based on the Science Fiction Work of Iain M. Banks', *Technology in Society* 34 (2012): 23–32. www.isiarticles.com/bundles/Article/pre/pdf/20144.pdf.
[71] Rumpala, 'Artificial Intelligences', 11.
[72] Baker, 'Scottish Utopian Fiction', 107.
[73] Baker, 'Scottish Utopian Fiction', 106.

"not infallible" and "there's [sic] lots of problems they can't handle",[74] and he outlined various constraints – both moral and political – which apply.[75] For example, while technically they can easily read the minds of human citizens, it is strictly forbidden for them to do so: "they will not look inside people's heads", Banks explains, "there's only one ship that ever did it."[76] Here, referring to the General Contact Unit (GCU) *Grey Area* (as explored in Chapter Six), Banks confirms that the humanist moral code maintained in the Culture restricts the Minds' actions in this way, but also makes it clear that the Minds have not achieved a standard of absolute perfection, despite how they may appear, as is necessary for godhead. As Banks explains in *Look to Windward*, the Minds are deliberately created as *im*perfect because the Culture discovered that "perfect AIs always sublime" (126–127), meaning that they leave permanently for another dimension, as explored below. Supporting this idea, Baker's analysis itself in fact relies upon the depiction of a particularly vulnerable Mind at the centre of *Phlebas'* narrative, eventually revealed as the Bora Horza Gobuchul,[77] who – damaged, threatened, near death – is forced into hiding for the dangerous knowledge it possesses. It is clear, therefore, that the Minds are not only fallible but far from immortal.

Furthermore, the Minds' powers rarely seem to stretch beyond the confines of the Culture's environments, otherwise – if their powers were truly god-like, covering the universe itself – there would be no conflict in the series that the Minds could not easily undermine. While their ability to manipulate energy into matter clearly indicates a high level of power, it is presented as a feat of engineering indicative of productive capacity, but not of supernatural or even merely natural omnipotence. Their powers in this regard are limited to the building of large-scale projects in space – the GSVs and Orbitals can be seen as extrapolations from currently existing structures like, for example, the International Space Station – and do not truly constitute a total god-like influence on the fundamental materials of the universe. No-one in the Culture worships the Minds, and their physical existence or abilities within Banks's fictions are never doubted; and existing as the result of the Singularity process, they are manmade, then self-developing. As outlined in this book, the Culture has developed over many decades as the result of several important shifts – while the Minds may well have helped

---

[74] Parsons, 'Interview: Iain Banks'. Web.
[75] Parsons, 'Interview: Iain Banks'. Web.
[76] Parsons, 'Interview: Iain Banks'. Web.
[77] The Mind eventually takes the same name as the novel's (by this point deceased) protagonist out of respect for him. See 'Epilogue', *Phlebas*, 471.

facilitate this process, and develop it further afterwards, they did not create the Culture, or the entities within it.

As we have seen in Chapter Two, the Minds are best understood as closer to a kind of secular state due to the nature of the various functions they perform, rather than as fulfilling a symbolic yearning for the divine or a narrative role more similar to that of gods. As a result of the Singularity, the Minds are in fact the highest level of *human* accomplishment possible: a simulated consciousness that replicates the human mind's cognitive abilities to the extent that it can become independent of its human creators, eventually superseding our possible intelligence. From a religious perspective, this would constitute blasphemy: "the sentient machines; the very image and essence of life itself, desecrated idolatry incarnate" (*Phlebas*, 334). To the atheistic Culture, however, this is merely a necessity if one is ever to rely upon a system that features such a being: gods must be created artificially if they are ever to exist. If the Minds do demonstrate "the continuing relevance of God and myth", as Baker argues, then Banks's series constitutes a blasphemous subversion: God did not create man, man created "God".

Raising similar issues, there are other types of being in the Culture universe that might be considered god-like, which Baker's analysis does not touch upon, but which have been examined in detail by Clarke, and briefly by Jackson and Heilman: the Sublimed.

Transcendence: Sublime, Sublimed, Sublimers

If a being is part of the Sublimed, it has passed into the realm of the Sublime: a dimension of pure energy located within the series' layered system of universes; henceforth, as one of the Sublimed, these entities have achieved a kind of heightened existence, granting them a deeper understanding of the universe. Sublimation is often, but not always, achieved by a civilisation en masse, as is the case with the Dra'Azon in *Phlebas*, a "Pure-energy superspecies long retired from the normal, matter-based life of the galaxy" (91), or the Gzilt who achieve this process – known as Subliming – at the climax of *The Hydrogen Sonata*. Seemingly any entity in this universe can become one of the Sublimed, including the Minds, drones, stored souls, or souls that have been uploaded into virtual space.[78]

The process of Subliming is usually instigated when an entity, or entities, is regarded to have reached a state of high achievement in

---

[78] Clarke, 'The Sublime in Iain M. Banks's "Culture" novels', 8.

their lives, feeling a sense of completion or often sheer boredom, and is able to transcend their physical bodily form, changing their base matter into pure energy. This, in fact, renders the process of Subliming as something like a larger-scale version of the process by which the Minds enable the Culture's postscarcity environment: using Csicsery-Ronay's terms, Subliming is the process of an individual, perhaps a Handy Man, combining with the Fertile Corpse, creating a new, altogether "Handier", entity.

Banks allowed a sense of mystery to develop around the Sublimed, amongst his characters, critics, and fans alike. This mystery and ambiguity was created by the fact that occasional references to the Sublimed are made in the series, since their introduction in *Phlebas*, yet their exact nature and function are left vague until *Hydrogen*. Banks even admitted that he decided to return to the subject of the Sublime in the final Culture book partly because "people at signings and in interviews began to ask about it".[79] It was only then that he "started to think about it properly and decided/realised that it was an important part of the whole context of the Culture and the rest of the civilised galactic scene".[80] There is certainly a sense of Banks developing his ideas as the series progresses, as discussed below. While most beings that pass into the Sublime seem to stay there, some do on occasion return to material reality for specific purposes. Initially in *Phlebas*, the Sublimed seem to pose a threat: the Dra'Azon guard the Land of the Dead (the planet of Schar's World), offering ominous warnings to the protagonists that "DEATH IS NEAR" (294), communicated via text on a monitor, yet they appear no further in the text. Later, in *Surface Detail*, Banks mentions the bizarre Bulbitions, entities that have passed into the Sublime and return briefly to the material plane to speak with the SC agent Yime. The Bulbitions seem to take the form of an individual's deepest subconscious psychological concerns (in Yime's case, implied anxiety stemming from the neutral gender identity that she temporarily adopts, as discussed in Chapter Four of this book), and are certainly unsettling if not actually obviously dangerous.

While Baker does not mention the Sublimed as examples of god-like beings in Banks's series, Jackson and Heilman describe the process as "a spiritual form of ascension", also noting the vast yet mysterious power with which it is associated.[81] Jim Clarke, while ultimately arriving at different conclusions, acknowledges that the Sublime features "hints of

---

[79] Banks, Q&A Session, 2012.
[80] Banks, Q&A Session, 2012.
[81] Jackson and Heilman, 'Outside Context Problems', 253.

religious and spiritual influence".[82] The word "sublime" has been defined as a "state of mind" that "marks the limits of reason and expression altogether with a sense of what might lie beyond these limits".[83] The sublime is also understood as being concerned with the "indescribable", and the "void" that remains unknowable to "finite beings".[84] Banks's descriptions of the Sublime often highlight the difficulty facing those who have passed into it to describe it in anything other than "vague, dreamy reports": "it is beyond comprehension, literally indescribable" (*Hydrogen*, 64). Given the connotations of the term, therefore, it is clear why Jackson and Heilman characterise Subliming as a spiritual ascension or transcendence, perhaps similar to the state of *moksha* (liberation of the consciousness from the material world) in Hinduism and Hindu philosophy.[85] Similarly, "sublime" is often used to refer to gods, or other divine beings, which, by their nature, seem to exist beyond words.[86] Cossont, the protagonist of *Hydrogen*, considers her understanding of the Sublime, stating that "like some ideas of God or whatever", the Sublime "was all around" (17), here perhaps likening it to the doctrine of Pantheism, which "identifies God with the universe".[87]

If this is true, then the Sublimed are suitably named (as with the self-descriptive moniker of the Minds), as the character Dorolow in *Phlebas* makes explicit: "This creature is virtually a god. I'm sure it can sense our moods and thoughts" (292). Supporting this reading, the Sublimed even have a kind of religious cult that worships them, known as the Sublimers, who:

> had turned what was a normal but generally optional part of a species' choice of fate into a religion. Sublimers believed that everybody ought to sublime, that every human, every animal, every machine and Mind ought to head straight for ultimate transcendence, leaving the mundane life behind and setting as direct a course as possible for nirvana. (*Excession*, 259)

Here Banks emphasises that, while Subliming is common and widespread, it is not generally deemed essential, yet it is a way of thinking that can

---

[82] Clarke, 'The Sublime in Iain M. Banks's "Culture" novels', 11.
[83] Philip Shaw, *The Sublime* (Oxon: Routledge, 2006), 211.
[84] Shaw, *The Sublime*, 211.
[85] Oxford Dictionaries, 'Moksha', Oxford University Press. www.oxforddictionaries.com/definition/english/moksha.
[86] Shaw, *The Sublime*, 1–2.
[87] Oxford Dictionaries, 'Pantheism', Oxford University Press. www.oxforddictionaries.com/definition/english/pantheism.

very easily fascinate and obsess people to the point of their dedicating their "mundane" lives to it, maybe even encouraging others to participate and turning it into a crusade. The Sublimers are ultimately portrayed as religious fundamentalists whose bigotry blinds them to the Culture's doctrine of pluralism, materialism, and freedom of choice (or, for those more sceptical of the Culture, perhaps the Sublimers are a reflection of the evangelical crusades in the name of atheism and utopia undertaken by Contact and SC).

Yet, as Clarke concludes, "Banks's Sublime is as firmly atheistic as the rest of his Culture mythos."[88] When he first began developing his notion of the Sublimed in *Phlebas*, Banks's descriptions – for example: "long retired from the matter-based life of the galaxy" (91) – did not render them in as resolutely rational a manner as in later texts. In *Hydrogen*, for example, the Sublime is portrayed as an "almost tangible, entirely believable, mathematically verifiable nirvana" (63), a description that seems designed to bring its connotations of religious transcendence within a rational framework. In the fictional cosmology of Banks's series, the universe as we know it in fact consists of several layered universes, between two of which is located the Sublime (*Hydrogen*, 16–17). Existing "parched, rolled, compressed and enfolded into the dimensions beyond the dimensions beyond the ones you could see and understand" (*Hydrogen*, 17), there seems nothing supernatural or spiritual about the Sublime, and it functions in much the same way as does virtual space within the series.

Either way, regardless of the extent to which it can be understood in rational terms, the Culture is clearly ideologically and morally opposed to the Sublime. The Culture could "in theory" have "sublimed anything up to eight thousand years ago [...] but the bulk of the Culture has chosen not to" (*Excession*, 82). To achieve Elderhood, as Subliming is also described in *Excession*, would not only require the Culture to stop the work of Contact and SC but negate its general existence as material culture, effectively removing its entire sense of purpose: "the very ideas, the actual concepts of good, fairness and of justice just ceased to matter once one had gone for sublimation" (*Excession*, 82). The Culture's view on Subliming can be seen as a continuation of its stance regarding mortality and immortality, as explored in Chapter Three of this book: its whole existence is geared towards providing the best possible life for its citizens in *this* life, on the material plane; the desire to leave utopia entirely behind is viewed by the Culture as "almost a personal insult" (*Windward*, 110). This view is implicit in the attitude of Culture citizen Byr Genar-Hofoen who, upon meeting a group of Sublimers,

---

[88] Clarke, 'The Sublime in Iain M. Banks's "Culture" novels', 11.

asks rhetorically, "You believe everybody should just disappear up their own arses, don't you?" To which the Sublimer, innocently unaware of Genar-Hofoen's cynicism, replies, "'Oh, no!' [...], her expression terribly serious, 'What we believe in takes one completely *away* from such bodily concerns...'" (*Excession*, 260). The Culture, which Genar-Hofoen still represents at this stage, not only chooses not to Sublime, but openly mocks the process and its advocates.

Despite the relative frequency of their appearance, the Sublimed remain one of the most mysterious entities in Banks's fictional universe, second perhaps only to the Excession. Yet, even if the Sublime is read in ultimately supernatural or spiritual terms, the Culture's attitude towards it is entirely commensurate with its rationalist, humanist outlook.

Conclusion

In *Metamorphoses of Science Fiction*, Darko Suvin famously argued that science fiction can be distinguished from fantasy by thinking of the former as cognitive estrangement and the latter as "the interposition of anti-cognitive laws into the empirical environment,[89] therefore associating SF with rationalism, materialism, and the possible, and fantasy with the supernatural, idealism, and the impossible. As the preceding chapter has demonstrated, Iain M. Banks implicitly intended for the Culture series to be understood as SF in Suvinian terms, and to be marked by this fundamental tendency towards rationalism and materialism as much as possible. Suvin's formulation of the relationship between SF and fantasy is therefore close to what Banks sees as the difference between science and religion,[90] and Ken MacLeod supports

---

[89] Darko Suvin, *Metamorphoses of Science Fiction: On the Poetics and History of a Literary Genre* (Bern, Switzerland: Peter Lang AG, 2016), 21.

[90] See Suvin, 'Estrangement & Cognition', *Metamorphoses*, 15–29; and Wegner, *Shockwaves of Possibility*, 10–13. Writing in *Metamorphoses*, initially published in 1979, Suvin was dismissive of the intellectual import of much fantasy writing, especially that published by Tolkien and in a Tolkienesque mode prior to the 1970s. Yet Suvin admits in his 2016 essay 'Considering the Sense of "Fantasy" or "Fantastic Fiction": An Effusion' that he has "been unable to do even partial justice to the burgeoning commercial genre of Fantasy" and he continues to provide "an experimental assay to see whether whatever sense I may draw from the accumulated splendors and miseries of fantastic fiction mostly from the mid-1970s, and from the secondary literature up to our days, can begin to make sense" of the "post-Tolkien corpus of 'heroic' plus 'horror' fantasy" (388–389).

this notion, commenting that he does not think Banks would have written a novel featuring elements of the supernatural or fantastic in an unambiguous manner: while Banks may have read such works for personal enjoyment, he would not have written them for professional publication, associating the ideological underpinnings of such forms with the irrational.[91]

Yet, as I have established, the Culture series is not entirely devoid of concepts that derive from religious and spiritual notions. Discussing these elements, Banks commented that "SF is now able to speak with some degree of authority" regarding "matters where only religious writing and faith previously seemed qualified to comment."[92] Calling concepts such as souls, afterlives, gods, and transcendence "dream fulfilment" (a term similar to Jameson's "wish fulfilment"[93]), Banks used his secular versions of such concepts to "propose alternative angles for looking at the same dreams."[94] The implication is that, when we come closer to actually achieving such dreams in this world, belief in something immaterial and outside the laws of physics will be understood as unnecessary and eventually die out. Therefore, Banks portrays the Culture as resisting ontological existence in anything other than the material plane, denying the virtual (on any kind of long-term basis), the spiritual, and the transcendent/energy plane of the Sublime as tantamount to an insult against the technoscientific and utopian forces that inspired their society in the first place. The Culture, too, demonstrates through humanism that religious belief is not necessary to live a moral life, and that coupled with such a system, technoscience can offer comfort and meaning for its citizens in this life; although, as we have seen in chapters Three and Four, the model of humanism that Banks followed also set certain limitations upon his progressive worldview. Having established this key break from religious thinking and organised religion, the final chapter of this book is concerned with aesthetic and creative practices in both the Culture itself and the Culture series.

---

[91] Ken MacLeod, 'The Culture & other stories', at 'The Life and Works of Iain (M.) Banks', Huddersfield Literature Festival, 6–7pm, 15 March 2014.
[92] Orbit Books website, 'An Interview with Iain M. Banks'. Web.
[93] See Jameson, 'How to Fulfill A Wish', *Archaeologies*, 72–85.
[94] Orbit Books website, 'An Interview with Iain M. Banks'. Web.

Chapter 6

Whole-Tone Scales Reaching Forever
Art in Utopia, Utopian Art

> "We shall never produce so satisfying a world that there will be no place for art." – B.F. Skinner, *Walden Two*

What do Culture citizens do on a day-to-day basis, if they are not agents of Contact or SC? Can art and creative culture exist in utopia? What function might they serve? What might they tell us about the nature of that utopia? How might a society truthfully represent itself to others without misrepresenting itself through ideology? Addressing such questions, this final chapter focuses on Banks's depictions of the Culture's internal environments, the social and cultural conditions of its GSVs and Os, briefly outlining the everyday culture of the Culture, as far as it is possible to do so, and addressing the problems of decadence and the death of art within utopia, before turning its focus toward the works of art that Banks depicts within the Culture texts. I provide an in-depth analysis of several examples from the series – Culture poetry ('Slight Mechanical Destruction' and 'Zakalwe's Song' from *Weapons*); the *Sleeper Service*'s living tableaux, the *Grey Area*'s torture museum, and the intricately designed ships in *Excession*; the extreme tattooing of Lededje's "Intagliate" body, and its subsequent digital rendering, in *Surface*; as well as three sonic examples: 'Expiring Light' from *Windward*, and, from *The Hydrogen Sonata*, both the musical occurrence 'The Sound' and the titular piece itself. I conclude with discussion of the Culture's attitude towards self-representation and aesthetics.

Everyday Life in the Culture

Several critics have observed that, despite Banks's intention to develop the Culture as a utopia, the texts in the series do not focus primarily upon analysing the details of the alternative society, as is often achieved in traditional utopian narratives through the guide–visitor relationship. In 1999, Simon Guerrier made the crucial observation that, rather than focusing upon the Culture's inner spaces, "it is *in* the liminal zones, in the boundaries between the Culture and other races, that [... Banks's] stories are all situated."[1] Kincaid concurs, arguing that Banks is not concerned with developing a substantial vision of a utopian political system: "If you concentrate on the rough edges of the Culture, those places where it rubs awkwardly against other neighboring civilizations, then you don't have to spend too much time thinking about how the centre actually works. And Banks doesn't do so."[2] Beyond citing textual examples that demonstrate a culture of hedonism, boredom, and liberalism, Kincaid argues, "all we really know of life [within the Culture] is that it is easy, very deliberately and specifically so."[3]

It is certainly clear that life is easy in the Culture – for those not involved in Contact or SC at least – and Guerrier and Kincaid are correct to draw attention to this important aspect of the series: this liminal focus enables Banks to further develop the form of the critical utopia, often highlighting the Culture's imperfections (its potential for imperialism) as well as enabling his fiction to achieve the accelerated narrative thrust of a space opera rather than the famously placid narratives of utopian fiction. Yet, observed across the entire series, Banks depicts more of the Culture's "centre", its culture, structure, and everyday life, than has been previously credited, and a more complex, if necessarily incomplete and fragmentary, picture emerges, as this book has worked to demonstrate.

The Culture is closer to the abundant and hedonistic Land of Cockaigne from medieval myth and literature than More's ascetic and pious community. Our first direct glimpse of life on a Culture Orbital is concerned with Fal 'Ngeestra, a kind of secular Oracle, and a peripheral character who, as with Yime in *Surface Detail*, Banks uses to provide exposition for and commentary on the text's main narrative. 'Ngeestra offers strategic advice to a drone whilst climbing a mountain on an O's "Plate", without the safety of her terminal. During her climb, she reflects upon the Culture and its values, describing "the things that really mattered in life, such as sport, games, romance, studying dead languages, barbarian societies and impossible problems, and climbing high mountains without the aid of a safety harness" (87). 'Ngeestra's list includes a wide range of activities – physical, mental and emotional,

---

[1] Guerrier, 'Culture Theory', 36.
[2] Kincaid, *Iain M. Banks*, 49.
[3] Kincaid, *Iain M. Banks*, 49.

ludic, scholarly, interpersonal, mathematical, linguistic, and so forth – neatly summarising much of what we do know of the Culture's culture. Yet, interestingly, she makes no direct mention of creative, artistic practice as such, a subject we shall return to shortly. The potentially dangerous sport in which 'Ngeestra indulges prefigures other such activities later in the sequence, such as the "wing-flying", or hi-tech hang-gliding, in Chapter Three, and the "lava-rafting" in Chapter Five, of *Look to Windward*. The Culture, then, provides opportunities for fairly extreme sports with full control over the parameters of danger. For those who prefer mental pursuits, game-playing is popular in the Culture, first appearing in Chapter Seven of *Phlebas* through the bizarre card-game Damage, and of course being central to *Player*, where Gurgeh becomes dissatisfied with his academic life of teaching and researching game-playing and trying to avoid attending parties. Game-playing is, in a sense, actually integral to the Culture, replacing the whims of the market with the Minds, who rely upon computer simulations and mathematical modelling to predict the outcomes of all aspects of society, especially SC's interventions, its battles, and other external conflicts. In *Windward*, one Mind even models the devastation inflicted by one of SC's attacks, in order to experience it virtually itself and ensure that the suffering it causes does not outweigh that which it prevents, while others in *Hydrogen* model the results of releasing key information about the Book of Truth to the Gzilt. From these glimpses into the everyday lives of relatively ordinary Culture citizens, we seem expected to deduce that Banks's utopia offers its citizens a range of options for pleasure and education, exploiting the full freedoms of such an advanced, limitless environment.

The Problem of Decadence

But abundance and hedonism potentially pave the road to decadence. Some critics have therefore challenged the Culture's utopianism on the grounds that it has gone too far, becoming culturally amoral or immoral. Farah Mendlesohn, for example, observes that "Christopher Palmer, Bruce Gillespie and Paul Kincaid have all suggested that Iain M. Banks's Culture, sunk as it is in leisure and the pursuit of pleasure, is an essentially decadent society."[4] And there is certainly evidence for this. The drug-fuelled sex orgies depicted in Chapter Ten of *Surface Detail*,

---

[4] Andrew M. Butler and Farah Mendlesohn, eds., *The True Knowledge of Ken MacLeod* (Reading: Science Fiction Foundation, 2003), 116.

perhaps, though they clearly operate within a system of consent and total physical safety, while stronger examples include its more extreme and morally suspect practices, such as the quasi-cannibalism performed onboard a Culture craft in 'State', and the playing of the dangerous game of Damage in *Phlebas*.

Described as "the most decadent game in history" (185), Damage "was just a card game: partly skill, partly luck and partly bluff" (195), but one that potentially involves death, suicide, and extreme emotional manipulation, played for financial "credits" as well as fame and prestige. The game prefigures the themes of other Culture texts such as *Player* and *Surface*, as well as those of cyberpunk fictions, through the motif of an elaborately developed virtual space of a boardgame or computer simulation which becomes both analogue of, and direct catalyst for, life/society itself. Damage acts as a bleak parody of life under Neoliberal capitalism: To "win" at the market-driven games of Globalisation, Banks suggests, the "hyper-rich dead beats" (185) who play it must risk their own mental and physical health, or that of those around them. This therefore suggests that the Minds and Hubs occasionally tolerate disturbing extremes, even for leisure purposes, as Sarble the Eye, "the most famous of the humanoid galaxy's freelance reporters", suggests (*Phlebas*, 186–187). Yet while Damage is played upon an Orbital, Vavatch does not belong to the Culture and instead acts as a kind of interzone or heterotopia,[5] as Banks would explain in a reply to a fan's letter: Vavatch's "condo-style ownership and neutrality are mentioned, if briefly, in the text", and "[t]he Culture simply provides the ships to evacuate the world"[6] prior to the O's demolition.

In 'State', however, Culture citizens are clearly seen to actively partake in disturbingly extreme behaviour. Here, Contact agents eat "vat-grown, ship food" (173), produced artificially onboard the *Arbitrary*. Working in accordance with its central maxim that "nothing and no-one is exploited", then, and as part of its overall technoscientifically enabled Second Nature, this implicitly allows the Culture to avoid the exploitation of animals – even plants – as well as enabling self-sufficiency in deep space – certainly a progressive goal, and also a topical one given that research into synthetic meat began, progressed, and was realised for the first time during Banks's lifetime. (In 1971, muscle fibres from a guinea pig were cultivated *in vitro*, while a 2005 paper by Jason Matheny, a director in US National Intelligence, popularised the concept,

---

[5] See McHale, 'Towards a Poetics of Cyberpunk', 9–11.
[6] Material relating to *Consider Phlebas*, Iain Banks Archive, University of Stirling.

referred to [coincidentally] as "Cultured meat"; and the first lab-grown burger was produced by a Maastricht University professor in 2013.[7]) Yet the origins of the Culture's meat raise ethical issues beyond those relating to animal rights: the feast consumed by the *Arbitrary*'s crew is developed from the cells of various dictators, politicians, and tyrants from Earth's history ("Stewed Idi Amin", "General Pinochet Chilli Con Carne", "Richard Nixon Burgers" [181]). Jude Roberts argues that this is tantamount to Culture protagonists endorsing "the transgression of a taboo that is considered to be the foundation of what it is to be human" using "symbolic and existential" violence.[8] Given that the Culture is a society that has supposedly achieved something near the zenith of human civilisation, such a transgression could suggest – as with the game of Damage – the possibility for decadence in the culture of utopia. Yet the feast scene, written in a wildly exaggerated tone and near-farcical manner, is clearly meant to be humorous, and determining its morality is dependent upon the extent of the differences perceived between physical and symbolic violence. Furthermore, the cultures of Earth as depicted in 'State' become a kind of control experiment for Contact, the continued decadence and deprivation of Earth humans acting as evidence of the necessity for intervention: compared with "us", at least, it is the Culture that appears morally superior.

Both the game Damage and the quasi-cannibalistic feast are certainly two of the most unpleasant practices to derive from the Culture, but their existence does not ultimately undermine the Culture's utopianism – they could even be seen to support it. Mendlesohn regards the Culture as decadent, but not in the same manner as Kincaid, Gillespie, and Palmer: the assertion that the Culture's hedonism equates to its decadence, she argues, "rings false because it has to contend with the outspoken endorsement by the Culture of leisure and pleasure as its whole point, and the very mark of civilization. The headlong flight into hedonism and away from 'reality' is the Culture's *raison d'etre*, not an indication of its decline."[9] Any indication of social decadence within the Culture can only exist within its utopian framework, which ensures that no real, long-lasting harm can occur, even in the most extreme cases: the

---

[7] See P.D. Edelman, 'Commentary: *In Vitro*-Cultured Meat Production', *Tissue Engineering* 11, no. 5/6 (3 May 2005), doi:10.1089/ten.2005.11.659; and BBC News, 'World's first lab-grown burger is eaten in London', 5 August 2013. https://www.bbc.co.uk/news/science-environment-23576143.
[8] Jude Roberts, '"Cannibals from Outer Space!": Symbolic Violence and the Cannibalism of the Other', in *The Science Fiction of Iain M. Banks*, Hubble, Norman, and MacCallum-Stuart, eds., 209.
[9] Mendlesohn, 'The Dialectic of Decadence', 116.

unbridled freedom achieved by the Culture, even at its most extreme, only supports its success. While a detailed analysis of the Culture's everyday life in this manner must necessarily remain incomplete, there is another method for establishing a stronger idea of the cultural detail and value of Banks's utopia.

The Death of Art in Utopia

Alongside the radical social and political changes that help to establish a utopian society, it is necessary to consider the associated effect this would have on the notions of art and creativity as we understand them; and considerations of art in utopia and the nature of utopian art have fascinated thinkers almost as much as utopian changes to economics, human nature, gender roles, and religion. Before it is possible to ask what art in utopia might look like, and who might produce it and why, we need to ask if it would in fact exist *at all*. R.C. Elliott discusses potential pitfalls in literary creation, suggesting that "[p]resumably the same substantive problems which have plagued writers trying to imagine what utopia would be like will face those who try, once utopian conditions are established, to create their own literature."[10] These problems may in fact prove to be so substantive that utopians simply do not, or *cannot*, create literature, and there are several cases to be made for the inevitability of the complete cessation of aesthetic practice within a utopian environment. As Elliott continues, "[t]o a degree that a literary artist helps bring about the conditions of utopia, he contributes to the death – or at least to the severe debilitation – of his art. It is a genuine dilemma" (128).

Art might be broadly defined as the products of deliberate creative and imaginative endeavour, often at least partly motivated by the desire for others to experience it and/or for financial gain. One potential problem leading to the "death of art" in utopia, then, is what Fredric Jameson describes as the "aestheticization of daily life", as occurs in Morris's *News From Nowhere*. In a postcapitalist society where labour has become unalienated, Morris suggested that creativity and imagination would become integral to employment, and what we conceive of as art would no longer exist as a separate category, as it would have blended seamlessly into daily life.[11] Utopia might also spell the death of art in another manner: if art, in a Marxist sense – at least the *best* art – fulfils

---

[10] Elliott, *The Shape of Utopia*, 122–124.
[11] Jameson, *Archaeologies*, 184.

a politically radical function, rendering society's ills visible and forcing it to confront them, then perhaps it serves no purpose in a utopian environment that has overcome its problems. By this understanding, art could lead to the development of utopia in the first instance, but would disappear once its purpose had been fulfilled. If this utopia ever developed problems again, perhaps radical art would resurface.

Another problem assumes that the desire to produce art would continue, regardless of utopian working conditions, but involves the removal of the deeper inspiration and motivations for producing art in the first place. As Elliott observes, "like heroism, great art may prove incompatible with the conditions of a stable and happy society."[12] He goes on to provide the example of the Vril-ya race from Edward Bulwer-Lytton's *The Coming Race* (1871) who, in their techno-spiritual utopia, "have only an insipid poetry of description". Because the Vril-ya "no longer experience the passions which motivated the great poetry of the past, the Vril-ya have no subject."[13] Elliott's discussion here follows on from the problem of boredom, suggesting that the art of utopians would necessarily reflect their own passion-less, insipid lives. His argument follows Adorno's definition of utopia as the absence of violence, suggesting that, if "the triumph of the artist" is "as Lionel Trilling has said, to shape the material of pain we all share," then "utopia tries to eradicate that pain. Its function is to lower the temperature of the culture, to reduce the amount of 'history' in it; for history, we know, is equivalent to pain."[14] Truly inspired art, then, seemingly cannot exist without reflecting a history of conflict.

To this list of problems we can add a third, for which Banks's series is a special case. The crucial role of posthuman AIs in the Culture narratives raises the issue of art produced by machines. As explained in *Windward* and *Hydrogen*, the Minds are capable of reproducing even the most complex forms of art produced by people to an incredibly high standard, and even producing works of their own, to a level of perfection that a human could not hope to achieve – a fact that could arguably decrease the significance of art produced by humans, even rendering it pointless.[15] (Such ideas reflect developments in AI contemporaneous with the Culture series: AI art had been developing for 50 years by 2018, when the first painting created by AI that uses algorithms to learn aesthetics by itself was auctioned for almost £8,000

---

[12] Elliott, *The Shape of Utopia*, 123.
[13] Elliott, *The Shape of Utopia*, 123.
[14] Elliott, *The Shape of Utopia*, 127.
[15] See *Windward*, 299–300; and *Hydrogen*, 187.

at auction in Christie's, London.[16]) The Minds and drones created several of the artworks analysed in this chapter, and we will return to this issue shortly.

Yet, despite these problems, art is clearly not dead in the Culture. Unlike Morris, who saw unalienated labour and satisfying employment as the key to the good life, the citizens of Banks's utopia have no need to work at all, so Culture citizens have literally centuries of time to fill, in their healthy, artificially extended lives. It follows, then, that many may choose to fill their time by utilising their imagination and creativity in whichever manner they see fit, fully supported by the limitless production capacity of their environments. Banks's close friend and musical collaborator, Gary Lloyd, assured me that Banks imagined there to be "the whole panoply of all music in the Culture,"[17] and following this I think it is fair to assume that Banks felt the same about the other arts. Yet the most immediate general observations to be made about art in the Culture series are that, firstly, it appears relatively infrequently, and secondly, that the majority of it – with one notable exception – is produced by individuals who are not citizens of the Culture, or exist in an ambiguous relationship with it (as we have seen is typical of Banks's characters more generally): dissidents, outsiders, non-conformists, the exploited, and the disillusioned. Discussing the role of art in the Culture, Banks as narrator – tongue firmly in cheek – indicates that it is not widely regarded as a positive pursuit: "Being a famous artist in the Culture meant at best it was accepted you must possess a certain gritty determination; at worst it was generally seen as pointing to a pitiably archaic form of insecurity and a rather childish desire to show off" (*Excession*, 198). His comments are clearly meant as comic irony, on the one hand, but, on the other, do suggest that artists definitely exist in the Culture, and do become well known, with this practice seen as serving little purpose other than to express the character of the artist. Even the most talented artists, Banks explains, "are not regarded in quite the same hallowed light as Contact members" (*Excession*, 198). If, as Elliott suggests, heroes and artists are both scarce in utopia, then perhaps both Banks's Handy "heroes" in Contact and SC, as well as its artists, necessarily operate on the Culture's fringes as they potentially threaten its utopian values. In this respect, much of the art in the sequence could be considered "Outsider Art" regardless of the technical training such artists have received.

---

[16] Thomas Graham, 'Art made by AI is selling for thousands – is it any good?' BBC website, 12 December 2018. http://www.bbc.com/culture/story/20181210-art-made-by-ai-is-selling-for-thousands-is-it-any-good.

[17] Gary Lloyd, email to author, 24 April 2016.

Art in Utopia and Utopian Art

While some see utopia as the death of art, R.C. Elliott, Jameson, and William J. Burling have argued for exploration of the art that is depicted in utopias as a crucial means of evaluating their quality and significance. Jameson, paraphrasing Elliott, compels us to "judge the quality of a given utopia on the basis of the art its creator attributed to his imaginary scenario."[18] Reasoning that art uniquely lays bare a utopia's shortcomings, Jameson argues that "[t]he work of art within the work of art thus itself becomes the miniature glass in which Utopia's most glaring absences are thus reproduced with minute clarity."[19] While Burling agrees with Jameson on the importance of focusing upon a utopia's artworks for similar reasons, their discussion on the most effective methodology for producing such an analysis places emphasis on different aspects of the artwork. For Jameson, critics should focus on the *content* of the described artworks, their aesthetics: the shortcomings of a utopia are concealed, he argues, "at an external level of political and social argument [and] of economic production," but can be, by the "purely aesthetic, suspended."[20] Burling, however, argues that Jameson has provided no clear framework or methodology for producing such an analysis,[21] and outlines his own as follows: "the mechanism of production is the crucial factor respecting art's form. While variations of content are interesting, they have far lesser ideological significance for art than those of form."[22] Burling defines what he calls a *"properly utopian artform"* as follows: *"a collective social practice that disempowers or exploits no-one, is ideologically transparent, and can be produced and/or consumed by any person in some variation."*[23] It is important to note, here, that Burling places the Culture's central axiom (that no-one and nothing is exploited) also as a defining aspect of utopian art. He finds a depiction of music from Le Guin's *The Dispossessed* to be "what Raymond Williams calls a *variation* of a presently understood art form, rather than the more properly dynamic and utopian matter of *innovation* that whole new mode of social relations would require", whereas the depiction of music in Kim Stanley Robinson's *Blue Mars* "tentatively but more fully achieves the

---

[18] Jameson, *Archaeologies*, 124, footnote.
[19] Jameson, *Archaeologies*, 185.
[20] Jameson, *Archaeologies*, 185.
[21] William J. Burling, 'Art as "The Basic Technique of Life": Utopian Art and Art in Utopia', in *Red Planets: Marxism and Science Fiction*, Bould and Miéville, eds. (London: Pluto Press, 2009), 47.
[22] Burling, 'Art as "The Basic Technique of Life"', 52.
[23] Burling, 'Art as "The Basic Technique of Life"', 63. Emphasis in original.

goal of historically legitimate utopian innovation."[24] The analysis that follows applies elements of Jameson and Burling's thinking (discussion of form and content), as well as Williams's dynamic of variation and innovation, to depictions of art in the Culture series.

Poetry under Special Circumstances: "an allegory of regress"

The importance of the poem 'Slight Mechanical Destruction' is perhaps easily overlooked when considering the complexity of the novel *Weapons* to which it forms an epigraph. Yet – written by Banks in March 1978 – it is of significance because, attributed to Rasd-Coduresa Diziet Embless Sma da' Marenhide (aka Diziet Sma), it is the only work of art depicted in the series to be created by a human Culture citizen with an un-complex relationship to her home. Sma is always *of* and *for* the Culture, always supporting its decisions and values, as we have seen. On one level, the poem prefigures the novel's central themes, expounding Banks's ideas of an amoral mercenary fighting for the "good guys", and offers cryptic clues about the narrative to follow. But Nick Hubble, reviewing *Poems* for *Strange Horizons*, argues that 'Slight Mechanical Destruction' "is not just the kernel of truth underlying the novel but the keystone of the entire Culture series," because "[w]hat the Culture merely know about the reality of the hierarchical societies of economies based on scarcity, Zakalwe viscerally embodies; by 'playing their game for real' [...] he gives it meaning."[25] While "Utopia spawns few warriors", as the poem's line goes, hired-gun outsiders such as Zakalwe are certainly exploited by Banks's utopia to ensure its self-preservation. Zakalwe as SC agent fights the Culture's battles, performs their missions, and as such experiences the real violence, inequality, and conflict that the pampered citizens of utopia can only read about, or experience through art. In this respect, the poem is Sma's response to the troubled relationship she has with her friend and colleague Cheradenine/Elethiomel.

The medium of poetry does not seem predisposed to meeting Burling's criteria for a properly utopian artwork. As a recognisable, familiar artform, such poetry is clearly an example of variation rather than innovation, in William's terms. This poem is also clearly an individual, deeply personal exercise; we are unsure where and in exactly in what form 'Slight

---

[24] Burling, 'Art as "The Basic Technique of Life"', 62. Emphasis in original.
[25] Nick Hubble, 'Poems by Iain Banks and Ken MacLeod', *Strange Horizons*, 12 October 2015. http://strangehorizons.com/non-fiction/reviews/poems-by-iain-banks-and-ken-macleod/.

Mechanical Destruction' is published (printed on paper? viewed on a computer screen? openly available on the Culture's data nets? kept in a personal collection?); and it is difficult to determine poetry – which is naturally drawn to individual interpretation – as "ideologically transparent". Yet, setting aside Sma's choice of words for poetic meaning, the language in which the poem is said to have been originally written – Marain, as used in the Culture, prior to the translation by Sma into English that we read in the novel – is a profoundly utopian form for meaning-making. Marain is said to have begun with a "linguistic blank sheet, yet with the accumulated knowledge of the hundreds of thousands known to those people and machines charged with the language's devising."[26] Banks is careful to distance Marain implicitly from the imperialistic practices that have helped to form English, describing the Culture's language as "culturally inclusive" yet with "no links to any of the main languages spoken by the people who came together to make up the Culture as a civilization."[27] In this way, the language of Banks's utopia can retain a sense of its multicultural history without symbolically imposing the dominance of any one culture over any other; it is a language designed, as with L.L. Zamenhof's Esperanto, to foster peace and inter-national/-galactic understanding. While the content of 'Slight Mechanical Destruction' cannot be said to be free from ideological content, it is at least a poem that eschews any imperialistic hegemony over the language in which it is written.

'Zakalwe's Song', a poem that forms part of the epigraph to *Weapons*, is attributed to a fictional, non-Culture poet, Shias Engin. That it is said to have been published in 'Volume IX: Juvenilia and Discarded Drafts' of Engin's *Complete Collected Poems* is a sly, self-deprecating joke on Banks's part, no doubt a reference to the fact that the original composition of the poem (December 1973) predates the rest of his published oeuvre. The language in which 'Zakalwe's Song' was written is not made clear, nor is any background relating to its fictional composer provided,[28] beyond speculation based upon the piecing together of clues from the main narrative. The influence of T.S. Eliot on Banks's writing is well documented, inscribed upon the series through the direct references to

[26] Banks, 'A Few Notes on Marain', Website of Trevor Hopkins. http://trevor-hopkins.com/banks/a-few-notes-on-marain.html.
[27] Banks, 'A Few Notes on Marain'.
[28] In an early draft of *Weapons* (circa 1974) – in which Banks experimented with a revolving "name cycle" for Zakalwe, with his name changing regularly throughout the text – Zakalwe at one stage introduces himself as "Engin. Shias Engin", in a clear allusion to the iconic introduction associated with Ian Fleming's character James Bond. – Iain M. Banks Archive, University of Stirling.

'The Waste Land' in the titles of two books within it (*Consider Phlebas*, *Look to Windward*) and 'Zakalwe's Song', too – with its inclusion of naturalistic dialogue, its influence from dramatic monologue, and its sense of confusion between the literal and symbolic – bears this influence. As Hubble explains, in describing "the conflict between the desire to stay and the impulse to leave, it is very much a poem about mortal finitude", quoting the final line: "The bomb lives only as it is falling."[29] This image – of the meaning of life lying in its journey rather than its destination – supports Banks's approach to utopianism as a matter of process and constant evolution. It also most explicitly mirrors the Culture's philosophy of resisting the urge to transcend its humanity, of living in the Real rather than the spiritual, the virtual or the Sublime, and reaffirms the central tenet of a techno-utopia, grounded in making the very best of what human culture can offer.

Excession and the Living Tableaux of War

Banks relished the freedoms afforded to him by the expansive modes of space opera to imagine strange forms of art and creative culture – all linked to the Culture in some way but not necessarily originating from within it. In the fourth-published Culture text *Excession*, for example, the Mind which inhabits and oversees the GSV *Sleeper Service* is afforded the opportunity to create a unique work of "living" art. With only two sentient, conscious inhabitants – the reclusive ex-Contact officer Dajeil Gelian and an AI, Gravious – the huge vessel of the *Sleeper Service* provides space for a multitude of flora and fauna, gathered from all over the galaxy, as well as maintaining Culture individuals who have agreed to be Stored onboard in suspended animation, as suggested by its name. By choosing to act as a vessel for Storage, the *Sleeper Service* is deemed to have adopted an unusual lifestyle, and again, like Ziller and Cossont, it exists on the fringes of the Culture (as do its inhabitants) as an officially "Eccentric" craft:

> When it Stored people it usually did so in small tableaux after the manner of famous paintings, at first, or humorous poses [...] the ship had always asked the permission of the Storees in question before it used their sleeping forms in this way, and respected the wishes of the few people who preferred not to be Stored in a situation where they might be gazed upon as though they were figures in a painting, or sculptures. (83)

[29] Hubble, 'Poems by Iain Banks and Ken MacLeod'. Web.

Based upon this description – which emphasises the consent of the Storees, the Culture's famously ludic attitude, and the ship's interest in art – the tableaux seem an innocent way for the Mind to pass time, out alone in deep space, providing the opportunity for Storees to participate in a unique artistic venture. These tableaux, to the Mind of the *Sleeper Service*, are its "master-work, its definitive statement" (205). Yet the *Sleeper Service*'s actions and motivations for the tableaux become more suspect and sinister as its interests develop in a morbid direction, and it begins focusing exclusively upon recreating especially gruesome scenes from historical battles, such as the Battle of Boustrago, and "the great sea battle of Octovelein".

Concerning the latter, the *Sleeper Service* appears to focus upon conveying the epic scale and dramatic complexity of the battle, which, at points, sounds almost picturesque in its descriptions of natural imagery:

> The air was crisscrossed by the smoky trails of the primitive rockets and the sky seemed supported by the great columns of smoke rising from stricken warships and transports. The water was dark blue, ruffled with waves, spattered with the tall feathery plumes of crashing rockets, creased white at the stem of each ship, and covered in flames where oils had been poured between ships in desperate attempts to prevent boarding […] The incomplete battle scene filled less than half of the bay's sixteen square kilometers. (205)

Here, Banks evokes the long-standing real-world tradition of paintings depicting naval battles – and comparable real-world examples of grand galleons leaking flames and pounding each with cannons are too numerous to mention.[30] The tone of the preceding passage, however, when compared with others that detail the ship's tableau of the 'Battle of Boustrago' – a particularly violent conflict from the Culture's distant history, which, as with the Twin Novae Battle mentioned previously, had been the "final, decisive battle" in a large-scale war – contrasts sharply (*Excession*, 79):

> Bodies lay scattered like twisted, shredded leaves amongst the torn-up grassland […] they all lay together, some with the collapsed shapelessness of death, some in a pool of their own internal organs,

---

[30] Notable examples include: 'The Battle of Trafalgar' by William Clarkson Stanfield, 1805; 'The Sinopskiy Battle on the 18th November of the 1853 year (Night after Battle)' by Ivan Aivazovsky, 1853; and 'Battle of Gibraltar' by Cornelis Claesz van Wieringen, 1607.

some missing limbs, some in a posture appropriate to their agony, thrashing or writhing or – in the case of some of the soldiers – supporting themselves on one limb and reaching out to plead for help, or water, or a *coup de grace* to end their torment. It was all quite still, frozen like a three-dimensional photograph, and it all lay, spread out like some military society's model scene made real, in General Bay Three Inner of the GSV *Sleeper Service*. (79–80)

The ship's focus for this tableau – notably different from the Battle of Octovelein – is clearly upon the gory aftermath of the battle, emphasising the pain, torment, and desperation of the dead, dying, and severely wounded, rather than the actions performed in the midst of the battle itself. As is made explicit, the tableau is very similar to dioramas created by real-world hobbyists and military enthusiasts, yet rendered on a one-to-one scale. As with the Hub in *Windward*, the Mind demonstrates an obsessive "working through" of violence and pain.

This becomes even more disturbing, as Banks notes, in the ship's attention to detail, carefully recreating the scene – every gout of blood and puff of smoke – with an obsessive accuracy:

> The details of the scene were as authentic as the ship could make them; it had studied every painting, etching and sketch of the battle and read every account, military and media report of it, even taking the trouble to track down the records of the diary entries of individual soldiers, while at the same time undertaking exhaustive research into the whole historical period concerned including the uniforms, weaponry and tactics used when the battle had taken place. (80)

The *Sleeper Service*, then, treads a fine line between providing a highly accurate recreation of a crucial historical scene as might be found in a museum, and exploiting the painful deaths of its subjects and the permission of its Storees, in a kind of House of Horrors. The tableaux, however, prove to be very popular. When the *Sleeper Service* "release[s] holograms of its more and more ambitious tableaux", it attracts significant attention from Culture people: Ulver Seich, one of the novel's viewpoint characters, expresses disappointment that she is unable to visit;[31] others are said to be drawn to it as they "thought it rather amusing"; others

---

[31] *Excession*, 340: "It looked like she wouldn't get to see even the remnants of the famous craft's tableaux vivants, and would have to make do with the Grey Area and its tableaux mortants."

because "they might be said to be forming part of a work of art"; and yet others because it is "fashionable" (84–85).

When an avatar of the *Sleeper Service*, known as Amorphia, enters the narrative, traversing the Battle of Boustrago in order to awaken an important Storee, the avatar offers an insight into its motivation for the tableau. Upon recovering, the Storee in question, Dajeil Gelian, observes the tableau surrounding her "for some time", and has her observations preempted by Amorphia: "'It is a terrible sight,' it said. 'But it was the last great land battle on Xlephier Prime. To have one's final significant battle at such an early technological stage is actually a great achievement for a humanoid species'" (87). By emphasising the significance of this battle – marking an end to almost all conflict – Amorphia suggests that it was motivated by a positive, progressive desire to remind the tableaux's viewers (who are implicitly mostly, if not all, from the Culture) about the unfortunate necessity for war in the past, and some of the "good" that has arisen from it, as well as providing a celebration of the fact that it can be removed altogether. Although Dajeil's response – "I was just thinking how impressive all this was. You must be proud" (*Excession*, 87) – could be read as sarcastic.

The Battle of Boustrago tableau, in particular, can be usefully compared with works by real-world artists such as Spanish Romantic painter and printmaker Francisco de Goya, especially 'The Disasters of War' (1810–1820), and contemporary *enfants terribles*, sibling duo Jake and Dinos Chapman, whose work often engages with that of Goya, particularly their sculpture 'Great Deeds Against the Dead' (2003). In 'The Disasters of War', a series of 82 etchings produced as a protest against various uprisings and wars affecting Spain during the early nineteenth century, Goya depicts various scenes of murder, torture, and execution, such as number 37, '*Esto es peor*' ('This is worse'), where the mutilated torsos and limbs of civilian victims are mounted on trees, in the aftermath of a war. As with the tableaux of the *Sleeper Service*, the cadaver in the tree within Goya's etching appears artistically arranged like a figure for a statue, and is depicted in considerable detail. An exhibition of Goya's work in London in 2015 reopened critical debate surrounding the violent content of this artist's work, focused on the question of whether it supports freedom from tyranny and repression, or glorifies it.[32] Similar debates surround the Chapman Brothers,

---

[32] See James Hall, 'My Highlight: Goya', *Guardian*, 3 January 2015. www.theguardian.com/artanddesign/2015/jan/03/my-highlight-goya-courtauld-national-gallery-james-hall; and Christopher Turner, '"I'd like to have stepped on Goya's toes, shouted in his ears and punched him in the

also, whose portfolio of controversies includes the direct alteration of mint-condition plates from 'The Disasters of War', printed by Goya himself (a piece the title of which anticipates its own controversy: 'Insult to Injury'), which was described by the Brothers as "rectification" and "improvement", but by critics as "desecration" and "defacement".[33] In direct relevance to the tableaux produced by the *Sleeper Service*, the Brothers produced 'Great Deeds Against the Dead' (2003), a life-sized, mixed-media recreation of *'Esto es peor'*, created from dismembered, fully castrated mannequins impaled upon a bare tree.

Regardless of the morbid nature of many of its obsessions, the *Sleeper Service* ultimately redeems itself in the narrative of Excession, when it plays a major role in ending the war at the novel's heart. It is revealed that the *Sleeper Service*, far from being a docile eccentric, disengaged from the politics of the Culture, has been part of a group of Minds known as the Interesting Times Games, engaged in a conflict between the Culture, an aggressive alien race, the Affront, and the mysterious and powerful entity the Excession itself. A sub-section of this gang, acting against the wishes of the Gang and the Culture at large, wished for the *Sleeper Service* to give over its vast hold space – currently filled with flora, fauna, and its elaborate tableaux – to a great fleet of Culture attack vessels, thereby ironically making the ship potentially responsible for such epic scenes of death and slaughter as it chose to represent with its art. In a wonderfully surreal continuation of its artistic inclinations, the *Sleeper Service* does perform this request, causing, "without warning […] Stored bodies and giant animals" to begin "popping into existence" across an Orbital, Teriocre, "inside the sports halls, on beaches, terraces, boardwalks and pavements, in parks, plazas, deserted stadia and every other sort of public space the Orbital had to offer" (*Excession*, 240–241) which suggests a more ludic sensibility for the bizarre, perhaps, rather than an unhealthy, obsessive interest in morbidity or actual sadism.

Ultimately, the *Sleeper Service* refuses to co-operate with the Gang, and uses its resources in a different manner in order to bring the war to a more peaceful conclusion. At the novel's finish, the *Sleeper Service* readies itself to perform the ultimate deed of heroism, sacrificing itself for the good of its people, although eventually the threat such destruction

---

face": The Chapman Brothers', *Tate Etc* 8 (Autumn 2006). www.tate.org.uk/context-comment/articles/id-have-stepped-on-goyas-toes-shouted-his-ears-and-punched-him-face.

[33] Jonathan Jones, 'Look What We Did', *Guardian*, 31 March 2003. www.theguardian.com/culture/2003/mar/31/artsfeatures.turnerprize2003.

represents seemingly causes the Excession to leave, just in time for the *Sleeper Service* to survive (428). This potential act of self-sacrifice, the *Sleeper Service* concludes, could be seen as "a kind of desperation at work", perhaps "an act of defiance", or maybe "it was even something close to an act of art" (428).

If the artistic tastes of the *Sleeper Service* tend towards the strange, they are eclipsed in this regard by the GCU *Grey Area* – also a key player in *Excession*'s narrative – which, in a similar manner to the *Sleeper Service*, uses itself as a venue for a kind of exhibition, yet one which is even more gruesome:

> The ship was like a museum to torture, death and genocide; it was filled with mementoes and souvenirs from hundreds of different planets, all testifying to the tendency towards institutionalized cruelty exhibited by so many forms of intelligent life. From thumbscrews and pilliwinks to death camps and planet-swallowing black holes, the Grey Area had examples of the devices and entities involved, or their effects, or documentary recordings of their use. Most of the ship's corridors were lined with weaponry, the larger pieces standing on the floor, others on tables; bigger items took up whole cabins, lounges or larger public spaces and the very biggest weapons were shown as scale models. (339)

Described as "like a museum to torture, death and genocide", Banks invites the reader to draw comparison between the *Grey Area*'s collection and really existing museums of a similar nature, such as the Torture Museum, and the Museum of Medieval Torture Instruments, both located in Amsterdam, Netherlands, and the Medieval Crime Museum, located in Rothenburg ob der Tauber, Germany.[34] It is an interesting fact, if possibly a coincidence, that the only city in the world to have more than one museum dedicated to such ghoulish subject matter is Amsterdam, which is known (perhaps stereotypically so) – like the Culture – as cosmopolitan, peaceful, and tolerant.

If the proceeding description of the *Grey Area* serves to indicate the tone and scale of its collection, the following list that Banks provides – featuring some 35 of the "thousands of instruments of torture" on display – indicates the somewhat obsessional extent of the ship's interests, as well as the huge time periods over which the items have been gathered:

---

[34] See the respective museums' websites: www.torturemuseum.com/; www.torturemuseumamsterdam.com/; and www.kriminalmuseum.rothenburg.de/.

> clubs, spears, knives, swords, strangle cords, catapults, bows, powder guns, shells, mines, gas canisters, bombs, syringes, mortars, howitzers, missiles, atomics, lasers, field arms, plasma guns, microwavers, effectors, thunderbolters, knife missiles, line guns, thudders, gravguns, monofilament warps, pancakes, AM projectors, grid-fire impulsers, ZPE flu-polarisers, trapdoors units, CAM spreaders and a host of other inventions designed for – or capable of being turned to the purpose of – producing death, destruction and agony. (339)

Featuring crude medieval weapons, such as clubs and spears, often roughly constructed from simple materials; far-future technology and staples of military SF and space opera such as grav- and plasma guns; and the even more complex-sounding ordinance suggested by the nova "grid-fire impulsers" and "ZPE flu-polarisers" – the paragraph is a huge list, both exhaustive and exhausting, of every conceivable type of arsenal. The presence of such a collection on board a vessel from the Culture seems perhaps somewhat incongruous – even for an Eccentric ship – given their supposedly peaceful nature. Given what Banks reveals about the *Grey Area* and its later role in the narrative, however, the content of the ship's collection seems appropriate to its nature, and therefore becomes sinister and concerning. The ship's moniker "*Grey Area*", suggesting connotations of uncertainty, dubiousness, and distrust, is significant as it is revealed that this was not the name it selected for itself (which is not stated), but one in fact chosen for it by the Culture: this rare incidence, of a Culture vessel being denied an official listing under its name of choice, is considered a grave insult, and clearly shows that the *Grey Area* is generally distrusted by the Culture.[35] The *Grey Area*'s bad reputation in the novel in fact extends beyond mere distrust: the ship is despised by its peers for its habit of reading the minds of Culture humans without their consent – perhaps the gravest wrongdoing it is possible for a Mind to commit, second to murder – therefore earning its pejorative nickname, "Meatfucker" (*Windward*, 249; *Excession*, 70–71). The ship therefore becomes a perfect exemplar of both names, performing a kind of rape of the psyche.

When Ulver Seich visits the *Grey Area*, her observations provide commentary on the nature of the items in the ship's collection, and draw attention to the somewhat detached way in which it is presented to an observer:

---

[35] See *Windward*: "To be denied your self-designated name is a unique insult in the Culture" (249).

She thought they might be more effective if they had contained the victims or the victims and tormentors, but they didn't. Instead they contained just the rack, the iron maiden, the fires and the irons, the shackles and the beds and chairs, the buckets of water and acid and electric cables and all the serried instruments of torture and death. To see them in action you had to stand before a screen. It was a little shocking, Ulver supposed, but kind of aloof at the same time. (*Excession*, 340)

Ulver observes that the various devices and weapons are presented in isolation from the human "victims" for whose torture they are designed, thus avoiding a visceral response to the actions, and also in isolation from the "tormentors", also avoiding an opportunity for the observer to analyse those capable of conducting such actions. While the torture is recreated on a "screen", the resulting effect is only "a little shocking", and her ultimate feeling of semi-aloofness suggests that her feeling of shock will be only temporary, and she will be able to leave the exhibits without being affected on a long-term or permanent basis.

Following this observation, however, Ulver goes on to suggest that her response is both cerebral and visceral. Initially she notes that, "It was like you could just inspect this stuff and get some idea of how it worked and what it did [...] and you could sort of ride it out [...] at the end of it you were still here, it hadn't happened to you" (340–341), which indicates that her experience was almost an impersonal, technical exercise. She follows this, however, by mentioning that, whilst "watching the screens [...] for a few seconds", she "nearly lost her breakfast; and it wasn't even humans who were being tortured" (340–341). The fact that the depictions on-screen almost made her physically sick indicate that she endured a deeper level of shock and distress during the exhibit after all; and her comment that "it wasn't even humans who were being tortured" suggests a feeling of pan-species empathy resulting from her experience – a more universal sense of horror at appalling acts of pain deliberately inflicted upon living creatures.

Ulver's next comments, however, indicate a further, more directly political, aspect of the *Grey Area*'s collection: "stopping this sort of shit was exactly what SC, Contact, the Culture was about, and you were part of that civilisation, part of that civilising... and that sort of made it bearable. Just if you didn't watch the screens" (340). As a Culture citizen, Ulver has adopted the values, messages, and ideologies of her civilisation, believing that the Culture is a force of moral progress in the galaxy, which is self-evidently, diametrically opposed to all forms of torture; as Banks stated: "What it boils down to is that a society that condones torture to protect itself doesn't deserve to be protected in the first place."[36] Viewing the *Grey Area*'s collection, horrific as it may be, is justified as it reaffirms everything she knows about herself and her background. In this regard, the collection operates in a similar manner to the 'Battle of Boustrago', as noted above, which sought to affirm the dominant narrative of the culture in which it was produced. It is interesting, at this stage, to recall the fact that, amidst the long list of *Grey Area* artefacts Banks provides, appears a knife missile – the Culture's most quintessential weapon. Whatever the real function of the *Grey Area*'s "grisly collection of memorabilia", when Ulver wonders "how many people had looked upon this," the ship's reply is vague: "apparently it regularly offered its services as a sort of travelling museum of pain and ghastliness, but it rarely had any takers" (341).

In contrast to the artworks produced by the *Grey Area*, and the majority of those on the *Sleeper Service*, Banks later describes one of the *Sleeper Service*'s tableaux that depicts a completely different scene, seemingly created with alternative motivations:

> the modest tableau on the balcony, which in its previous existence, before the GSV had decided to go Eccentric, had been part of a café with a fine view of the bay. Here were posed seven humans, all with their backs to the view of the empty bay and facing the hologram of a calm, empty swimming pool. The humans wore trunks; they sat in deck chairs around a couple of low tables full of drinks and snacks. They had been caught in the acts of laughing, talking, blinking, scratching their chin, drinking. (206–207)

Initially, the tableau may perhaps seem included purely for comic effect, achieved by its sharp contrast with the battle-focused tableaux previously described. Immediately following the preceding quotation, however, Banks states that the tableau in fact depicts "some famous painting, apparently. It didn't look very artistic to Gravious. It supposed you had to see it from the right angle" (207).

Here, Banks may be referring to 'People in the Sun', painted by Edward Hopper in 1960, currently owned by the Smithsonian American Art Museum, which depicts three men and two women, dressed formally, seated in deck chairs, and facing out over "mountains, sky, and grass," an "abstracted environment that veers between a real view

---

[36] James Knight and Murdo McLeod, 'Iain Banks', *Vice*, 2 December 2009. https://www.vice.com/en_uk/article/jmdm8y/iain-banks-274-v16n12.

and a stage set."[37] As noted in the description provided by the Museum, "People in the Sun suggests a crowd of tourists who feel obliged to take in a famous scenic view, but do so with little pleasure."[38] Following this observation, the expressions of Hopper's tourists indicate an arguably neutral response to the scenery that they observe, which can easily be interpreted as boredom. The human figures from Banks's tableau, however, are notable for the distinct range of their expressions and gestures – "laughing, talking, blinking, scratching their chin, drinking" – and, while there is nothing immediately unusual or striking about these commonplace and familiar actions, the fact that they were singled out for depiction, by both Banks and the *Sleeper Service*, draws attention to this very ordinariness. Perhaps this "modest tableau on the balcony" is included to enliven an otherwise potentially morbid and depressing exhibition, by capturing seven different individuals, each expressing a different aspect of everyday human activity: focusing upon life as it is lived, amongst so much death and suffering. Considered alongside the *Sleeper Service*'s other works, it establishes a dialectic of pain, torture, and death on the one hand, and freedom, life, and utopia on the other.

Lededje's Intagliation in *Surface Detail*

Lededje Y'breq, the protagonist of *Surface Detail*, can be understood – like the *Sleeper Service*'s tableaux – as an example of a living work of art. Referred to as an "Intagliate", Lededje "was covered, head to foot, in what was called a congenitally administered tattoo. Lededje had been born tattooed, emerging from the womb with the most fabulously intricate patterns indelibly encoded at a cellular level onto her skin and throughout her body" (69). Lededje is a woman who originates from the pan-human society known as the Sichultian Enablement; while Lededje and her people become involved with the Culture in the novel, the creation of her elaborate "tattoo" initially has no direct relation to the Culture, yet later in *Surface Detail* the Culture is required to remake Lededje's tattoo, as discussed below, which can be used to provide a degree of insight into its own practices.

It is straightforward to understand the extrapolation that Banks has performed to arrive at the notion of Intagliation. Beginning with the

---

[37] Edward Hopper, 'People in the Sun', 1960, oil on canvas, 40⅜ x 60⅜ in. (102.6 x 153.4 cm) Smithsonian American Art Museum. Gift of S.C. Johnson & Son, Inc. 1969. americanart.si.edu/collections/search/artwork/?id=10762.
[38] Hopper, 'People in the Sun'. Web.

concept of cosmetic tattooing – inserting indelible ink into the dermis layer of the skin in order to change the pigment and decorate a person's body – as is commonly practised in various cultures worldwide, Banks postulates that a society with a higher level of technological capability would be able to administer such markings throughout the entirety of a human body, both inside and out: the markings are noted to appear also on an Intagliate's teeth, the whites of their eyes, the pores of their skin, their organs, and their bones (69). While the use of tattooing for purely aesthetic purposes is mentioned in Banks's Culture series,[39] Intagliation is not voluntary: her markings identify Lededje as a chattel slave, the property of "Mr Joiler Veppers, President and Prime Executive Officer of the Veprine corporation; the richest man in the world [...] in charge of the most powerful and profitable company that had ever existed" (80). Allowing for something of a grim pun on the term "branding", Lededje's tattoos consist of "fabulous scroll work", the basis of which is the brand logo for Veppers' company: "the letter V standing for Vespers, or the Vesperine corporation that he commanded" (75). Lededje's father, Grautze – Veppers' business partner and sworn "blood brother" – had arranged "a momentous, reputation-securing, history-making, world-changing deal" (73) which they sealed in blood, using a pair of ceremonial daggers, rather than in print. Following the failure of this deal, however, Grautze was forced to comply with the outrageously draconian debt laws enforced by the ultra-capitalist Sichultian system:

> if a commercial debt could not be fully settled, or the terms were deemed not entirely sufficient due to shortage of funds or other negotiables by one of the partners, then the defaulting or inadequately provisioned side could compensate by undertaking to have a generation or two of their progeny made Intagliate, signing over care and control, indeed the ownership, of those to whom they were indebted or at a fiscal disadvantage. (71)

Having no choice but to hand over his wife and daughter, Grautze commits suicide using the dagger with which he sealed the initial deal, despite Veppers' assurance that Lededje and her mother would be cared

---

[39] In *Excession*, it is noted about the character Genar-Hofoen that he has a bodily adornment removed: "It had been a whim after a drinking session (as had an animated obscene tattoo he'd removed a month later)." The notion of an animated tattoo clearly displays another example of Banks's extrapolation in this regard; the notion of an animated tattoo also features prominently in China Miéville's *Kraken* (2010).

for, with his wife eventually throwing herself from a tower, years later (75). In a lifetime of actions marking nothing less than a total betrayal of his friend and partner, Veppers subjects Lededje to exploitation, and physical and mental abuse, and rapes her multiple times. Following an unsuccessful escape attempt, Veppers kills Lededje, only for her to be resurrected by the Culture, and one key plot thread of *Surface* follows Lededje's attempts to gain vengeance upon Veppers, working alongside the Culture. This revenge narrative is linked with the novel's other key plot thread, concerning the existence of virtual hells, by the fact that the physical location of the computer substrate that enables the hells to exist is underneath the Veppers' company itself.

As this description makes clear, Lededje's markings, therefore, originate from a society with an entirely different culture to that of the Culture. Through the sub-plot concerning Lededje and her revenge on Veppers, Banks enables some of his bitterest, most Juvenalian satire directed at the capitalist economic system, particularly Neoliberal ideas surrounding free markets, privatisation, and market competition. Lededje is personally owned by Veppers as a human chattel slave who can be bought and sold as a commodity, in the same manner as black Africans once were in the Americas and across Europe, and becomes effectively an example of what Cedric Robinson called "racial capitalism".[40] As Naomi Klein explains, "The cotton and sugar picked by enslaved Africans was the fuel that kick started the Industrial Revolution. The ability to discount darker people and darker nations in order to justify stealing their land and labour was foundational".[41] Similarly, the branding of Lededje's skin marks her as simultaneously a subaltern other and exploited victim of capitalism, on which the Vesperine Corporation relies. Every part of her body is marked to indicate her total ownership by the Vesperine Corporation, reifying Lededje into a unit of capital that can be traded on the stock markets, a literal slave to the corporate, global, Neoliberal agenda.

As with Banks's depictions of artists in *Windward*, *Hydrogen* and *Excession*, Lededje is an outsider figure from an early age, easily identifiable as such through her markings: "When she began to mix with them, the other toddlers and younger children from the estate seemed in awe of her [...] the other children had no markings, boasted no astounding design upon their skins" (*Surface*, 70). The fact that the signifier of difference for Lededje is her skin invites the reader to associate her

---

[40] See Jodi Melamed, 'Racial Capitalism', *Critical Ethnic Studies* 1, 1 (Spring 2015): 76–85.
[41] Klein, *No Is Not Enough*, 95.

treatment with discourses of race and ethnicity, and her "legal" indenture as Intagliate with colonial slavery. While such a reading is viable in the sense that Lededje can be viewed as a symbol of any woman who has been ostracised, exploited, and abused by the society from which she originates, her suffering, however, does not result from prejudice against her unusual appearance, but in fact vice versa: her markings symbolise cruelty and prejudice, specifically related to class. While Lededje has clearly been abused by her owner, the Sichultians at least have laws that supposedly ensure the protection of the Intagliate, with some slaves considering their positions a privilege, as – inevitably coming from poor backgrounds – their servitude allows them to live alongside rich people, sharing the fruits of their wealth (70–71). When this detail is explained, the tone of Banks's authorial voice – sarcastic and insincere – highlights the preposterous nature of the argument (72).

Lededje's markings afford her the opportunity to meet another outsider figure, who takes a strange and obscure interest in her Intagliate body, ostensibly for aesthetic reasons. In the fifth chapter, shortly after she is revived by the Culture, Lededje relates a story to the avatar Sensia, about an unusual incident she once experienced whilst attending a reception held by Veppers, several years previously. Lededje was approached by a being identifying itself as Himmerance, who describes himself as follows: "I am a wanderer; an explorer [...] a cultural translator [...] and a collector of images of whatever I consider to be the most exquisite beings, wherever my travels take me" (88). While he does not reveal it to Lededje at the time, Himmerance is an avatar of a former Culture ship, *Me, I'm Counting*, which is considered independent. Later described by a different Mind as "Hooligan-class LOU" (90), and like the *Sleeper Service* "declared as an Eccentric" (85), Himmerance asks to "take an image" of Lededje for his "private collection" (86). Assuming that the stranger means a nude photograph of her for his own sexual gratification – further exploitation – she initially writes him off as "just an old perv after all" (85). Assuring her that his interests in her body are "purely due to the intagliation you have suffered", Lededje asks "What do you do with these images?" to which he replies, "I contemplate them. They are works of art, to me" (86).

While the content of this artwork – Lededje's uniquely decorated body – seems an understandable choice for aesthetic presentation, the particular form of Himmerance's art is also interesting. The avatar explains that: "It would be an image of your entire body, not just both inside and out, but of its every single cell, indeed its every atom, and taken, in effect, from outside the three dimensions one normally deals with" (85). Lededje confirms that Himmerence here is referring to a position "from hyperspace" (85), effectively meaning that the image would be rendered in four dimensions. Himmerence proceeds to show Lededje some other images from his collection that prove to be rare and beautiful cosmic anomalies, and to explain the science behind them: "This is just the three-dimensional view one would have of a stellar field-liner entity [...] A particularly fine specimen [...] creatures who live within the magnetic lines of force in, mostly, the photospheres of suns" (86). Despite its initially unsettling nature, Lededje ultimately treats Himmerence's request as a kind of strange compliment, warily securing a surprise gift in return, and agrees for her image to be taken. This encounter also serves as a neat opportunity for Banks to establish a plot device, when the avatar is revealed to have seeded Lededje with a neural lace as her surprise gift, thus enabling her to be resurrected by the Culture.

Following these various interpretations of Lededje's markings – as corporate branding, as marker of difference, as fetishised aesthetic object – Banks gives them a final purpose in the climax of *Surface Detail*'s revenge sub-plot: the personal confrontation between Veppers and Lededje. When finally Veppers is killed, his death is administered with a kind of poetic justice: Lededje's markings – which she has the Culture reapply following her "death" as she feels incomplete without them – were actually the disguise used by one of the Culture's AI bodyguards, a knife missile, which attaches itself to Veppers, and efficiently crushes him to death (614–616), although Lededje was unaware. Banks's graphic and unusual descriptions make this scene one of pure gothic extravagance and abject horror: Veppers' head "seemed to crumple and shrink into itself, becoming a far-too-thin tall cylinder that disappeared in a spray of blood" (616). Veppers' death is ironic because he is killed by something resembling an item of his own creation, becoming himself Intagliate if only for a short while and symbolically experiencing the suffering he caused to others; and also because the markings – regarded as a creation of great aesthetic beauty – were co-opted for a particularly gruesome demise. Yet this scene has a deeper significance. While Lededje's tattoo originates from outside the Culture, and therefore the pain and subjugation with which the former is associated is largely unrelated to the latter, the fact that the Culture is prepared to remake the tattoo provides insight into its own ethos. By remaking it, the Culture appropriates the tattoo into its own culture, however temporarily, and the purpose for which SC remakes the tattoo – the crushing of a Culture enemy – therefore demonstrates them perpetrating violence. SC would perhaps justify this as an act of corporal punishment, legitimate as it is performed only in extremely rare instances. Also, shortly before instigating the coup de grace, a Mind asks Lededje if she wishes the death of her oppressor and rapist to be quick or slow, both a demonstration of compassion and symbolic displacement of responsibility for Veppers' death away from itself and the Culture, and onto Lededje and the Sichult (616). As with the *Sleeper Service*, it is an artwork whose ideological content seems to suggest two sides to Banks's civilisation: the utopian Culture and an SC capable of revenge and retaliation.

Music in the Culture Series

Of all the forms of art depicted throughout his oeuvre, including both mainstream and SF, Banks provides the most sustained and detailed engagement with the art of music, publishing four novels that prominently feature professional musicians/composers as protagonists (*Canal Dreams*, *Espedair Street*, *Look to Windward* and *The Hydrogen Sonata*), and several others that make numerous incidental references to music and musicians, both real and fictional. As for the reasoning behind Banks's privileging of music over the other arts in this manner, it is straightforward to understand that, on one level, it merely reflects his own personal taste: Banks's appreciation for music is well-documented and he was an accomplished composer in the fields of rock and classical music, a hobby that he maintained throughout much of his life. Yet there is a deeper reason for his privileged discussion of music that is more directly pertinent to the themes of this book, relating to the unique challenges presented to writers in their attempts to depict both utopia and music in the printed literary work – an issue that we will return to below.

While references to music in Banks's texts may often be insignificant in terms of the overall plot, he still uses them to strengthen the themes with which he is concerned. In *The Wasp Factory*, for example, protagonist Frank/Frances attends a gig by the fictional punk band The Vomits, listening to the "howling, crashing music" that "thundered through the sweaty room."[42] By having Frank hear the band's overtly phallic lyrics, full of hypermasculine posturing and insecurity ("Ma gurl-fren's left me un ah feel like a bum, / ah loss ma job an when ah wank ah can't cum…"), and state that "this sounded like it would be fun," Banks adds further layers of comic irony to his text, which is concerned with misconceived gender identity, and its socio-cultural construction. Elsewhere, Banks allows references to provide subtle characterisation:

[42] Banks, *The Wasp Factory*, 75.

Prentice in *The Crow Road* and Cameron in *Complicity* both listen to rock/indie acts from the 1990s, such as The Pixies and Faith No More, reflecting their countercultural leanings and left-wing political stances.[43] Similarly, there are several passing references to music in the Culture series, often forming part of the backdrop to parties, ceremonies, and other key events. For example: in *Player*, string players perform near Gurgeh as he meets his game-playing match in Professor Boruelal, and a band from the Empire of Azad display their cruelty by performing "wailing" music upon instruments formed from human skin and bones (220); in *Excession*, Ulver Seich is recruited into SC at a dance, given momentum by music (102–103); and in *Weapons*, music tinkles softly as the complexity of Zakalwe's true identity is revealed (369).

There are two instances in the Culture series, however, when a musical composition is integral to a text's narrative, forming a nexus point for various plot strands, as well as the socio-political themes with which the texts are concerned.

'Expiring Light' in *Look to Windward*

As is typical of Banks's space opera, *Look to Windward*, the sixth-published text in the Culture series, features a complex multi-stranded narrative with shifting viewpoint characters, all subtly interwoven, building to coalesce as a dramatic climax: two key plot strands include an attempt at violent retribution against the Culture by military veteran Major Quilan, following the death of his wife during the Chelgrian civil war, and disillusioned celebrity composer Mahria Ziller, writing and premiering the grandest piece of his career, 'Expiring Light'. Ziller and 'Expiring Light' are intrinsically linked to the wider politics of the novel, concerned with the socio-political consequences of a hugely destructive historical battle (the Twin Novae Battle) that took place between the Culture and Ziller's people, the Chelgrians. The Chelgrians fought alongside the Idirans and against the Culture in the Idiran–Culture war, as forms the background for the events in *Phlebas*. The Culture was responsible for inadvertently instigating a catastrophic civil war on Chelgria after one of its supposedly benign interventions failed. Many decades later, the Culture commissioned Ziller to compose 'Expiring Light' as a commemoration of the "gigadeaths" that resulted from the destruction of two planets during the Twin Novae Battle, an event significant enough to end the war. Premiered thousands of years after the war, 'Expiring

---

[43] Banks, *The Crow Road*, 384.

Light' is timed to coincide with the appearance of the supernovae that resulted from the battle.

This fictional symphony has several interesting and revealing parallels with the real-world 'Symphony in Three Movements' by Igor Stravinsky. In my personal correspondence with Banks's friend Gary Lloyd, with whom he composed several pieces of music, Lloyd has confirmed that – as far as he is aware – Banks did not have this specific piece in mind, but he was generally aware of Stravinsky's life and work.[44] Eric Walter White notes that 'Symphony in Three Movements', composed between 1942 and 1945 amidst World War Two, was linked in Stravinsky's mind "with a concrete impression, very often cinematographic in origin, of the war"[45] – and Stravinsky sometimes simply called it his "war symphony".[46] Given this knowledge, parallels can be drawn between the Twin Novae Battle – an atrocity of enough magnitude to conclude a bitter war – and the destruction of Hiroshima and Nagasaki in 1945, the final stage in ending World War Two. Furthermore, both Ziller and Stravinsky composed their respective symphonies whilst living as expatriates in exile from their place of origin (a detail from Stravinsky's life of which Lloyd assures me Banks was definitely aware, even if it was not his primary inspiration for the piece).[47] Ziller lives "half outcast, half [in] exile" (*Windward*, 20) on Masaq', ostracised from his home planet, Chelgria, after he criticised the draconian caste system enforced there. Russian-born Stravinsky began composing 'Symphony in Three Movements' shortly after moving to the United States, this move in part motivated by a marked low point in the popularity of his music,[48] but also, like Ziller, by a desire to compose undisturbed under conditions of "tranquility" and "security", in "an atmosphere

---

[44] Gary Lloyd, email to author, 26 April 2016.
[45] Eric Walter White, *Stravinsky: The Composer and his Works* (London: Faber and Faber, 1966), 96.
[46] Charles M. Joseph, *Stravinsky Inside Out* (New Haven and London: Yale University Press, 2001), 120.
[47] Lloyd has, however, proudly informed me that Banks was inspired by one of his own compositions: "When Iain was writing about the composition in *Look To Windward* that he was in fact using as his guide, model and inspiration a piece of mine that I wrote for [the] *son et lumiere* shows entitled 'Ignition'. The largest of these shows took place in Llandrindod Wells in 1996 with an audience of 11,000 people. I had a small choir bolstering up the recorded version of the piece which was what usually would be used at the events I was involved in, and I conducted it from a pontoon that was covered in ignition sites. It was deafening, the fireworks, not the music." Gary Lloyd, email to author, 26 April 2016.
[48] White, *Stravinsky*, 91–92.

of [political] neutrality."[49] Ziller may now live on the safe haven of a Culture Orbital, but this fact does not stop him from regularly criticising his new-found home and its people, as he does those he left behind. Refusing to assimilate into this society, Ziller appreciates the Culture's liberal environments as they provide him with the space and facilities to compose undisturbed, as well as the venue and audience for his symphony; but, at the same time, he bitterly criticises Culture people for their supposedly hedonistic, valueless, and artificial lives. In fact, his impression of the Culture goes beyond mere criticism and dislike to hatred and loathing: it is telling that, at one stage, Ziller remarks that "Happily, that hatred *does* provide vital inspiration for my work" (*Windward*, 65).

'Expiring Light' is performed at the climax of a long concert programme featuring several shorter pieces, the whole of which Banks makes clear has been carefully arranged so that its overall form mirrors its subject matter: the Idiran–Culture war itself:

> The music accumulated. Each piece, he realized, was slowly contributing to the whole. Whether it was Hub's idea or Ziller's, he didn't know, but the whole evening, the entire concert programme had been designed around the final symphony. The earlier, shorter pieces were half by Ziller, half by other composers. They alternated, and it became clear that the styles were quite different too, while the musical philosophies behind the two competing strands were dissimilar to the point of antipathy. [...] The evening was the war. The two strands of music represented the protagonists, Culture and Idirans. Each pair of antagonistic pieces stood for one of the many small but increasingly bitter and wide-scale skirmishes which had taken place, usually between proxy forces for both sides, during the decades before the war itself had finally broken out. The works increased in length and in the sensation of mutual hostility. (376)

Through this description, it is clear that the programme is intended to represent the chronology of the war, with each of the various musical works commissioned representing each of its battles. By deliberately placing "antagonistic pieces" (with musical aesthetics that are "dissimilar to the point of antipathy") side by side, the programme is used to mirror the conflict of a battle between factions with opposing political ideologies: a sonic "war" to convey a physical war. In this manner, it operates in a similar manner to the Game of Azad in *Player*, where the different tactics

---

[49] White, *Stravinsky*, 93.

offered by the Culture and by the Empire of Azad represent the broader cultures of these two enemies. From his descriptions, Banks does not explicitly state which particular musical style corresponds with which side in the conflict, and it is possible only to glean general impressions of the symphony's overall tonality, from certain passages in the text.

Banks describes the start of Ziller's piece in the following manner:

> The symphony *Expiring Light* began with a susurration that built and engorged until it burst into a single clashingly discordant blast of music; a mixture of chords and sheer noise that was echoed in the sky by a single shockingly bright air burst as a huge meteorite plunged into the atmosphere directly above the Bowl and exploded. Its stunning, frightening, bone-rattlingly loud sound arrived suddenly in a hypnotic lull in the music, making everybody – certainly everybody that Quilan was aware of, including himself – jump. (377)

Here Banks suggests the tonality of the piece using adjective-heavy lyrical language. Close analysis reveals a strong impression of the use of musical dissonance, which is also a prominent feature of Stravinsky's 'Symphony in Three Movements'. Dissonance is often understood in relation to its opposite, "consonance", the latter of which is defined as "a harmonious sounding together of two or more notes" [...] with an "absence of roughness", and relief of "tonal tension."[50] Dissonance, therefore, can be understood as a combination of notes that creates a sensation of aural "roughness" and disharmony, leading to sensations of discomfort in the listener – arguably an appropriate tonality for depicting war in sonic form. In the above quotation, Banks potentially expresses dissonance using the adjective "clashingly", which suggests notes in conflict like soldiers on a battlefield, before he makes its presence more explicit with the musical term "discordant", which is a synonym for dissonance. These terms are shortly followed by the phrase "sheer noise", again implying note combinations so exceedingly harsh in tone as to be heard as completely un-pitched, non-musical sounds. Elsewhere, the symphony is described in similarly violent terms: as "screaming" (*Windwood*, 377) and "battering" (378) the concert audience. Interestingly, Banks supports his preceding descriptions of the symphony's beginning, by allowing the music to be "echoed" by acts of real, physical destruction – the burst

---

[50] Brian C.J. Moore and Claude V. Palisca, 'Consonance', Grove Music Online, *Oxford Music Online*, Oxford University Press. www.oxfordmusiconline.com.v-ezproxy.brunel.ac.uk:2048/subscriber/article/grove/music/06316.

and explosion of a meteorite – inviting the reader to interpret these violent acts as visual analogues for the tonal content of the music they accompany.

As well as using harsh tones to convey the mood of war, Banks's descriptions of 'Expiring Light' are further enhanced by a particularly surreal register, which is achieved by the deliberate confusing and overlapping of four different elements. Firstly, commencing just as the light from the first nova (named Portisia) explosion becomes visible, the actual, physical destruction of Portisia is visible to the audience in the sky above the Bowl. Secondly, projections of "visuals of the war and more abstract images" also fill the sky (377). Thirdly, Banks uses metaphoric language to describe the music, which draws upon similar destructive and war-like imagery. Finally, much of this chapter (16: 'Expiring Light') is written from the third-person limited perspective of Quilan, whose perception is doubly impaired by general feelings of guilt, doubt, and despair, as well as the presence of another individual's consciousness (that of General Huyler) within his own.[51] This surreal, overlapping effect is arguably used by Banks to echo the state of "cognitive dissonance"[52] that Quilan is experiencing at this point in the narrative: torn between a committed duty to infiltrating the Culture in order to perform an act of terrorism against them, whilst, in the process, slowly developing a significant degree of respect for them, in an inversion of Gurgeh's developing relationship with Azad in *Player*. The following paragraph, in which the symphony is linked by direct simile to ambiguous images of destruction, exemplifies the effect in question:

> Somewhere near the furious centre of the work, while the thunder played bass and the music rolled over it and around the auditorium like something wild and caged and desperate to escape, eight trails in the sky did not end in air bursts and did not fade away but slammed down into the lake all around the Bowl. (377)

The fact that the trails "slammed into the lake" would seem to indicate that Banks is here describing the real fall-out of Portisia's nova, although

---

[51] At this stage in the novel's narrative, Quilan has the consciousness of General Huyler embedded within his own, in order to help him conduct his act of terrorism/revenge against the Culture; this allows Huyler to access some of Quilan's thoughts, but supposedly only those necessary in order to complete their task.

[52] Simon Blackburn, 'Cognitive Dissonance', in *The Oxford Dictionary of Philosophy*, updated 2016 (Oxford University Press, 2008). www.oxfordreference.com/view/10.1093/acref/9780199541430.001.0001/acref-9780199541430-e-603.

the paragraph follows a passage outlining the accompanying projected visuals, with no clear delineation between topics. In the next paragraph, the concert audience is *literally* shaken by the physical force of the lake-strikes – confirming Banks's previous reference as relating to the real destruction – and *figuratively* shaken by the music's startling effect:

> The entire Bowl, the whole kilometre-diameter of it, shook and quivered as the waves created by the lake-strikes smashed into the giant vessel. The music seemed to take the fear and terror and violence of the moment and run screaming away with it, pulling the audience behind like an unseated rider caught in the stirrup of their panic-stricken mount. (377)

In the second sentence, Banks uses simile to cast the audience as a terrified equestrian, with the music of the symphony itself representing the wild horse they struggle to control. This comparison serves to emphasise how the audience is affected physically and emotionally by Ziller's creation: temporarily trapped in an unpredictable moment, the listeners are seemingly forced into passivity by the sheer vehemence of the music, and unable to break free.

Quilan's state of mind at this stage, described using the oxymoron "terrible calmness", seems to mirror in some ways the terrified passivity of the rest of the audience, and – as he is the viewpoint character for this chapter – the reader is privy to the psychological effects he experiences in response to the music:

> It was as though his eyes formed a sort of twin tunnel in his skull and his soul was gradually falling away from that shared window to the universe, falling on his back forever down a deep dark corridor while the world shrank to a little circle of light and dark somewhere in the shadows above. Like falling into a black hole, he thought to himself. Or maybe it was just Huyler. (378)

The effects of listening to music will of course vary according to the individual subject, and in this case Quilan's perspective is complicated a great deal, as previously mentioned, by grief, guilt, political ambivalence, and the presence of General Huyler within his consciousness. In paragraphs following the preceding quotation, the symphony seems to enable Quilan to experience a period of reflection and revelation, overwhelming in its intensity. Finally, descending to the nadir of his psychological "black hole", Quilan discovers that Huyler is no longer within him, and instead the former communicates internally with an SC drone who reveals that

Quilan's plan to enact revenge upon the Culture by destroying the Masaq' Orbital had been discovered and rendered impossible. Quilan's experience is written in a manner that heightens the already surreal tone of the section, almost to the extent of a dream-like blurring of reality and vision, or as Quilan makes explicit, as "if he'd been fed a drug" (378). Within this virtual dream- or drug-like space, Quilan alternates between periods of near-solipsistic self-reflection and feelings of unity with all of his surroundings: "he watched from a thousand angles, he was the stadium itself, its lights and sounds and very structure" (380). Upon revealing that the Culture was aware of his revenge almost from the outset, the drone encourages Quilan to "listen to the end of the symphony", which is described using the metaphor of a wave: "[t]he music rose like the bulging bruise of water from an undersea explosion, an instant before the smooth swell ruptures and the spout of white spray bursts forth" (380). Here, Banks uses natural imagery in order to symbolise Quilan's rising doubts about the suicide mission and act of terrorism that he has come to the Culture to enact.

Ultimately, through 'Expiring Light', *Look to Windward* forms a mediation on the ways in which artistic practice can clash and collude with the cultures in which it is created, the role of art as memorial of war and conflict, and a fascinating example of the difficulties arising from attempting to describe music in writing effectively.

The Hydrogen Sonata and 'The Hydrogen Sonata'

Published thirteen years after *Windward*, *The Hydrogen Sonata* – the tenth and final Culture text – features a fictional musical work prominently in its narrative, this time featuring a musician, Vyr Cossont, and not a composer as such, as protagonist. 'The Hydrogen Sonata' itself, subtitled the "26th String-Specific Sonata For An Instrument Yet To Be Invented", is an experimental and avant-garde musical work, and is closely associated with Cossont throughout the novel. The sonata is generally regarded as highly unpopular due to its extreme complexity and inaccessibility to most listeners, and as such has achieved a notorious and even semi-mythical status throughout the Culture's galaxy, with even its composer, Vilabier, supposedly treating it as a joke (125). Nevertheless, Cossont has made it her life's task to perform a perfect solo rendition of the piece, spurred on by its reputation as "near impossible to play acceptably, let alone perfectly" (13).

As with 'Expiring Light', parallels can be drawn between Banks's depictions of 'The Hydrogen Sonata' and a real-world counterpart, in this case the piece 'Time and Motion Study II', written by the English composer Brian Ferneyhough between 1973 and 1976, around the time Banks began developing his series. Ferneyhough's 'Study' shares a similar renown to Vilabier's sonata: once described as "the ultimate in complexity,"[53] Ferneyhough's score includes: "labyrinthine"[54] notation on up to five staves simultaneously; "mind-bending rhythmic density;"[55] and extensive annotations indicating the emotional timbre of each passage, which are bizarre, abstract, and idiosyncratic.[56] While a perfect rendition of 'Time and Motion Study II' is perhaps not actually *impossible*, or a task that would literally require an entire lifetime to achieve – nor, in fact, is perfection an attribute even *expected* for it by its composer[57] – an extremely high level of virtuosity *is* required to perform it to a satisfactory degree; and, such is the detailed nature of the score, any performer must dedicate a huge amount of time to the piece, in order to satisfy the substantial demand placed upon them by the composer. At one stage, Cossont refers to the 'The Hydrogen Sonata', sarcastically pointing out that the "score *is* beautiful" (124), and her description here, then, could easily refer to Ferneyhough's piece also, as pictured in Figure 1.

The compositional complexity of 'The Hydrogen Sonata' and 'Time and Motion Study II' is also reflected in terms of performance. Vilabier's sonata is written for a solo performer of an instrument known as "The Antagonistic Undecagonstring" or elevenstring, which is described in such a way as to suggest a cello and a piano, but also a bicycle due to the necessity for a performer to sit partly inside the instrument's body (12). Similarly, Ferneyhough's 'Study', written for solo cello, requires its performer to be both surrounded by, and wired up to, a complex arrangement of footpedals, microphones, and speakers – like "strapping

---

[53] Tom Service, 'A Guide to Brian Ferneyhough's Music', *Guardian*, 10 September 2012. www.theguardian.com/music/tomserviceblog/2012/sep/10/contemporary-music-guide-brian-ferneyhough.

[54] Service, 'A Guide to Brian Ferneyhough's Music'. Web.

[55] Service, 'A Guide to Brian Ferneyhough's Music'. Web.

[56] Brian Ferneyhough, 'Time and Motion Study II: for solo cello and electronics' (London: Peters, 1978). Annotations include: "violent but reserved, coldly inscrutable"; "with passionate dedication and self-transcendence"; and "with the utmost imaginable degree of violence".

[57] Service, 'A Guide to Brian Ferneyhough's Music'. "The point is, if Ferneyhough wanted his scores [...] to be a sort of straitjacket for the performer, to determine precisely what they should be doing at every microsecond of the piece, he would have become an electronic or electro-acoustic composer."

WHOLE-TONE SCALES REACHING FOREVER   247

Figure 1.
Extract from
*Time and Motion
Study II* by Brian
Ferneyhough
(EP7223) ©
Copyright 1978
by Peters Edition
Limited, London.
Reproduced by
kind permission
of Peters Edition
Limited, London.

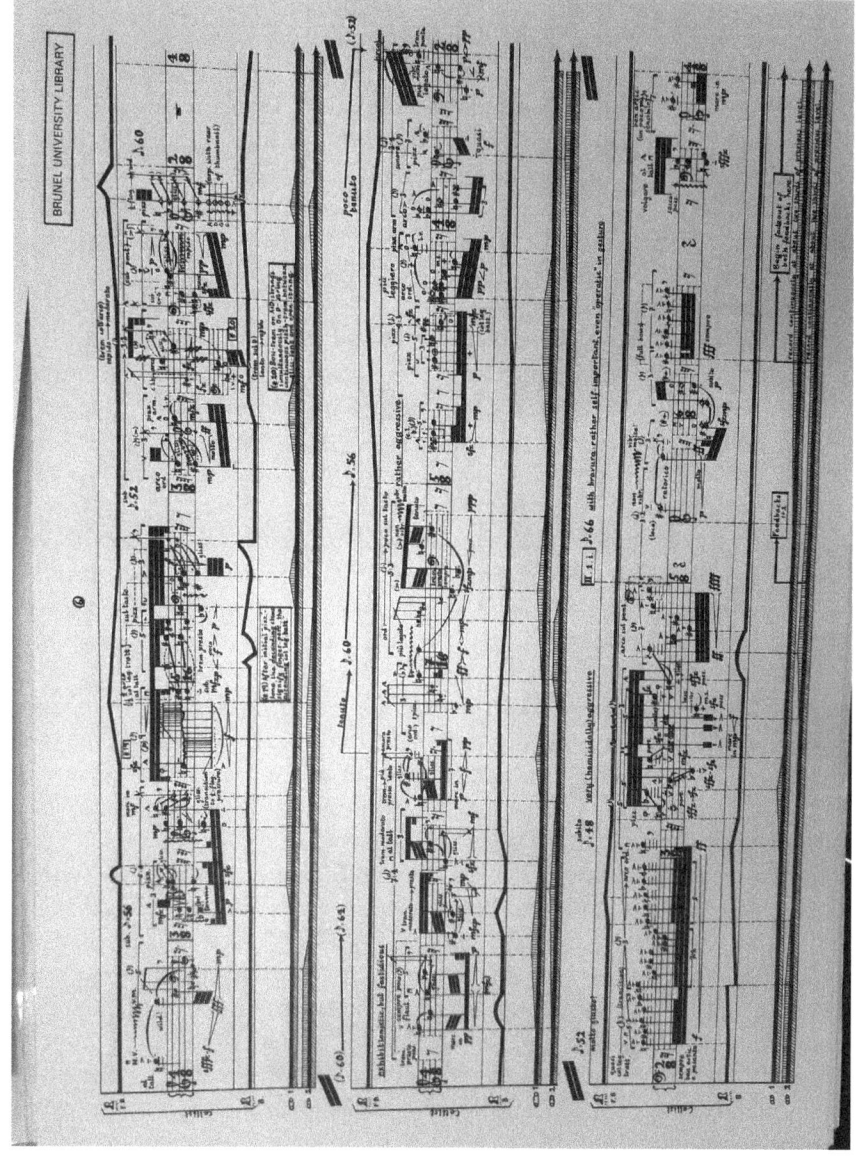

the performer into a sort of musical electric chair"[58] – just as Cossont must sit partially inside her elevenstring in order to play it.

When describing the sound of the sonata itself, Banks does occasionally rely upon metaphor, as with his treatment of 'Expiring Light', but he offers much more concrete detail of its harmony and tonality, possibly a reflection of his own increased interest in composition later in life. 'The Hydrogen Sonata' is a work characterised by high levels of dissonance ("clashing... atonal music" [127]; "I do detect a degree of discordant tonality" [128]) in a much more explicit manner than 'Expiring Light'. In an interview, Banks explains that 'The Hydrogen Sonata' was intended as a satire of atonal music, reflecting his own musical preferences: "I'm not a traditionalist in many things, but I am when it comes to music; I like melody. I can't be getting on with atonal music. I keep trying."[59] Even Vilabier himself admits writing the piece to "prove how easy it was to write such... mathematical... programmish... music" (*Hydrogen*, 125) and the sonata seems notoriously unpopular for its inaccessibility. It is no coincidence that the only people who seem to appreciate 'The Hydrogen Sonata' within Banks's novel are academics, computers, and androids.[60] It is significant that – in brief snippets of a symphony composed by Banks and aired during his final BBC interview – Banks consciously used as few chords as possible, and only single melody lines:[61] in other words, the exact opposite of 'The Hydrogen Sonata', which is noted for its almost total lack of melody.[62] It is not unreasonable, then, to suggest that the Culture's music may be composed along these lines, given the highly personal construction of Banks's utopia, although the series does provide evidence for alternatives, as we will see below.

In a sub-plot of *Hydrogen*, Banks describes another sonic occurrence – portrayed as more natural, and overwhelmingly beautiful – that contrasts with the supposedly "programmish", "soulless" nature of Vilabier's sonata. Known simply as 'The Sound', this "sky-filling, soul-battering, ear-splitting" (329) noise, created by wind passing through deliberately created tunnels cut into a planet's mountain range, is powerful enough to cause QiRia, an individual old enough to have known Vilabier, to dedicate later stages of his long life to hearing 'The Sound' from its source through an extra set of ears, grafted in place of his eyes (326–337).

---

[58] Service, 'A Guide to Brian Ferneyhough's Music'. Web.
[59] BBC Radio Scotland, 'Interview with Iain M. Banks', *The Book Café*, 8 October 2012. www.bbc.co.uk/programmes/p00zjf0f.
[60] See *Hydrogen*, 124 and 286–287.
[61] BBC Radio Scotland, Interview. Web.
[62] See *Hydrogen*, 127.

Compared to "a slow, sonorous hymn in a language you would never understand" (328); "an orchestra of hundreds of gigantic organs all playing [...] at the same time" (329); and a "god bellowing in your ear" (331), Banks's descriptions of 'The Sound', scattered across several pages, rely upon science-fictional extrapolations of familiar musical practices as well as the scale of the divine in a similar manner to his descriptions of 'Expiring Light' years earlier. These descriptions contrast with those of 'The Hydrogen Sonata', which Banks in fact seldom describes directly; when he does do so, he uses distinctly less-enthused language. There is a sense that 'The Sound' moves Banks more than the sonata.

But while Banks does use 'The Hydrogen Sonata' to satirise atonal music, his touch is playful and light-hearted, and his writing indicates a greater enthusiasm and interest in discussing the complex metaphoric potential of the piece's aesthetics, rather than as a piece of music in its own right. The piece's title, 'The Hydrogen Sonata', rather like the term "science fiction" itself, is a near oxymoronic term that mixes concepts from art and science, establishing an ontological spectrum between "objective truth" and "human creation". Following this, Banks develops a complex metaphor interlinking musical concepts and terms with concepts from particle physics and cosmology, often synonimically or homonymically, such as through the word "string". The Antagonistic Undecagonstring, for example, was deliberately designed by Vilabier with eleven strings, not seemingly for a specific musical reason, but in order to represent the dimension known as "the Sublime", transcendence into which forms the pinnacle of the Gzilt's (the civilisation from which both Vilabier and Cossont originate) goals. In order to understand this metaphor, it is necessary to understand the fictional cosmology that Banks imagined for his Culture series. Banks developed his own variation of the familiar SF trope the "multiverse", or coexisting, layered universes – he explained, "think of an onion"[63] – and the Sublime is said to be located in layers seven to eleven (*Hydrogen*, 17). Therefore, Vilabier wrote the sonata for an eleven-stringed instrument, linking it with the "vast, infinite, better-than-virtual ultra-existence" (63) that is the Sublime. In turn, Vilabier chose a stringed instrument as opposed to, say, an instrument with valves or keys, to allow for a pun on the word "string", relating the physical components of the instrument to the one-dimensional objects postulated in the concept of String Theory in particle physics. This metaphor is strengthened by Banks's description of the sonata's introductory passage: here, a "single high note" signifies "a hydrogen nucleus", followed by a "wavering chord" that represents "the

---

[63] Iain Banks, 'A Few Notes on the Culture'. Web.

concept of a sole electron's probability cloud." Together, "the first note and the first chord represented the element hydrogen" (286).

While there is relatively little further in-depth description of the piece in the novel, it is possible and worthwhile to speculate briefly about the broader implications of the above analysis on Banks's intended metaphorical significance for 'The Hydrogen Sonata' as a whole. Given the repeatedly stated complexity and length of the piece – seemingly the absolute pinnacle of baroque intricacy and grandiosity in the music of the known galaxy – it is reasonable to suggest that the piece represents nothing less than the grandest imaginable story: that of the universe's expansion, and the emergence of life within the cosmos itself. Ferneyhough, too, expresses the radical musical philosophy behind his music using metaphors from particle physics:

> We need to speculate about modes of reality and works of art do this for us. The work of art is not there just to entertain but to continually take apart and re-assemble the *molecules of meaning* which for us constitute reality. We must continually deconstruct them and reconstruct them in other formulations to see what their mode of reality, for a moment, might be.[64]

For Ferneyhough, then, art of any kind – but especially music – performs one of science fiction's most basic functions: speculation on the nature of our current reality; but, perhaps more importantly – as with Banks's novels – it allows the artist also to "reconstruct" that reality, and conceive it in a new manner.

As well as fulfilling this metaphorical role in the story, 'The Hydrogen Sonata' is linked with the novel's social and political themes, largely through the protagonist, Vyr Cossont. Cossont is an important performer of the sonata, and not its composer, Vilabier (about whom little is known except that he was probably an academic).[65] Born into the religious Gzilt civilisation, where all choose a Life Task to pass the time spent in a corporeal body in this universe before they Sublime, Cossont chooses for her Life Task the challenge of performing 'The Hydrogen Sonata' perfectly, a task that almost no others have accomplished. Like Ziller, Cossont occupies a liminal and ambiguous position relating to her home culture. While at the start of the novel she does lives with the

---

[64] Optic Nerve Limited, 'Electric Chair Music', 23 February 2015, retrieved from Youtube. Emphasis added. www.youtube.com/watch?v=sykB4znEk2Q.
[65] The piece was first performed to an audience of academics. See Banks, *Hydrogen*, 126.

Gzilt, Cossont seems to have chosen her Life Task as much to distance herself from the conservative and militaristic Gzilts, who do not afford musical and martial discipline the same level of respect, as from a love of creativity and music. Cossont proudly displays both her social and her musical non-conformity by wearing a jacket emblasoned with the offensive logo of her old musical group 'The Lords of Excrement'. In fact, her rebellion and dedication go deeper: in order for a solo performer to play 'The Hydrogen Sonata', which uses the elevenstring's full harmonic range, they are required to have an extra pair of arms surgically grafted onto their bodies – as Cossont has done. While she views this as an improvement or adaptation, and it can easily and perfectly be undone, it induces shock and disgust among her family members, many of whom call her a "freak", and threaten her with discrimination and social ostracism (*Hydrogen*, 31). Throughout the novel, Cossont is very reluctant to practise the piece, however, and even transporting the "coffin-like" (176) elevenstring seems a chore. Cossont's desire to rebel against the social, political, and religious structure of the Gzilt seems to leave her trapped, as, while practising the unpopular sonata is in itself an act of rebellion, this nevertheless helps her achieve her life task, an act of social conformity. Her dichotomy is somewhat resolved at the novel's conclusion: though she *does* eventually complete her Life Task, Cossont also flings the instrument into space afterwards, listening as it "hummed emptily" (517).

As John Clute describes in his review of *Hydrogen*:

> The book can be read as an almost totally unguarded paean to the deeply conjoined joys of making something and finding something out: all in the full and explicit realization that in the end nothing means squat, in the explicit understanding that doing meaning is to make meaning last, but only until you stop.[66]

Cossont's way of "doing meaning" in the book has been up to now the Life Task assigned by her culture. In flinging away the elevenstring, Cossont achieves a symbolic rejection of the Gzilt. But by sharing the Culture's view that "doing meaning" in the material plane of reality is more beneficial than in the energy plane of her people, Cossont achieves a much more literal rejection of her family and home culture by choosing not to Sublime alongside them, and to remain in relative

---

[66] John Clute, 'Somewhere More Interesting than Arrival', *LA Review of Books*, 16 October 2012. https://lareviewofbooks.org/article/somewhere-more-interesting-than-arrival/#.

isolation on Gzilt. *Hydrogen* concludes with the end of one kind of meaning for her, then, and also with another beginning, marked by a new sense of freedom: "First, she would go home. After that, she had no idea what she might do" (517). Performing 'The Hydrogen Sonata' has been for Cossont a way to reassemble what Ferneyhough calls the "molecules of reality", literally and figuratively, into an image of personal meaning: the sonata may have little *intrinsic* meaning for her, but it is in its performance, in the human act of *striving* toward a challenging goal, that Cossont found her true Life Task. In the final pages of the final text in the sequence, Banks returned to the central insight of his first written Culture work: for Cossont, as in 'Zakalwe's Song', "the bomb lives only as it is falling."

Utopia, Art, and Representation

Hydrogen and *Windward*, then, (alongside *Player* as Wegner observes)[67] can be considered at least partial examples of the *Künstlerroman*, or the novel of the artist, in which the creative process of artistic production is explored throughout the artist's life. In his essay on the subject, 'A Philosophical View of the Novel of the Artist', Ernst Bloch observes a kind of utopianism in the structure of such works, observing that, in the words of Caroline Edwards: "Unlike the structure of the detective novel (another of Bloch's favoured genres) which gathers evidence to illuminate crimes that occurred in the past, the novel of the artist thus 'brings out something new' in its straining towards the future (Bloch 1988: 267)."[68] In this way, Bloch's discussion introduces a more fundamental connection between the novel of the artist and the novel of utopia: the mutual, inevitable un-representability of their central topic. As Wegner explains, "The authentic Künstlerroman maintains a fidelity to the concrete Utopia in a paradoxical fashion, by way of an acknowledgment of a certain failure in its project: the failure to represent precisely the new thing, the work of art itself".[69] Just as Banks inevitably "fails" to produce a complete representation of his utopia – of the entire Culture itself in his series – he could never hope to represent the fictional

---

[67] Wegner, *Shockwaves*, 73.
[68] Caroline Edwards, 'Uncovering the "gold-bearing rubble": Ernst Bloch's Literary Criticism', in *Utopianism, Modernism, and Literature in the Twentieth Century*, Reeve-Tucker and Waddell, eds. (Palgrave Macmillian UK, 2013), 182–203.
[69] Wegner, *Shockwaves*, 109.

creative works (the *Sleeper Services*'s tableaux, Lededje's Intagliation, the game of Azad, etc.) described within, authentically or in their entirety, either: they can only ever be truly experienced at first hand. This is also especially true of the *musical* works that Banks invented, due to the uniquely abstract nature of the sonic arts, which convey meaning primarily through emotion but cannot directly represent the world.[70]

Yet this failure – this emptiness in representation – is important because, through these figures of utopia, the utopian form "educates our desire" for something new. Discussing Bloch's essay in *Marxism and Form*, Jameson explains that, "For Bloch, however, this emptiness of the work within a work, this blank canvas at the center, is the very locus of the not-yet-existent itself; and it is precisely this essentially fragmentary and aesthetically unsatisfying structure of the novel of the artist which gives it its ontological value as a form and figure of the movement of the future incomplete before us".[71] As "blank canvases", then, 'The Hydrogen Sonata' or Lededje's Intagliation may ultimately be "fragmentary and aesthetically unsatisfying", yet we can recognise within them an orientation towards the unknowable future by the very presence of their "empty" cores; and thus we return to the notion of the Culture embodying Jameson's concept of the future as disruption, and as a vessel for thinking the break.

The Culture demonstrates an awareness of the utopian potential of unrepresentability, working to control and limit the ways in which *it itself* is represented. In accordance with its decentralised nature, Banks notes that the Culture has no "emblem or logo", as it "refused to place its trust in symbols. It maintained that it was what it was and had no need for such outward representation. Just as it could not imprison itself with laws, impoverish itself with money or misguide itself with leaders, so it would not misrepresent itself with signs" (*Phlebas*, 14). Therefore, the Culture bears no flag, no symbol, or no anthem: when a Culture ambassador in *Player* is required to pretend his people *do* have an anthem, the first melody he whistles is taken from a dirty and offensive ballad (124); and as General Huyler from *Windward* notes, distastefully given his martial background, Culture citizens do not wear uniforms of any kind.[72] The Culture's name reflects this desire, suggesting a wish to be known only *through* its culture, through its people and the things they

---

[70] See Roger Scruton, 'Representation in Music', *Philosophy* 51, no. 197 (July 1976): 273–287.

[71] Jameson, *Marxism and Form*, 131–132, quoted in Wegner, *Shockwaves*, 109.

[72] "They still don't have uniforms? This is a whole society run by fucking dissidents." – Banks, *Windward*, 74.

do, the way they live, the way they think; therefore becoming "ideologically transparent", as Burling argued properly utopian art should be. In this way, the Culture wishes to exist *beyond representation altogether* – beyond potential *mis*representation – and therefore to be understood only as it is, as the *thing-in-itself*. By refusing any kind of "branding" – by choosing "no logo" like some off-shoots of the justice globalism movement – the Culture distances itself from the centralised, corporate ethos of the businesses, empires, hegemonies, and other entities from which it revolted against initially, which may misrepresent themselves through marketing for financial gain – as in *Surface*, where the literal branding of Lededje's skin also operates as a metaphor for corporate slavery. Similarly, the Culture's refusal to label or brand itself is an attempt to avoid a broader "crisis of representation". In *Mythologies* (1957), Roland Barthes challenges the notion that artistic modes such as Realism are able to describe the world with a level of objectivity and accuracy as they conceal a semiotic level, one of many *representations* of reality (like Ferneyhough's "modes of reality"), and portray this as something natural.[73] As such, the Culture forms a response to the postmodern world in which, as Jameson expounded, signs lost their power to meaningfully signify,[74] a process which continues in the current era of "post truth" and "alternative fact".[75]

While the Culture's intentions do largely bear out in the series, we have already seen that Sma's poetry in *Weapons* goes some way to representing the Culture, albeit in an oblique manner, and there are in fact further occasions where Banks provides us with images of art that work to symbolise both the structure and the philosophy of his personal utopia. Of these, the most significant occurs at one stage in *Matter*: protagonist Djan Seriy Anaplian listens to a piece of music in which she hears "the influence of the Culture" (her chosen society) "signaled by a chord sequence constructed from mathematically pure whole-tone scales reaching forever down and up" (95). Djan's comment is entirely extraneous to the central and peripheral narratives of the novel, yet it is interesting, not just as a unique example of Culture self-representation, but also because Banks uses the form of atonal, whole-tone music – satirised four years later in *Hydrogen* – to do so.

---

[73] See Roland Barthes, *Mythologies* (London: Random House, 2000).
[74] See Frederic Jameson, *Postmodernism; or The Cultural Logic of Late Capitalism* (London: Verso, 1991).
[75] See Jon Sopel, 'From "alternative facts" to Rewriting History in Trump's White House', BBC, 25 July 2018. https://www.bbc.co.uk/news/world-us-canada-44959300.

Again, while Banks struggled to enjoy atonal music in his personal life, he was clearly alert to the symbolic potential of the mode. While the potentially dissonant *content* of this figurative whole-tone music (similar to 'Expiring Light' and 'The Hydrogen Sonata') could confirm Jacques Attali's assertion that music's order "simulates the social order," whereas "its dissonances express marginalities"[76], this dissonance could be seen as a byproduct of the music's *form*. Several critics have identified certain sonic aesthetics as indicating social models of utopia metaphorically,[77] for example, by suggesting that the structuring of atonal, twelve-tone music is more egalitarian and therefore more utopian than tonal music since, by its definition, "all notes must be represented equally," whereas "tonal music selects certain notes according to the key and scale being used."[78] The twelve-tone row was certainly a key figure of utopian art for both Bloch and Theodor Adorno.[79] The Culture is like whole-tone scales, then, because *social equality* is fundamental to the former just as a *formal equality* (evenly spaced notes) is to the latter. The notes are *mathematically* pure, suggesting the logic and rational organisation that the Culture recognises in itself; and the notes reach up and down *forever*, mirroring the Culture's lack of finite spatial boundaries. So we must return to 'The Hydrogen Sonata', then, hearing in the egalitarian modernism of its whole-tone scales an indication of Bloch's utopian "straining towards the future" (an indication that even suggests a kind of symbolic link between the sonata and the Culture itself).

Once we recognise this, aesthetic patterns similar to the logic of the whole-tone scale that reoccur in the series can be clearly identified, especially in variations of the fractal: "a curve or geometrical figure, each part of which has the same statistical character as the whole."[80] In *Excession*, the *Sleeper Service* secretly stores a host of battle ships that have been patterned in a procedure known as Baroquing: "fractally

[76] Michael J. Griffin, 'Utopian Music and the Problem of Luxury', *Utopian Studies* 16, no. 2 (2005): 255.
[77] Marshall Brown and Michael Kennedy, 'Origins of modernism: musical structures and narrative forms', in *Music and Text: Critical Inquiries*, Steven Paul Scherp, ed. (Cambridge: Cambridge University Publishing, 2006), 90.
[78] Brown and Kennedy, 'Origins of modernism', 90.
[79] See, for example, Moya K. Mason's discussion of 'Theodor Adorno's Theory of Music and its Social Implications' on her personal website (http://www.moyak.com/papers/adorno-schoenberg-atonality.html) or Michael Gallope's 'Ernst Bloch's Utopian Tone of Hope', *Contemporary Music Review* 31, 5–6 (2012): 371–387.
[80] Oxford Dictionaries, 'Fractal', Oxford University Press. www.oxforddictionaries.com/definition/english/fractal.

inscribed with partially random, non-predictable designs", "covered with these curious, whorled patterns and motifs" (226–227). As with Lededje's Intagliation, the patterns do not stop at the craft's surface, but repeat internally, going "down to the atomic level" (227). These fractal processes of both Intagliation and Baroquing serve as camouflage for a potentially violent purpose – the ships are warships (227), whilst Lededje's Intagliation were remade by the Culture, disguising a knife missile, itself a kind of bodyguard and security device.[81] Yet such images – whole-tone scales, Intagliation, Baroquing – also suggest the fundamentally fractal shape of the Culture: gradually expanding through the galaxy, replicating itself in repeating forms (such as the Orbitals and GSVs, Contact's notion of "strength in depth"), with its central values inscribed at every level. As MacLeod notes using fractal language, with the Culture, "there is the sense of a toolkit that *scales up*".[82] Crucially, each form, each "tool in the kit", is represented equally in relational terms at every level, with no one part allowed to dominate: an inversion of Globalisation as Socialisation.

This discussion brings us back to Sma's Culture poem 'Slight Mechanical Destruction, in which Hubble identifies a similarly fractal logic. Arguing that the poem "turns on a lack of congruence between essence and metaphor", Hubble identifies the Culture's wariness of representation and its potential for ideological distortion back in Banks's earliest written piece for the series, which also happens to be the strongest artistic statement produced by his utopia. To Hubble, with this poem, "Banks's whole body of work comes into focus as an infinite *fractal* repetition of the designation by Sma of Zakalwe's trajectory as 'an allegory of regress'".[83] From *Phlebas* to *Hydrogen*, therefore, the series explores the Culture's continual expansion of radical egalitarianism throughout the galaxy in inverse relation to the older philosophies of romance, tradition, and heroism that Zakalwe embodies.

Finally, in tracing the logic of the twelve-tone scale and the fractal throughout the series, we can recognise the careful, symbolic representations of the Culture that Banks discreetly introduced into his texts,

---

[81] This mechanism of attack/defence clearly resembles animal predators, such as the Poison Dart Frog, native to Central and South America, or the Flamboyant Cuttlefish, native to Northern Australia and Southern New Guinea, which cover their dangerous nature with beautiful patterns to confuse their prey, or lull it into a false sense of security.

[82] Ken MacLeod, 'Phlebas Reconsidered', 1–3, in Butler, Mendlesohn, *The True Knowledge*, 1. Emphasis added.

[83] Hubble, 'Poems by Iain Banks and Ken MacLeod'. Web. Emphasis added.

which form a powerful system of subconscious, emblematic resonances that signify the depth of its utopian currents.

Conclusion

Walter Benjamin famously concluded 'The Work of Art in the Age of Mechanical Reproduction' (1970) by arguing that: "the logical result of Fascism is the introduction of aesthetics into political life," which means that "Communism responds by politicizing art."[84] Following this, the Culture series itself demonstrates Banks's dedication to creating art that embodies Benjamin's notion, suffused with a profound progressive political radicalism. Banks provides texts that challenge both the logic of fascism and the way in which communism has been misrepresented, and misused in history. Nowhere is this embodied more effectively than in Banks's dedication to utopianism, into which analysis of the artworks within the Culture – Jameson's miniature glass – provides unique insights. Art has become an esoteric activity, viewed as eccentric, quaint, or even a waste of time, despite the Culture's society offering every citizen unlimited creative possibilities. Therefore depictions of art in the Culture series itself are sparse in number and, while they are clearly artworks *in* utopia, they frequently cannot be considered utopian works of art according to Jameson's understanding or Burling's framework. Furthermore, art is seemingly more common amongst AIs than amongst humans. It is the creations of the Minds – with their obsessive tendencies toward cataloguing, collecting, and painstaking reproduction – that seem to characterise the Culture's art just as much as Sma's poetry or Ziller's symphony. Further demonstrating Banks's pro-AI stance, providing the Minds with an urge toward artistic expression works to humanise them and challenge the conventional depiction of AI as capable only of mathematical, rational logic. The Culture is limitless in nature yet its art mostly takes the form of what Burling calls variation: its tableaux, poems, and symphonies are recognisable as the result of bourgeois individualist practice, rather than the radically new, utopian collective approach to art that Burling calls innovation. As such, it reflects Jameson's parallax reading of SF in Banks's series, where the utopian/ socialist imagination is limited by the constraints of capitalist reality. Much of the art depicted in the series is concerned with war and violence of some kind, analysis of which reveals a kind of residual memory of pre-utopia in an aesthetic, psychoanalytic method. In a similar manner

---

[84] Walter Benjamin, *Illuminations* (London: Jonathan Cape Ltd, 1973), 243.

to the *Grey Area*'s torture museum and the *Sleeper Services*'s tableaux, 'Expiring Light' serves the dual purpose of keeping the memory of past mistakes alive in the public imagination and of allowing the pampered citizens of utopia to experience the violence that has been abolished from their society in symbolic form. Yet, as Jude Roberts reminds us in her study of cannibalism in the Culture, the Culture itself is also still capable of perpetrating such symbolic violence. Finally, it is ironic that the form of an atonal, serial composition should provide the most appropriate aesthetic representation of Banks's personal utopia given that it is the musical form that he most struggled to appreciate. Yet this did not stop him from connecting the daring innovators of modernist music with the radical breaks from political, aesthetic, and generic tradition that he intended many aspects of his Culture series to embody.

Concluding Postscript

"The imagination is the goal of history. I see culture as an effort to literally realize our collective dreams." – Terence McKenna.

While there was something slickly science fictional in the Falcon 9's elegant reverse landing onto the *Of Course I Still Love You* in March 2019, the SpaceIL ship *Beresheet* was reported to have crash-landed on the moon on 11 April. Yet Banks did not intend for the Culture's technoscience to look as slick as SpaceX, regularly explaining that its ships were functional and practical, and compared them with modular furniture: shunning special effects, Banks wanted the Culture's ships to demonstrate its commitment to a transparent, neutral self-representation. The next few years promise further milestones for the Culture series. Scheduled for publication in 2021, Ken MacLeod's book *The Culture: Notes and Drawings* will reveal many of Banks's original illustrations for the first time, providing "a unique insight into the Culture, including its history, language, technology, philosophy and values."[1] The book is sure to prompt further discussion on the Culture's visual aesthetics, as was the long-awaited Amazon TV adaptation, until it was unfortunately cancelled in August 2020.[2]

Despite the risks of rogue entrepreneurs like Musk, it is difficult not to find a degree of excitement in the increased interest in space travel in recent years. Yet the early decades of the twenty-first century seem

---

[1] Katherine Cowdry, 'Drawings by the late Iain M Banks to be published', *Bookseller*, 14 February 2018. https://www.thebookseller.com/news/orbit-publish-culture-drawings-iain-m-banks-731691.

[2] James Vincent, 'Amazon cancels TV adaptation of Iain M. Banks' sci-fi Culture series', *Verge*, 26 August 2020. https://www.theverge.com/2020/8/26/21402585/amazon-cancels-tv-adaptation-culture-series-iain-m-banks-consider-phlebas.

to echo the apocalyptic tone of the mid-1970s in which Iain M. Banks wrote his Culture series. During the time of the SpaceX/SpaceIL launch, the UK was embroiled in a turbulent period of mass protest, fierce debate, sharp social divide, and political turmoil relating to the EU "Brexit" Referendum. In this we can even recognise something of the Subliming vote taken by the Gzilt in *Hydrogen*: a society-wide decision on changing its culture for years to come, its democracy muddied by ambiguity and misinformation.

The UK would eventually leave the EU on 31 January 2020, and, completing final work on this manuscript in May 2020, Britain's future relations with the EU still remain uncertain. Furthermore, the world's future has been dramatically shaken by the Covid-19 pandemic. While the pandemic – a tragic and destructive global pattern – is nothing like the positive apocalypses discussed in this book, we can only hope that some constructive changes will arise from it, enabling the world to heal, even to thrive. It can be difficult to maintain Banks's bold hope for the future, yet we need his un-shaking sense of optimism now more than ever.

Banks found such hope in the near limitless horizon of technology and science, tempered by a core belief in humankind's potential for compassionate thinking, collective action, and reasoned logic. This found its apotheosis in his passion for the possibilities of space travel and of humankind dispersing across the galaxy, and the recently reinvigorated missions of both the private and public spheres claiming to work toward making such a future feasible. We can only hope that those intending to make the *technologiade* process a historical reality take heed of the Culture's injunction against exploitation, and of SF's warnings against imperial expansion, in the quest for a global and galactic Second Nature. Reading the Culture series is to recognise something of the real-world West in the actions of SC and Contact, and something of the liberal democratic enclaves of the developed world in the societies of the Culture itself, in those spaces where Banks's imagination most directly brings the post-Cold War context in which it operated along with him. Yet we simultaneously acknowledge the power present in those glimpses of radical Otherness provided by Banks's vision of a future after economic, biological, social, and political limitations that is no less attractive for the idiosyncrasies of his uninhibited imagination.

In this book, I have expanded upon my reading of the Culture as a kind of utopia by examining the extent to which certain fundamental shifts or breaks away from less utopian societies have necessarily been achieved, and the process by which it has effected such changes. Indeed, in many ways, Banks provided us with the name for these processes from the outset. When he re-drafted *Use of Weapons* in 1974, re-naming his newly conceived personal utopia "the Culture" instead of "the Aliens", Banks could not have chosen a more apt term. The word "culture" was famously described by Raymond Williams as "one of the two or three most complicated words in the English language"[3] – a suitable term, then, for a creation that has attracted such an array of often contradictory understandings and has resisted easy categorisation. Yet the term is accurate for a reason more profound than this shared sense of complexity: the Culture simply *is* culture, in almost all understandings of the word; and it allows for these various definitions and understandings of culture to combine, overlap, and become interrelated. The Culture is a way of thinking: undergoing a certain process of "refinement of mind, taste, and manners," as well as of "intellectual development."[4] The Culture is "the distinctive ideas, customs, social behaviour, products, or way of life of a particular nation, society, people, or period."[5] The Culture is "a way of life", a "social environment", and "a group of people", who subscribe to a particular philosophy, practice, and attitude.[6] The Culture is a collection of artificial environments, whose inhabitants are linked primarily by shared achievements, practices, customs, worldviews, behaviours: linked by and representative of a *shared utopian culture*. The Culture is something that you *do*, as well as somewhere you live. The Culture is to be Culture*d*, nurtured, utopianised. The Culture is fractal and twelve tonal because its fundamental values and philosophies run through it at every level, forming a broader, inter-locking utopian pattern.

To return to the self-reflexion of Fal 'Ngeestra in *Consider Phlebas*, perhaps the occasion where her question "so, who are we?" is answered most explicitly in the series occurs in 'The State of the Art'. As one of the Minds explains:

> what are we supposed to be about, Sma? What is the Culture? What do we believe in, even if it is hardly ever expressed, even if we are embarrassed about talking about it? *Surely in freedom, more than everything else.* A relativistic, changing sort of freedom, unbounded by laws or laid-down moral codes, but – in the end – just because it is hard to pin down and express, a freedom of a far

---

[3] Raymond Williams, *Keywords* (London: Fourth Estate, [1976] 2014), 90–92.
[4] Oxford Dictionaries, 'Culture', Oxford University Press. www.oed.com.v-ezproxy.brunel.ac.uk:2048/view/Entry/45746?result=1&rskey=1Tguyt&.
[5] Oxford Dictionaries, 'Culture'. Web.
[6] Oxford Dictionaries, 'Culture'. Web.

higher quality than anything to be found on the planet beneath us at the moment. (161, emphasis added)

The planet beneath them, to which the Mind refers, is none other than the planet Earth during the 1970s, and the scene serves to highlight the difference and distance between Banks's utopia and ourselves. The Culture's freedom is freedom *from* – from our scarcity, our conflicts, our alienated labour, and our inequalities. Banks always intended the Culture to be a place in which he would like to live, if something like it could ever be realised, and MacLeod pointed out that it is ironically a rare example of a utopia in which many people would actually wish to live.[7] I, for one, would agree. Like most utopias, the Culture series does not offer a method by which we might change our planet from that which Banks's characters find beneath them. But it does remind us to look up to the Culture as representative of the peaks to which we should constantly aspire, regardless of our ability to ever definitively achieve them.

The Culture is Banks's most famous creation within SF and it is to the works concerned with it that he brought his most personal and most profound ideas. I hope the series will be considered Banks's masterwork, and that it may eventually be regarded outside of the SF sphere, alongside *The Wasp Factory*, as amongst the finest works of literature. The texts have an extended utopian value and significance that lies in the nature of the Culture itself, forming a multivalent utopian force in which individuals can participate – a truly utopian culture. By turns exuberant, humorous, sarcastic, satirical, playful, and angry, Banks utilised many voices whilst writing this series, all singing the same message: we should never stop fighting for a more peaceful world, we should never lose our hope to pessimism, and we should always regard human culture as the highest of values.

The Culture is not just the most ornate and expansive fictional endeavour of Banks's 28-year career as publishing writer: it is one of the most radical creations in all of SF. Given the originality, complexity, and wonderful ambiguities of Banks's work, it is no surprise that the British Library's 2011 exhibition *Out of this World* described the Culture as one of the most extraordinary settings in modern literature.

---

[7] MacLeod, 'Iain Banks: A science fiction star first and foremost'. Web.

Bibliography

Abbot, Phil. 'Utopians at play'. *Utopian Studies* 15, no. 1 (2004): 44–62.
Abelove, Henry, Michèle Aina Barale, and David M. Halperin, eds. *The Lesbian and Gay Studies Reader*. New York: Routledge, 1993.
Aldiss, Brian W., ed. *Space Opera: An Anthology of Way-Back-When Futures*. London: Book Club Associates, 1974.
— *The Detached Retina*. Liverpool: Liverpool University Press, 1995.
Asimov, Isaac. *Foundation*. London: Voyager, [1953] 1995.
Attebery, Brian. *Decoding Gender in Science Fiction*. New York: Routledge, 2002.
Atwood, Margaret. *In Other Worlds: SF and the Human Imagination*. London: Virago, 2011.
Baccolini, Raffaella, and Tom Moylan, eds. *Dark Horizons: Science Fiction and the Dystopian Imagination*. London: Routledge, 2003.
Baker, Timothy C. 'Scottish Utopian Fiction and the Invocation of God'. *Utopian Studies* 21, no. 1 (2010): 91–117.
Banks, Iain. *The Wasp Factory*. London: Macmillan, 1984.
— *The Crow Road*. London: Abacus, 1992.
— *Whit*. London: Abacus, 1995.
— *Walking on Glass*. London: Abacus, [1985] 1998.
— *The Bridge*. London: Macmillan, [1986] 2000.
— *Dead Air*. Great Britain: Abacus, [2002] 2003.
— *Transition*. Great Britain: Little, Brown, 2009.
Banks, Iain, and Ken MacLeod. *Poems*. St Ives: Little, Brown, 2015.
Banks, Iain M. *Consider Phlebas*. London: Orbit, [1987] 1988.
— *The Player of Games*. London: Orbit, [1988] 1989.
— *Use of Weapons*. London: Orbit, [1990] 1992.
— *The State of the Art*. London: Orbit, [1991] 1993.
— *Excession*. London: Orbit, [1996] 1997.
— *Inversions*. London: Orbit, [1998] 1999.
— *Look to Windward*. Great Britain: Orbit, 2000.
— *Matter*. London: Orbit, 2008.
— *Surface Detail*. London: Orbit, 2010.
— *The Hydrogen Sonata*. London: Orbit, 2012.
Barthes, Roland. *Mythologies*. London: Random House, [1957] 2000.
Baumann, Fred. 'Humanism and Transhumanism'. *New Atlantis*, no. 29 (Fall 2010): 68–84.

Benjamin, Walter. *Illuminations*. London: Jonathan Cape Ltd, 1973.
Bogstad, Janice M. 'Men Writing Women'. *Women in Science Fiction and Fantasy 1* (2009): 170–178.
Bookchin, Murray. *Post-Scarcity Anarchism*. London: Wildwood House, 1974.
Bostrum, Nick. 'The Transhumanist FAQ'. In *Readings in the Philosophy of Technology*. David Caplan, ed. Maryland: Rowman and Littleford Publishers, Inc., 2009.
Bould, Mark, Andrew M. Butler, Adam Roberts, and Sherryl Vint, eds. *The Routledge Companion to Science Fiction*. Oxon: Routledge, 2009.
— *Fifty Key Figures in Science Fiction*. Oxon: Routledge, 2010.
Bould, Mark, and China Miéville, eds. *Red Planets: Marxism and Science Fiction*. London: Pluto Press, 2009.
Braidotti, Rosi. *The Posthuman*. Cambridge: Polity Press, 2013.
Brown, Carolyn. 'Utopias and Heterotopias: The "Culture" of Iain M. Banks'. In *Impossibility Fiction: Alternativity, Extrapolation, Speculation*. Derek Littlewood and Peter Stockwell, eds. Amsterdam: Rodopi, 1996.
Brown, Chris. '"Special Circumstances": Intervention by a Liberal Utopia'. *Millennium – Journal of International Studies* 30, no. 3 (2001): 625–633.
Brown, James. 'Not Losing the Plot: Politics, Guilt and Storytelling in Banks and MacLeod'. In *The True Knowledge of Ken MacLeod*. Andrew M. Butler and Farah Mendlesohn, eds. 55–75. Reading: Foundation Studies in Science Fiction, 2003.
Brown, Marshall, and Michael Kennedy. 'Origins of modernism: musical structures and narrative forms'. In *Music and Text: Critical Inquiries*. Steven Paul Scherp, ed. Cambridge: Cambridge University Publishing, 2006.
Buckell, Tobias. *Crystal Rain*. Tor Books, 2006. Ebook.
Burling, William J. 'Art as "The Basic Technique of Life": Utopian Art and Art in Utopia'. In *Red Planets: Marxism and Science Fiction*. Mark Bould and China Miéville, eds. 47–66. London: Pluto Press, 2009.
Butler, Andrew M. 'Thirteen Ways of Looking at the British Boom'. *Science Fiction Studies* 30, no. 3 (November 2003): 374–393.
Butler, Andrew M., and Farah Mendlesohn, eds. *The True Knowledge of Ken MacLeod*. Reading: Science Fiction Foundation, 2003.
Cabell, Craig. *Iain Banks: The Biography*. John Blake Publishing Ltd, 2014. Ebook.
Caroti, Simone. *The Generation Starship in Science Fiction: A Critical History, 1934-2001*. North Carolina: MacFarland and Co, 2011.
— *The Culture Series of Iain M. Banks: A Critical Introduction*. North Carolina: MacFarland and Company, Inc., Publishers, 2015.
Channel 4. 'Iain Banks'. *The English Programme: Scottish Writers*. Warwick: Channel 4, 1996.
Christie, Mike. 'Review: "The State of the Art"'. *Foundation: The International Review of Science Fiction*, 49.
Christie, Thomas. 'Chapter Two: Iain M. Banks's *The State of the Art* (1989) and Ken MacLeod's *The Stone Canal* (1996)'. In *Notional Identities: Ideology, Genre and National Identity in Popular Genres*. 25–71. Newcastle upon Tyne: Cambridge Scholars Publishing, 2013.

Clarke, Arthur C. *Childhood's End*. London: Pan Books Ltd, [1954] 1956.
— 'Hazards of Prophecy: The Failure of Imagination'. In *Profiles of the Future: An Enquiry into the Limits of the Possible*. 14–21. Profiles of the Future: An Enquiry into the Limits of the PossibleLondon: Harper and Row, [1962] rev. 1973.
— *2001: A Space Odyssey*. London: Arrow Books Limited, [1968] 1988.
Clarke, Jim. 'The Sublime in Iain M. Banks's "Culture" novels'. *Vector* 281 (Winter 2015): 7–11.
Clute, John. *Pardon This Intrusion: Fantastika in the World Storm*. Essex: Beccon Publications, 2011.
Colebrook, Martyn, and Katharine Cox, eds. *The Transgressive Iain Banks: Essays on a Writer Beyond Borders*. North Carolina: McFarland Press, 2013.
Coombs, Herbert Cole. *The Return of Scarcity: Strategies for an Economic Future*. Cambridge: University of Cambridge Press, 1990.
Craig, Cairns. 'Player of Games: Iain (M.) Banks, Jean-Francois Lyotard and Sublime Terror'. In *The Contemporary British Novel since 1980*. James Acheson and Sarah C.E. Ross, eds. 229–239. New York: Palgrave Macmillan, 2005.
Csicsery-Ronay Jr., Istvan. *The Seven Beauties of Science Fiction*. Middletown, CT: Wesleyan University Press, 2008.
— 'Empire'. In *The Routledge Companion to Science Fiction*. Mark Bould, Andrew M. Butler, Adam Roberts, and Sherryl Vint, eds. 362–372. Oxon: Routledge, 2009.
Danczak, Felix. 'Look to Windward: T.S. Eliot's *The Waste Land* as a Template for the sf of Iain M. Banks'. *Vector* 264 (Autumn 2010): 23–28.
Davies, William. 'The New Neoliberalism'. *New Left Review* 101 (September–October 2016): 124–127.
Davis, Laurence. 'Morris, Wilde and Le Guin on Art, Work, and Utopia'. *Utopian Studies* 20, no. 2 (2009): 213–248.
Dawkins, Richard. *The God Delusion*. London: Transworld Publishers, 2006.
Delany, Samuel. 'The Necessity of Tomorrow(s)'. In *Starboard Wine*. 1–14. Middletown, CT: Wesleyan University Press, 2012.
Descartes, Rene. 'Letter to Princess Elizabeth (28 June 1643)'. In *Philosophy Then and Now*. N. Scott Arnold, Theodore M. Benditt, and George Graham, eds. 58–63. Oxford: Blackwell Publishing, 1998.
Devor, Holly. 'Gender Role Behaviors and Attitudes'. In *The Lesbian and Gay Studies Reader*, H. Abelove, M.A. Barale, and D. Halperin, eds. New York: Routledge, 1993.
Dillons Review. 'Inversions: An Interview', *Dillons Review* 16 (May–June 1998).
Dodou, Katherina. 'Evading the Dominant "Reality" – the Case of Iain Banks's *Walking on Glass*'. *Studia Neophilologica* 78 (2006): 28–38.
Donnellan, Craig. *Our Ageing World*. Cambridge: Independence Educational Publishers, 2002.
Duggan, Robert. 'Iain M. Banks, Postmodernism and the Gulf War'. *Extrapolation: A Journal of Science Fiction and Fantasy* 48, no. 3 (Winter 2007): 558–577.

Edwards, Caroline. 'Uncovering the "gold-bearing rubble": Ernst Bloch's Literary Criticism'. In *Utopianism, Modernism, and Literature in the Twentieth Century*. A. Reeve-Tucker and N. Waddell, eds. (Palgrave Macmillian UK, 2013): 182–203.

Elliott, Robert C. *The Shape of Utopia: Studies in a Literary Genre*. London: University of Chicago Press, 1970.

Falconer, Rachel. *Hell in Contemporary Culture*. Edinburgh: Edinburgh University Press, 2005.

Falcus, Sarah. 'Gender in *The Wasp Factory*, *Whit* and *The Business*'. In *The Transgressive Iain Banks*. Martyn Colebrook and Katharine Cox, eds. North Carolina: McFarland Press, 2013.

Ferguson, Kathy E. 'Patriarchy'. In *Women's Studies Encyclopedia* 2. Helen Tierney, ed. Westport, CT: Greenwood Publishing, 2009.

Ferneyhough, Brian. 'Time and Motion Study II: for solo cello and electronics'. London: Peters, 1978.

Fischer, John Martin, and Ruth Curl. 'Philosophical Models of Immortality in Science Fiction'. In *Immortal Engines: Life Extension and Immortality in Science Fiction and Fantasy*. Geroge Slusser, Gary Westfahl, and Eric S. Rabkin, eds. 3–13. Athens: University of Georgia Press, 1996.

Foucault, Michel. 'Of Other Spaces, Heterotopias'. In *Other Spaces: The Affair of the Heterotopia*. Roland Ritter and Bernd Knaller-Vlay, eds. Austria: Haus der Architektur, 1998.

Fukuyama, Frances. 'The End of History?' *National Interest* 16 (Summer 1989): 3–18.

— *The End of History and the Last Man*. Free Press, 1992.

— *Our Posthuman Future: Consequences of the Biotechnology Revolution*. Farrar, Straus and Giroux, 2002.

Gallope, Michael. 'Ernst Bloch's Utopian Tone of Hope'. *Contemporary Music Review* 31, 5–6 (2012): 371–387.

Gamble, Sarah. 'Patriarchy'. In *The Routledge Companion to Feminism and Postfeminism*. New York: Routledge, [1999] 2006.

Garnett, David. 'Interview: Iain Banks'. *Wired Journal*. (Winter 1989): 51–69.

Germana, Monica. 'Special Topic 1: The Awakening of Caledonias? Scottish Literature in the 1980s'. In *The 1980s: A Decade of Contemporary British Fiction*. Emily Horton, Philip Tew, and Leigh Wilson, eds. 51–74. Bloomsbury Publishing PLC, 2014. ProQuest Ebook Central.

Goodway, David, ed. *For Anarchism: History, Theory, and Practice*. London: Routledge, 1989.

Greenland, Colin. 'Consider Phlebas by Iain M. Banks'. *Foundation: The International Review of Science-Fiction* 40. (Summer 1987).

Gregory, Brad S. 'The Insights and Oversights of the "New Atheists"'. *Logos* 12, no. 4 (Fall 2009): 17–55.

Grey, John. *Straw Dogs: Thoughts on Humans and Other Animals*. London: Granta Books, 2002.

— *Black Mass: Apocalyptic Religion and the Death of Utopia*. St Ives: Penguin Books, 2007.

Griffin, Michael. 'Utopian Music and the Problem of Luxury'. *Utopian Studies* 16, no. 2 (2005): 247–266.
Guerrier, Simon. 'Culture Theory: Iain M. Banks's "Culture" as Utopia'. *Foundation: The International Review of Science Fiction* 28, no. 76 (Summer 1999): 28–38.
Haddock, David, ed. *The Banksonian*. Issues 1–16 collected. Self-published.
Hardesty, William. 'Mercenaries and Special Circumstances: Iain M. Banks's Counter-Narrative of Utopia, Use of Weapons'. *Foundation: The International Review of Science Fiction* 76 (Summer 1999): 39–46.
— 'Space Opera without the Space: The Culture Novels of Iain M. Banks'. In *Space and Beyond: The Frontier Theme in Science Fiction*. Gary Westfahl, ed. 115–123. London: Greenwood Publishing Group, 2000.
— 'Space Opera'. In *The Cambridge Companion to Science Fiction*. Edward James and Farah Mendlesohn, eds. 197–208. Cambridge Companions to Literature. Cambridge: Cambridge University Press, 2003.
Hardt, Michael, and Antonio Negri. *Empire*. United States of America: Harvard University Press, 2000.
Howe, Stephen. *Empire: A Very Short Introduction*. Oxford: Oxford University Press, 2002.
Hubble, Nick. 'Science Fiction in the U.K.' In *Sense of Wonder: A Century of Science Fiction*. Leigh Ronald Grossman, ed. Wildside Press, 2011. Ebook.
Hubble, Nick, John McLeod, and Philip Tew, eds. *The 1970s: A Decade of Contemporary British Fiction*. London: Bloomsbury Publishing PLC, 2014.
Hubble, Nick, and Aris Mousoutzanis. *The Science Fiction Handbook*. London: Bloomsbury Academic, 2013.
Hubble, Nick, Joseph Norman, and Esther MacCallum-Stewart, eds. *The Science Fiction of Iain M. Banks*. Exeter: Glyphi Publications, 2018.
Interzone 16. 'Interview with Kim Newman'. Cited in David Haddock, ed., *The Banksonian: An Iain (M.) Banks Fanzine* 4 (November 2004).
Jackson, Patrick Thaddeus, and James Heilman. '"Outside Context Problems": Liberalism and the Other in the Works of Iain M. Banks'. In *New Boundaries in Political Science Fiction*. Donald M. Hassler and Clyde Wilcox, eds. 235–258. South Carolina: University of South Carolina, 2008.
Jacobs, Allan. 'The Ambiguous Utopia of Iain M. Banks'. *New Atlantis: A Journal of Science Technology* (Summer 2009): 45–58.
James, Edward. *Science Fiction in the 20th Century*. Oxford: Oxford University Press, 1994.
Jameson, Fredric. 'The Politics of Theory: Ideological Positions in the Postmodernism Debate'. *New German Critique*, no. 33 (Autumn, 1984): 53–65.
— *Late Marxism: Adorno, or, The Persistence of the Dialectic*. London & New York: Verso, 1990.
— *Postmodernism; or The Cultural Logic of Late Capitalism*. London: Verso, 1991.
— *Archaeologies of the Future: The Desire called Utopia and Other Science Fictions*. London: Verso, 2005.
— *Valences of the Dialectic*. London: Verso, 2009.
— *Representing Capital: A Reading of Volume One*. London: Verso, 2011.

Joseph, Charles M. *Stravinsky Inside Out*. New Haven and London: Yale University Press, 2001.
Kateb, George. *Utopia and its Enemies*. New York: Schochen Books, 1972.
Keen, Tony. Paper given at 'The State of the Culture: a One-day Symposium on Iain M. Banks's "Culture" series'. Brunel University London. 11 September 2013.
Kerslake, Patricia. *Science Fiction and Empire*. Liverpool: Liverpool University Press, 2007.
Khanin, G.I. 'The 1950s – the Triumph of the Soviet Economy'. *Europe-Asia Studies* 55, no. 8 (December 2003): 1,187–1,211.
Kincaid, Paul. *Modern Masters of Science Fiction: Iain M. Banks*. Oxfordshire: University of Illinois Press, 2017.
Klein, Naomi. *No Is Not Enough*. St Ives: Penguin Books, 2017.
Kulbicki, Michal. 'Iain M. Banks, Ernst Bloch and Utopian Interventions'. *Colloquy: Text, Theory, Critique* 17 (August 2009): 34–43.
Kurzweil, Ray. *The Singularity is Near*. New York: Viking, 2005.
Lamont, Corliss. *The Philosophy of Humanism*. London: Pemberton Publishing Co Ltd, [1949] 1965.
Larbalestier, Justine. *The Battle of the Sexes in Science Fiction*. Middletown: Wesleyan University Press, 2002.
Law, Stephen. *A Very Short Introduction to Humanism*. Oxford: Oxford University Press, 2011.
Le Guin, Ursula. *City of Illusions*. 1967.
— *The Dispossessed*. St Albans: Panther Books Ltd, [1974] 1976.
— *The Left Hand of Darkness*. London: Orbit, [1969] 1992.
Leckie, Anne. *Ancillary Justice*. London: Orbit, 2014.
Levitas, Ruth. 'In eine bess're Welt entrückt: Reflections on Music and Utopia'. *Utopian Studies* 21, no. 2 (2010): 215–231.
— *Utopia as Method*. Hampshire: Palgrave MacMillian, 2013.
Lippens, Ronnie. 'Imachinations of Peace: Scientifications of Peace in Iain M. Banks's *The Player of Games*'. *Utopian Studies: Journal of the Society for Utopian Studies* 13, no. 1 (2002): 135–147.
Littlewood, Derek, and Peter Stockwell, eds. *Impossibility Fiction: Alternativity – Extrapolation – Speculation*. 57–74. Amsterdam: Rodopi, 1996.
Luckhurst, Roger. *Science Fiction*. Cambridge: Polity, 2005.
Lukács, Georg. 'Reification and the Consciousness of the Proletariat'. In *History and Class Consciousness: Studies in Marxist Dialectics*. Cambridge, MA: MIT Press, 1971.
MacLeod, Ken. *Cosmonaut Keep*. Great Britain: Orbit, 2000.
— *Dark Light*. Great Britain: Orbit, 2001.
— *Engine City*. Great Britain: Orbit, 2002.
— 'Phlebas Reconsidered'. In *The True Knowledge of Ken MacLeod*. Andrew M. Butler and Farah Mendlesohn, eds. Reading: Foundation Studies in Science Fiction, 2003.
— *Learning the World*. London: Orbit, 2006.
— 'Telephone interview'. 2:05pm, Friday 17 May 2013.

Mangum, Teresa. 'Longing for Life Extension: Science Fiction and Late Life'. *Journal of Aging and Identity* 7, no. 2 (2002): 69–82.
Martingale, Moira. *Gothic Dimensions: Iain Banks – Time Lord.* Quetzalcoatl Publishing, 2013.
Matthews, Race. 'Iain M. Banks: The "Culture" Science-Fiction Novels and the Economics and politics of Scarcity and Abundance'. *Metaphysical Review* 28/29 (August 1998): 9.
McCarthy, Gerry. *Futura Reviews*, June 1988, Dublin. In the Iain Banks Archive, University of Stirling.
McCracken, Scott. *Pulp: Reading Popular Fiction.* Manchester: Manchester University Press, 1998.
McHale, Brian. 'Towards a Poetics of Cyberpunk'. In *Beyond Cyberpunk: New Critical Perspectives.* Graham J. Murphy and Sherryl Vint, eds. New York: Routledge, 2012.
Melamed, Jodi. 'Racial Capitalism'. *Critical Ethnic Studies* 1, 1 (Spring 2015): 76–85.
Mendlesohn, Farah. 'The Dialectic of Decadence and Utopia in Iain M. Bank's Culture Novels'. *Foundation: The International Review of Science Fiction* 93 (2005): 116–124.
— 'Iain M. Banks: *Excession*'. In *A Companion to Science Fiction*, David Seed, ed., 556–567. Oxford: Blackwell Publishing, 2005.
— *Rhetorics of Fantasy.* Middletown, Conn: Wesleyan University Press, 2008.
Middleton, Tim. 'The Works of Iain M. Banks: A Critical Introduction'. *Foundation: The International Review of Science Fiction* 76, no. 5 (Summer 1999): 5–16.
Milburn, Colin. 'Nanotechnology in the Age of Posthuman Engineering: Science Fiction as Science'. *Configurations* 10, no. 2 (Spring 2002): 261–295.
Millar, Gavin. 'Scottish Science Fiction: Writing Scottish Literature Back Into History'. *Etudes Ecossaises* 12 (2009): 121–133.
Miller, Gavin. 'Iain (M.) Banks: Utopia, Nationalism and the Posthuman'. In *The Edinburgh Companion to Contemporary Scottish Literature.* Berthold Schoene, ed. Edinburgh: Edinburgh University Press, 2007.
Moody, Harry R. *Aging: Concepts and Controversies.* Los Angeles: Pine Forge Press, 2010.
Moorcock, Michael. 'Guest Editorial'. *New Worlds* 129 (April 1963). Reprinted in Edward James, ed. *Science Fiction in the 20th Century.* Oxford: Oxford University Press, 1994.
— ed. *Best SF Stories from New Worlds 8.* St Albans: Panther Books Ltd, 1974.
More, Thomas. *Utopia.* England: Heron Books, [1516], n.d.
Morris, William. *News From Nowhere.* Oxford: Oxford University Press, [1890] 2003.
Morrison, Jago. *Contemporary Fiction.* London: Routledge, 2003.
Moskowitz, Sam. *Seekers of Tomorrow.* United States: World Publishing Co., 1966.
Moylan, Tom. *Demand the Impossible: Science Fiction and the Utopian Imagination.* Germany: Peter Lang AG, Internationaler Verlag der Wissenschaften, 2014.

Murphy, Graham J., and Sherryl Vint, eds. *Beyond Cyberpunk: New Critical Perspectives*. New York: Routledge, [2010] 2012.

Murray, Isobel. 'Interview with Iain Banks, 29th November 1988'. In *Scottish Writers Talking*. Isobel Murray, ed. East Linton: Tuckwell Press, Ltd, 2002.

Nairn, Thomas. 'Iain Banks and the Fiction Factory'. In *The Scottish Novel Since the Seventies: New Visions, Old Dreams*. Graham Wallace and Randall Stevenson, eds. 127–135. Edinburgh: Edinburgh University Press, 1993.

Newman, Michael. *Socialism: A Very Short Introduction*. Gosfort: Oxford University Press, 2005.

Nolan, Val. '"Utopia is a way of saying we can do better": Iain M. Banks and Kim Stanley Robinson in Conversation'. *Foundation: The International Review of Science Fiction* 43, no. 119 (2014): 65–77.

Oxford Dictionary of Philosophy. 'Soul'. Oxford: Oxford University Press, 2005.

Paik, Peter, Y. *From Utopia to Apocalypse*. Minneapolis: University of Minnesota Press, 2010.

Palmer, Christopher. 'Galactic Empires and the Contemporary Extravaganza: Dan Simmons and Iain M. Banks'. *Science-fiction Studies* 26, no. 77 (March 1999).

Parrinder, Patrick, ed. *Science Fiction: A Critical Guide*. Suffolk: The Chaucer Press, 1979.

Plato. *Republic*. St Ives: Penguin Books, 2003.

Pohl, Frederik. 'Introduction'. In E.E. "Doc" Smith. *The Skylark of Space*. Connecticut: Easton Press, 1991.

Porion, Stéphane. 'Reassessing a Turbulent Decade: the Historiography of 1970s Britain in Crisis'. *Etudes Anglaises* 69, no. 3 (2016): 301–320.

Prucher, Jeff, ed. *The Oxford Dictionary of Science Fiction*. Oxford University Press, 2006.

Rennison, Nick. 'Iain Banks'. In *Contemporary British Novelists*. 18–22. Oxfordshire: Routledge, 2005.

Reynolds, Alastair. *Revelation Space*. London: Gollancz, 2000.

— *Chasm City*. London: Gollancz, 2001.

Roberts, Adam. *Science Fiction*. Cornwall: Routledge, 2010.

Roberts, Jude. 'Culture-al Subjectivities: the Constitution of the Self in Iain M. Banks's Culture Texts'. PhD Thesis. University of Nottingham, 2013.

— 'Iain M. Banks's Culture of Vulnerable Masculinities'. *Foundation* 43, no. 117 (Spring 2014): 46–60.

— 'A Few Questions on the Culture'. In Paul Kincaid. *Modern Masters of Science Fiction: Iain M. Banks*. Oxfordshire: University of Illinois Press, 2017.

— '"Cannibals from Outer Space!": Symbolic Violence and the Cannibalism of the Other'. In *The Science Fiction of Iain M. Banks*. Hubble, Norman, and MacCallum-Stewart, eds. 195–211. Exeter: Glyphi Publications, 2018.

Robinson, Kim Stanley. *Green Mars*. London: Harper Collins, [1993] 1994.

— *Blue Mars*. New York: Bantam Books, [1996] 1997.

— *Red Mars*. London: Voyager, [1992] 2009.

Rothbard, Murray N. 'Karl Marx: Communist as Religious Eschatologist'. *Review of Austrian Economics* 4, no. 1 (December 1990): 123–179.

Russ, Joanna. *The Female Man*. Ayelsbury: Hazell Watson And Viney Ltd, 1977.
Sage, Victor. 'The Politics of Petrification: Culture, Religion, History in the Fiction of Iain Banks and John Banville'. In *Modern Gothic: A Reader*. Victor Sage and Allan Lloyd, eds. Manchester: Manchester University Press, 1996.
Salamon, Gayle. *Assuming a Body: Transgender and Rhetorics of Materiality*. New York: Columbia University Press, 2010.
Sandbrook, Dominic. *State of Emergency. The Way We Were: Britain 1970–1974*. London: Penguin, 2011.
Sargent, Lyman Tower. 'The Three Faces of Utopianism Revisited'. *Utopian Studies* 5, no. 1 (1994): 1–37.
— *Utopianism: A Very Short Introduction*. New York: Oxford University Press, 2010.
— 'Theorizing Utopia / Utopianism in the Twenty-First Century'. In *Spectres of Utopia*. Artur Blaum and Ludmila Gruszewska, eds. Lublin: Peter Lang GmbH, 2012.
Schoene-Harwood, Berthold. 'Dams Burst: Devolving Gender in Iain Banks's *The Wasp Factory*'. *Ariel* 30, no. 1 (1999): 131–148.
Scholes, Robert, and Eric S. Rabkin. *Science Fiction: History, Science, Vision*. Oxford: Oxford University Press, Ltd, 1977.
Scruton, Roger. 'Representation in Music'. *Philosophy* 51, no. 197 (July 1976): 273–287.
Shaw, Philip. *The Sublime*. Oxon: Routledge, 2006.
Slusser, George, Gary Westfahl, and Eric S. Rabkin, eds. *Immortal Engines: Life Extension and Immortality in Science Fiction and Fantasy*. London: University of Georgia Press, 1996.
Smith, E.E. "Doc". *First Lensman*. St Albans: Granada Publishing Ltd, 1971.
— *The Skylark of Space*. Sussex: Granada Publishing Limited, 1974.
— *Triplanetary*. St Albans: Granada Publishing Ltd, 1975.
Sprague de Camp, L. *Science-Fiction Handbook: The Writing of Imaginative Fiction*. New York: Hermitage House, 1953.
Steger, Manfred B. *A Very Short Introduction to Globalization*. Oxford: Oxford University Press, 2003.
Steinmetz, George. *State/Culture: State-Formation after the Cultural Turn*. Ithaca, NY: Cornell University Press, 1999.
Suvin, Darko. *Positions and Suppositions in Science Fiction*. Kent, Ohio: Kent State University Press, 1988.
— 'Theses on Dystopia 2001'. In Michal Kulbicki. 'Iain M Banks, Ernst Bloch and Utopian Interventions'. *Colloquy: Text Theory Critique* 17 (August 2009): 34–43.
— *Metamorphoses of Science Fiction: On the Poetics and History of a Literary Genre*. Bern, Switzerland: Peter Lang AG, 2016.
Tew, Phillip. *The Contemporary British Novel*. London: Continuum, 2007.
Tripp, Anna. *Gender*. London: Palgrave, 2007.
Verne, Jules. *Journey to the Centre of the Earth*. New York: Oxford University Press, 1992.

Vint, Sherryl. 'Iain M. Banks: The Culture-al Body'. In *Bodies of Tomorrow: Technology, Subjectivity, Science Fiction*. 79–102. London: University of Toronto Press Ltd, 2007
— Cultural Imperialism and the Ends of Empire: Iain M. Banks's *Look to Windward*'. *Journal of the Fantastic in the Arts* 18, no. 1 (Winter 2008): 83–98.
Ward, Colin. *Anarchism: A Very Short Introduction*. Oxford: Oxford University Press, 2004.
Wegner, Phillip E. *Life Between Two Deaths, 1989–2001: U.S. Culture in the Long Nineties*. United States of America: Duke University Press, 2009.
— *Shockwaves of Possibility: Essays on Science Fiction, Globalization, and Utopia*. Bern, Switzerland: Peter Lang AG, 2014.
Wells, H.G. *The Time Machine*. New York: Bantam Books, 1973.
Westfahl, Gary. 'Space Opera'. In *The Cambridge Companion to Science Fiction*. E. James and F. Mendlesohn, eds. 197–208. Cambridge: Cambridge University Press, 2003.
Westlake, Donald E. *Murderous Schemes: An Anthology of Classic Detective Stories*. Oxford: Oxford University Press, 1996.
Wheeler, Pat. 'Issues of Gender, Sexuality and Ethnicity'. In *The Science Fiction Handbook*. Nick Hubble and Aris Mousoutzanis, eds. London: Bloomsbury Academic, 2013.
White, Eric Walter. *Stravinsky: The Composer and his Works*. London: Faber and Faber, 1966.
Williams, Evan Calder. *Combined and Uneven Apocalypse*. Zero Books: Winchester, 2011.
Williams, Raymond. *Keywords*. London: Fourth Estate, [1976] 2014.
Winter, Jerome. *Science Fiction, New Space Opera, and Neoliberal Globalism: Nostalgia for Infinity*. Melksham: University of Wales Press, 2016.
Woodcock, George, ed. *The Anarchist Reader*. Fontana: Glasgow, 1980.
Žižek, Slavoj. *Welcome to the Desert of the Real!* London: Verso, 2002.

Electronic Resources

Academy of Medical Sciences. 'Rejuvenating Ageing Research'. September 2009. https://acmedsci.ac.uk/file-download/35180-ageingwe.pdf.
Adams, Stephen. 'Chapman Brothers' Hell Back From The Flames'. *Telegraph*, 29 May 2008. www.telegraph.co.uk/news/uknews/2050329/Chapman-brothers-Hell-back-from-the-flames.html.
Aegard, John. 'Ambiguous Reparations: Iain M. Banks' Look To Windward'. *Strange Horizons*, 18 December 2000. www.strangehorizons.com/2000/20001218/look_to_windward.shtml.
Aguilar-Millan, Stephen, Ann Feeny, Amy Oberg, and Elizabeth Rudd. 'The Post-scarcity World of 2050–2075'. *Futurist* 44, no. 1 (January 2010). https://www.researchgate.net/.../216807965_The_Post-Scarcity_World_of_2050-2075.
Alderman, Naomi. *Science Fiction: On Other-World Wars*, 23 October 2010. www.guardian.co.uk/books/2010/oct/23/surface-detail-iain-banks-review.

BIBLIOGRAPHY

Angus, Kat. 'Katee Sackhoff returns to Earth'. *Canwest News Service*, 2 September 2009.
Aplin, Marc. 'Fantasy Fiction; Iain M. Banks Interview – Part One'. 26 October 2012. fantasy-faction.com/2012/iain-m-banks-interview-part-one.
Arnott, Steve. 'The Culture: Iain Banks's Greatest Creation?' 11 September 2015. www.thepointhowever.org/index.php/culture/159-the-culture-iain-bank-s-greatest-creation.
Bailey, Melissa. 'First Uterus Transplant in the US Gives 26-Year-Old Woman Chance at Pregnancy'. *StatNews*, 25 February 2016. www.statnews.com/2016/02/25/uterus-transplant/.
Banks, Iain M. 'A Few Notes on Marain'. Website of Trevor Hopkins. N.d. http://trevor-hopkins.com/banks/a-few-notes-on-marain.html.
— 'A Few Notes on the Culture'. *Vavatch*, 10 August 1994. www.vavatch.co.uk/books/banks/cultnote.htm.
— 'Divided Over "Our Boys"'. *Guardian*, 22 March 2003. www.guardian.co.uk/theguardian/2003/mar/22/guardianletters6.
— 'Out of this World'. *Guardian*, 12 July 2008. www.theguardian.com/books/2008/jul/12/saturdayreviewsfeatres.guardianreview5.
— 'Stop funding for faith schools'. *Times*, 16 August 2009. www.timesonline.co.uk/tol/news/uk/scotland/article6797769.ece.
— 'Small step towards a boycott of Israel'. *Guardian*, 3 June 2010. www.guardian.co.uk/world/2010/jun/03/boycott-israel-iain-banks.
— 'Reconsider Blair book signing'. *Guardian*, 18 August 2010. www.guardian.co.uk/politics/2010/aug/18/reconsider-blair-book-signing.
— 'Iain,' comment on mckryn66, 'Live Webchat: Iain Banks'. *Guardian*, 6 July 2011. www.theguardian.com/books/booksblog/2011/jul/06/live-webchat-iain-banks.
— 'Scotland and England: what future for the Union?' *Observer*, Sunday 28 August 2011. www.guardian.co.uk/culture/2011/aug/28/scottish-independence-snp-iain-banks.
— 'Why I'm supporting a cultural boycott of Israel'. *Guardian*, 5 April 2013. www.theguardian.com/books/2013/apr/05/iain-banks-cultural-boycott-israel.
BBC News. 'Ageing Gene Discovered'. 17 April 2003. http://news.bbc.co.uk/1/hi/health/2952417.stm.
— 'Blair Impeachment Campaign Starts'. 27 August 2004. http://news.bbc.co.uk/1/hi/uk_politics/3600438.stm.
— 'World's first lab-grown burger is eaten in London'. 5 August 2013. https://www.bbc.co.uk/news/science-environment-23576143.
BBC Radio 4. 'Iain Banks: *The Wasp Factory*'. *Bookclub*, 10 November 2011. www.bbc.co.uk/programmes/b016w0nf.
BBC Radio Scotland. 'Interview with Iain M. Banks'. *The Book Café*, 8 October 2012. www.bbc.co.uk/programmes/p00zjf0f.
Beauchamp, Scott. 'The Future Might Be a Hoot: How Iain M. Banks Imagines Utopia'. *Atlantic*, 15 January 2013. www.theatlantic.com/entertainment/archive/2013/01/the-future-might-be-a-hoot-how-iain-m-banks-imagines-utopia/267211/.

Bettcher, Talia. 'Feminist Perspectives on Trans Issues'. *Stanford Encyclopedia of Philosophy*. Edward N. Zalta, ed. (Spring, 2014). plato.stanford.edu/entries/feminism-trans/#PhenTransEmb.

Blackburn, Simon. 'Cognitive Dissonance,' in *The Oxford Dictionary of Philosophy*, updated 2016. Oxford University Press, 2008. www.oxfordreference.com/view/10.1093/acref/9780199541430.001.0001/acref-9780199541430-e-603.

Bowring, M.A. 'Resistance Is Not Futile: Liberating Captain Janeway from the Masculine–Feminine Dualism of Leadership'. *Gender, Work & Organization* 11 (2004): 381–405. doi:10.1111/j.1468-0432.2004.00239.

British Science Fiction Association. 'About the British Science Fiction Awards'. N.d. www.bsfa.co.uk/bsfa-awards/.

Chalmers, David. 'The Singularity: a philosophical analysis'. Singularity Institute, 2010. http://consc.net/papers/singularity.pdf.

Clute, John. 'Somewhere More Interesting than Arrival'. *LA Review of Books*, 16 October 2012. https://lareviewofbooks.org/article/somewhere-more-interesting-than-arrival/#.

— 'Greenland, Colin'. In *The Encyclopedia of Science Fiction*. John Clute, David Langford, Peter Nicholls, and Graham Sleight, eds. London: Gollancz, 2018. Updated 31 August 2018. http://www.sf-encyclopedia.com/entry/greenland_colin.

— 'Smith, E E'. In *The Encyclopedia of Science Fiction*. John Clute, David Langford, Peter Nicholls, and Graham Sleight, eds. London: Gollancz, 2018. http://www.sf-encyclopedia.com/entry/smith_e_e.

Clute, John, and David Langford. 'Planetary Romance'. In *The Encyclopedia of Science Fiction*. John Clute, David Langford, Peter Nicholls, and Graham Sleight, eds. London: Gollancz. Updated 4 December 2013. http://www.sf-encyclopedia.com/entry/planetary_romance.

Clute, John, David Langford, and Cheryl Morgan. 'Transgender SF'. In *The Encyclopedia of Science Fiction*. John Clute, David Langford, Peter Nicholls, and Graham Sleight, eds. London: Gollancz, 2018. http://www.sf-encyclopedia.com/entry/transgender_sf.

Colebrook, Martyn. 'Reading Double, Writing Double'. *The Bottle Imp* 8 (November 2010): 5. www.arts.gla.ac.uk/ScotLit/ASLS/SWE/TBI/TBI Issue8/Colebrook.pdf.

Cowdry, Katherine. 'Drawings by the late Iain M Banks to be published'. *Bookseller*, 14 February 2018. https://www.thebookseller.com/news/orbit-publish-culture-drawings-iain-m-banks-731691.

Daoust, Phil. 'Brushes with Doom'. *Guardian*, 2 September 2000. www.theguardian.com/books/2000/sep/02/sciencefictionfantasyandhorror.iainbanks.

DePaulo, Bella. 'Asexuals: Who Are They And Why Are They Important?' 23 December 2009. www.psychologytoday.com/blog/living-single/200912/asexuals-who-are-they-and-why-are-they-important.

Dictionary.com. 'Neuter'. Random House, Inc. www.dictionary.com/browse/neuter.

BIBLIOGRAPHY

Dowd, Maureen. 'Elon Musk's Billion-Dollar Crusade To Stop The A.I. Apocalypse'. *Vanity Fair*, April 2017. https://www.vanityfair.com/news/2017/03/elon-musk-billion-dollar-crusade-to-stop-ai-space-x.

Drew, Julie. 'Cultural Composition: Stuart Hall on Ethnicity and the Discursive Turn'. In *Race, Rhetoric, and the Postcolonial*. Gary A. Olson and Lynn Worsham, eds. 205–239. Albany: State University of New York Press, 1999.

Duke, Barry. '"Faith is basically bananas", says dying "Evangelical Atheist" Iain Banks'. *Freethinker*, 4 April 2013. www.freethinker.co.uk/2013/04/04/faith-is-basically-bananas-says-dying-evangelical-atheist-iain-banks/.

Edelman, P.D. 'Commentary: *In Vitro*-Cultured Meat Production'. *Tissue Engineering* 11, no. 5/6 (3 May 2005). doi:10.1089/ten.2005.11.659.

Elmhurst, Sophie. 'Is Richard Dawkins destroying his reputation?' *Guardian*, 9 June 2015. https://www.theguardian.com/science/2015/jun/09/is-richard-dawkins-destroying-his-reputation.

Encyclopedia Britannica. 'Heaven'. Encyclopedia Britannica Inc., 2016. www.britannica.com/topic/heaven.

— 'Limbo'. Encyclopedia Britannica Inc. Online Library Edition. www.britannica.com/topic/limbo-Roman-Catholic-theology.

— 'Soul'. Encyclopedia Britannica Inc. Online Library Edition. https://www.britannica.com/topic/soul-religion-and-philosophy.

F, Justin. 'The History Of Drones (Drone History Timeline From 1849 To 2019)'. *Drone Enthusiast*. N.d. https://www.dronethusiast.com/history-of-drones/.

Farnell, David. 'Preemptive regime change in Iain M. Banks's *The Player of Games*', *Fukuoka University Review of Literature & Humanities* 41, no. 4 (16 January 2010). https://fukuokau.repo.nii.ac.jp/index.php?action=pages_view_main&active_action=repository_action_common_download&item_id=1052&item_no=1&attribute_id=22&file_no=1&page_id=13&block_id=39.

Flynn, Tom. 'What is Religious Humanism – really?' *Center for Inquiry*, 23 August 2012. www.centerforinquiry.net/blogs/entry/what_is_religious_humanism_--_really/.

Genome News Network, 'Genetics and Genomics Timeline: 1973'. http://www.genomenewsnetwork.org/resources/timeline/1973_Boyer.php (Accessed 29 March 2019).

Gevers, Nick. 'Look to Windward'. *SF Site*. 2000. http://books.guardian.co.uk/departments/sciencefiction/story/0,6000,367256,00.html.

— 'Cultured futurist Iain M. Banks creates an ornate utopia'. *Science Fiction Weekly*, 15 May 2008. archive.is/FgDHg

Graham, Thomas. 'Art made by AI is selling for thousands – is it any good?' BBC website, 12 December 2018. http://www.bbc.com/culture/story/20181210-art-made-by-ai-is-selling-for-thousands-is-it-any-good.

Grayling, A.C. 'Humanism's faith in reason represents our best hope', 3 March 2013. *Guardian*. www.theguardian.com/commentisfree/2013/mar/03/humanism-religion-reason-our-best-hope.

Grossman, Lev. 'Lord of the Ringworld: In Praise of Larry Niven'. *Time*, 13 June 2012. entertainment.time.com/2012/06/13/lord-of-the-ringworld-in-praise-of-larry-niven/.

Guinness World Records. 'Oldest Person Ever'. www.guinnessworldrecords.com/world-records/oldest-person.

Hale, Thomas N., and Anne-Marie Slaughter. 'Hardt and Negri's Multitude: The Worst of Both Worlds'. *Open Democracy*, 25 May 2005. https://www.opendemocracy.net/en/marx_2549jsp/.

Hall, James. 'My Highlight: Goya'. *Guardian*, 3 January 2015. www.theguardian.com/artanddesign/2015/jan/03/my-highlight-goya-courtauld-national-gallery-james-hall.

Hari, Johann. 'Heaven: A Fool's Paradise'. *Independent*, 21 April 2010. www.independent.co.uk/opinion/faith/heaven-a-fools-paradise-1949399.html.

Hart, Hugh. 'Strong Women Steer Battlestar Galactica's Final Voyage'. *Wired*, 15 January 2009. https://www.wired.com/2009/01/women-steer-bat/.

Hartwell, David G., and Kathryn Cramer. 'How Shit Became Shinola: Definition and Redefinition of Space Opera'. *SF Review*, 3 August 2003. www.sfrevu.com/ISSUES/2003/0308/Space%20Opera%20Redefined/Review.htm.

Hodge, Bob, and Vishay Mishra. 'What was postcolonialism?' *New Literary History* 36, no. 3 (2005): 375–402. muse.jhu.edu.ezproxy.brunel.ac.uk/journals/new_literary_history/v036/36.3mishra.html.

Hopper, Edward. 'People in the Sun'. 1960. Oil on canvas. 40 3/8 x 60 3/8 in. (102.6 x 153.4 cm). Smithsonian American Art Museum. Gift of S.C. Johnson & Son, Inc. 1969. americanart.si.edu/collections/search/artwork/?id=10762.

Horwich, David. 'Culture Clash: Ambivalent Heroes and the Ambiguous Utopia in the Works of Iain M. Banks'. *Strange Horizons*, 21 January 2002. www.strangehorizons.com/2002/20020121/culture_clash.shtml.

Hubble, Nick. 'Poems by Iain Banks and Ken MacLeod', *Strange Horizons*, 12 October 2015. http://strangehorizons.com/non-fiction/reviews/poems-by-iain-banks-and-ken-macleod/.

—— 'Iain M. Banks by Paul Kincaid'. *Strange Horizons*, 18 December 2017. http://strangehorizons.com/non-fiction/reviews/iain-m-banks-by-paul-kincaid/.

Hughes, Colin. 'Doing the Business, Profile: Iain Banks'. *Guardian*, 7 August 1999. www.guardian.co.uk/books/1999/aug/07/fiction.iainbanks.

Hugo Awards, The Official Site of the. '2005 Hugo Awards'. www.thehugoawards.org/hugo-history/2005-hugo-awards/.

Humanism. 'Tributes Pour In For Our Distinguished Supporter Iain Banks'. June 2013. https://www.humanism.scot/what-we-do/news/tributes-pour-in-for-our-distinguished-supporter-iain-banks/.

Humanist Society Scotland website. 'About Humanist Society Scotland'. https://www.humanism.scot/what-we-do/about-hss/

Intersex Society of North America, The. 'What is Intersex?' 1993–2008. www.isna.org/faq/what_is_intersex.

Jeffries, Stuart. '"A Man of Culture" (Interview with Iain Banks)'. *Guardian*, 25 May 2007. www.theguardian.com/books/2007/may/25/hayfestival2007.hayfestival.
Johnson, Greg L. 'Excession'. *SF Site*, 1998. www.sfsite.com/03a/exc28.htm.
— 'Matter: A Review'. *SF Site*, 2008. www.sfsite.com/06a/mt273.htm.
Jones, Gwyneth. 'Review of *Matter*'. *Strange Horizons*, 14 April 2008. http://strangehorizons.com/non-fiction/reviews/matter-by-iain-m-banks.
Jones, Jonathan. 'Look What We Did'. *Guardian*, 31 March 2003. www.theguardian.com/culture/2003/mar/31/artsfeatures.turnerprize2003.
Jordison, Jim. 'Iain Banks's *The Bridge*: the link between his mainstream and SF work'. *Guardian*, 23 September 2014. www.theguardian.com/books/2014/sep/23/iain-banks-the-bridge-link-mainstream-literature-science-fiction.
Kaveney, Roz. *The Culture's Latest Conflicts. Independent*, 15 August 2010. www.independent.co.uk/arts-entertainment/books/reviews/surface-detail-by-iain-m-banks-2106657.html.
Kelly, Stuart. 'Does Elon Musk really understand Iain M Banks's "utopian anarchist" Culture?' *Guardian*, 18 June 2018. https://www.theguardian.com/books/booksblog/2018/jun/19/elon-musk-iain-banks-culture-novels.
— 'Iain Banks: The Final Interview'. *Guardian*, 15 June 2013. https://www.theguardian.com/books/2013/jun/15/iain-banks-the-final-interview.
Kinson, Sarah. 'Interview with Iain Banks'. *Guardian*, 7 February 2008. www.guardian.co.uk/books/2008/feb/07/iainbanks?INTCMP=SRCH.
Knight, James, and Murdo McLeod. 'Iain Banks'. *Vice*, 2 December 2009. https://www.vice.com/en_uk/article/jmdm8y/iain-banks-274-v16n12.
Langford, David. 'Singularity'. In *The Encyclopedia of Science Fiction*. John Clute, David Langford, Peter Nicholls, and Graham Sleight, eds. London: Gollancz, 2018. 25 October 2018. http://www.sf-encyclopedia.com/entry/singularity.
Lawrence, Felicity. 'Sweatshop campaigners demand Gap boycott'. *Guardian*, 2 November 2002. https://www.theguardian.com/uk/2002/nov/22/clothes.globalisation.
Le Guin, Ursula. 'American SF and the Other'. *Science Fiction Studies* 7, vol. 2:3. (November 1975). http://www.depauw.edu/sfs/backissues/7/leguin7art.htm.
Leach, Antonia. 'Iain M. Banks – Human, Posthuman and Beyond Human'. *Elope* 15, no. 1 (June 2018): 69–81. revije.ff.uni-lj.so/elope.
Leatham, Xantha. 'Dying Wish of Scots Author Revealed'. *Scotsman*, 15 February 2015. www.scotsman.com/lifestyle/dying-wish-of-scots-author-iain-banks-revealed-1-3690835.
Leith, William. 'A Writer's Life: Iain Banks'. *Telegraph*, 3 November 2003. www.telegraph.co.uk/culture/3605692/A-writers-life-Iain-Banks.html.
Lewis, Martin. 'The Centauri Device, M. John Harrison'. *SF Site*, 2002. www.sfsite.com/04a/cd125.htm.
Liptak, Andrew. 'Amazon is developing a series based on Iain M. Banks' sci-fi novel *Consider Phlebas*', *Verge*, 21 February 2018. https://www.theverge.com/2018/2/21/17035618/amazon-culture-series-iain-m-banks-television-show.

MacLeod, Ken. 'Iain Banks: A science fiction star first and foremost'. *Guardian*, 10 June 2013. www.theguardian.com/books/2013/jun/10/iain-banks-ken-macleod-science-fiction.

— 'Ken MacLeod on Iain Banks'. *Internationalist Socialist Network*, 23 July 2013. http://internationalsocialistnetwork.org/index.php/ideas-and-arguments/analysis/193-ken-macleod-on-iain-banks-use-of-calculators.

— 'Use of Calculators'. *Early Days of a Better Nation*, 26 July 2013. http://kenmacleod.blogspot.com/2013/07/use-of-calculators.html.

Marx, Karl. *A Contribution to the Critique of Political Economy*. Marxists.org, [1859] 1999. https://www.marxists.org/archive/marx/works/1859/critique-pol-economy/.

Mason, Moya K. 'Theodor Adorno's Theory of Music and its Social Implications'. http://www.moyak.com/papers/adorno-schoenberg-atonality.html

McGinty, Stephan. 'Iain Banks marries in his favourite place'. *Scotsman*, 8 August 2013. www.scotsman.com/lifestyle/books/iain-banks-marries-in-his-favourite-place-1-2882190.

Merriam-Webster. 'Mother'. www.merriam-webster.com/dictionary/mother.

Miller, Henry I. 'Designing Improved Humans: Playing Cat and Mouse with Genetic "Enhancement"'. *Genetic Engineering News* 28, no. 6 (5 March 2008). www.genengnews.com/gen-articles/designing-improved-humans/2402/.

Mitchell, Chris. 'Iain Banks: *Whit* and *Excession*: Getting Used to Being God'. *Spike*, 3 September 1996. www.spikemagazine.com/0996bank.php.

Moore, Brian C.J., and Claude V. Palisca. 'Consonance'. Grove Music Online. *Oxford Music Online*. Oxford University Press. www.oxfordmusiconline.com.v-ezproxy.brunel.ac.uk:2048/subscriber/article/grove/music/06316 (Accessed 30 March 2019).

Morton, Oliver. 'A Cultured Man'. *Wired* 2.6, June 1996. yoz.com/wired/2.06/features/banks.html

Mullan, John. 'Iain Banks Obituary'. *Guardian*, 10 June 2013. https://www.theguardian.com/books/2013/jun/09/iain-banks-dies-59-cancer.

Musk, Elon. (@elonmusk), 'If you must know, I am a utopian anarchist of the kind best described by Iain Banks'. Tweet, 16 June 2018, 3:55pm. https://twitter.com/elonmusk/status/1008120904759402501?lang=en.

National Records of Scotland. 'Religion (detailed)'. Scotland's Census 2011. https://www.scotlandscensus.gov.uk/documents/censusresults/release2a/rel2A_Religion_detailed_Scotland.pdf.

New Humanist. 'Q&A: Iain Banks'. *New Humanist* 127, no. 4 (July/August 2012). https://newhumanist.org.uk/articles/2832/qa-iain-banks.

Office for National Statistics. 'Overview of the UK Population', 21 July 2017. https://www.ons.gov.uk/peoplepopulationandcommunity/populationandmigration/populationestimates/articles/overviewoftheukpopulation/july2017 (Accessed 27 April 2020).

Ontario Humanist Society. 'In memoriam: Iain Banks, novelist, humanist, "evangelical atheist"'. 10 June 2003. http://www.ontariohumanists.ca/events/in-memoriam-iain-banks-novelist-humanist-evangelical-atheist-national-humanist.

Optic Nerve Limited. 'Electric Chair Music'. [Video file]. 23 February 2015. Retrieved from YouTube: www.youtube.com/watch?v=sykB4znEk2Q

Orbit Books website. 'An Interview with Iain M. Banks on the 25th Anniversary of the Culture'. 2012. www.orbitbooks.net/interview/iain-m-banks-on-the-25th-anniversary-of-the-culture/.

Oxford Dictionaries. 'Apocalypse'. Oxford University Press. www.oxforddictionaries.com/definition/english/apocalypse.

— 'Culture'. Oxford University Press. www.oed.com.v-ezproxy.brunel.ac.uk:2048/view/Entry/45746?result=1&rskey=1Tguyt&.

— 'Fractal'. Oxford University Press. www.oxforddictionaries.com/definition/english/fractal.

— 'Liberal'. Oxford University Press. www.oxforddictionaries.com/definition/english/liberal.

— 'Minarchy'. Oxford University Press. www.oxforddictionaries.com/definition/english/minarchy.

— 'Moksha'. Oxford University Press. www.oxforddictionaries.com/definition/english/moksha.

— 'Mother'. Oxford University Press. www.oxforddictionaries.com/definition/english/mother.

— 'Pantheism'. Oxford University Press. www.oxforddictionaries.com/definition/english/pantheism.

— 'Utopia'. Oxford University Press. www.oxforddictionaries.com/definition/english/utopia.

Parsons, Michael. 'Interview: Iain M Banks talks "Surface Detail" with Wired'. *Wired*, 14 August 2010. www.wired.co.uk/news/archive/2010-10/14/iain-m-banks-interview.

Poole, Stephen. 'Culture Clashes: Review: *Matter* by Iain M. Banks'. *Guardian*, 8 February 2008. www.theguardian.com/books/2008/feb/09/fiction.iainbanks.

Robertson, John. 'Iain Banks: Stop Funding for Faith Schools'. *Times*, 16 August 2009. www.thesundaytimes.co.uk/sto/news/uk_news/article182309.ece.

Rumpala, Yannick. 'Artificial Intelligences and Political Organization: an Exploration Based on the Science Fiction Work of Iain M. Banks'. *Technology in Society* 34 (2012): 23–32. http://isiarticles.com/bundles/Article/pre/pdf/20144.pdf.

Rundle, James. 'Interview with Iain M. Banks'. *SciFiNow*, 13 August 2010. http://www.scifinow.co.uk/news/interview-iain-m-banks/.

Russ, Joanna. 'When it Changed'. In *American Futures*. Indiana University of Pennsylvania, [1972] 2013. www.americanfuturesiup.files.wordpress.com/2013/01/russ-when-it-changed.pdf.

Samuel, Leah. 'With Womb Transplants a Reality, Transgender Women Dare to Dream of Pregnancy'. *StatNews*, 7 March 2016. https://www.statnews.com/2016/03/07/uterine-transplant-transgender/.

Scott, Peter. 'Meritocracy is in retreat in twenty first century higher education'. *Guardian*, 1 September 2015. www.theguardian.com/education/2015/sep/01/higher-education-class-degree-university-inequality.

Scottish Government, The. 'Analysis of Religion in the 2011 Census'. 17 May 2006. https://www.gov.scot/publications/analysis-religion-2001-census/pages/2/

Secularism.org. 'Profile of Iain Banks'. www.secularism.org.uk/iainbanks.html.

Service, Tom. 'A Guide to Brian Ferneyhough's Music'. *Guardian*, 10 September 2012. www.theguardian.com/music/tomserviceblog/2012/sep/10/contemporary-music-guide-brian-ferneyhough.

SFX. 'Interview: Iain M. Banks, Part Two'. 13 October 2010. www.sfx.co.uk/2010/10/13/interview-iain-m-banks-part-two/.

Shaw, Dave. 'Summary of Rosi Braidotti's *The Posthuman* (Part 1)'. 14 June 2015. https://medium.com/open-objects/summary-of-rosi-braidotti-s-the-posthuman-part-1-12e79316940f.

Shrieking Man, The. 'Iain M Banks: Imperialist Propagandist?' 23 March 2008. hismastersvoice.wordpress.com/tag/iain-banks/.

Silver, Stephen H. 'Iain M. Banks: The Algebraist'. *SF Site*, 2004. www.sfsite.com/~silverag/banks.html.

Socialist International, The. 'The Declaration of the Socialist International'. 30 June to 3 July 1951. https://www.socialistinternational.org/about-us/declaration-of-principles/.

Sopel, Jon. 'From "alternative facts" to Rewriting History in Trump's White House'. BBC. 25 July 2018. https://www.bbc.co.uk/news/world-us-canada-44959300.

Soyka, David. 'Transition: A Review'. *SF Site*, 2010. www.sfsite.com/01a/tr311.htm.

Sparks, Matthew. 'Top Scientists Call for Caution Over Artificial Intelligence'. *Telegraph*, 13 January 2015. https://www.telegraph.co.uk/technology/news/11342200/Top-scientists-call-for-caution-over-artificial-intelligence.html.

Stableford, Brian M., Peter Nicholls, Mike Ashley, and David Langford. 'New Worlds'. In *The Encyclopedia of Science Fiction*. John Clute, David Langford, Peter Nicholls, and Graham Sleight, eds. London: Gollancz, 2018. Updated 31 August 2018. http://www.sf-encyclopedia.com/entry/new_worlds.

Telegraph. 'Obituary: Iain Banks', 9 June 2003. www.telegraph.co.uk/news/obituaries/culture-obituaries/books-obituaries/10108884/Iain-Banks.html.

Trotsky, Leon. 'What Is Proletarian Culture, and Is It Possible?' *Marxists.org*, [1923]. www.marxists.org/archive/trotsky/1923/art/tia23c.htm.

Turner, Christopher. '"I'd like to have stepped on Goya's toes, shouted in his ears and punched him in the face": The Chapman Brothers'. *Tate Etc* 8 (Autumn 2006). www.tate.org.uk/context-comment/articles/id-have-stepped-on-goyas-toes-shouted-his-ears-and-punched-him-face.

Tuttle, Lisa. 'Women in SF'. In *The Encyclopedia of Science Fiction*, John Clute, David Langford, Peter Nicholls, and Graham Sleight, eds. London: Gollancz, 2018. http://www.sf-encyclopedia.com/entry/women_in_sf.

Walter, Damien G. 'A plea to Iain M Banks'. *Guardian*, 19 February 2010. http://www.guardian.co.uk/books/booksblog/2010/feb/19/iain-m-banks-culture.

Index

9/11 attacks 3, 14, 16, 45, 183

adventure fiction 40–41, 58, 67, 71, 91, 118, 142–143, 154–155, 167
ageing 118–140
Aldiss, Brian 20–21, 24, 119
Anaplian, Djan Seriy 115, 150–154, 163, 165–167, 176, 254
anarchism 1–2, 22, 27–29, 38, 49, 53, 81–82, 85–88, 97, 187
artificial intelligence (AI) 6, 10, 41, 68, 73–77, 91–93, 165, 183, 192, 203–205
atheism 182, 189, 209
atonal music 248–249, 254–255, 258

Baker, Timothy C. 188, 190–192, 202, 204–207
Banks, Iain
  The Bridge 13, 17, 25
  The Business 15
  Canal Dreams 15
  Complicity 15, 239
  Consider Phlebas 3, 6, 12, 14, 23–26, 28, 40, 42–43, 45, 50, 52, 54, 56, 64, 70, 79, 83, 89, 93–95, 112, 117, 158–159, 163, 180, 182–184, 190–192, 203, 205, 215–216, 234, 239, 253, 256, 259, 261, 263, 266, 268, 277
    see also Gobuchul, Bora Horza
  The Crow Road 15
  'Descendent' 16
  Excession 5, 15–16, 42–43, 47, 54, 56, 79, 86, 90, 130, 139, 141, 148–149, 151, 153, 158, 160–163, 171–173, 202, 208–209, 210, 213, 215, 220, 224–231, 234–235, 238, 239, 245–246, 248–256, 260, 263
    see also Genar-Hofoen
  'A Gift from the Culture' 16, 69, 189
  The Hydrogen Sonata 6, 8, 17, 44, 50, 57, 80, 89, 92, 122, 131, 163, 180, 182, 187, 206–209
    see also Cossont, Vyr
  Inversions 15–16, 19, 38, 41, 44, 55–59, 61–67, 76, 79, 94, 144, 163, 166, 186
    see also Oelph; Vosil, Doctor
  Look to Windward 15–17, 28–29, 42, 44–45, 54, 56, 74, 87, 93, 112, 117, 136, 169–170, 180, 182, 205, 209, 213, 215, 219, 224, 226, 230, 235, 238–241, 245, 252, 253, 263
    see also Ziller, Mahrai
  Matter 15, 18, 44, 56, 58, 115, 141, 150–151, 153–154, 163, 165–167, 182, 254
  The Player of Games 11–12, 24, 19, 28, 42–43, 45, 47–48, 56, 58, 61, 65, 69, 79, 80, 83, 89, 91–92, 94, 95, 99–100,

281

102–106, 115, 121, 141, 153–156, 158–159, 160, 162, 168, 215–216, 229, 239, 241, 243, 252–253, 263, 268, 275
   see also Gurgeh, Jernau Morat; Sma, Diziet
'Slight Mechanical Destruction' 11, 18, 213, 222–223, 256
A Song of Stone 15
'The State of the Art' 6, 12, 43, 56, 79, 111, 129, 134, 140, 159, 163, 164, 199, 216–217, 261
   see also Sma, Diziet
Surface Detail 17, 44, 57, 79, 81–82, 89, 92, 111, 113, 121, 136–138, 141, 147, 149, 163, 173, 180, 182, 193–194, 197–202, 207, 213–216, 219, 233, 235, 237, 254, 256
Use of Weapons 9–11, 15–16, 18–19, 43, 54, 56, 76, 79, 95, 111, 117, 122–123, 125, 127, 129, 132, 136, 138, 140, 163–164, 183, 202, 213, 222–223, 239, 254
   see also 'Slight Mechanical Destruction'; Zakalwe; 'Zakalwe's Song'
Walking on Glass 17, 25
The Wasp Factory 12–13, 25, 144–145, 177, 181–182, 184, 238, 262–263
Whit 15, 182
'Zakalwe's Song' 8, 18, 213, 223–224, 252
Baudrillard, Jean 189
Bloch, Ernst 45, 252–253, 255, 266
Braidotti, Rosi 116–117, 182–183
the British Empire 44
Buckell, Tobias 119, 123
Butler, Andrew M. 23, 26

capitalism 9, 22, 24, 26, 35, 39, 52, 67, 71, 78, 83, 85–86, 92, 98, 109, 180, 189, 216, 235, 254

Caroti, Simone 29, 90
Christianity 182–183, 190, 196
Clarke, Arthur C. 41, 59, 128, 155, 160, 203
Clarke, Jim 188, 197, 207
Clute, John 25, 26, 143, 165, 251
Colebrook, Martyn 85n
colonialism 29, 40, 43–44, 48, 50, 54, 67, 91–92, 118, 146, 154, 164, 236
communism 15, 69, 86, 190, 257
Contact 7–8, 38, 42–46, 53, 60, 64, 79, 81, 86, 90–92, 94–96, 98, 106, 112, 123, 124, 127, 129, 132–133, 138, 155, 160–164, 176, 189, 205, 209, 213–214, 216–217, 220, 224, 231, 256, 260
Cossont, Vyr 245, 250
Csicsery-Ronay Jr., Istvan 2, 19–20, 23, 34–35, 38, 40–42, 55, 59, 67, 71, 75, 89, 91–92, 115, 154–155, 160, 164–165, 167–168, 179, 203, 207, 265
   The Seven Beauties of Science Fiction 35
   see also the Fertile Corpse; the Handy Man; the Shadow Mage; the *technologiade*; the Tool Text; the Wife at Home; the Willing Slave
cyberpunk 39–40, 75, 90, 114, 119, 123, 131, 135–136, 155, 165, 192–193, 197–198, 201, 216, 269–270

Dawkins, Richard 184, 189
death 5, 8, 14–15, 19, 27, 59, 60–61, 105, 108, 111, 118, 123–124, 129, 131–139, 156, 166, 192–196, 198–199, 201–202, 205, 207, 213, 216, 218, 221, 225–226, 228–231, 233, 237–239, 266, 272
   see also mortality
Dick, Philip K. 118, 131

Duggan, Robert 46, 182, 189
dystopia 23, 27, 29, 32, 37, 44–45, 70, 75, 90, 104–105, 115, 119, 168, 201

Eliot, T.S. 223
empire 3, 12, 17, 22, 24, 27, 29, 35, 37–38, 42–44, 46–51, 53, 55–58, 65, 84, 105–107, 124, 254
Empire (Hardt & Negri) 37–38, 51–52, 55, 64, 67, 69, 83, 85
Europe 3–4, 6, 11–12, 15, 18–19, 58, 77, 84, 117, 165, 235
the European Union (EU) 18–19, 260

Ferneyhough, Brian 246, 247, 250, 252, 254
the Fertile Corpse 42, 71–73, 207
Foucault, Michel 52
Fukuyama, Frances 31–32, 113, 114

Genar-Hofoen 130, 141, 149, 160, 161, 162, 163, 172, 209–210, 234
gender 19–20, 22, 30, 34, 41, 104, 140–152, 154, 156, 159–160, 164–167, 170–171, 173–176, 181, 187, 207, 218, 238
genetic engineering 83, 98, 111, 114–116, 119–120, 127, 132, 148, 275
Gibson, William 135, 155, 192, 198
Globalisation 8, 18–19, 37, 39, 45, 51, 55–56, 67, 71, 106–107, 117, 216, 256
globalism 37, 51, 54–56, 69, 71, 83, 254
Gobuchul, Bora Horza 26, 54, 56, 94, 159, 183–184, 203, 205
Gothic 13, 30, 40, 118, 203, 237
Greenland, Colin 23, 24, 165
Gurgeh, Jernau Morat 12, 43, 56, 79, 83, 91, 94–96, 98–108, 115, 117, 141, 153–168, 215, 239, 243

Haddock, David 23
the Handy Man 41, 43, 56, 79, 93, 115, 141, 143, 149, 150, 154–156, 158–161, 163, 165–168, 172, 176, 190, 207, 220
the Handy Woman 44, 57, 72, 115, 142–143, 149, 150, 164, 166–167, 172, 176, 190, 220
Harrison, M. John 23–25
Heinlein, Robert 22, 23, 142, 146, 176
Hubble, Nick 10, 19, 28, 58, 63, 67, 222, 224, 256
humanism 116, 117, 118, 139, 179, 181, 182, 185, 186, 194, 211

immortality 111, 118, 135, 136, 137, 138, 139, 194, 199, 209
imperialism 3, 16, 29, 35, 37, 38, 39, 44, 48, 49, 50, 51, 54, 55, 64, 67, 84, 85, 117, 146, 214
Islam 189, 198

Jameson, Fredric 8, 30–33, 42, 71, 77, 85, 109, 128, 211, 218, 221–222, 253–254, 257
Archaeologies of the Future 44, 93
Representing Capital: A Reading of Volume One 68n
Valences of the Dialectic 45, 68

Keen, Tony 72n
Kerslake, Patricia 29, 38, 44, 48–51, 55, 85–86
Kincaid, Paul 12, 17, 29, 57, 65, 90, 130, 214, 215, 217
Klein, Naomi 235
Kurzweil, Ray 73

Le Guin, Ursula 23, 39, 144, 177
The Dispossessed 22, 105, 221
The Left Hand of Darkness 169, 173
Leon, Trotsky 30, 31
liberal(ism) 28, 29, 31, 45, 69, 81, 84, 85, 87, 90, 94, 161, 214, 241, 260

libertarian(ism) 2, 56, 69, 84, 85, 86, 87, 90, 114n
Linter, Dervley 132–134, 140, 141, 159, 160–161, 163–164, 169, 187–188, 199

MacLeod, Ken 4, 5, 6, 10, 15, 16, 18, 23, 24, 25, 71, 75, 77, 86, 112, 210, 256, 259, 262
Martingale, Moira 30, 59, 145, 188, 203
Marx, Karl 30, 82, 190
Marxism 31, 87, 94, 99, 108, 218, 253
Mendlesohn, Farah 52, 55, 79, 86, 129, 130, 161, 162, 197, 215, 217
Miéville, China 234n
the Minds 7, 11, 33–34, 46, 50, 54, 66, 73–74, 77, 79–80, 86–96, 101, 109, 111, 139, 142, 143, 186–188, 195, 202–208, 215–216, 219–220, 224–226, 228, 230, 238, 257, 262
modernism 67, 71, 105n, 255
Moorcock, Michael 21, 24
mortality 118, 131, 194, 209
    see also death
Moylan, Tom 35, 69, 70, 71
murder 57, 58, 60, 61, 62, 83, 83n, 86, 87, 123, 124, 126, 127, 132, 136, 193, 227, 230
Musk, Elon 1, 2, 27–28, 75, 81, 85, 259

Neoliberalism 4, 8, 9, 11, 14, 17, 35, 67, 69, 180, 202
New Wave of SF 21, 26, 70–71, 142–143, 176, 195, 252–253
New Space Opera 4, 23, 25, 119, 143, 165

Oelph 59–61, 64–67, 144

postcolonialism 29, 44, 48, 48, 50, 54, 67, 91, 92, 118, 146, 154, 164, 236

postmodernism 8, 45, 71
(post)scarcity 34, 49, 50, 69, 76, 77, 78, 80, 84, 85, 87, 89, 98, 102, 105, 113, 150, 158, 199, 207

racism 41, 98, 113–114
rejuvenescence 111, 118
religion 13, 44, 50, 97n, 180–189, 191, 194, 196, 198, 208, 210, 211, 218
revolution 31, 33, 34, 44, 70, 76, 90, 113, 235
Reynolds, Alastair 23, 75, 119, 123
Roberts, Jude 30, 85, 117, 137, 143, 145, 182, 217, 258
Robinson, Kim Stanley 71, 77, 119, 129, 221
Robinsonaide 41, 56
robot 41, 166
Russ, Joanna 142–144

science fiction 13, 20, 21, 23, 25, 26, 40, 41, 71, 91, 104–105, 142, 144, 177, 204, 210, 249–250, 259
Scotland 3, 4, 9, 12, 15, 22, 181, 183
Second Nature 42, 71–72, 89, 114, 116, 180, 197, 216, 260
secularism 2, 26, 50, 58, 118, 180, 181, 183, 185, 186, 187, 190, 191, 196, 200, 203, 204, 206, 211, 214
senescence 111, 118, 119, 122, 127, 131, 133
the Shadow Mage 41–43
Sma, Diziet 11–12, 81, 83, 126, 132–134, 140, 142–143, 159–160, 163–164, 168, 222–223, 230, 254, 256–257, 261
Smith, E.E. 'Doc' 19, 20, 24, 39, 176
    Lensman
    Galactic Patrol 146
    The Skylark of Space 41, 72, 142, 143
    Triplanetary 160

INDEX

socialism 5, 15, 24, 26, 28, 31, 37, 38, 44, 49, 69, 78, 81, 82, 83, 84, 86, 88, 94, 186, 257
the Soviet Union 3, 15, 31, 77
space opera 4, 10, 12, 14, 17, 19, 20, 21, 22, 23, 24, 25, 26, 35, 38, 39, 40, 41, 42, 43, 56, 67, 71, 77, 89, 115, 118, 130, 141, 142, 143, 144, 146, 147, 148, 154, 158, 160, 161, 163, 164, 165–166, 176, 177, 214, 224, 230, 239
Special Circumstances (SC) 7, 38, 42–46, 53, 58, 79, 83, 89, 91–92, 94–96, 100, 122–124, 125, 129, 132, 137–138, 150, 154–156, 158–160, 163, 165–167, 172, 175, 176, 186, 190, 193, 207, 209, 213, 214, 215, 220, 231, 237, 238, 239, 244, 260
Star Trek 22, 39, 92, 165
Star Wars 1, 12, 22
Stravinsky, Igor 240, 242
the Sublime 8, 15, 19, 44, 50, 57, 135, 139, 173, 180, 187, 205–211, 224, 229, 249–251
Suvin, Darko 40, 63, 203, 210

technologiade 34, 35, 37, 38, 40, 41, 42, 44, 53, 54, 55, 56, 57, 61, 63, 65, 66, 71, 75, 79, 111, 113, 129, 146, 167, 168, 186, 202, 260
terraforming 72
terrorism 3, 16, 17, 19, 37, 41, 45, 81, 243, 244, 245n
Thatcher, Margaret 11–13, 17, 69, 99, 107
Thatcherism 11, 13, 17
Tolkien, J.R.R. 106
the Tool Text 35, 39, 41, 59, 75, 89, 95, 116, 139, 154, 164, 256
transgender 148, 150, 156, 152, 171, 174, 177
Trump, Donald 38

utopia(nism) 1, 3, 9, 10, 11, 14, 27, 28, 29, 30, 37, 43, 44, 45, 46, 49, 52, 53, 56, 59, 63, 64, 65, 68, 70, 73, 77, 78, 82, 83, 84, 86, 87, 90, 103, 105, 109, 112, 115, 128, 129, 130, 131, 132, 133, 134, 135, 139, 141, 142, 147, 148, 149, 163, 168, 171, 176, 177, 179, 184, 185, 186, 188, 189, 190, 196, 202, 204, 209, 211, 213, 215, 217, 218, 219, 220, 221, 222, 223, 224, 233, 238, 248, 252, 253, 255, 256, 257, 259, 260, 262
  anti-utopia 29, 71, 91, 97, 113, 129, 159
  critical utopia 35, 38, 40, 54, 69, 91, 214
  personal utopia 1, 29, 81, 186, 254, 258, 261
  techno-utopia 42, 69, 71, 111, 180, 197

Veppers, Joiler 57, 193, 202, 234–238
Vint, Sherryl 27, 29, 44, 45, 49, 51, 52, 55, 64, 84, 85, 117, 122, 139, 140, 145, 153, 170, 173, 177, 186, 189
Vosil, Doctor 58–62

Wheeler, Pat 144
the Wife at Home 41, 141, 142, 143, 166, 167, 168
Williams, Evan Calder 34–35
Williams, Raymond 221–222, 261
the Willing Slave 41, 91–93
Winter, Jerome 22, 24, 39

Zakalwe (Elethiomel/Charedenine) 8, 10–13, 18, 43, 54, 56, 79, 117, 122–128, 131–132, 135–138, 140, 148, 161, 183, 202, 213, 222–224, 239, 252–256
Ziller, Mahrai 87, 187, 224, 239–242, 244, 250, 257
Žižek, Slavoj 14